W9-BJN-117

Safeguarding Psychiatric Privacy

Safeguarding
Psychiatric Privacy:

Computer Systems
and Their Uses

EDITED BY

EUGENE M. LASKA, Ph.D.

RHETA BANK, M.A.

Rockland Research Institute

A WILEY BIOMEDICAL PUBLICATION

JOHN WILEY & SONS, New York • London • Sydney • Toronto

Copyright © 1975 by John Wiley & Sons, Inc.

All rights reserved. Published simultaneously in Canada.

No part of this book may be reproduced by any means,
nor transmitted, nor translated into a machine language
without the written permission of the publisher.

Library of Congress Cataloging in Publication Data:
Main entry under title:

Safeguarding psychiatric privacy.

  (A Wiley biomedical-health publication)
  Includes bibliographical references and index.
  1. Multi-State Information System. 2. Psychiatry—
Medical records—Access control. 3. Privacy, Right of.
I. Laska, Eugene. II. Bank, Rheta.

RC455.2.M38S23   651.5   75-15570
ISBN 0-471-51831-X

Printed in the United States of America

10 9 8 7 6 5 4 3 2 1

Authors

Boris M. Astrachan, M.D., Professor of Clinical Psychiatry, Yale University School of Medicine, and Director, Connecticut Mental Health Center, New Haven, Connecticut.

Rheta Bank, M.A., Director of Educational Services at the Information Sciences Division, Rockland Research Institute, Orangeburg, New York.

Charles W. Cobb, Ph.D., Director of Information Systems Development, Connecticut Department of Mental Health, Hartford, Connecticut.

Jeffrey L. Crawford, Ph.D., Director, Automated Medical Records (For the Developmentally disabled) Project, Information Sciences Division, Rockland Research Institute, Orangeburg, New York.

William J. Curran, J.D., Frances Glessner Lee Professor of Legal Medicine at the Harvard School of Public Health, Harvard University, Boston, Massachusetts.

Jean Endicott, Ph.D., Evaluation Section, Biometrics Research, New York State Department of Mental Hygiene and Department of Psychiatry, Columbia University, New York, New York.

Barry M. Goldwater, Jr., United States Congress, Washington, D.C.

Ann B. Goodman, M.A., M.S., Information Sciences Division, Rockland Research Institute, Orangeburg, New York.

Gilbert Honigfeld, Ph.D., Associate Director, Clinical Research Department, Sandoz, Inc., East Hanover, New Jersey.

Nathan S. Kline, M.D., Director, Rockland Psychiatric Institute, Orangeburg, New York.

Edward I. Koch, U.S. Congress, Washington, D.C.

Eugene M. Laska, Ph.D., Director, Information Sciences Division, Rockland Psychiatric Institute, Orangeburg, New York.

Michael S. Levine, Chief of Statistics and Record Center, Connecticut Mental Health Center, and Lecturer, Department of Psychiatry, Yale University School of Medicine, New Haven, Connecticut.

Morris Meisner, Ph.D., Information Sciences Division, Rockland Research Institute, Orangeburg, New York.

Myron Pulier, M.D., Information Sciences Division, Rockland Research Institute, Orangeburg, New York.

Carole Siegel, Ph.D., Information Sciences Division, Rockland Research Institute, Orangeburg, New York.

George M. Simpson, M.B., Ch.B., M.R.C. Psych., Principal Research Psychiatrist, Rockland Research Institute, Orangeburg, New York.

Robert L. Spitzer, M.D., Evaluation Section, Biometrics Research, New York State Department of Mental Hygiene and Department of Psychiatry, Columbia University, New York, New York.

Zebulon Taintor, M.D., Director, Multi-State Information System, Information Sciences Division, Rockland Research Institute, Orangeburg, New York.

Gary L. Tischler, M.D., Associate Director, Connecticut Mental Health Center and Associate Professor of Clinical Psychiatry, Yale University School of Medicine, New Haven, Connecticut.

Oscar P. Weiner, M.S.S.A., Chairman, Utilization Review Committee, Connecticut Mental Health Center, and Associate Professor of Social Work in Clinical Psychiatry, Yale University School of Medicine, New Haven, Connecticut.

Alan F. Westin, Ph.D., Professor of Public Law and Government, Columbia University, New York, New York.

Baila Zeitz, Information Sciences Division, Rockland Research Institute, Orangeburg, New York.

To

David and Esther
Estelle
Jeffery, Lori, Mark and Matthew

Preface

Many studies show that a person with a mental disease spends much of his or her life suffering from it. If hospitalized or treated once, the individual is likely to need further hospitalization or treatment at some other time. Given this pattern, it is natural to assume that analysis of information describing the manifestations of mental illness, the development of symptoms, the treatments prescribed, and the course of the illness during and after treatment will contribute to a discovery of causes and, possibly, prevention techniques and to an understanding of the best methods of therapeutic intervention.

In this context, in 1967 the United States Department of Health, Education, and Welfare through the National Institute of Mental Health granted funds to the Information Sciences Division of the Rockland Research Institute for the creation of an automated psychiatric record system. The result, the Multi-State Information System, is a system for keeping records about individuals needing care and about the delivery of care. The system is to be used for facility and program administration, for research, and, especially, for improving the therapeutic rehabilitation of the patient.

The use of modern computing equipment and data processing techniques in psychiatry, however, is not without danger to individual privacy and to the confidential relationship between clinician and patient. Yet it is possible to gather and analyze information without trampling on human rights. Data can and must be protected from improper scrutiny, misuse or disclosure by means of physical and technical security and by legislation. Though aware of the dangers of automation, society seems to have concluded that the potential benefits of automation make it worth the risk, so long as one proceeds with caution and under constant public vigilance.

The desire to share the experiences gained by users of the Multi-State Information System and to describe efforts to protect the privacy and confidentiality of the data stored in it have inspired this book. It is an attempt to bring some perspective to the issues surrounding utilization of automated psychiatric information systems and basic human rights to privacy.

We are grateful to the staff of the Information Sciences Division who have expended considerable effort in the development of the Multi-State Information System and have thus contributed to this book. Parts 1 and 2 were written by Jon Bangs, Jeffrey Crawford, Peter Dannenberg, Vincent Dimiceli, Bruce Fairman, Nurhan Findikyan, Robert Kaufl, George W. Logemann, Morris Meisner, Donn Morrill, Mary Jo Ohliger, Bernice Proctor, Myron Pulier, Robert Schore, Carole Siegel, Leonard Spivak, Joseph Wanderling, Stanley Wasylyk, Baila Zeitz, William Zeitz, Peter Ziek, and us. Special thanks for editorial assistance, painstakingly and patiently performed, are due to Robert Schore. The tedious task of manuscript preparation was beautifully accomplished by Mary Lima, with the assistance of Vivian Gualano, Mary Stebbins, and Patricia Douglas. Photographic expertise was supplied by Sidney Bernstein.

We also thank our many colleagues in the mental health community whose support, contribution to, and enhancement of the work of this Department have strongly contributed to those components of MSIS that may be called a success. Included are not only the contributors to this volume but others too numerous to mention. One person whose constant encouragement and involvement requires special mention is Dr. Earl Pollack. He acted as MSIS project officer for NIMH from 1967 to 1974. Often times the solutions to problems that served to decrease our frustration levels were effected at the cost of raising his. Vivian Gualano falls into the same category and we ask her to accept our sincerest appreciation.

EUGENE M. LASKA
RHETA BANK

Orangeburg, New York
May 1975

Acknowledgments

A great many people have contributed to the development of the Multi-State Information System. Below is a partial list of our colleagues and associates for whose efforts we are extremely grateful. A complete listing would be impossibly long—we, therefore, extend our gratitude and appreciation to the many friends, colleagues, staff members, and collaborators not listed here.

Dr. Nathan S. Kline created the Rockland Research Institute and a unique environment fostering innovative research and development.

Dr. George W. Logemann was for six years the Associate Director of the Division and his herculean efforts guided the technical development of MSIS.

Drs. Morris Meisner and Carole Siegel from the very beginning provided formal mathematical collaboration, consultation, and support.

Dr. Earl Pollack of the National Institute of Mental Health was Project Officer for the MSIS grant. His very special encouragement we most appreciate.

Dr. George M. Simpson consulted on many aspects of the MSIS clinical system.

Drs. Robert L. Spitzer and Jean Endicott were the principal workers in the *Ad Hoc* Committee on Forms, which guided the development of an integrated set of forms that are the core of the MSIS clinical record.

Abbott Weinstein was for five years co-principal investigator of the MSIS grant and guided the development of the local services system used by the New York State Department of Mental Hygiene.

Cecil Wurster of the National Institute of Mental Health worked closely with both ISD staff and state participants.

Members of the Liaison Committee reviewed the statistical and legal data requirements of each participating state and designed the basic census-keeping forms.

Members of the Community Mental Health Center Users Group consulted on the design of those modules of MSIS that are especially suitable for the needs of community mental health centers.

Members of the Committee of Commissioners reviewed plans and advised on the development directions taken by MSIS.

Members of the MSIS staff labored long and hard to make plans turn into operational systems.

E. M. L.
R. B.

Contents

PART 4. LEGAL AND SOCIAL ISSUES

Safeguarding Psychiatric Privacy

1 Perspectives

Introduction

A revolutionary change in mental health service delivery has permeated all types of psychiatric facilities in the past two decades. First, the introduction of psychotropic drugs by 1955 had a dramatic effect in alleviating symptomatology and maladaptive behavior, made possible the return of countless patients from the chronic wards of state hospitals to their homes, and enabled others to remain in their communities and receive treatment from outpatient facilities. The reduction of patient populations in massive state institutions, more clearly seen by the early 1960s, caused administrators of these hospitals to reevaluate the roles and functions of these facilities; thus began a gradual transition of the state hospital into a multimodality psychiatric center which has yet to achieve final form and, in all likelihood, will remain in a state of perpetual transition to reflect everchanging mental health practices.

Second, the Community Mental Health Center Act of 1963 marked the clearest display yet of federal concern and involvement in mental health service delivery by providing funding and staffing grants with a concomitant commitment to criteria that clearly delineated the growing emphasis on community-based programs and on alternatives to long-term hospitalization for psychiatric patients. The inclusion of some mental health benefits in Medicare and Medicaid legislation is another logical extension of growing federal interest. Now all treatment modalities and alternatives will be available regardless of socioeconomic lines: no longer will state hospitals be the province of the poor; no longer will outpatient psychotherapy be exclusively for the middle class.

Third, changes in society itself have produced new attitudes toward psychiatric treatment, and much of the social stigma has been dissipated. This has fostered greater utilization of psychiatric service.

Finally, the growth of consumerism has brought to ordinary citizens a role in administering and reviewing governmental services including mental health, so that the programs of mental health facilities are no longer the exclusive domains of the medical professional: legislators, taxpayers, citizens, and users of the service all have input into program planning, and all demand to know how funds are spent and what results are obtained. The psychiatric administrator is now accountable for programs and service delivery to the board of directors of the facility, the state department of mental health, the state legislative committee, the legislature, the taxpayer, the federal funding source, professional bodies, third party payers, and so on. The professional mental health specialist is also faced with the challenge to prove usefulness and effectiveness to Professional Standards Review Organizations (PSRO) and utilization review committees and to meet criticisms inherent in recent court decisions pertaining to the patient's right to effective treatment.

Accountability, utilization review, evaluating effectiveness, program planning, and budgeting are administrative activities dependant upon data, properly gathered and readily disseminated. The clinician who desires to achieve a more objective base of operations and the researcher who aims to determine the effectiveness and viability of various treatment procedures also rely on data systems which allow inspection of a multitude of variables.

Data have always been collected in mental health facilities. Administrators have always had need to keep track of patients, staff, costs, requisitions, clinical procedures, and dispositions and have always had a variety of manual means supplemented by simple office equipment to accomplish the task. Indeed, even a computer can be used as an elaborate typewriter with capabilities for memory and retrieval.

If an information system is conceivable without the use of computers, why should a computer with its associated expense, with the aura it creates, and with the concerns it raises be introduced. Similar questions are raised by the smaller developing countries or by mental health facilities struggling for funding: Would not the best use of the mental health dollar be spent on direct patient care and the expense of computers be deferred to more productive economic times? Cost-conscious administrators ask to be shown that computers reduce patient days, minimize expenses, and/or improve treatment.

As the scope of mental health treatment expands, as new therapeutic modalities are introduced, as the functions of psychiatric facilities broaden, as new drugs are tried, and as new educational and preventive programs are used, the range of information that needs to be tracked, analyzed, organized, compared, and reviewed becomes quite formidable. Countless psychiatric facilities exist with manually maintained massive files of thousands of patients who have passed through the doors and received therapy with varying treatment outcomes. Yet despite the accumulation of this information, it remains unavailable to the clinician, researcher, and administrator because retrieval problems are insurmountable as can be illustrated by the example of a single patient who upon readmission to a psychiatric hospital may be prescribed a similar drug regimen as previously despite its prior lack of success or unfortunate side effects. Difficulty in retrieving this patient's previous chemotherapy even though documented in a manually maintained chart results in the loss of this knowledge to the present treating psychiatrist and possibly unnecessary extensions of treatment time.

More broadly, consider the administrator or researcher who would like to review the success of a particular therapeutic modality on a specific group of patients. The information is there in the records, but scores of workers would have to delve for months to locate such data which could be available in moments through computer-organized collection and retrieval procedures. Computer technology grew out of the needs to organize data in usable ways and to expedite analytic processes and calculations.

In the changing mental health delivery system, more is needed than the simple procedures previously available. A viable information system means that a sufficient number of variables reflecting mental health operations will be collected and that these variables will be presented quickly in a variety of formats with data analyzed, sequenced, and reorganized in as many ways as needed.

Nobody argues with the need for computing equipment for use in the housekeeping functions of mental health institutions. The requirements for keeping track of valuable resources are the same in this activity as in most other activities of society. Payroll, accounts payable, accounts receivable, inventory, and amount of laundry utilized must be monitored. The uniqueness of the utilization of computing in the field of mental health derives from the need for what might be lifetime information on individuals requiring professional intervention.

A mental health information system can be designed to follow the trends and statistics of an entire service delivery system, a single facility, or the problems of care given to an individual patient during his lifetime. While system, institution, and patient could all survive without the presence of the computer, its introduction has the potential of evaluating service delivery systems, of expediting the functioning of that institution, and of monitoring the course of the patient's stay within a facility in order to see that he does more than merely "survive," that he receives objective, clinically valid treatment wherever in the mental health service delivery system he is, and that such intervention enhances the quality of his life. The total information system is as revolutionary as the growth and development that have been the most recent characteristics of mental health delivery systems.

The introduction of computers has brought polarized reactions either of awe or trepidation. The application of computer technology to mental health problems brings this same divergent response further complicated by concerns about the effects of this technology upon privacy, confidentiality, and the safeguarding of individual rights. These issues are discussed in the ensuing chapters of this book. The need to develop protection mechanisms to insure privacy and maintain confidential records can best be examined by first understanding the scope of a psychiatric information system, the nature of the data it accumulates, and the uses of this system as part of mental health service delivery.

The goals of a computerized information system in mental health may be envisioned along several broad lines:

1. *Individual Patient Record Keeping.* The system is designed to assist clinicians in the management of individual patient care by taking note of key facts in the patient's psychiatric, social, and medical history: documenting treatment interventions; keeping track of problems and treatment goals; and recording outcomes.

Maintaining extensive records during the course of the lifetime of an individual is among the most complex tasks which can be performed. No individual can ever really get to know another on the basis of simple external facts. Even if these were known, their organization into a comprehensive, simple context would be difficult. Enter the computer system and the hope that it can shuffle, correlate, integrate, and reorganize the data into a cohesive presentation for the clinician both to meet his requirements for ordinary record keeping and to aid his interpretive processes which result in therapeutic decisions and treatment-goal planning.

In addition, complete patient records enhance the monitoring of service delivery, especially safeguarding against illegal or unnecessary involuntary commitments.

2. *Facility Management.* On the simplest level, a system would provide the basic housekeeping needs: payroll, billing, accounts receivable and payable, purchasing, inventory—the same computer applications found in business, industry, and government.

Administration, however, is broader than usual business functions and includes monitoring patients being served, allocating resources, evaluating key treatment indices such as discharge or readmission rates, displaying the resources for serving patients, and generally noting the quality of care.

Administrative data is needed on two levels: within the facility by administration for its own monitoring, budgeting, planning, and day to day operations, and as the basis for accountability reporting to professional and funding groups.

3. *Planning and Evaluation.* Mental health professionals can no longer conduct their practice within an "ivory tower." Particularly in psychiatry, the mental health professional may be more vulnerable than most to the demand that he prove that appropriate treatment has been offered and that he establish the value of his outcomes. Recent court decisions based on patient claims of lack of treatment have underscored the need for continued self-evaluation and activity documentation.

Established practices are no longer taken for granted as psychiatrists from one school of thought delve into other theories, and increasing numbers of therapists stake claim to eclectic practices. Newer forms of medical record keeping such as the problem-oriented record or records that measure patient goal attainments are being developed. All this information can be used for program planning, for monitoring treatment, and for developing new service standards.

4. *Research Support.* Information systems accumulate large data bases on which epidemiological, demographic, and other investigative researches can be carried out, including the determination of optimal strategies for therapeutic intervention. The analytic and computational capabilities of the computer compliment the research design, allowing complex data-manipulation activities.

5. *Regional Management of Mental Health Service Delivery.* A regional information system can be designed so that it helps administrators to facilitate continuity of care, to balance relationships among organizations, to monitor services rendered, to insure the availability of needed services within regional areas and, in general, to review the way in which service providers and residents of an area interact. Growing interest has developed, particularly in view of economic realities, in eliminating duplications of service through better area-wide coordination, controlled referral patterns, and balanced programs of service keyed to the needs of target populations within designated catchment areas.

6. *State and Local Government Management of Mental Health Resources.* The same information system that supports individual facility activities can be used to aggregate the data so that it facilitates management of large mental health delivery systems.

7. *National Assessment of Mental Health Delivery Systems.* Data is used to insure that recipients of federal support implement programs as required by law. National trends on the problems of the mentally ill and on the utilization of service-delivery agencies can be reviewed and lead to planning of new federal programs.

8. *Protection of Privacy and Confidentiality.* An automated information system must incorporate into the system design technical and legal safeguards of the data.

9. *Education and Training.*   By helping to describe existing mental health delivery systems and the patients served, a good information system provides the basis for training mental health professionals, informing the public, and motivating funding sources.

PURPOSES OF THIS BOOK

This book discusses the use of computer technology in mental health facilities and the social and legal issues arising from such use. The computer's role includes and goes beyond normal bookkeeping chores and helping to maintain patient records; the computer is used as a clinical instrument in diagnosis, treatment, and monitoring; as an administrative instrument in planning, resource allocation, and peer review; as a research tool; and as a library of information about patients, therapies, trends, and treatment modes.

Part 1 of this book is historical. The development of computers and their impact on society and on psychiatry, in particular, is traced. The evolution of medical–psychiatric record keeping is also documented as prelude to a discussion of how computer technology impacts record-keeping practice. In addition, some of the existing mental health information systems in various countries, states, and individual facilities are described.

Part 2 is a description of a particular mental health information system, the Multi-State Information System (MSIS), and is illustrative of the extensive use to which such a system may be put.

Part 3 is a series of contributions from users which describe some of the applications particular agencies have made of this information system. These papers show some of the actual uses of the system, relate the kinds of things that can be accomplished with the data collected, and demonstrate how the delivery of mental health services is enhanced by computer technology.

Part 4 addresses itself to the legal and social issues raised by electronic data collection in mental health including the pooling of technical resources for underdeveloped nations and the need for protection of individual rights. The collected papers are from lawyers, from congressional leaders in the United States, and from MSIS personnel and serve to delineate the problems of data security. Some of the solutions adapted by MSIS to address these problems are presented.

Brief History of Computers

Civilization, from earliest recorded times, has been imbued with a natural curiosity to expand knowledge of its encompassing environment and surrounding universe. The history of today's modern electronic computer begins with mankind's earliest desires to understand nature, record the knowledge acquired, and systematically recall this information when needed.

In prehistoric days, pictorial representations on cave walls and symbolic language served the purpose of recording and transmitting knowledge. As civilization advanced, commerce and trade developed within and among neighboring groups with a concomitant need for accurate mathematical systems to aid in keeping count of populations, objects, and possessions. Concern with the heavens and the unseen powers within the universe resulted in the development of astronomy. Mathematics and astronomy were seen as the keys to understanding the universe. Spoken language, the art of writing, and systems of counting, while indeed helpful, were recognized as being insufficient by themselves for the task of recording, storing, analyzing, and communicating vast amounts of information. Innately inventive, a number of early cultures in different locations and at different points in time simultaneously turned to devising mechanical aids that would afford both reliability and speed to help in the process.

HISTORICAL DEVELOPMENTS

The earliest forerunner of the computer, the abacus, has been traced back to the 6th century, B.C., where it was in use in China. Similar counting devices employing beads and strings were developed independently, but within three centuries of each other, in Japan and in the Mediterranean lands of the Greek and Roman era. Simplistic in design and still in use today, it met the need for a reliable, fast device that would expedite arithmetical processes. Sundials and water clocks were other inventions of this period that provided means for mathematical and astronomical calculations.

During the Middle Ages and the Renaissance, the perfection of the lever and the gear promoted the construction of mechanically operated clocks and rotating models of the planets; the increase in commerce and shipping encouraged the invention of advanced calculation devices such as the compass and the slide rule and the development of bookkeeping and accounting systems. The invention of the printing press has been well documented historically, but it is noted here because of the impact it made on promoting communication and social interchange and on increasing the need for solutions to problems created by the information explosion.

Increasingly, scientists and inventors turned their talents to the problems of information handling. Recently discovered papers of Leonardo di Vinci show that he had an early plan for an automatic calculating machine. William Schikard, in 1623, designed a "calculating clock" using a system of rods and gears but it was not successfully implemented. In 1642 in France, Blaise Pascal to assist his father, a tax collector, devised a calculating machine capable of addition. His machine was built, and historians regard it as the first operating digital computer. Between 1663 and 1673 Sir Samuel Morland in England developed three partially successful calculators with capabilities for addition, multiplication, and trigonometric functions. In Germany in 1671 Gottfried Wilhelm von Leibnitz devised a calculator with the ability to multiply. Built by 1694 this machine made possible the mechanical calculation of trigonometric and astronomical tables.

In 1780 Joseph Marie Jacquard, motivated by what he regarded as the inefficiency and tedious routine of the weaving loom on which he worked, designed an automated operation utilizing a series of cards with punched holes to control the feeding of the threads in proper sequence through the loom to form varied designs. This idea, seemingly far removed from computational mechanisms, would have greater significance a century later.

The 18th century found many scientists working to perfect calculating machines capable of automating mathematical processes. These machines tended to be bulky, gear driven, and not truly reliable. Johann Helfrich von Muller was responsible for designing in 1782 a machine utilizing gears and cranks that could perform the four basic processes of addition, subtraction, multiplication, and division.

Still no one had designed a machine that could operate with little human intervention and that could remember its calculations. An English scientist, Charles Babbage, became interested in the task and made it virtually his life's work. As a result of his efforts, he is regarded by some as the "father of the computer," for the machines he designed ultimately incorporated functions that are part of the electronic computing equipment in use today.

Babbage's first major design was for his difference engine which was to have the capability of calculating mathematical tables based on differences of figures and of presenting the results not as numbers on machine dials but in a series of tables, typeset and printed by the machine. However the cost for this machine was excessive and the needed materials were not available, so work on it stopped in 1833.

Babbage meanwhile had developed the ideas for a different kind of machine that he called an analytic engine. This machine would have more versatile functions, perform rapidly, and be cheaper and simpler to construct. Powered by steam energy, this machine would perform all arithmetical processes, in any series or combinations, and solve any mathematical problem. There were to be four basic parts: a "store" that served as a memory bank for numbers and results, a "mill" where the arithmetic calculations took place, a "sequencer" to direct operations, and an input and output mechanism capable of printing results on paper tape or punching them on cards. The functions of today's computers are input, storage, control, logic, and output, divisions consistent with Babbage's earlier thinking. Babbage was laughed at by many of his associates, and while initially supported by some government funds, eventually lost financial backing for his work, and during his lifetime was unable to see his own machine fully built. However he did live to see his principles implemented in a calculating machine built by George Scheutz of Sweden in 1853. This machine was exhibited at the Paris World's Fair, 2 years later, and then put into use at an observatory in the United States. A small part of the mill section of the analytic engine was built by Babbage's son after his father's death, but again material, cost, and the limited technology of the day made Babbage's basic inventions only theoretical successes.

A computing machine was planned by William Thomson in England in 1876 but was not built until 1930 by Vannevar Bush at the Massachusetts Institute of Technology. Other efforts in the late 19th and early 20th centuries centered around the perfection and widespread utilization of adding machines, comptometers, and similar business equipment.

The next major figure in computer development, Herman Hollerith, a statistician for the United States Census Bureau, was concerned with the lengthy time needed to process the results of the 1880 census; by the time the data was fully analyzed through traditional hand computation, it was found no longer useful. Winning the backing of census officials, he set to work on a tabulating machine to be used for the 1890 census. He received inspiration from two very divergent sources: by observing an anonymous railroad conductor using a hole puncher to punch passenger tickets and by turning his attention to Jacquard's automated weaving loom and the use of punched cards to control it. Hollerith's tabulating machine performed data processing utilizing punched cards where holes punched in various places on the cards indicated the response to different questions asked on the census. The punched holes properly registered on the tabulating machine which sorted the cards. The census count for 1890 proceeded twice as rapidly as had the 1880 census, and an initial general population count was available before the year was out. Hollerith went on to perfect his equipment further for use in subsequent census counts and in business. The same device was incorporated into the maintenance of Social Security data in later years.

ELECTRONIC COMPUTERS

By the 1930s business and government offices were well equipped with a variety of computational machinery. Generally all these machines were based on mechanical operations and were limited in how fast they operated or in how complicated a problem they could handle without a human operator controlling the machine through all facets of its operation. Memory systems and programming had not yet been developed.

In 1939 Howard Aiken and a team of engineers at Harvard University initiated work on a large-scale, electromechanical computer with capabilities for more automated advanced mathematical processes. Spurred on by military demands of World War II, the Automatic Sequence Control Calculator, the Mark I, was completed in 1944 by International Business Machines Corporation (IBM). Put into use by the United States Navy to calculate trajectories for ballistic missles, Mark I basically consisted of a series of 78 adding machines and office calculators linked together by a roll of programmed perforated paper. The Mark I computer now performed in minutes, and even in seconds, calculations that previously had taken large teams weeks of around-the-clock operations. In addition, Mark I was designed to operate from remote terminals using telephone lines and was also able to operate without human intervention once a program was started. It remained in use until 1959.

The need for even speedier computations spurred work on an all-electronic computer, one that did not need the more laborious mechanical parts. The United States Army authorized development of the Electron Numerical Integrator and Calculator (ENIAC) which was designed by J. P. Eckert and J. W.

Mauchly at the University of Pennsylvania. Built as a secret project during World War II, it actually did not become operational until 1946 after the war had ended. In the ENIAC mechanical parts were replaced with electronic valves and relays, with a resultant improvement in speed and capabilities, but its operation was impeded by the time-consuming tasks of setting up problems, of setting appropriate switches, and of making the various plug and socket connections. Its initial work, like that of Mark I, was in the area of computing the trajectories of ballistics. The development of electronic computers was greatly speeded by the impetus of military needs.

Other machines developed in the late 1940s and early 1950s included the BINAC by Eckert and Mauchly, in which the use of magnetic tape to store information and crystal diodes that replaced switches greatly improved speed and efficiency over the ENIAC. Aiken went on to develop the Mark II (1947), Mark III (1950), and Mark IV (1952).

Maurice V. Wilkes at Cambridge University, England, built the Electronic Delay Storage Automatic Calculator in 1949, one of the first stored-program computers. John von Neuman completed the Electronic Discrete Variable Automatic Computer (EDVAC) by 1950, providing for branching, looping, modifying sequences, and obtaining instructions from memory. IBM built the Selective Sequence Electronic Calculator (SSEC) by 1948. The Automatic Calculating Engine (ACE) was completed in England in 1950 and the Eastern Automatic Computer (SEAC) at the Bureau of Standards was in operation by 1951.

The first machine built for commercial use was the Universal Automatic Computer (UNIVAC) designed by Eckert and Mauchly who had formed their own company. The machine became operational by 1951. Its initial use was for the United States Bureau of the Census, but it became noted as the first computer available to business and industry. It could store programs and had a compiler which translated programs into machine language. The success of UNIVAC, in essence, marked the close of the experimental era of computer development. Electronic computing now emerged as an important new component of the everyday scene and as a new industry with professional and technical personnel. By 1953 the market for commercially produced computers greatly expanded in the United States.

Since 1955 cost factors have decreased, computer processes have been expedited to function at faster speeds, memory-storage units have increased in their retention capacities, and subsidiary equipment and processes such as minicomputers, smaller remote terminals linked to central computers and time-sharing procedures, have developed.

The earliest electronic computers operated with vacuum tubes and have become known in the industry as "first-generation" computers. They were large, took up much space, and performed computations in milliseconds (thousandths of a second). Bell Laboratories developed the transistor in 1948, and a gradual changeover chiefly between 1956 and 1959 from tube to transistorized machines was made. Computers that were transistorized became known as "second generation" computers, took up less space, and increased computer speed to microseconds (millionths of a second). The "third generation" of computers utilized integrated circuits, were on the market by 1965, and performed in nanoseconds (billionths of a second).

Programming systems have advanced with changes in machine design from the wiring techniques used at the end of World War II to the machine language code of the late 1940s and early 1950s to the relatively machine-independent procedure-oriented languages (FORTRAN, ALGOL, COBOL) of the late 1950s and early 1960s to problem-oriented languages approximating a stylized natural language in the middle 1960s and to a concentrated (but not successful) effort to establish a universal procedure-oriented language (PL/1) in the late 1960s.

While initial research and experimentation in computer design has been centered in the United States and Great Britain, other countries including France, Germany, the Soviet Union, Japan, Sweden, Switzerland, Canada, and Australia to lesser degrees have been engaged in computer development.

In the generic sense, the term "computer" refers to any electronic or mechanical device that performs arithmetic or logical computations. Thus, in the broad sense, the term would correctly describe pocket calculators, adding machines, telephone switching systems, air defense systems, and commercial data processing systems. In the sense normally implied in every day use, however, the term refers to a particular subset of these devices: the digital computer.

A digital computer is a high-speed, electronic, internally programmed device. In the digital computer, the binary digit, or bit, is adopted as the elementary unit of information. All information is coded in terms of bits, and all operations in the computer are performed at this elementray level. Since each bit can have only 0 or 1 as values, data are represented internally as strings of 0's and 1's.

There are further classifications of digital computers which are possible, but two are of usual interest. Computers can be designed in such a way as to suit one specific class of operations. Those which are designed to handle great numbers of calculations with relatively small amounts of data are referred to as "scientific computers." Those which are designed to handle great amounts of data with relatively small numbers of calculations are referred to as "commercial computers." Both classes of machine can usually accommodate both types of work, but with differing, relative degrees of efficiency. If the computer is not designed especially to suit one specific class of problems, then it is referred to as a "general purpose computer."

Modern digital computers have a distinctive architecture when compared with early computers. Both for purposes of design and for implementation, three major functions are distinguished: input/output, processing, and memory. These different functions are translated into the computer architecture as physically identifiable subsystems, depending on the scale of the system. Large-scale, commercial systems are usually comprised of many discrete pieces of equipment, each of which serves one of the basic functions. Each "box" in the system is interconnected with others by cables, which are the paths for control information as well as data. In small-scale, "mini systems" on the other hand, there are fewer discrete units, but the basic functional units are still distinct and identifiable.

The input/output (I/O) subsystem controls the operation of the various peripheral devices and transfers information between these devices and the memory. The most common peripheral devices are magnetic tapes and disks, card readers and punches, and paper tape readers and punches, but a wide variety of special-purpose equipment is usually available to suit application requirements. On command from the processor, the I/O subsystem activates the device designated. Data is either transferred from the device to memory (input) or from memory to the device (output). The data which are transferred are usually envisioned as information to be processed by a particular program, but programs can also be stored on I/O equipment for retrieval and execution on command.

The memory subsystem stores all information which is directly processed by processing subsystem. This information includes both computational data and program instructions. Memory is organized into basic units of information, called words, which represent a fixed number of bits. The number of bits per word varies with the design of the system and is typically 16 to 24 for small- to medium-scale computers and upwards of 32 to 36 bits for larger-scale machines. The word is usually the smallest unit of information transferred between the subsystems, although further subdivisions are possible.

The function of the processing subsystem (processor) varies in detail depending on the general class of work for which the computer is intended, but can generally be said to include arithmetic/logic operations and program control. The operation of the processor is controlled on a step-by-step basis by a set of instructions called a program. Any intended computer operation must be stated in terms of elementary operations such as add, subtract, compare, branch, read, write, skip, and so on and must be initially introduced into the memory from some input device. Subsequently the processor control unit selects commands from memory and presents them to the arithmetic/logic unit for execution. The control unit can be directed to alter its normal sequential selection sequence, as in the case of a branch, which permits the processor to exercise decision functions that have been preprogrammed.

The general power of computers stems from the fact that the average computer is able to execute several million basic operations per second, while controlling a wide variety of I/O equipment.

AREAS OF USE

The first computers were constructed for use in mathematical and engineering applications. As mentioned above many subsequent developments were motivated by military necessity. Scientific problems also provided an impetus since complex computations can shorten or replace costly experiments in meteorology, quantum chemistry, nuclear physics, and space exploration. In the United States, commercial versions of prototype computers, many built for the armed services, the space agencies, and the Atomic Energy Commission, were subsequently marketed for the private sector. Soon these machines were utilized in business for processing large volumes of data but with relatively simple computations in such areas as clerical inventory control, payroll processing, and mailing-list maintenance.

In the late 1960s computers began to be used more and more for management purposes, including the generation of statistics, summaries, timetables, and production schedules. Computers began gaining importance in such diverse areas as education, library science, printing, telephone switchi g, legal research, and medical applications.

By the early 1970s computers were in general governmental and business use in every major industrialized country of the world. The United States holds the lead in the extent of governmental and commercial utilization of computers and in the number of actual installations of computers and terminals. While in 1950 only 15 computers were installed and in use in the United States, by 1960 the number of installations had increased to an estimated 5000. In 1970 there were over 40,000 computers in use, and by the end of the decade, experts anticipate over 100,000 computer installations.

The largest users of computers are governments, where the emphasis is on social and economic development. Japan, England, Canada, and the countries of Western Europe also make widespread use of computer technology at ever-increasing rates. The smaller, developing countries of Africa, Asia, and the Near East are entering the field. Demography, economic planning, taxation, social insurance, public health, and resource management are areas of particular importance for both industrialized and developing countries.

A variety of examples of computerized information systems illustrate pragmatic uses of computers. The United States' military defense system is based upon the computerized systems of the Strategic Air Command. Midflight space corrections are ordered instantly after consulting real-time output from the computers of the National Aeronautic and Space Administration. Airline reservation systems, department store inventories, and tickets to Broadway shows are handled by computers. Urban planning, traffic control, industrial automation, telephone systems, and television production also typify the diverse application of computer technology. More esoteric roles played by computers are in widely different areas such as computer-assisted instruction, social dating, off-track betting, and machine games. Some computer engineers predict for the 1990s, a computer in every home to help the housekeeper shop, plan menus, and control internal home climate; to keep the employed members of the family in contact with the "office"; to give the student access to library catalogs and his university; and to give the citizen the opportunity of voicing his opinion instantly on legislative issues.

THE COMPUTER IN MEDICINE

The medical field illustrates an important use of the computer for the benefit of mankind. The potential in this area is in the computer's ability to retain information, both in terms of medical literature and in terms of patient's clinical records, and to perform real-time functions, that is collecting instant, current data on an ongoing problem or situation and comparing it at once with stored information on the problem. In terms of a medical patient, information on an individual's present symptoms and biological functions and processes sent immediately into a computer can be analyzed in terms of past information about that patient and compared with knowledge and norms. The computer can then indicate an analysis, make suggestions for possible diagnosis, detail further tests needed, and delineate possible modes of therapy.

The Latter Day Saint's Hospital in Salt Lake City, Utah, since 1954 has made just such use of computer technology on an extended scale, particularly in cardiovascular research, patient monitoring of vital life signs, laboratory test analyses as well as medical instruction and statistical studies.

The Kaiser Foundation Hospital in Oakland, California, has developed a prototype data information system (1) that has been introduced in multiphasic health testing centers throughout the United States. An individual receiving an annual preventive examination has most tests performed and analyzed through a computer link, may answer a medical questionnaire recorded on a machine, and may have his medical record as part of the computer's memory bank.

The National Institute of Health in Bethesda, Maryland, where much cancer research has been centered, is developing an information system based on the findings of over 100,000 research papers. The Fox Chase Center for Cancer and Medical Sciences in Philadelphia, Pennsylvania, is studying radiation therapy utilizing computers. The United States Public Health Service has devised a computer program to standardize cardiogram analysis. Mt. Sinai Hospital in New York City has linked its computer by telephone to rural towns in West Virginia 500 miles distant, so that instant cardiogram findings are made available to physicians. Downstate Medical Center in Brooklyn, New York, maintains a computer with over 100 terminals, automating medical records, providing ready access to the physician of a patient's previous medical history and therapies and freeing nurses from clerical chores. Computers also control blood distribution networks with listings of donors, availability, and recipients. A computer link exists between the emergency room of Boston's Logan Airport and the Massachusetts General Hospital.

Computers in psychiatry (2) have played a role in simulated interviews and in administering, scoring, and standardizing intelligence and personality tests, chiefly on an experimental and research basis. In terms of service delivery in mental health, computers function in the realms of data collection, psychiatric/medical record keeping, psychotropic drug monitoring, evaluation of patient treatment and goal attainments, and in the establishment of a total mental health information system. It is to these ends that the following chapters of this volume are addressed.

REFERENCES

1. M. F. Collen, "The Multi-Test Laboratory in Health Care of the Future," *Hospitals*, **41**, May 1967.
2. N. S. Kline and E. M. Laska, Eds., *Computers and Electronic Devices in Psychiatry*, Grune and Stratton, New York, 1968.

BIBLIOGRAPHY

W. Desmonde, *Computers and their Uses*, Prentice-Hall, Englewood Cliffs, 1971.

H. Goldstine, *The Computer from Pascal to von Neumann*, Princeton University Press, Princeton, 1972.

C. C. Gotlieb and A. Borodin, *Social Issues in Computing*, Academic Press, New York, 1973.

N. Hawkes, *The Computer Revolution*, E. P. Dutton, Ed., New York, 1972.

IBM, Instructors Guide, *Special Academic Computer Concepts Course for University, Library, and Museum Executives and Scholarly Associations in the Humanities*, IBM, 1968.

J. G. Kemeny, *Man and the Computer*, Charles Scribner's Sons, New York, 1972.

G. B. F. Niblett, *Digital Information and the Privacy Problem*, Organization for Economic Co-Operation and Development, Paris, 1971.

J. M. Rosenberg, *The Computer Prophets*, Macmillan, New York, 1969.

K. R. Stehling, *Computers and You*, World Publishing, New York, 1972.

Brief History of
Psychiatric-Medical Records

The keeping of medical records is as old as the practice of medicine. Early murals recorded medical achievements on the walls of caverns in Spain; later records of surgical procedures include tracings on clay tablets, hieroglyphs on Egyptian tombs, and long rolls of papyrus and parchment. In Greece where the Asclepiadae practiced medicine in temples called Aesculapia as early as 1134 B.C., columns among ruins in Epidaurus were marked with names of patients, brief case histories, and comments on whether or not the patients were cured (1).

Hippocrates, born about 460 B.C., practiced the principles of precise observation and exact description. He drew his basic knowledge of medicine from the case reports collected in the Aesculapia of Cos. Hippocrates' writings, although chiefly of historical value, contain descriptions of convulsive disorders that are still acknowledged as accurate. He kept detailed case reports and taught his sons, also physicians, to record all findings. His emphasis on facts, rather than faith, is revealed in his writing; during the period of Hippocrates and his disciples, medical care was closer in spirit to modern medicine than it was for the following 1500 years (2).

19

During the Graeco–Roman period, Galen (about A.D. 130–201) is known to have based his teaching on case reports. He had access to the Aesculapian tablets as well as to libraries. Unfortunately the quality of medicine and of medical records reflected the general deterioration in moral and spiritual status from Byzantine through early medieval times, a period of approximately 1000 years.

St. Bartholemew's Hospital, London, England, was founded during medieval times. Some of the records of its first patients still exist. Under King Henry VIII (1509–1547), rules for government of the hospital were written. Detailed instructions on safekeeping of the records as well as the collection of demographic information and statistics on diseases, cures, and deaths were enumerated in these rules.

When William Harvey became physician to St. Bartholemew's Hospital in 1609 part of his responsibility, as outlined in a document that still exists, was the keeping of case records.

Andreas Vesalius (1514–1564), who obtained his degree from the University of Padua, kept detailed records of surrepitious dissections (prohibited at that time by the Roman Catholic Church); these records contributed greatly to the knowledge of anatomy. Medieval medicine had become progressively more removed from reality, concerned with logical inference and rational elaboration rather than observation. Medical writings were chiefly philosophical treatises rather than case records. Vesalius emphasized the importance of seeing, doing, and recording rather than speculating. He was the first to hold the appointment of professor of anatomy at the University of Padua; the University was one of the first in Europe to provide a medical curriculum. Once Papal decree made dissection legal in 1556, the meticulous recording of observations on human anatomy was practiced, and these observations were made available for reference and study.

In the United States Benjamin Franklin was one of the prime movers in the establishment of the first incorporated hospital in 1752. Many of the earliest records of Pennsylvania Hospital were actually written by Franklin. Basic information on the first patients admitted still exists; after 1803 a more detailed record was kept of some cases. Histories were begun in 1873, and the file remains unbroken to the present.

The New York Hospital opened in 1771 and maintained a register from 1793. Many of the histories written after 1808 follow a routine similar to that of today. Some attempt at indexing disease was started in 1862, and a disease nomenclature was adopted in 1914. Massachusetts General Hospital, which opened in 1821, has a complete file of clinical records with all cases cataloged. This hospital employed the first medical records librarian, Mrs. Grace Whiting Myers, who later became the first president of the Association of Record Librarians of North America.

Although teaching hospitals had been keeping records for several hundred years, medical records did not receive serious attention from other medical institutions until 1902, when the American Hospital Association discussed problems of lack of uniformity and general indifference on the part of some doctors toward medical records. In 1905, at the 56th meeting of the American Medical Association, physicians themselves discussed the need for complete records and the reluctance of doctors in general to overcome their dislike of the effort necessary to maintain these records; this problem still exists (1).

STANDARDS FOR MEDICAL RECORDS

In 1913 the American College of Surgeons was founded. In order to elevate the standards of surgery, a national standardization of hospitals was proposed. Part of an editorial in the May 1919 issue of *Hospital Management* stated (3):

> The basis of standardized service is to know what the hospital is doing, and to record its work in such a way as to enable an appraisement to be made of it. . . . Records, therefore, are a prime essential in any program of hospital standardization. . . . Case records are the visible evidence of what the hospital is accomplishing. . . . Not to maintain case records properly is like running a factory without a record of the product.

When records compiled by candidates for fellowship were examined by the College, major deficiencies quickly became apparent; steady improvement in medical records began with hospital standardization.

Medical records personnel organized in 1929, bringing a rise in status for these workers and a concomitant improvement in the quality of the record. Increasingly stringent educational requirements for records personnel have been noted.

In 1952 the Joint Commission on Accreditation of Hospitals composed of members of the American Medical Association, the American Hospital Association, the American College of Surgeons, and the American College of Physicians assumed the responsibility for establishment of standards for hospitals in the United States. Accreditation requirements have further raised standards for medical reports (1). .

STANDARDS FOR PSYCHIATRIC RECORDS

The Hospital Accreditation Program was geared to the acute, general hospital. In 1970 the Accreditation Council for Psychiatric Facilities was created to implement standards specifically for psychiatric facilities (4, 5).

LEGAL ASPECTS OF MEDICAL RECORDS

Hospitals and other health care institutions in every state are required, either by statute or by administrative regulation, to maintain medical records. In addition, standards are set by the hospitals themselves, by professional organizations, and by accreditation groups. Minimum requirements as to what information must be present in the medical record are most often found in hospital-licensing regulations.

There is no question that the medical record is the property of the hospital; however the hospital has the responsibility for protecting the record from "unauthorized access." The personal data contained in the record are confidential because of the special relationship between patient and physician—a relationship that in many states extends by law to other medical professionals. The record is protected from unauthorized inspection by law in some states and by administrative practice in others (1).

The principle of confidentiality makes it imperative that whenever the record is to be used outside the confidential relationship written authorization be obtained from the patient. But even this seemingly simple rule is fraught with questions, particularly, although not exclusively, in the case of psychiatric records. Suppose, for example, that the patient himself demands access to information in his record that the physician thinks would be detrimental to his well being. Or suppose the relatives of an "incompetent" patient demand access to information on the patient's behalf. Since the very nature of psychiatric records often demands sensitive workups of immediate family members, the clinician may well be extremely reluctant to allow the patient's family access to this material. Thus access to records and rules governing this access must take questions of clinical judgment into account; current administrative and legal policies vary widely on this issue.

Not infrequently the medical record is used as evidence in court, most recently in successful suits brought by patients against the hospital (6, 7). A good record, which shows clearly the treatment given the patient, by whom given, and when given, affords protection to the hospital and the physicians involved, whereas incomplete or inaccurate records can result in serious liabilities.

Proliferation of automated methods for recording, storing, and retrieving medical record information has been accompanied by new problems of confidentiality.

CONTENTS OF THE PSYCHIATRIC RECORD

The medical record is a compendium of information about the patient, a storehouse of the knowledge concerning the patient and his care. To be complete the record must contain sufficient information to identify the patient clearly, to justify the diagnosis, and to record the results (1). A hospital record is typically begun in the admitting department, where identifying data are collected. The nurse adds the bedside record; the attending physician and co-workers add their notes documenting complaints, onset, and course of illness, personal and family history, report of physical examination, and a plan for study and treatment while the patient is in the hospital. Additional reports may include x-ray, laboratory, electroencephalogram and surgical procedures, all of which are filed by separate departments. Nurses record observations, medications, treatments, and other services rendered. The attending physician records progress of the patient and eventually composes a Discharge Summary.

For the psychiatric record, much additional information is required. A psychiatric history (anamnesis) is taken, and a mental status is performed for each patient admitted. Social service reports, psychological evaluations, legal papers, records of treatment including all therapeutic activities, and progress notes are needed. A final diagnosis based on nomenclature of the *Diagnostic and Statistical Manual* of the American Psychiatric Association must be included (8). The Discharge Summary should be a recapitulation of the course of the patient's illness and treatment during the hospital stay.

INADEQUACIES OF THE RECORD

Although general standards for the psychiatric record are specified in the Accreditation Manual (5), specific instructions on how to meet these standards do not exist. The past hundred years have seen tremendous growth in types of data available and needed, and steadily increasing demands on the medical record to accommodate these needs; yet the medical record has changed little over this period. In recent years the litany of criticism has grown more vociferous, particularly regarding the structure and format of the record or the lack thereof. Greenes et al. (9) state:

> Most medical records remain a chronologic repository of data and are not organized according to diagnostic or therapeutic problems. Relevant records may frequently not be located. One may find notes pertinent to a particular aspect of a patient's health only by leafing through an entire volume. Terminology is inconsistent, data are not organized in well defined formats, and notes are often illegible.

Organization of the record, according to Gordon (10), is rarely systematized even in research centers. In service hospitals the record is a "jumbling together of pages" that is apparently "prepared more in keeping with custom or in compliance with hospital regulations than for reference during the illness."

One type of information, decisional data, is rarely found in the medical record (11); it is usually impossible to tell, for example, why a schizophrenic patient receiving Stelazine was suddenly switched to Thorazine. Last complains that "... a patient's clinical record is little more than a partly chronological, incomplete and disjointed account of symptoms, physical signs, special investigations, progress and treatment. . . Rarely is an attempt made to delineate the decision-making process" (12).

The various inadequacies of medical records in general and psychiatric records in particular can have far-reaching consequences considering the multiplicity of uses for these records. First and foremost, the record is an account of clinical management of the patient. Perhaps at one time the skilled physician could keep track of his entire practice in his head; indeed many doctors even today claim that they can provide good care without a formal record, resent efforts to standardize record keeping and feel that record keeping uses time and thus detracts from patient care. But the masses of data produced today are too complex to be "stored" in the human brain. Then too, patients come in contact with several clinicians of various disciplines and skills and an array of consultants and paraprofessionals, all of whom must have a standard record of information about the patient in order to provide proper care and to inform their colleagues of what is being done (11).

The record is also important in clinical research that requires not only complete data, but data that is systematically organized for ease of retrieval. Leafing through one patient's entire record to obtain relevant pieces of information is sometimes a necessary headache; performing the same exercise on whole groups of records is an impossibility. Evaluation of treatment is an area of clinical research that demands follow-up data; even in the best research centers, these data are rarely available (11).

Data are used not only clinically, but for a variety of administrative purposes. Recent years have brought about a "crisis of accountability." Increasing use of the records for audit, for peer review, for precise documentation of services in order to claim reimbursement from third-party payors is demanding that doctors (13) nurses (14) and social workers (15) upgrade the source document of patient care. Accreditation committees examine the records of a hospital carefully. J. D. Wallace, Secretary General of the Canadian Medical Association, states that "in the majority of cases in which a hospital does not achieve accreditation or is dropped from full accreditation to provisional or non-accreditation, medical records are the cause" (13).

ATTEMPTS TO UNDERSTAND "BAD" RECORDS

A number of investigators impressed with the repetitiveness of the criticism aimed at medical records have attempted to isolate the reasons behind the problems. Smith, Sjoberg, and Phillips state that "institutional records are products of systems of norms, the organization of a hospital being one such system. It follows that we must understand these norms if we are to understand the contents of the records" (16). Garfinkel (17) has found an "organizational rationale" for the state of records. The comparative cost of finding out various kinds of information accounts for the fact that some data are more frequently available than others. To determine sex and age of a new admission, for example, is relatively simple while an occupational history would be costly and time consuming. Another factor is the lack of agreement on what should constitute the "core" of information. The service-oriented clinician, the experimental psychologist, the hospital administrator, and the epidemiologist have different data requirements. Garfinkel concludes also that the record is not really an unsystematic, disorganized jumble of looseleaf paper for the knowledgeable reader. "The possibility of understanding is based on a shared practical and entitled understanding of common tasks between writer and reader" (17).

Mumford (18) makes a distinction between research/teaching institutions and patient-oriented clinics. In research setting the need for sharing information among colleagues promotes better quality medical records whereas the service-oriented facility tends to see time spent on data recording as wasted. Nathanson and Becker (19) conclude, too, that where the sharing of information is considered important, notably in facilities where the team approach is paid more than lip service, the quality of records is highest.

COMPUTERIZATION OF THE RECORD

Many of the attempts to improve the quality of the traditional record have focused on automation. In the early and middle sixties, it seemed as though computers could indeed solve many of the problems. Computers provide legible reports; they can store, file, and retrieve quickly vast quantities of information. Several groups have successfully addressed themselves to the problem of automating psychiatric records (20) and have provided quantities of legible, organized information never before available.

Evaluation of these systems is now appearing in the literature. One senses, together with the great pride in what has been accomplished, the disappointing realization that automation in itself is no panacea. Barnett reflects that "the initial wave of optimism and enthusiam generated by beguiling promises of an immediately available total hospital computer system has passed" (21). The realization has grown that "we do not know in systematic terms how clinicians use medical records, and, perhaps even less how they use output from automated information systems" (22). Feinstein, in a conference on medical information systems, summarizes the problem (11): "A computer system that has no defined clinical purpose and that neatly stores data in an arbitrary manner, however elegant, can provide neither quality in the data nor quality in the scientific goals for which the data are used."

NEW APPROACHES TO ORGANIZING THE RECORD

A major rethinking of the organizational structure of the record is problem orientation, an approach developed by Lawrence Weed (23); the philosophy of problem orientation is detailed in Part 3. Much enthusiasm for this approach has been voiced in the literature; proponents include doctors (12), nurses (19), rehabilitation workers (24, 25), and social workers (15). The most frequently cited advantages are that the Problem Oriented Record (POR) provides a structure, a systematic way of recording and storing all of the activities of various staff members and the logic of clinical decisions. The record is readable, patient oriented, and at least on a rudimentary level, readily auditable. Not surprisingly, the most enthusiastic proponents of the POR may be found in research/teaching institutions. The POR is currently operational on a manual basis in many of the teaching institutions in the United States and its use is spreading; whether service institutions will follow suit cannot yet be determined.

Grant and Maletzky (26) have applied the POR to psychiatric record keeping and have stressed the use of "clear statements of behavioral excesses, deficits, or inappropriateness in the problem list." A limited pilot study of an automated Problem-Oriented Psychiatric Record has been undertaken (27). It is hoped that a structured approach to psychiatric records coupled with the undeniable advantages of computerization will do much to improve the quality and increase the usefulness of these documents.

REFERENCES

1. E. R. Huffman, *Medical Record Management,* 6th ed., Physicians' Record Company, Berwyn, Illinois, 1972.

2. L. S. King, Ed., *A History of Medicine,* Penguin Books, Middlesex, 1971.

3. Editorial on Hospital Standardization, *Hosp. Manage.,* May 1919.

4. *Standards for Psychiatric Facilites,* American Psychiatric Association, Washington, 1969.

5. *Accreditation Manual for Psychiatric Facilites 1972,* Joint Commission on Accreditation of Hospitals, Chicago, 1972.

6. *Wyatt, v. Stickney,* April 13, 1972, 344 F. Supp. 373.

7. *Wyatt, v. Stickney,* June 2, 1972, 344 F. Supp. 387.

8. *Diagnostic and Statistical Manual of Mental Disorders,* 2nd ed., American Psychiatric Association, Washington, 1968.

9. R. A. Greenes, G. O. Barnett, S. W. Klein, A. Roblins, and R. E. Prior, *New Engl. J. Med.,* **282** (1970), 307–315.

10. B. L. Gordon, *J. Am. Med. Assoc.,* **212** (1970), 1502–1507.

11. A. R. Feinstein, *Comput. Biomed. Res.,* **3** (1970), 426–435.

12. P. M. Last, *Med. J. Aust.,* **1** (1973), 946–950.

13. J. D. Wallace, *Can. Med. Assoc. J.,* **109** (1973), 1136.

14. M. Woody and M. Mallison, *Am. J. Nurs.,* **73** (1973), 1168–1175.

15. R. A. Kane, *Soc. Work,* **19** (1974), 412–419.

16. J. O. Smith, G. Sjoberg, and V. A. Phillips, *J. Soc. Psychiatr.,* **15** (1969), 129–135.

17. H. Garfinkel, *Studies in Ethnomethodology,* Prentice Hall, Englewood Cliffs, 1967, pp. 185–207.

18. E. Mumford, *Interns: From Students to Physicians,* Harvard University Press, Cambridge, 1970.

19. C. A. Nathanson and M. H. Becker, *Med. Care,* **11** (1973), 214–223.

20. J. L. Crawford, D. W.. Morgan, and D. T. Gianturco, Eds., *Progress in Mental Health Information Systems: Computer Applications,* Ballinger, Cambridge, Mass. 1974.

21. G. O. Barnett, *New Engl. J. Med.,* **279,** (1968), 1321–1327.

22. E. S. Pollack, C. D. Windle, and C. R. Wurster, "Psychiatric Information Systems: An Historical Perspective," in J. L. Crawford, D. W. Morgan and D. T. Gianturco, Eds., *Progress in Mental Health Information Systems: Computer Applications,* Ballinger, Cambridge, 1974, pp. 319–331.

23. L. L. Weed, *Medical Records, Medical Education, and Patient Care,* Case Western Reserve University Press, Cleveland, 1970.

24. "The Histories and Physical Examinations Are Not Enough," *Arch. Phys. Med. Rehabil.,* **54** (1973), 188–189.

25. R. L. Milhous, *Arch. Phys. Med. Rehabil.,* **53** (1972), 182–185.

26. R. L. Grant and B. M. Maletzky, *Psychiatr. Med.,* **3** (1972), 119–129.

27. G. H. Honigfeld, M. Pulier, E. Laska, R. Kaufl, and P. Ziek, "An Approach to Problem-Oriented Psychiatric Records," in J. L. Crawford, D. W. Morgan and D. T. Gianturco, Eds., *Progress in Mental Health Information Systems: Computer Applications,* Ballinger, Cambridge, 1974, pp. 107–135.

The Functions of Medical-Record-Keeping Procedures

JEFFREY L. CRAWFORD, Ph.D.

The medical record is considered to be the cornerstone of patient care. Behaviors of physicians, psychologists, nurses, administrators, and lawyers are directly influenced by information contained in the patient's chart. Record-keeping procedures may influence decisions to change medications, begin psychotherapy, establish community prevention programs, begin litigation, change staff/patient ratios, and even add a new wing to a hospital.

As is usually the case where a document involves multiple disciplines, there are attempts to improve procedures for transmitting and acquiring information. Plans to improve the medical record include changing the format of data entry from source oriented to problem oriented (1–5), replacing free text (narrative) with checklist formats (6–10), and automating the record contents, a trend whose popularity is increasing at a very fast pace (11, 12). Large, complex management information systems are being developed utilizing medical record data. National trends of peer and utilization review, national health insurance proposals, and the development of Professional Standards Review Organizations (PSROs) place increased pressure on medical-record-keeping procedures to provide timely, accurate patient-based data for a variety of purposes and persons.

The movement to change the structural components, the nature of the information recorded, and the procedures for data collection, entry, and retrieval in record-keeping procedures necessitate an analysis of the basic functions of record keeping. Once the functions are delineated, perhaps a more coherent effort to implement change may result.

The information contained in the medical record attempts to fulfill at least the basic clinical, administrative, and accountability needs and also serves as the raw material for research.

Clinical information describes the patient's responses to treatment, adaptation to the treatment setting, and so forth. Administrative functions of the record provide the ward or unit manager and hospital administrator with information necessary for smooth organizational functioning. Accountability functions of the record allow the hospital professional staff to monitor the quality of care received by patients, to correct faults as well as to reward sound procedures. Clinical research functions allow, for example, the determination of those treatment modalities most effective with different patient classes. Thus the medical record in theory, at least, fulfills four critical functions in the medical management of patients.

CLINICAL FUNCTIONS

The clinical function of the record, documenting the patient's responses to treatment modalities from surgical procedures to electroshock therapy, is generally considered the most important. The Joint Commission on Accreditation of Hospitals (JCAH) (13) lists several clinical functions of the psychiatric record as follows:

1.   Serving as a basis for planning and insuring continuity of patient care.
2.   Providing the means of communication among the physicians and any professionals who contribute to the patient's care.
3.   Furnishing evidence that documents treatment modalities and observations of patient responses to the specific treatments.
4.   Allowing the practitioner to determine the patient's condition during any phase of the treatment episode and to delineate the procedure performed.
5.   Providing information to consultants for opinion after examination of the patient and the patient's medical record.
6.   Insuring that another practitioner can determine what has transpired in the management of a patient and can determine the patient's response to treatment in the event that this physician assumes the case.

Clearly the most important clinical function of the record is accurate, reliable information transmission to the disciplines responsible for the management of the patient. Clinical personnel who observe the patient in a variety of settings (occupational therapist, chaplain, social service personnel, ward nurses and nursing aids, dietician, and radiologist, to name a few) need a forum to transmit their observations into verbal form. The patient's physician or the team responsible for clinical management must take the information, sort the reliable from the unreliable, integrate the remainder, and develop a treatment plan. This plan usually includes statements about behaviors that should be increased in frequency (e.g., more verbal interaction with other patients in the case of a chronic schizophrenic patient), decreased in frequency (e.g., hyperactive behavior in the case of the manic patient), and those behaviors that should be stabilized (cleanliness, etc.). Once the behaviors have been delineated, a plan for reaching the desired outcomes is elaborated. Plans can range from general (group therapy 3 times a week for 10 weeks) to specific (reinforce with a smile and words of praise any attempts at social interaction). When the staff documents behavioral outcomes and treatment plans, monitoring the patient's progress becomes a major clinical staff function. The Progress Note section of the record takes prominence in delineating the success or failure of the treatment plan. Typically, staff record their day-to-day observations of patient behavior there. Weekly "chart rounds," which can involve the treatment team or the entire staff, are held, the contents of the record playing an important role in patient-oriented decisions. During the chart rounds the staff integrates the various comments from several different sources, makes decisions concerning the efficacy of treatment and as a result does or does not make changes in the treatment plan. In this sense the medical record functions as a research document, where "scientists" record behavior, relate treatment plans to behavioral change or nonchange, integrate the concomitant information, hypothesize the possible reasons for the observed behavior, manipulate the patient's environment by changing a treatment plan, observe the behavior that follows from the manipulations, record the behavior . . . and the process continues until the patient leaves the treatment environment.

The clinical function of the record does not end when the patient departs from the immediate care of the ward or unit staff. The record serves as the basis for the future treatment of the patient whether he reports to the same physician regularly or presents himself as an emergency to the hospital (14). In fact, continuity of care is an ever present theme in justifying medical-record-keeping procedures (15–18). In inpatient psychiatric facilities where readmission rates are high, returning patients are not always assigned to the unit that provided care previously. The medical record is the only source of information that continuously documents services provided and responses to treatment. The treating physician relies on the recorded observations of others for initial treatment decisions (e.g., patient may have a history of poor responses to chlorpromazine but better responses to trifluoperazine). Thus the record plays an important role, insuring that the patient receives the type of care that has in the past proven most effective.

Continued, documented, legible, reliable, accurate, and retrievable patient information helps the clinical staff meet their goals for continuous improvement in applying medical services to patients.

Another clinical function of medical records has been suggested, namely, their use in preventing disorders (19). Information collected in the medical record is used to forestall dysfunction by reducing rates of occurrence of particular disorders in the population at large over extended time periods, promoting psychological health, education, and welfare (20). Data contained in the record, such as diagnosis, demography, and location (residence) aggregated for specified time periods may identify the distribution of behavioral disorders and possible determinants. The mental health professional takes his clinical skills into the community (as opposed to the institutional setting) and implements procedures to reduce the incidence and prevalence of psychopathology (21). The emphasis upon service delivery in the community places an increased pressure on medical-record information. Demographic analyses of communities must be interfaced with the demographic characteristics of populations currently being served so that high-risk subgroups (those persons who have a higher probability of "contracting" the disorder) can be identified, coordination of services enhanced, and community well-being facilitated. The ability to extract and aggregate data quickly from the medical record is critical to the community/clinical orientation. It is in this area that automating the medical record may prove to be of greatest value.

ADMINISTRATIVE FUNCTIONS

The daily behavior of health administrators in the planning, operation, and budgeting of clinics, hospitals, and medical centers is influenced by medical-record-keeping procedures. Administrative decisions concerning resource allocation, expansion or deletion of services, building programs, hiring patterns, food-service decisions, and inventory management are based, to a large extent, on medical-record information that delineates: where and when, who receives what types of services, provided by whom, for what frequency and duration, and at what cost.

The vast increases in the number of individuals accessing mental health service delivery units and the inefficient mechanisms for resource allocation and service delivery indicate that mental health administrators must design, manage, and operate new health care systems to achieve the integration of local, state, and federal services (22). As the clinician assumes the role of the clinical administrator, the reliance on timely, accurate information becomes critical for program management. To assist in this difficult task, mental health administrators have turned to automation as a potential solution (12).

Automating the medical record for administrative purposes resulted in the development of management information systems (MIS) that provide organized methods of data selection related to the internal operation of an organization. The MIS supports the planning, control, and operational functions of an organization by selecting data pertaining to particular organizational functions and transforming them into the information needed for decision making by persons who plan, administer, monitor, evaluate, and finance services. Computer-support procedures for medical/administrative information recording usually result in a more structured and complete patient record.

It is obvious that the input needed to answer many types of administrative questions comes from the medical record. From computerized records administrators can ask questions such as the following:

- What is the average length of stay for inpatients?
- What types of service is a particular unit rendering?
- Do different treatment modalities result in differing readmission patterns?
- To what community agencies are patients referred?
- What combination of direct and indirect patient services are most cost effective?

The fact that human service programs operate under increasing pressures for management control, for accountability to public and private funding sources, for planning the most effective utilization of scarce resources, and for justifying to consumer groups established patterns of service delivery indicates that the medical record will become an even more important administrative document in the future.

ACCOUNTABILITY FUNCTIONS

Current trends in the health delivery system indicate an increased concern with issues of program accountability and with the development of standards and criteria for evaluating the quality of care delivered. The impetus for program monitoring and accountability comes from several sources as follows:

1. Court rulings, following the precedent of *Wyatt v. Stickney,* require mental health facilities to meet clear standards for effective treatment
2. National health insurance plans mandate reimbursement for only those

mental health services of *demonstrated efficiency* for cases where *need* and *likely benefit* for the services have been rendered and a claim for payment has been initiated.

3. The Bennett Amendment (P.L. 92-603) established Professional Standards Review Organizations (PSROs) that monitor the appropriateness of resource utilization and the quality of institutional services provided under Medicaid, Medicare, and Maternal and Child Health Care Programs. This federal legislation provides for evaluating the following:

   a. The necessity for institutional admission.
   b. The duration of institutional services.
   c. The appropriateness of the level of institutional care.
   d. The adequacy and relevance (quality) of the services provided.

4. Third-party payors will most likely develop PSRO-like programs for evaluating the quality of services for inpatient and outpatient programs not covered by Social Security Acts. In the very near future, service delivery of all health care facilities will be closely monitored.

Professional Standards Review Organizations are to be established in areas designated by the Secretary of Health, Education, and Welfare prior to January 1, 1976. Since PSRO legislation will have impact quite soon, a discussion of the components of professional review and the relationship to medical-record-keeping procedures is relevant here.

According to Decker and Bonner (23), professional review usually involves evaluation of the following:

   1. The services provided (based on diagnosis).
   2. The patient's medical needs and the level of services provided.
   3. The amount (volume) of provided service.
   4. Appropriateness of the outcome, including complications, provisions for aftercare procedures, indication for discharge.
   5. Appropriateness of services provided to populations.

Professional review is a detailed procedure requiring precise documentation in the medical record. Aside from the complete documentation in the record, the information must be easily retrieved in meaningfully defined formats. Further complexities arise when population profiles must be extracted from the record through aggregating procedures. Current manual modes of record keeping may not be able to meet the demands of PSRO legislation.

Professional review legislation requires each PSRO to establish standards and criteria for assessing quality of care, while at the same time developing norms for frequency and duration of service and standards for desired compliance. The medical record now becomes the critical (and perhaps only) document that contains the information needed for review. The success or failure of the PSRO is contingent upon the medical-record-keeping procedures developed in the PSRO designated area.

All psychiatric medical records must meet the standards explicated by the Joint Commission on Accreditation of Hospitals (13). Their *Accreditation Manual for Psychiatric Facilities 1972* mandates that "an adequate medical record shall be maintained for every patient of a psychiatric facility."

The manual explicates:

> The medical record shall contain sufficient information to identify the patient clearly, to justify the diagnosis, to delineate the treatment plan and to document the results accurately.

Specifically, the record should include:

1. Identification data and consent forms
    a. Patient's name
    b. Address
    c. Date of birth
    d. Date of admission
    e. Next of kin
    f. Consents
    g. Legal status as deemed necessary
2. Source of referral
3. History of the patient
    a. Chief complaint
    b. Details of present illness
    c. Inventory of systems
    d. Past history
    e. Social, vocational, and family history
4. Report of physical examination
5. Report of neurological examination
6. Consultation
    a. Psychological testing
    b. Educational evaluation
    c. Sociovocational appraisal
    d. Pathology and clinical laboratory
    e. Radiology examination
    f. Surgical treatment
    g. Psychiatric and other medical treatment
    h. Any other diagnostic and therapeutic procedures performed

7. Report of psychiatric evaluation
   a. Mental status
   b. Psychodynamics and sociodynamics
   c. Precipitating stress and premorbid personality
   d. Tentative diagnosis
   e. Development of treatment plan
   f. Prognosis based on that plan
8. Treatment plan
9. Medical orders
10. Observations
    a. Documentation of treatment plan
    b. Chronological report of patient's progress
11. Report of actions and findings
12. Discharge summary
    a. Provisional diagnosis
    b. Primary final diagnosis (physical and psychiatric)
    c. Secondary final diagnosis (physical and psychiatric)
    d. Clinical resume
       (1) Recapitulation of the significant findings and clinical course of patient's hospitalization
       (2) Condition upon discharge
       (3) Recommendations and arrangements for future treatment including prescribed medications and follow up programs

The inclusion of these data constitutes an "adequate" medical record. The criteria of the JCAH standards for record keeping can clearly meet the needs delineated by PSRO legislation and peer and utilization review committees. (Peer review involves the application of collective professional judgment to individual and group medical performance, while utilization review evaluates the necessity for and the quality of care.)

The more fundamental issue with regard to current medical-record-keeping procedures is the ability to access, process, and output the data in the record to appropriate sources for review purposes. Current manual procedures are not capable of meeting the large-scale review functions mandated by law. Consequently, an automated data processing mechanism is necessary to create a centralized, systematized, easily accessible, and retrievable data base. In most manually stored hospital record systems, the information on a particular patient may be stored in various locations, e.g., the chart in the ward, the psychologist's file, and the social worker's personal records. Professional review would involve extensive search for complete information on one patient. Yet PSRO legislation mandates that aggregated data, as well, be made available for consumer and provider profiles. Although the patient information may exist in the manual-record-keeping facilities, the cost of retrieval is high and the time needed to aggregate data exorbitant. As a result of PSRO legislation, medical records will be increasingly automated. In fact, Decker and Bonner (24) devote approximately one-third of their book to data processing systems. It seems quite obvious that the medical records of the future will best fill the accountability functions through automation. As the interrelationship between automation and accountability functions becomes more complex, the medical record will play an increasingly important role in decisions regarding health care delivery.

RESEARCH FUNCTIONS

The carefully documented medical record can provide researchers with information delineating the relationship among behavioral disorder, treatment modality, and behavioral change. In fact, it seems reasonable to suggest that the information contained in the record should be as precise as the notes of a research scientist as he documents his observations. Medical personnel do, in fact, function as researchers in their daily patient-oriented activities. Staff observe the patient's behavior, document their observation, aggregate the data (usually according to some vague conceptual rather than precise schemata), discuss the results, hypothesize which variables are responsible for the observed behavior, manipulate the environment (e.g., increase or decrease medication), observe . . . and the process continues.

Psychiatric staff use the methods of scientific procedure, yet the nature of the recording instruments is far from adequate. Instruments that emphasize the description or topography of behavior that can be quantified need to be included in the medical record. This shift to a research orientation will result in staff behavioral changes. Psychiatric staff could begin monitoring the patients' behavior as they do temperature and blood pressure, recording their findings on reliable and valid instruments. New relationships among classes of variables will emerge, and treatment decisions will become more meaningful. The scientific foundation of psychiatry can only be enhanced.

STUDY AREAS ON MEDICAL RECORDS

Although the medical record has been accorded primary importance in assuring overall quality of patient care, there are many aspects of record-keeping procedures that need investigation. These include the following:

1.   Specifying the *actual* relationship of the medical record to treatment decisions.

2. Delineating the information that is absolutely necessary for the clinical management of psychiatric patients.

3. Documenting how the record is used by professional and paraprofessional staff.

4. Analyzing the portions of the record that are used and not used and the reasons for these behaviors.

5. Developing automated procedures that facilitate clinical as well as administrative and accountability functions.

6. Evaluating the impact of automated record-keeping procedures on patient care.

7. Experimenting with different formats for entering and storing medical data so that information retrieval can best be facilitated.

Much has been written about the functions of medical records. Yet we do not know how clinicians, program managers, lawyers, and review committees use them. The future of medical record research is best summarized by Pollack, Windle and Wurster (25):

> This seems to leave us in a situation where we are developing systems for needs which are as yet unspecified and for uses which cannot be articulated. Although this is somewhat an oversimplification of reality, it seems clear that more studies are needed to determine systematically what specific information is needed, . . . with accountability as the highest priority, and to find ways of meeting these needs in a coordinated and, above all, economical way.

REFERENCES

1. G. Honigfeld, M. Pulier, E. M. Laska, R. Kaufl, and P. Ziek, "An Approach to Problem Oriented Records," in J. L. Crawford, D. W. Morgan, and D. T. Gianturco, Eds., *Progress in Mental Health Information Systems: Computer Applications,* Ballinger, Cambridge, Mass., 1974, pp. 107–120.
2. R. L. Grant and B. M. Maletzky, *Psychiatr. Med.,* 3 (1972), 119–129.
3. R. S. Ryback and J. S. Gardner, *Am. J. Psychiatr.,* 3 (1973), 312–316.
4. L. L. Weed, *N. Engl. J. Med.,* **278** (1968), 652–657.
5. L. L. Weed, *Medical Records, Medical Education and Patient Care,* Press of Case Western Reserve, Cleveland, Ohio, 1969.
6. L. Craig, F. Golenzer, and E. Laska, "Computer Constructed Narratives" in N. S. Kline and E. Laska, Eds., *Computers and Electronic Devices in Psychiatry,* Grune & Stratton, 1968, pp. 59–80.
7. E. Laska, G. Simpson, and R. Bank, *Compr. Psychiatr.,* **10,** 2 (March 1969), 136–146.
8. M. F. Collen, *J. Med. Assoc.,* **195** (1966), 830–833.
9. P. Hall, C. Mellner, and T. Danielson, *Methods of Information in Medicine,* **6** (1967), 1–6.

10. R. D. Yoder, *Hospitals,* **40** (1966), 75–85.

11. E. Laska, A. Weinstein, G. Logemann, R. Bank, and F. Breuer, *Compr. Psychiatr.,* **8,** 6 (Dec. 1967), 476–490.

12. J. L. Crawford, D. W. Morgan, and D. T. Gianturco, Eds., *Progress in Mental Health Information Systems: Computer Applications,* Ballinger, Cambridge, Mass., 1974.

13. *Accreditation Manual for Psychiatric Facilities 1972,* Joint Commission on Accreditation of Hospitals, Chicago, 1972.

14. L. G. McCampbell, *J. Tenn. Med. Assoc.,* **62** (1969), 928–932.

15. J. Anderson, "Aims of Medical Information," in J. Anderson and J. M. Forsythe, Eds., *Information Processing of Medical Records,* North Holland, 1970, pp. 22–27.

16. J. L. Crawford, "Computer Applications in Mental Health: a Review," in J. L. Crawford, D. W. Morgan, and D. T. Gianturco, Eds., *Progress in Mental Health Information Systems: Computer Applications,* Ballinger, Cambridge, Mass., 1974.

17. A. Feinstein, *Clinical Judgment,* Williams and Wilkins Co., Baltimore, 1967.

18. N. Tallent, *Psychiatr. Quart.,* **37** (1963), 642–665.

19. J. Anderson, "Aims of Medical Information," in J. Anderson and J. M. Forsythe, Eds., *Information Processing of Medical Records,* North Holland, 1970, pp. 22–27.

20. E. Cowen, *Ann. Rev. Psychol.,* (1974), 423–472.

21. B. Bloom, *Community Mental Health: A Historical and Critical Analysis,* General Learning Corp., 1973.

22. D. J. Levinson and G. L. Klerman, *Administration in Mental Health,* (1972), 47–64.

23. E. M. Laska, "The Multi-State Information System," in J. L. Crawford, D. W. Morgan, and D. T. Gianturco, Eds., *Progress in Mental Health Information Systems: Computer Applications,* Ballinger, Cambridge, Mass., 1974, pp. 231–252.

24. B. Decker and P. Bonner, *PSRO: Organization for Regional Peer Review,* Ballinger, Cambridge, Mass. 1973.

25. E. Pollack, C. Windle, and C. Wurster, "Psychiatric Information Systems: An Historical Perspective," in J. L. Crawford, D. W. Morgan, and D. T. Gianturco, Eds., *Progress in Mental Health Information Systems: Computer Applications,* Ballinger, Cambridge, Mass., 1974, pp. 319–331.

Brief History of Information Systems in Mental Health

The growth of computer technology and the concurrent need for better means of maintaining mental health information led to the development of automated information systems in this field in the early 1960s. Generally these systems were initiated on a research and demonstration basis and, through the present, though some are funded through service delivery organizations, many are funded through research-oriented agencies. Mental health information systems utilizing computers have been established in many countries on federal, state, and regional bases as well as in individual facilities. Some, though not all, of these systems are described below.

NATIONAL COMPUTERIZED INFORMATION SYSTEMS

United States. The growing recognition of mental illness as a major problem combined with the lack of uniform data on the true nature and scope of its dimensions, brought about in 1951 in the United States, under the leadership of the National institute of Mental Health (NIMH), active steps to create uniform reporting procedures and to foster the statistical analysis of the resulting data. In 1955 the introduction of psychoactive drugs as a form of therapy began the dramatic reduction of the populations of mental hospitals and made community resources more appropriate places for the treatment of the mentally ill. This trend was augmented by the Community Mental Health Center Act of 1963 which emphasized the community rather than the traditional state hospital as the center of the mental health service delivery system and brought with it a need to provide means to follow patients as they moved through a variety of treatment settings. With the expanded number of treatment modalities and of kinds of resources available, the complexity of statistical data needed to describe the mental health delivery system was increasingly difficult to attain through traditional manual reporting methods (1).

The NIMH, as a federal agency, has the responsibility for providing national leadership in mental health. For many years, the Institute has required that the various states and federally funded community mental health centers submit statistical data which are then integrated by computer into reports describing national trends.

In addition, NIMH provides financial support to a number of research and development projects in the automation of psychiatric records with the objectives of providing tools for improved patient care and more efficient use of personnel, developing institutional management information systems, building research data bases, and facilitating the reporting of data useful for state and national program planning and evaluation. One of the earliest projects at Camarillo State Hospital in 1962 (2) was a pioneer for more complex efforts such as the Multi-State Information System, the Missouri Standard System of Psychiatry, the Fort Logan system, and the Institute of Living system; these are described below.

Indonesia.   The government of Indonesia collects data on psychiatric patients in all of its mental health facilities. These data are processed by computer programs which produce narrative reports in English and Indonesian as well as cross-tabulations used for planning and epidemiological studies. This system is more fully explained in Part 3.

Yugoslavia.   The Republic of Croatia in Yugoslavia, with a 4.5 million population, maintains 5 mental hospitals and 19 psychiatric units in general hospitals. A psychiatric case register of all patients diagnosed as alcoholic or psychotic was started in 1963 on a manual basis by the Department of Chronic Diseases, Institute of Public Health. To date, 30,000 patients have been identified, representing 1% of Croatia's adult population, with the incidence of chronic schizophrenia paralleling the United States' experience.

With an increase in the numbers of persons in the register and the kinds of information collected, manual procedures were found to be increasingly inefficient. By 1969 plans were initiated for changing to an automated computer system and with technical and financial assistance from the United States via the National Institute of Mental Health, a computerized system was established (3).

In Croatia computerization offered distinct capabilities not possible with the manual system: admission and under-care rates could be computed by various demographic variables and correlated with the general population census of 1971; correlations with death records could help in establishing mortality tables and defining risks for certain categories of released patients; community centered follow-up studies would become possible; data could be more readily correlated with other psychiatric registers elsewhere.

With the available data, a follow-up study is now underway on patients diagnosed as schizophrenic who were hospitalized during 1963 and 1964. The study will determine the interaction of certain variables, the effect of illness upon the family, community, and health resources, and the effect of treatment on the course of illness and on present levels of functioning. Methodology includes the use of survey forms by a field study unit, follow-up psychiatric examinations, a review of the register files, and the design of questionnaire forms. Long-range goals are to provide data that will assist in reducing length of hospitalization, readmission rates, and chronicity and will abet the patient's readjustment to his community.

Russia. The Scientific Statistics Center of the Serbsky Medical Institute of Forensic Psychiatry in Moscow is attempting to maintain a computer registry of psychiatric patients in local health centers throughout the country. The registry contains demographic, socioeconomic, and treatment information. The current aim is to create mathematical models concerning morbidity and prevalence to be used in administering and planning psychiatric services (4).

Israel. The State of Israel has adapted the Multi-State Information System as the national mental health registry. Data will be used for planning, epidemological studies, research, and program evaluation. For specific details, see Part 4.

COMPUTERIZED INFORMATION SYSTEMS ON A STATE LEVEL

At present the majority of state departments of mental health utilize to some extent data processing systems to handle psychiatric information. Examples in the United States include California, Connecticut, Hawaii, Massachusetts, Missouri, New York, Rhode Island, South Carolina, and Tennessee which have developed data systems of their own or are utilizing the Multi-State Information System (see Part 2). In a survey conducted by the National Association of State Health Program Directors in 1971 (5), of 38 states responding, 34 were actively engaged in processing mental health data. Twenty-four of these were processing business data and at least some rudimentary clinical data. Three were processing clinical information only and seven were processing business data only. With the need to justify budget expenditures, the need to monitor funds expended on treatment programs, and the need to review and upgrade the quality of individual care, many states have begun to more fully utilize automated systems of data collect and analysis (6).

Missouri.   In 1966 the Missouri Institute of Psychiatry in collaboration with the Missouri Division of Mental Health began the development of an automated psychiatric information system to provide both clinical and administrative information (7, 8). Currently about 20 Missouri institutions participate in the system and these consist of clinics for the mentally retarded, state schools and hospitals for the mentally retarded, mental health centers, and state hospitals for the mentally ill. Data are transmitted from each of 10 major mental health facilities to a computer located at the Institute's facility in St. Louis.

The information system consists of three components: (1) the clinically oriented Standard System of Psychiatry (SSOP), (2) administrative systems, and (3) a Census System that interfaces with both SSOP and the administrative systems. The Census System captures demographic and movement information, while SSOP collects clinical information by means of such clinical instruments as the Minnesota Multiphasic Personality Inventory (described below), the Community Adjustment Profile Scale, and a Mental Status Examination. Fund encumberance, cost accumulation, and itemized billing are carried out by the administrative systems. The system maintains a common data base for all participating institutions and generates a variety of clinical and census reports, as well as a series of business outputs.

Data is collected on checklist forms that are completed by clinicians, technicians, clerks, nonprofessional staff, patients, and relatives. No form used by a clinician is more than one page in length, and narrative comments in addition to the checklist are maintained. The forms completed relate to patient admission, demographic, and movement information; mental status, intelligence, physical examination, social functioning, and environmental factors; inpatient behavior, community adjustment, alcohol use and Minnesota Multiphasic Personality Inventory (MMPI); and various laboratory tests and billing data.

Output from the system in the form of narrative printouts includes the Admission Checklist highlighting problems and positive findings; the Mental Status Examination listing positive findings; the physical examinations detailing all findings and a summary of positive findings; and narrative descriptions derived from the Behavior Scales, Community Adjustment Profile, and Alcohol Questionnaire. Factor scales and comparative data are also derived from the latter three forms as well as a scale for the MMPI. Census, statistical, and patient-movement reports in a variety of daily and monthly formats are also generated.

An Outpatient Contact System is operational for community mental health centers detailing patient contacts and forms of therapy, providing automated appointment rosters, and identifying patients not seen for extended periods of time.

In various phases of development are: an Evaluation Index based on statistics related to length of care, transfers, readmissions, terminations, average time in the community, and similar factors; a Cost Effectiveness Measure utilizing reports of symptom reduction from the Missouri Impatient Behavior Scale and adjustment pre- and posthospitalization as reported on the Community Adjustment Profile; a series of actuarial reports affording aggregate data about types of patients; and automated clinical summaries. A community services system will be developed to record community contacts by mental health centers that are not directly patient related. A Problem Oriented Medical Record Progress Note is also being tested.

Illinois.   The Department of Mental Health in Illinois is regionalized into eight zones. Each zone has an inpatient facility and a community network including such resources as an outpatient clinic, a sheltered workshop, day programs, and programs for retarded children. The objective of regionalization was to provide comprehensive mental health care within the zone centers, rather than referring patients to the state hospitals. An automated information system serving east central Illinois on a decentralized regional basis developed out of needs to provide new forms of statistical reporting. The H. Douglas Singer Zone Center (see below) also has developed computer systems.

The design developed is primarily a staff reporting system, as opposed to systems based on patient data. This kind of reporting can effectively correlate costs of the delivery of services, reduce concerns about confidentiality that patient data banks frequently arouse, and provide needed management data as a large variety of staff activities (training, consultation, education, community meetings, contacts with nonpatients) can be accounted for in this system.

The forms used in the system are a Patient Cover Sheet containing demographic information and a statement of the problem area, a Staff Reporting Form which is a description of staff activity by case, program, and/or activity, and a form that provides for case terminations. More than 50 output reports are possible from this system. The type of reports and frequency are determined by administrative and clinical needs. Some of the more frequently utilized outputs are: Summary of Case Activity, indicating case volume and activity which provides documentation for funding sources; Caseload by Age and Marital Status; Service Hour Effort by Work Area or by Program; Individual Staff Report summarizing a clinician's monthly activity; and an Individual Client Profile with demographic data which is made a part of the patient's record and used in case terminations.

Evaluation measurements have been made of cost–benefit factors, and goal-attainment scales have been derived where requested. The automated system does allow for ready budgetary analysis of programs and recovery of funds from insurance and third-party sources.

Case Registers.   Case Registers utilizing electronic data processing devices have existed for more than 10 years in the State of Maryland (9, 10) and in Monroe County, New York (11). Other registers, many of them manual systems, exist in Dutchess County, New York (12), Hawaii (13), North Carolina (Tri-County Register) (14). Scandinavia, Yugoslavia, England, and Scotland also have case registers.

Registers provide unduplicated patient counts enabling scrutiny of patient movement among facilities and/or services, review of service patterns, and development of patient profiles. A case register is particularly useful as a method for evaluating mental health services, either by utilizing data in the register or by utilizing the register as a source for sample populations to be studied more intensively. In addition, output from a register provides many clinical leads or hypotheses for future testing.

Victoria Province, Australia.   Computing systems in mental health are by no means confined solely to the United States. The Victoria government in Australia utilizes a computer to maintain a case register of inpatients and outpatients of all mental health facilities in the province. This sytem, developed over the last 10 years, is a statistical system whose main use is for program planning and epidemiological studies.

Province of Saskatchewan, Canada.   An automated information system was developed in the Province of Saskatchewan beginning in 1966 to encompass inpatients and outpatients in all of the province's psychiatric facilities (15). A Registration and Continuing Record Form is completed at the point of initial contact and covers demographic, etiological, and clinical data in summary form. A Patient Contact Form is filled out for every contact made by professionals, listing type of service received by the patient, who provided the service, location, and duration.

Information is entered at a centralized computer facility, and a printout is returned to the originating agency. The computer maintains a temporary active case register for all patients, and information can be updated with little effort.

Output from the system is also in the form of summary data which becomes a part of record keeping, research, and planning activities. Future plans call for placing computers at major regional centers instead of the current practice of relying on a single central facility.

COMPUTER SUPPORT IN AMERICAN, MILITARY PSYCHIATRY

Computer Support in Military Psychiatry (COMPSY) began as a pilot project in 1968 and is based at the Department of Psychiatry and Neurology, Walter Reed Army Medical Center in Washington, D.C., and at the Mental Health Consultation Services at Fort Benning, Georgia and Fort Meade, Maryland. The goals for the project were to provide for a psychiatric information system to objectify and systematize information following a patient from initial iden- tification to his return into the military milieu and to establish an information system that would link all the mental health agencies of the military com- munity and provide for evaluation and for research into the epidemiology of mental health in the military. The design objective was to facilitate information flow among facilities and test the feasibility of an army-wide system (16). The COMPSY system consists of a psychiatry Registry with basic patient-identify- ing information from Walter Reed Army Medical Center and from the services at Fort Benning and Fort Meade.

Walter Reed Hospital.   The Walter Reed Inpatient System was adapted from the work done at the Institute of Living (see below) and includes a modification of the automated scoring and reporting system of the Minnesota Multiphasic Personality Inventory, automated nursing notes utilized on a behavior modifi- cation ward, and a Mental Status Examination.

The system now includes information such as census rosters, 24-hour nurs- ing report, daily activities schedule, MMPI scoring, nursing note, monthly summaries, and mental status examinations. Since computer terminals were not installed on wards, the project was developed with little need for on-line real time data; the computer record was not a substitute for the written medical record.

Mental Health Consultation Centers.   The mental health information system for the Mental Health Consultation Center (MHCS) was developed at Fort Benning, Georgia, and the model was later adapted to Fort Meade, Maryland. Since the program and record-keeping procedures of the MHCS's vary among military posts, an army-wide standardized computer system was not feasible, nor could the use of computer technology to teleprocess information between MHCSs and inpatient facilites at larger medical centers be made practical as originally conceptualized. Instead, the system was designed to take into account the fact that the MHCS functions as a community mental health center in a network of other services providing social service and mental health functions on a military base, and so could be modified by an MHCS according to its unique needs. The information system established at these two posts coor- dinated services to particular patients and families and obtained epidemio- logical data for planning and administration of mental health services.

At Fort Benning five agencies participated in the mental health information system. Data entered on the computer system came from a Contact Cover Sheet providing identifying data and a Basic Information Sheet detailing demographic and biographical information obtained during initial interviews. Additional forms were developed to cover the needs of specific agencies for intraagency use.

This system has been responsible for reducing duplication of services, coordinating treatment plans on behalf of a patient, motivating further communication between agencies, and providing for follow-through on interagency referals. It has brought about a focus on the family as the unit of treatment rather than on the individual soldier-patient. A cost-justification evaluation study of the system is being made.

COMPUTER UTILIZATION AT INDIVIDUAL FACILITIES

Camarillo State Hospital, Camarillo, California.   Camarillo State Hospital, Camarillo, California, administered by the State Department of Mental Hygiene, is the largest inpatient state hospital in California. From 1962 to 1965 Camarillo, with funding from the National Institute of Mental Health, was the setting for a psychiatric data automation project which despite its limitations has come to be regarded as a prototype for information systems. The goal of this project was to develop a patient data system to service a large mental hospital with concomitant experimentation and analysis to ascertain its practicality.

Technical accomplishments of the project included the establishment of a Master Patient File containing identifying information and utilized in the preparation of lists, summaries, notifications of patients due for quarterly progress notes or annual physical examinations. The system was manually maintained utilizing punched cards, and in the third year of this project was converted to a computer system with the added feature of producing case-summary data retrievable from teletype terminals. The project also established a Clinical Information Laboratory in one of the treatment units maintaining computer records of case-history data including diagnoses, progress notes, medications, and therapies. As part of this project, clinical staff received training in computer technology.

The project goal was not fully realized; the 3-year time span was found to be insufficient for planning, and tradition-minded staff were resistant to the unique innovations. However the feasibility of some type of computerized information system was demonstrated, and an analytical and experimental design was drawn up. Camarillo was the first large inpatient facility to attempt some work in utilizing computer technology as a tool in mental health services (1).

The Institute of Living, Hartford, Connecticut. The Institute of Living is a privately operated inpatient facility located in Hartford, Connecticut. A computerized information system was begun in 1962, and expanded 2-years later with funding from the National Institute of Mental Health (17).

The goals of the automation project were the elimination of substantial amounts of paper work in the hospital and the ability to gain rapid access to information. In its early stages, the hospital was linked with a multiuser shared commercial system, which proved not to be feasible since response times and availability were too frequently delayed. By installing its own equipment and providing for auxillary generators in the event of power failures, the hospital developed 24-hour accessibility and reliability. Also, the MUMPS programming language developed at Massachusetts General Hospital for medical settings has been adapted to this computer system. The original goal of eliminating all written reports has not been achieved because of an inadequate number of terminals in the present system and because of curtailment of federal funding. At present the patient information includes admissions and demographic data, patient movement data, special services, physical examinations, mental status examinations, medications, nursing notes, educational therapy notes, special behavior reports, and diagnoses. The Minnesota Multiphasic Personality Inventory is also used.

Through statistical analysis of individual and aggregate data, predictive and evaluative programs in areas such as chemotherapy, diagnostic classifications, predicting disruptive behavior, and identifying potential runaways have been developed. A sequential analysis program determines when significant changes have occurred. Nursing notes have been automated throughout the hospital, eliminating tedious clerical duties; these notes are readily available to clinical staff through display on cathode-ray video terminals and as printouts. This form has over 200 checklist statements organized into a variety of behavioral areas such as personal habits, social behavior, verbalization, appearance, and mood and provides for 19 factor scales rating areas such as thought disorganization, depression, anxiety, and negativism. Computer output of nursing notes consists of a narrative summary and a profile of the 19 factor scores. Unusual changes in behavior can be rapidly detected, patients can be ranked against their ward group to determine their degree of adaptivity, and the report allows for comparisons over a 9-day period. Cross-sectional and longitudinal studies of patient progress are also possible.

The Department of Educational Therapy developed a patient observation form covering 11 categories, and computer output is a narrative Patient Observation Report.

Hospital operations have been added to the computer system providing for financial payroll and billing procedures, statistical analysis, and scheduling such as nursing coverages.

H. Douglas Singer Zone Center, Rockford, Illinois.   This center provides in-patient and outpatient services for psychiatric, alcoholic, and mentally retarded patients for a nine-county region in northwestern Illinois and is operated by the State Department of Mental Health. The Zone Mental Health Data Service includes an Electronic Data Processing Section. The data processing unit has developed an automated Patient Information and Management System to follow its own patients and to augment the coordination of services among smaller agencies in this region, while the Evaluation Section has been conducting long-term follow-up studies (18).

The Patient Information and Management System functions through all aspects of a patient's admission and treatment by this facility. At the initial planning conference an Identification Form that gathers basic demographic and identifying information is completed. An Evaluation Form is also filled in and provides for a symptom checklist with a five-point severity scale for each symptom; the clinician's diagnosis; a listing of prior contacts with social service agencies; a section for Transitional Service Guidelines inquiring into a patient's housing, financial, occupational, and social resources (to help in the patient's readjustment to community life); and a Social Competence Assessment concerned with family, personal, and interpersonal relationships.

The completion of these two forms, taking about 20 minutes, provides three types of output: an Admission Form in narrative format that highlights the patient's demographic and psychosocial characteristics and his symptomatology, a computerized diagnosis where the symptom pattern is evaluated against a set of symptom norms, and a printout of three possible diagnoses together with the clinician's diagnosis. The information is computer stored in a patient data base, and programs have been written to analyze this data.

On admission, an Admission Card providing for identifying data is also completed, activating a patient file on the computer that will keep track of drugs prescribed, therapies received, and statistical data on the length of the patient's treatment. The computer provides as output, preprinted cards for each patient with identifying data that are completed periodically as the patient continues in care. These include a series of service cards to keep track of changes in status, therapy, drug prescriptions, and legal status; a linking card (describing community services on behalf of the patient), and a Termination Card. When completed the termination card automatically removes the patient from the active file.

Output from these service cards provides for a daily hospital census, a census of the separate clinical units, and a Patient Daily Activity Report listing therapies, drugs, and linking activities of the patient. Monthly output data includes an Episode Summary Report summarizing the Daily Activity Reports, and a monthly Caseload Summary for each clinician. A Ninety Day Notice is printed for clinicians listing outpatients who have not had clinical contact with this time span. Another Monthly Report summarizes the patient flow, treatment rendered, and cost figures providing needed administrative, statistical, and fiscal information.

Fort Logan Mental Health Center. This state-operated mental hospital provides inpatient and outpatient treatment, day, evening, or 24-hour hospitalization, a halfway house, family care, and community lodges. Treatment orientation is based on concepts of milieu therapy and open-door policies, and programs are provided in the areas of alcoholism, child, adolescent, and adult psychiatric units, geriatrics, and vocational services.

An automated patient and information management system has existed since 1961 when this facility first opened and includes most of the information routinely recorded in the patient's chart for both clinical and administrative uses. Maintained by the Program Information and Analysis Department, automated devices at the facility consist mostly of key-punch, optical scan, and tabulating equipment; the center does not maintain its own computer or terminals. Analyses are done on nearby computers available either at the University of Colorado or at the State Capitol. The center recognizes the use of outside computers as less than an optimal arrangement, and processes have been designed to expedite data collection, storage, and retrieval operations (19).

The Record System for each patient includes demographic and historical data, ratings of pre- and posthospital adjustment, clinical evaluations, treatment summaries, summaries of patient movement through various programs, and discharge evaluations. Information is obtained from admitting office clerks, ward personnel, and clinicians, and this information is retained both in the patient's chart and in the data processing unit.

A Resource Utilization Monitoring System was the outgrowth of a program begun in 1968 to identify and plan for the chronic patient and to predict the kinds of demands caring for this type of patient places upon the center. Analysis was based on demographic traits, the mental status examination, and utilization of various treatment resources.

The Workload Analysis, designed to help in budget planning, analyzes statistics on patients admitted, patients evaluated, patients referred to other agencies, patients attending the Center daily, and patients discharged, and compares these figures with ratios of work performed in each service category, resulting in a weighted workload index.

The Automated Tri-informant Goal Oriented Progress Note was developed for clinical and administrative use as a measure of treatment effectiveness. Computer output provides a narrative report of selected goals and treatment methods and a response rating scale listing goal statements, their preassigned importance, a six-point rating scale of goal attainment, methods selected for each goal, and a six-point rating scale for the method used with each goal.

Treatment goals as seen by the patient and his relatives are also recorded after a semistructured interview.

An Output Value Analysis is a system designed to estimate the economic value of a program's output balanced by program cost, taking into account a patient's estimated economic productivity and estimated benefit for his response to treatment. Statistically derived indices evaluate investment return and treatment effectiveness and provide accountability and fiscal data.

SPECIAL PROJECTS IN AUTOMATED PSYCHIATRIC DATA

The Minnesota Multiphasic Personality Inventory. The Minnesota Multiphasic Personality Inventory developed at the University of Minnesota by Starke Hathaway and J. C. McKinley in the early 1940s has become the most widely used structured test of personality. The subject is required to give true–false answers to 566 statements. The test yields scores on 4 validity scales which describe the subject's test-taking attitude and on 10 clinical scales which describe various aspects of the subject's personality. In addition, a large number of scales have been designed for special purposes or for use with specific populations.

Automated scoring procedures have been developed at the Mayo Clinic and are available commercially in the United States and in Western Europe. Four other computer services have programs to score and interpret the MMPI, so that a diversity of reports are available depending upon user and purpose, and different scales and bases are utilized by the different computer services (14).

Other Automated Test Data. Other tests that have been automated to some extent are the California Psychological Inventory (in conjunction with the MMPI) and the Rorschach. The objective scoring of the Rorschach, as opposed to the clinician's traditional subjective interpretation, was part of the original design of this examination. Perceptanalysis, a system of Rorschach scoring, was developed in 1957 by Zygmunt Piotrowski who later utilized a computer to validate his system, but routine use of the program has not developed. Work has also proceeded in the automation of the Wechsler Adult Intelligence Scale and the Peabody Picture Vocabulary Test, both of which yield IQ scores, but these systems have yet to be fully developed (14).

REFERENCES

1. J. L. Crawford, D. W. Morgan, and D. G. Gianturco, *Progress in Mental Health Information Systems,* Ballinger, Cambridge, Mass., 1974.

2. *Psychiatric Data Automation Project Final Progress Report,* Task Document 1.5.5, Camarillo State Hospital, Mental Health Project Grant R-11 MH 889, July 16, 1965.

3. K. Gorwitz, B. Z. Locke, F. J. Warthen, "An Automated Psychiatric Case Register in Yugoslavia" in B. S. Brown and E. F. Torrey, Eds. *International Collaboration in Mental Health,* United States Department of Health, Education, and Welfare, Rockville, Md. 1973.

4. A. S. Kiselev, *Am. J. Psychiatr.,* **128,** (Feb. 1972), 8.

5. H. D. Schnebbe and R. J. Kreimer, "Use of Electronic Data Processing Equipment in State MH-MR Hospital Systems," Study #210, National Association of State Mental Health Program Directors, August 1971.

6. G. A. Ulett, "Computer Communications and Common Sense Answers to State Mental Health Problems," paper presented at the seminar on the Computer Challenge to State Government, 18th Biennial General Assembly of the States, Council of State Governments, Chicago, 1966.

7. I. W. Sletten and G. A. Ulett, *Mo. Med.,* (May 1968), 357–364.

8. I. W. Sletten and G. A. Ulett, *Psychiat. Ann.,* **2** (Dec. 1972), 42–57.

9. *Maryland Psychiatric Case Register: Description of History, Current Status and Future Users,* United States Department of Health, Education, and Welfare, Public Health Service, December 1967.

10. W. Phillips, Jr., and A. R. Bahn, "Computer Processing in the Maryland Psychiatric Case Register," paper presented at the Public Health Records and Statistics Conference, Washington, D.C., June 1966.

11. *"Description of Psychiatric Case Registers,"* unpublished provisional document, United States Public Health Service, March 1968.

12. E. Gruenberg, Ed., *Evaluating the Effectiveness of Community Mental Health Services,* Mental Health Materials Center, New York, 1966.

13. *Session Laws of Hawaii,* Fourth, State Legislature, Regular Session of 1967, Section 81-5 and Chap. 48B, RLH 1955, 1965 Supplement.

14. L. B. Alltop, I. Wilson, W. Raby, and C. Vernon, "State Psychiatric Record (Patient) Linkage System," unpublished paper, supported by NIMH Grant I-DII MH 1297-1 (no date).

15. R. I. Lanyon, Collection of unpublished materials, supported by NIMH Grant MH 20233.

16. D. W. Morgan and S. I. Frenkel, "Computer Support in Military Psychiatry," in J. L. Crawford, D. W. Morgan, and D. T. Gianturco, Eds., *Progress in Mental Health Information Systems,* Ballinger, Cambridge, Mass., 1974.

17. B. C. Glueck, "Computers at the Institute of Living," in J. L. Crawford, D. W. Morgan and D. T. Gianturco, Eds., *Progress in Mental Health Information Systems,* Ballinger, Cambridge, Mass., 1974.

18. J. M. Kaplan and W. G. Smith, "An Evaluation Program for a Regional Mental Health Center," in J. L. Crawford, D. W. Morgan and D. T. Gianturco, Eds., *Progress in Mental Health Information Systems,* Ballinger, Cambridge, Mass., 1974.

19. N. C. Wilson, "An Information System for Clinical and Administrative Decision-Making Research and Evaluation," in J. L. Crawford, D. W. Morgan, and D. T. Gianturco, Eds., *Progress in Mental Health Information Systems,* Ballinger, Cambridge, Mass., 1974.

Fiscal and Administrative Issues

Rising costs of general medical care and mental health services are an important factor in the demands upon psychiatric administrators for increased accountability in fiscal matters and cost consciousness. In federal fiscal year 1972, $83.4 billion was spent on medical care, representing 7.6% of the gross national product. Compared with a 1950 expenditure of $10.4 billion, this dramatic increase of the past two decades has been attributed to an inflationary economy, population growth, a greater utilization of medical services, and newly discovered technologies and medications (1). Other factors increasing costs are inequitable distribution of manpower and facilities, inadequacies in the availability and delivery of services, lack of quality controls, and poor coordination in the health delivery system (2).

Appropriate data-collection and -utilization techniques enable administrators of mental health programs to analyze programs, determine costs, and recover expenses from third parties while simultaneously satisfying internal information needs. Modern data gathering needs to reflect such factors as the investment of professional time in community education, consultation, and prevention; newer therapeutic modalities (such as day treatment centers and partial hospitalization); changes in goals that seek to reduce chronicity among psychiatric patients; and evaluations of program effectiveness. Administrative activities such as planning, budgeting, and service expansion need to be based on readily available, objective data on costs, patients, personnel, facilities, existing programs, catchment populations, and other factors organized in an easily understood format.

The concept of public accountability has grown in recent years in reation to increasing governmental expenditures for mental health services. The concern of overseeing bodies is for demonstrations of effectiveness in meeting human needs within a fiscally viable structure that allows administrators to cost-justify expenditures. With increases in funding sources, there has been a concomitant increase in accountability reporting. Data are needed by state departments of mental health, the National Institute of Mental Health, local county or municipal agencies, specialized groups studying specific problems, insurers who carefully scrutinize claims for service prior to reimbursement, and community groups who play a role as consumers of the service. Data for each group have to be presented in unique, idiosyncratic formats and may include overlapping or singular features. An insurer may require data only on the particular patients insured, while a governmental body may require data on all patients. To illustrate the complexity of the data collection and presentation task, a typical community mental health center with a budget over $1 million may obtain funds from 10 or more sources, each with different reporting and programming requirements. The center itself may be an operation of many participating organizations working together to deliver coordinated services, each retaining its own programming and associated budgetary needs (3).

The demands for improved cost consciousness has necessitated the updating of bookkeeping and data collection to be more in accord with sound accounting principles that serve the purposes of satisfying funding and policy setting bodies and for internal fiscal management (4). As facilities grow larger, take on more functions and services, and increase staff and budgets, manual systems of recording data no longer suffice. Concerns with accountability, cost-consciousness, and programming within fiscal limits motivate administrators to seek better data-collection and reporting systems by turning to computerization.

AUTOMATING DATA COLLECTION

Well thought out and carefully implemented automated techniques are more apt to provide information that is accurate, reliable, and timely than existing means. The computer, fulfilling the need for accurate up-to-date reports at frequent intervals in a wide variety of formats, is a means of keeping up with demands being placed upon mental health service agencies and is equally viable for the inpatient hospital, outpatient clinic, or multifunction community mental health center.

Whether or not computerization is right for a particular agency depends upon many unique factors. The decision is reached by balancing the objectives hoped for in automating against the cost factors involved and by evaluating the capabilities of particular equipment and systems to process contemplated applications. Computers and associated equipment are expensive; applications programming, systems programming, and electronic data processing personnel are needed. A small facility, with an adequate and easily managed manual record- and account-keeping system, might not be able to cost justify a computer system for its administrative and fiscal purposes. Careful study needs to be made to determine the optimal point where the benefits of computerization outweigh the incremental costs. Sharing staff and equipment among several facilities represents another option.

Overall, the goal of any innovation in a mental health facility is to provide improved services to the community and to patients in care. The automation of administrative and fiscal processes needs to be analyzed, balancing this overall objective with the specific objectives computerization might accomplish. Among these aims are better administrative controls with improved utilization of facilities and personnel, more effective cost consciousness in planning that could lead to reduced expenses through improved fiscal management, reduction of lost charges, faster collection of accounts receivables, reduction of capital tied up in inventory, more accurate accounting and faster payment from third-party insurance funds. Automatic data processing also affords more accurate and reliable data to provide for planning, capital management, and reporting to overseeing groups such as boards, legislatures, and other funding sources.

Introduction of a computer and data processing to a mental health facility does not of itself assure that benefits will be derived; the end result can only be evaluated in terms of the applications of a computer system and the manner in which it is used. The most frequent starting tasks of computer facilities are in administrative- and business-data applications, particularly in patient billing, accounts receivable, payroll, inventory regulation, purchase control, and other traditional accounting functions. Other uses of computerization in the realms of clinical, record-keeping, and research applications are in relatively earlier stages of program development.

A series of indirect benefits derived from a computer information system also needs to be considered. Any automated system requires knowing organization, structure, and information flow; a detailed systems analysis of present operations is a by-product of automating existing manual systems. A systems analysis of operations and subsequent automation imposes a discipline upon users that requires that tasks be performed consistently in standardized ways that have proved to be efficient, forcing the user to think with clarity and precision about the tasks at hand. Automation creates an extensive body of easily retrievable data and statistics that opens a potential for evaluative and research applications not possible with hand-tabulation methods, so that developing trends and changing relationships can be discovered sooner and so be used for future planning (5).

Cost consciousness, a vital asset to any mental health facility, is a balance of maximized patient service effectiveness and minimized costs. It may be achieved by careful systems analysis of organizational functions, and often, by adherence to authorized procedures. Computerization will not automatically produce more effective cost controls in a facility. As in its other applications, the computer needs to be recognized as a tool, used to meet specific goals by generating the data needed for administrative decision making. Accordingly, information pertaining to cost factors can be retrieved and can be used administratively to improve fiscal management. However this function in itself can not cost justify a computer system installation, and studies have not sufficiently demonstrated that costs of computer systems have been paid for by improved recovered costs and reduced expenses. Cost consciousness, as aided by computer technology, needs to be considered as only one of many possible uses in deciding whether automation is appropriate for a particular facility.

SYSTEM VARIATIONS

Paralleling administrative exploration on whether to computerize its functions is the question of the type of automated system to consider. The range of possibilities include the large-scale multiunit shared system such as the Multi-State Information System, an in-house system serving a single facility, a commercial service bureau system which typically performs bookkeeping and accounting functions, and specialized application systems that perform in restricted areas such as research or drug monitoring. The system that best meets the needs of a particular facility is dependent upon the size of the institution, cost factors, tasks computerization will be expected to perform, required processing speed, and the range of information to be computer stored.

Shared Systems

A large-scale multiunit time-shared system offers the use of advanced electronic equipment with greater potentials for speed, the ability to process several programs simultaneously, and larger memory-storage capabilities; all at greatly reduced capital cost to the individual user since the equipment and cost are shared by many facilities. Programming costs are also reduced by the use of common programs. Data bases provide a common body of information that serve the needs of the various users linked into the system. Typically, facilities are tied to a central computer installation through telephone lines, with each facility maintaining its own terminal, key-punch equipment or other devices to prepare machine-readable input for computer processing. In the absence of teleprocessing equipment, facilities can utilize centralized computers through mail or hand delivery, although this is slower.

A multiunit time-shared system is generally considered to be an on-line, real-time system. On-line means the facility has ready access to the computer, usually through its own teleprocessing terminals. Real-time refers to the user's ability to process data and secure return information that serves an instant purpose. The shared system usually has the capability to process information relating to a wide variety of a facility's activities.

Batch processing is a variation of a shared system where real-time data is not needed. Various processing operations are performed at set times on a scheduled basis, with similar tasks being performed at the same time.

Shared commercial service bureau systems offer more limited services usually in the business areas of patient billing, accounts receivable, and general accounting. Often these systems effectively correlate these procedures with the requirements of private and governmental insurance. Limitations are the narrow service area, the lack of flexibility in meeting the unique requirements of individual users, and the inability to expand into other areas without increasing cost factors.

The advantages of a shared system are in the benefits it brings to the individual facility entering the system. Automated processes can begin sooner, at less initial capital cost, with less extensive investment in personnel, equipment, and facilities. The shared system offers experienced, qualified personnel, lessening the administrative burden upon the participant facility. In addition, reliability, accuracy, and quality controls are usually already built into the system. The shared system can be entered in steps—one application at a time. A problem associated with a shared system is the lessening of a facility's controls over certain aspects of the system. For example, certain applications needed by one facility may not be available, and each facility must conform to the requirements of the already-developed shared system. Cost factors in a shared system can become substantial if long-term commitments are required or if cost factors are inequitably prorated among users. The facility in time becomes dependent upon the continuous operation of the shared system and would face many problems should the system fail.

In-House Systems

An in-house system is one designed for use within a single facility, with the computer, associated teleprocessing equipment, and data processing personnel located within the agency using it. An in-house system is installed at greater capital and personnel expense to the facility. It is maintained under the control of that facility so that its applications, programs, and designs can be developed in accordance with the desires of the facility. Factors to be considered must include the space a computer and other electronic data processing equipment take up, additional supplies needed, desired speed and applications, and future plans for automation. Capital expenses for a small computer system for the smaller facility are usually less than for participating in a shared system, but personnel costs for the facility significantly increase final overall expenses (6, 7). Some large in-house computer centers utilize facility management firms to operate their computer system thus lessening the highly specialized technical knowledge required of facility administration.

ADMINISTRATIVE/FISCAL APPLICATIONS OF COMPUTER SYSTEMS

Electronic data processing of administrative and fiscal data is the primary use for computers in 60 to 80% of all kinds of business and governmental installations, and medical and mental health facilities are no exception to this rule. It is usually the first area to be considered in determining whether automation offers benefits to particular facilities (8). Descriptions are given below of some of the most frequent administrative and fiscal applications of computer processing in mental health settings.

Census

Data on patient populations are needed as the basis for a variety of daily, monthly, and other periodic reports tracking factors such as total patient census for the facility, length of time in care, movement through various services of the facility, demographic variables among the population, and treatment modalities utilized.

Admission is a crucial point for gathering the identifying and demographic information needed and is readily adaptable to an automated process. Input through key-punch cards or mark sense forms, for example, provides the data needed for the admission report and the identifying information that will head Discharge and Change of Status Reports, as well as forms needed by various divisions of the facility, such as occupational therapy, social service, and psychology. The Admissions Report can be the form of notification to other departments that a patient has been admitted. For the inpatient, additional output instruments and department reports are possible, perhaps providing a dietary worksheet or bed and ward assignment. Financial data can become the basis for patient billing and insurance claim outputs.

More sophisticated equipment includes teletypewriters, cathode ray display tubes, and other terminals at the admissions location of the facility to determine immediate space, determine bed availabilities, and give notifications to various departments and nursing stations which also have terminals. Although most frequently found in larger inpatient services, this capability might also be useful for high-volume, multilocation outpatient services.

An automated admission/discharge/change of status system has the capability immediately of updating facility utilization, existing vacancies, program capacities, and locations of patients within the services of the facility. Many of the forms used can have identifying information preprinted by the computer based on data previously collected. Statistical information generated is useful in analyzing program utilization, tracing movement through services, tracking trends, and projecting future needs (6).

Patient Billing

Patient-billing procedures provide for the recording of charges for room, board, laboratory tests, medications, therapy, and other professional services. An automated system offers immediate entry of charge information so that a bill listing a statement of charges accrued can be readily printed at discharge or at periodic intervals. Problems in setting up an automated billing system revolve around assuring that charge information from all service areas of the facility are obtained and around the divergent requirements and payment plans of third-party payers including government plans such as Medicare and Medicaid and private insurers.

Input into the system is most usually through key-punched cards or through prepunched cards made up at admission with tables of charges in each service category already stored in the computer. Output from the computer system is in the form of a Discharge Billing Statement with the prorated amounts due from the patient and from third-party payors differentiated. Periodic bills for long-term patients and billing summaries for already discharged patients are also possible. Entries in the general ledger can be made from these billing statements. Automated patient billing also provides a basis for income and revenue reporting. The computer can be programmed to identify the source and amounts of income realized, to relate the income to appropriate cost centers in the facility, and to produce revenue reports in appropriate formats on a periodic basis. Income from each department can be ascertained, comparisons can be made between actual and projected revenues, and the amounts of insurer rebates can be delineated (6).

Cost of a computerized system is greater than manual and business machine tabulations but provides for acquiring additional detailed information and managerial analysis reports and is more timely and accurate. Automated billing frequently results in increased revenue and fewer lost transactions for the facility. An effective system assures that charge information is entered from all service areas where charges can be incurred. Discharge billing reflects an up to the minute status of accrued charges and is useful as it is often more difficult to secure payment or reimbursement for charges that are unbilled at the time of discharge. Although a facility cannot always count on this increased revenue sufficiently balancing the cost factors in installing this kind of system, there have been cases where automation of the billing system has paid tremendous dividends. This is usually an indication that the former billing system was incapable of keeping up with increased requirements for detailed information or with increased service volume or both.

Accounts Receivable

The accounts receivable system is generally interfaced with patient billing. Accounts receivable represent amounts due from patients and from third-party payors. An automated system sets up an accounts receivable file and through entries (often key-punched cards) keeps track of payments made, balances, credits, and other charges.

Information contained in an accounts receivable file provides patient identifying data, third-party information, a record of payments, an account balance, and payment dates. Input into the system is through the patient billing process, admission reports, cash receipts, and adjustments. Output reports available include account listings, status reports analyzing account payments, insurance accounts receivable, and delinquency reports of accounts that have been outstanding for a predetermined period of time. Reports describe the file of any single patient and the status of the entire facility or of any of its components. The administrator can receive an aged trial balance of all accounts receivable or separate reports on accounts receivable from patients and from insurers. Aging an account means determining the amount of time an account has been outstanding for the purpose of assigning delinquent statuses. Reports can be listed in order of aging. Automated dunning procedures are possible. A daily cash report and a daily billing report are useful for controlling cash flow.

This kind of information is useful in overall fiscal management, reducing the level of amounts past due by automated follow-up procedures and projecting future needs and financial borrowing capacities against accounts receivable and the revenues eventually anticipated.

Cost Finding and Rate Setting

Cost finding and rate setting are accounting techniques that contribute to effective fiscal management. Cost finding is the process of determining costs actually incurred in providing care. The method involves establishing cost centers and ultimately charging all relevant costs—direct and indirect—to particular final producing functions or activities.

One model of this method utilizes the five basic services of the community mental health center as cost centers (inpatient, partial hospitalization, emergency care, outpatient, consultation). The costs of the various components of each service are charged to the service in which they are incurred. Direct costs might include professional staff salaries, food and commodity costs, drugs, and so on. In the instance of staff salaries, these may have to be prorated among the services to the extent that a particular staff member may function in more than one service. Indirect costs would be those related to administrative, housekeeping, and similar functions necessary for the overall functioning of the facility, but not a component of direct patient care.

Another model of the cost-finding method involves determination of cost centers by a particular organizational unit (adult, children, diagnostic, drug, alcoholism) and determination of the associated direct and indirect cost variables by services offered. There is no universal scheme to a cost-finding procedure; the particular model to be followed is designed to meet the unique needs of the agency, although some federal and private insurers require adherence to a particular method.

Rate setting is the means of establishing equitable rates for patient services based on the determination of actual incurred costs, such as actual number of hours of staff–patient contacts (for professional staff), pharmaceutical and laboratory expenses for drugs and tests administered, laundry and food expenses where offered as part of a particular service, and the prorated portion of indirect expenses attributable to the particular service the patient is receiving. In practice, all these factors are frequently adjusted for projected costs as well.

Cost finding and rate setting are useful in meeting the information requirements of funding bodies. These techniques are helpful in analyzing and justifying the use of mental health resources by developing accurate and equitable rates, explaining resource utilization, forming the basis for reimbursements, and providing for patient billing. Internally they are a basis for a facility's own administrative analysis of its program and associated expenses. They make possible program evaluation by comparing costs with the revenue generated, finally determining the level of subsidy needed to maintain the program.

Cost finding and rate setting need to be based on a budgetary and planning or management information system that has gathered adequate data on patients, staffing, programming, facilities, and overall expenses. The procedure is manually possible, but it is immensely expedited by the ability of the computer to process data speedily and to assure the accuracy and timeliness of the information generated (9, 10).

Purchasing and Inventory

Nonautomated purchasing and inventory control systems involve detailed and voluminous paper work. More effective cost consciousness can be introduced into a facility by increased knowledge of inventory already on hand and control of the purchasing procedures, Inventory, including supplies, equipment, drugs, and food, can be recorded on punched cards or other input media that are computer readable. Purchasing, distribution to different departments, returns to stock, returns to vendors are all computer processed. Maximum and minimum inventory levels for various items can be established and stored in computer memory, providing for automatic generating of purchase orders for reordering items approaching minimum levels, and rejecting new purchase orders for items found to be in stock at maximum levels. Mathematical algorithms such as the Economic Order Quantity (EOQ) can be computerized to indicate the most economical reorder point.

In present manual purchasing systems, a department initiates a request and obtains approvals for the purchase, inventory is checked to see if the item is on hand, and stockroom records are adjusted to reflect the requisition and determine if new ordering is needed. The price factor is calculated and the item is ordered or delivered from stock. This is highly adaptable to a computerized automated system after a careful systems analysis of the existing purchasing–inventory control procedure.

Outputs from the system make possible the automation of the purchasing process, interfacing this process with the accounts payable and general ledger systems, analysis of supplies and costs by departments and cost centers, reports on the value of inventory on hand, usage reports, and budgetary reports.

Accounts Payable

Accounts payable is usually interfaced with the general accounting system and with the purchasing system. It represents expenditures to be made by a facility, other than payroll. Input data consists of a list of vendors doing business with a facility, invoice information related to goods, selling price, delivery dates, returned products and appropriate crediting, and check lists. Output reports possibly include a vendor list of approved suppliers to a facility with code numbers, a periodic invoice credit activity list reporting all billing and credits reflecting net purchasing, a purchase order list of goods awaiting delivery, an accounts payable list of monies due that can also be listed by specific vendors, and cash disbursements in total and by vendor.

Budgetary Systems

The budget as a management tool has received wide recognition in not-for-profit organizations, particularly those financed directly by tax revenues. Computerization of the budget allows for rapid reporting of trends which might result in overexpenditures and for alerting individual departments of the status of their budgets. In a flexible budgeting environment, midyear adjustments may be made without a tedious manual recalculation of totals. A budgetary system may be programmed to reject overbudget expenditures.

Sophisticated computer programs may also be used as aids in planning future budgets based upon past expenditures weighted by staff projections of future needs. High-speed computer processing allows administration to compare several alternative budgets simply by changing input data.

General Ledger

The general ledger is the principal instrument of the accounting department and keeps track of financial transactions, cash flow, income, disbursements, accounts receivable, and accounts payable. It is a straightforward business procedure typically performed through a hand posting, manual method or with the aid of some business tabulating machines. The process is efficiently converted to an automated system if the funneling of all information is assured and can be converted from hand posting to data processing formats. The conversion to data processing of the functions of payroll, accounts receivable, and accounts payable are already a major part of the task and the input from these sources can automatically be processed into the general ledger. The department originating information can begin the data flow by transmitting the information on appropriate computer-readable forms. An automated general ledger can make available as output financial statements, balance sheets and statistical data needed for budget preparation (6).

Personnel

With 80% of the cost of mental health programs attributable to personnel costs, statistics and analysis generated on personnel can be useful in determining staffing formulas and equitable allocations of staff among programs and services. The salary associated with each staff member is useful in determining the cost of each service category, program, and professional or occupational category. Filled and vacant staff positions and source of funding for different staff lines can also become known, providing administrative and staff feedback on the equitable distribution of personnel among services while identifying problem areas.

Biographical data can be provided on staff related to educational and experience levels and analysis of workloads by cases, areas of service, or time. Such data provides the basis for reporting expenditures for staffing programs.

Payroll

Automated processing of payroll data is one of the most common computerized activities. The efficiency this procedure has introduced into industry, business, hospitals, and government departments is equally applicable to the mental health facility. This function is typically performed by commercial computer service bureaus or by in-house systems, and can be fully or semi-automated.

Input into the system would initially provide for employee files listing identifying and employment data and data reflecting employment and payroll procedures. A completely automated system could have a direct tie-in with employee time clocks, which is quite expensive, but might be justified in a large facility. Output from the system consists of printed payroll checks and associated records, with all deductions, hours worked, overtime, and tax information accounted for. Managerial reports possibly would provide for an analysis of the distribution of labor by work categories in the components of the facility, and statistical information useful for administrative decision making related to personnel.

Food Service

Computer programs have been developed that provide for menu planning that meets nutritional standards, offers variety, and is cost conscious. The purchasing of raw food is based upon information from the system on anticipated menus with the ultimate goal of lowering food costs and improved control over food inventory and purchasing. Systems also can be designed to plan for meal preparation and distribution based upon current patient census in each component and particular dietary requirements or even menu choices.

Maintenance

The maintenance department is generally charged with the maintenance, repair, and renovation work for buildings and grounds. Two basic functions that can be automated pertain to preventive maintenance scheduling and work-order requests. Preventive maintenance requires an inventory of all items within a facility requiring periodic service. Computer output is a report of maintenance actions required, issued on a predetermined period basis with followup on completion of the tasks. Work orders on needed repairs are possible on a variety of hand or computer forms which list area, department making request, and work needed. Maintenance can later add information related to time involved and materials used. The administrative benefit of the reports generated is in cost control and analysis (6).

Grants Management

Mental health facilities with large research units or university affiliations are frequently the recipients of a variety of grants for staffing, research, evaluation, and capital expansion. Such grants may emanate from the National Institute of Mental Health, the Department of Health, Education, and Welfare, other government bodies, or private foundations. Each grant carries with it certain requirements, life cycles, renewal dates, and reporting requirements on varying schedules. The length of time a grant remains active often does not follow the fiscal year of the agency. A computer system can be set up for grant management by keeping track of the minutiae associated with each grant including its related reporting and staffing requirements. A smaller facility with fewer grants can arrange such a system manually on a tickler file basis, but the larger facility with a multitude of grants would benefit by automation.

Special Projects

Future planning for a mental health facility requires careful thought and evaluation as to needs, existing programs, and analysis of what is required. Effective administrative decision making is based on consideration of all available data surrounding the particular issues, and the computer offers this information in an organized format as an aid to the decision-making administrative process. One such issue in agency planning might entail a demographic analysis of a catchment area used to decide upon kinds of program expansion and locations of new facilities. Data can be collected and processed to offer information relative to analysis based on statistics from the U.S. Census Bureau, from local governmental statistics, and from the agency's own statistics on patient population serviced. Tables are produced, data offered, and mathematical models applied to determine optimal areas to be looked into.

Issues such as lease versus purchase decisions on plant and equipment can also be analyzed, using data on the cost factors of each arrangement, by applying a mathematical model that takes into account different cost variables, depreciation scales, and programming uses. Many other discrete decisions that require sifting large amounts of data or complex mathematical calculations may be performed advantageously by computer. Of course the necessary programming staff must be available for these tasks.

CONCLUSION

The ever-rising cost of health care in the United States has brought closer governmental and public scrutiny into cost factors for medical and mental health services. The use of mental health agencies by the consumer has also increased because of better acceptance of treatment and the larger variety of available therapeutic modalities. A number of government and private insurance plans are in different stages of development, providing for some mental health coverage and opening new sources for financial reimbursement to psychiatric facilities. However increased cost and utilization has created a demand for better administrative and fiscal control in the management of mental health facilities.

Effective administration and decision making leading to programming and planning needs to be based on analysis of all available information. The cost of mental health care has also engendered careful financial controls, cost consciousness, and procedures to insure recovery of costs from different resources. The ability to do this requires an accurate method of data collection. The need for extensive bodies of data for administrative and fiscal management often leads to the decision for automation. Computer-generated information is organized, accurate, reliable, and timely, and data that meets these criteria are needed for accountability reports, for securing reimbursement, and for internal fiscal controls.

REFERENCES

1. United States Department of Health, Education, and Welfare, *The Size and Shape of The Medical Care Dollar,* Washington, D. C., 1972.
2. I. S. Falk, "Financing for the Reorganization of Medical Care Services and their Delivery," in J. B. McKinlay, Ed., *Economic Aspects of Health Care,* Milbank Fund-Prodist, New York, 1973.
3. S. Feldman, "Problems and Prospects: Administration in Mental Health," *Adm. Ment. Health,* Winter 1972.
4. D. L. Salsbery, *Accounting Guidelines for Mental Health Centers and Related Facilities,* Western Interstate Commission for Higher Education, Boulder, Colorado, 1971; National Institute of Mental Health, Rockville, Md., 1972.
5. R. M. Barnette, Jr., "Benefits in the Use of Computer Services," in M. B. Squire, Ed., *Current Administrative Practices for Psychiatric Services,* Thomas, Springfield, Ill., 1970.
6. United States Public Health Service, *Comprehensive Hospital Computer Applications Program,* National Technical Information Service, Springfield, Va., 1972.
7. J. P. Singer, *Datamation,* May 1969.
8. J. L. Crawford, "Computer Applications in Mental Health: A Review" in J. L. Crawford, D. W. Morgan, and D. T. Gianturco, Eds., *Progress in Mental Health Information Systems,* Ballinger, Cambridge, Mass., 1974.
9. J. E. Sorensen and D. W. Phipps, "Cost Finding: A Tool for Managing Your Community Mental Health Center," in *Adm. Ment. Health,* Winter 1972.
10. J. E. Sorensen and D. W. Phipps, *Cost-Finding and Rate-Setting for Community Mental Health Centers,* Association of Mental Health Administrators, Lansing, Michigan, 1971.

2　Multi-State Information System

Components of the System

INTRODUCTION

MSIS is an automated mental health information system that gathers data pertaining to patient information and direct and indirect staff services as an aid to the clinician in record keeping, diagnostic considerations, and treatment planning and as an aid to the administrator by producing reports that meet internal management and external accountability requirements. Data stored in the system's computer banks are also useful in planning, budgeting, research, evaluation, development of statistical methodology—all for purposes of the enhancement of mental health treatment modalities.

Information entered into the system is prepared at its source by the participating facility on computer-readable forms. The information is entered through a computer terminal linked by telephone to the MSIS computer at the Information Science Division of the Rockland Research Institute where data are processed and stored. Reports are generated from the central computer to a facility through its terminal. Mail or hand delivery may substitute for the telephone line linkage of terminal to computer, reducing the speed by which data are processed. In some instances the MSIS system is set up on independent computers in consultation with liaison personnel. At this time the system serves programs run by state departments of mental health, individual mental health facilities, and some overseas countries.

The operations of the system can best be understood by delineating the flow of data, components of the system, and the kinds of output reports and services available from MSIS.

Recording Information

MSIS has designed forms which collect various types of data (table 1). While the MSIS offers all these data-recording opportunities and more (a facility may design its own additional data-collection instruments) to record data on any given patient, the individual facility or mental health program uses only those instruments which are appropriate for the individual patient. Moreover, they were designed as an integrated set so that the same data need be recorded only once.

MSIS Terminal Activities

Completed forms are sent from the various locations to a terminal where the data on the forms are prepared for transmission to the MSIS computers. The documents are either key punched or scanned optically. Both the key punching and the optical scanning result in a deck of cards which is then placed in the card reader of the terminal.

The computer communicates with the terminal over telephone lines connected to it and receives all data from the cards. After the data have been processed, reports are transmitted to the terminal over the telephone lines. These reports are produced on the printer of the terminal and distributed by terminal personnel to the appropriate locations.

Data Flow

Once information has been recorded on forms as part of the clinical process, the data are either sent by mail or transmitted from terminals to a central computer. The computer checks the data for completeness, internal consistency, and accuracy. Using the Error Analysis and other reports, for example, Missing Data Reports, generated by the system, the staff of each facility adds information or modifies or corrects the information recorded for each patient as needed, using for the most part the same forms originally used to enter the data. Specific detailed material not captured on the forms may be added to the patient's manual record, and missing information, when it becomes known, may be added at any time to the computer files to make the record complete.

Clinical, administrative, and research reports are transmitted from the computer center and printed at the appropriate terminal or are sent by mail. Whenever basic information is added to the patient's record, a corresponding

Table 1

Types of Information	MSIS Form	Form Code	Examples of Information Recorded
Demographic	Admission Form	MS5	Basic descriptors of a patient: sex, birth date, address, marital status, name, ethnic group, religion, household composition
Administrative	Admission Form Change in Status Form Termination Form	MS5 MS6 MS5A	Legal status, ward/clinic assignment, income, census tract of home residence, prior psychiatric service, and referral sources and disposition of the case.
Patient problem and progress	Psychiatric Anamnestic Record Mental Status Examination Record Periodic Evaluation Record Periodic Evaluation Record for Community Facilities Psychiatric Diagnosis Recording Form Problem Appraisal Scales	PAR MSER PER PER-C PDRF PAS	Clinical appraisals of a patient's psychiatric condition: mental status examination, periodic progress evaluations, diagnoses, appraisals of problems and case history
Treatment and service data	Direct Patient Service Form Drug Order Form Direct Patient Service Form	DPS DPS	Types of services rendered, time spent in a given contact, prescriptions, other treatment modalities
Other staff services	Indirect Services Form Ancillary Services Recording Sheet	IDS ADS	Services performed by the staff of a facility not directly related to patient care: contacts made, indirect service such as consultation and community education, ancillary service such as x-ray, administrative functions
Other patient data	General Applications Data Recording Sheets	GAS	Other details about patients: accidents, fiscal data, dietary restrictions

report is produced by the computer; for example, when an Admission Form is submitted, a note reflecting that information is returned to the facility and when a Mental Status Examination Record is submitted, a narrative report is returned. Many of these reports are in narrative format, and they substitute, in part, for those usually dictated by clinicians and typed.

Reports that summarize data such as census lists, drug histories, patient movement histories, and summaries of direct services received are produced at the request of the facility. In addition, the entire range of data collected on patients is available on request for retrieval in unending combinations and variety.

COMPONENTS OF THE SYSTEM

Admission, Change in Status and Location, and Termination

The first act of any medical-record-keeping system, manual or automated, is opening a patient file and putting basic patient information into it. Similarly for MSIS, once the identity and the initial location of the patient are established on the computer file, other information can be inserted into the record. The first document, therefore, that must be completed on a patient is an Admission Form (Figure 1). Information about changes in status or location are added as the patient progresses to termination. In order that the location and status of each patient be recorded, three kinds of MSIS documents are utilized: the Admission Form (MS5), the Change in Status and Location Form (MS6) (Figure 4), and the Termination Form (MS5A) (Figure 6). Although the forms illustrated here are machine or optically scanned, the data may be entered into the computer through key punching as well.

When a patient appears for service, the facility gathers some basic demographic information which establishes the identity and the corresponding case number of the patient and places him in a given service location with a particular status. If the patient is an inpatient, location refers to building and ward; otherwise, it refers to the service which maintains primary responsibility for his treatment program. Also recorded onto the Admission Form are data on address, occupation, marital status, prior psychiatric service, referral source, and an appraisal of the presenting problems. Although space on the form is provided for identifying information such as name and address, such items are optional; a facility may choose to identify each record by a case number only even though it may impact complete utilization of the information system.

The data collected on the form are sent to the MSIS computers that check the information, initiate the patient's record, and produce the Error Analysis

Report (Figure 2). This report notes recording errors which the computer has found and indicates whether the data from each form submitted have been accepted into the computer files. Whenever the data are faulty or missing, the Error Analysis Report contains a message detailing the error and suggesting remedial procedures; when no errors are detected, a message notes that the data were entered into computer storage.

An Admission Note (Figure 3) produced by the computer containing all the information recorded on the Admission Form is returned to the facility. The note may be used as the face sheet for the patient's chart after it has been checked by the personnel at the facility as another verification that the intended information has been entered correctly.

The same Admission Form can also be used to alter the information already on the patient's file, that is, to update, correct, or delete items on the computer record. Instructions, transaction, or "action codes" on the form tell the computer what to do with the data on the form.

Changes in Status and Location

As a patient proceeds through a treatment program, he may change from an outpatient to an inpatient to a day care patient and, perhaps, may subsequently also receive service from a succession of units. A variety of data-collection instruments all capturing the same basic information are available for recording these changes.

One commonly used vehicle for recording these data is the optically scannable Change in Status Form where one page is used per patient (Figure 4). In parts of facilities where many changes may occur in relatively short periods of time (such as ward to ward transfers), a single form for each transaction would be cumbersome, so a data recording sheet (Figure 5) with many lines is used, and a single line entry is made for each change. This sheet often functions as a supervisor's daily report or as a unit census report. Other versions have been designed by individual facilities and, in some cases, by state Departments of Mental Health.

Termination

When a patient no longer participates in the treatment program, the case should be terminated. Termination information can be entered into the computer record utilizing a Change in Status Form, generally appropriate for terminations occuring from inpatient status, or alternatively, the Termination Form (MS 5A) (Figure 6) designed especially for use in community-based facilities. The Termination Form allows for recording the disposition of the case, the referrals, the final diagnosis, and a summary of all of the services

FORM MS 5 (5-70)

ADMISSION FORM*

	ADMISSION OR ACTION				2. FACILITY NAME	3. FAC. CODE	4a. WARD/UNIT	4b. STATUS	5. CONSECUTIVE NO.
	FIRST	RE	U	C	D (TRM)	R. S. H.	016	OPC-100		123456

10. LEGAL STATUS (inpatients only)
11. LEGAL STATUS DATE month-day-year
12. ADMISSION DATE month-day-year — 01-03-72

13. NAME last STEWART first NANCY middle initial / maiden name
7. SEX F 8. AGE 24 9. DATE OF BIRTH month-day-year 12-01-47
6. CASE NUMBER OR ID NUMBER 146 2167

14b. USUAL ADDRESS no. and street or rd. 123 QUINN STREET
city, town or village ORANGEBURG, N.Y. state zip code 10962 county ROCK.
14a. CATCH. AREA XY
14c. ADDRESS CODE 987654

15. SOCIAL SECURITY NO. 123-45-6789
16. OCCUPATION SECRETARY 061
17. NAME AND LOCATION OF LAST PSYCHIATRIC OR RETARDATION FACILITY OR SERVICE RCCMHC

MARK ONLY ONE CHOICE EXCEPT AS SPECIFIED—USE ONLY NO. 2 PENCIL

18. CONSECUTIVE NUMBER

	1	2	3	4	5	6	7	8	9
0	1								
0		2							
0			3						
0				4					
0					5				
0					6				

19. ACTION CODE 1st Re
20. EMERGENCY Yes No
21. VETERAN Yes No
22. CITIZENSHIP U.S. Other Unknown
23. ENVIRONMENT Farm City/Village Rural Non-farm

24. RELIGION
Protestant Roman Catholic Jewish
None Other Unknown

25. ETHNIC GROUP
White Negro American Indian Puerto Rican
Oriental Other Unknown (1) See Instructions

26. PRESENT MARITAL STATUS
Never Married Married Remarried Separated

30. FACILITY CODE

	1	2	3	4	5	6	7	8	9
0	1	2	3	4	5	6	7	8	9
0	1	2	3	4	5	6	7	8	9
0	1	2	3	4	5	6	7	8	9

31. SOURCE OF REFERRAL
Self Mental Health Center Institution for Retarded
Family or Friend Mental Hospital Other Retardation Facility
Clergy General Hosp.- Psychiatric Unit Court or Correction Agency
School General Hosp.- Other Unit Public Health or Welfare Agency
Police (Excluding Court or Correction Agency) Nursing Home Division of Vocational Rehabilitation
Private Psychiatrist Psychiatric Clinic Voluntary Agency
Other Private Physician Other Psychiatric Facility Other

32. TIME SINCE LAST PSYCHIATRIC OR RETARDATION SERVICE
NO PRIOR SERVICE WITHIN SAME DAY WITHIN 7 DAYS WITHIN 30 DAYS WITHIN 6 MOS. WITHIN 1 YEAR OVER 1 YEAR IN-PATIENT OTHER LAST SERVICE WAS—

CODE FOR LAST FACILITY OR SERVICE

	1	2	3	4	5	6	7	8	9
0	1	2	3	4	5	6	7	8	9
0	1	2	3	4	5	6	7	8	9
0	1	2	3	4	5	6	7	8	9

76

33. PRIOR PSYCHIATRIC OR RETARDATION FACILITY OR SERVICE (Mark ALL which apply)

NONE :::::   UN-KNOWN :::::

INPATIENT

::::: This Facility

::::: Mental Hospital

::::: Mental Health Center

::::: General Hospital

::::: V. A. Hospital

::::: Partial Hosp.

::::: Institution for Retarded

::::: Other

ALL OTHER

::::: This Facility   ::::: Private Psychiatrist

::::: Mental Health Center   ::::: Other Private Therapist

::::: Nursing Home   ::::: Retardation Facility

::::: Residential Treatment Center   ::::: School, Special Class

::::: Hostel or Halfway House

::::: Psychiatric Clinic   ::::: Penal Institution

::::: Other Psychiatric Facility   ::::: Other

35. OVERALL SEVERITY OF CONDITION

NOT ILL :::::   SLIGHT :::::   MILD :::::   MODERATE :::::   SEVERE :::::

36. PROBLEM DURATION LESS THAN

WEEK :::::   MONTH :::::   1 YEAR :::::   2 YEARS :::::   2 YEARS & OVER :::::

37. WRITE PSYCHIATRIC DIAGNOSIS OR IMPRESSION (Include Code, Use APA Manual II, 1968)

| 2 | 9 | 4 | . | 3 |

Psychosis associated with drug abuse

COMPLETED BY   *M. Brown*   **DATE**   *1/3/7~*

::::: Divorced/Annulled   Widowed :::::   Unknown :::::

27. HOUSEHOLD COMPOSITION (Mark ALL which apply)

::::: Lives Alone   ::::: With Children   ::::: With Others

■■ With Spouse   ::::: With Siblings   ::::: In Institution   Unknown :::::

::::: With Parents   ::::: With Other Relatives

28. EDUCATION—HIGHEST GRADE COMPLETED

UNGRADED	1-2	3	4	5	6	7	8	9
0			VOC. BUS. OR TECH.	COLL. 1	COLL. 2	COLL. 3	GRAD. SCHOOL	UNKNOWN
10	11	12						

29. WEEKLY FAMILY INCOME (Average Net Dollars)

| WELFARE | BELOW 50 | 50-99 | 100-149 | 150-199 | 200-299 | 300 AND OVER | UNKNOWN |

NO. OF INDIVIDUALS ON FAMILY INCOME

| 1 | 2 | 3 | 4 | 5 | 6 | 7 | 8 | 9 AND OVER | UNKNOWN |

34. PROBLEM APPRAISAL (Mark ALL which apply)
Consider 2 wks. preceding interview

PHYSICAL FUNCTION DISTURBANCE
- ■■ Sleep Problems
- ::::: Eating Problems
- ::::: Enuresis, Soiling
- ::::: Seizures, Convulsions
- ::::: Speech Articulation Problems
- ::::: Other Physical Problems

INTELLECTUAL DEVELOPMENT
- ::::: Inadequate

SOCIAL RELATIONS DISTURBANCE
- ::::: With Child
- ■■ With Mate, Spouse
- ■■ With Other Family
- ■■ With Other People

SOCIAL PERFORMANCE DISTURBANCE
- ■■ Job
- ::::: School

OTHER SIGNS AND SYMPTOMS
- ■■ Suicidal Thoughts
- ::::: Suicidal Acts, Gestures
- ::::: Anxiety, Fears, Phobias
- ::::: Obsessions, Compulsions
- ■■ Depressed Mood, Inferiority
- ::::: Somatic Concerns, Hypochondriasis
- ■■ Social Withdrawal, Isolation
- ::::: Dependency, Clinging
- ::::: Grandiosity

- ■■ Suspicion, Persecution
- ::::: Delusions
- ■■ Hallucinations
- ■■ Anger, Belligerence, Negativism
- ::::: Assaultive Acts
- ■■ Alcohol Abuse
- ■■ Sexual Problems
- ■■ Narcotics, Other Drugs
- ::::: Anti-Social Attitudes, Acts
- ::::: Agitation, Hyperactivity
- ::::: Disorientation, Impaired Memory
- ::::: Speech Disorg., Incoherence
- ■■ Slowed up, Lack of Emotion
- ::::: Inappropriate Affect, Appearance, Behavior
- ::::: Daily Routine, Leisure Time Impair.

*Supported in part by NIMH Grant No. 14934, a Multi-State Information System for Psychiatric Patients

IBM H9867T

LE986H NEI

Figure 1 Admission Form.

STATE   : VT   VERMONT   PROCESSED AT ISD: APR 7,1971 18:58
FACILITY : 71   STARTED BY ISD.:   APRIL 5, 1971 21:30
DELIVER TO : BUILDING 10   BATCH NUMBER: 9955

MULTI-STATE INFORMATION

ERROR ANALYSIS FOR BUILDING 10

PROC DATE 5/14/71   PROC TIME 18:35

PATIENT NAME	CASE NUMBER	ACTN FORM	ACTN CODE	TRANS DATE	WARD	DATE SENT	TIME SENT	ERROR CODE	ERROR MESSAGE
BROWN, LOU	401901	ADM3	MISS	05/14/71	10	05/05	21:30		TRANSACTION REJECTED. CORRECT PROBLEM(S) LISTED BELOW AND RESUBMIT THE FORM.
								AD301	ACTION CODE INVALID - NOT F,R,C OR U
CRANT, ANN	507805	ADM1	RE	01/01/70	69	04/05	21:30		TRANSACTION ACCEPTED AS RECORDED
POOK, WILL	609806	ADM1	UPDT	05/14/71	69	04/05	21:30		TRANSACTION ACCEPTED AS RECORDED
RILEY, PHIL	802801	ADM1	FRST	01/01/70	69	04/05	21:30		TRANSACTION PARTIALLY ACCEPTED CORRECT ERRORS NOTED BY SUBMITTING A FORM USING ACTION CODE 'CORRECT'.
								AD230	ADMISSION STATUS FIELD MISSING
								AD232	CASE OR ID. NUMBER FIELD MISSING
								AD114	DATE OF BIRTH MISSING
								AD120	NEW LEGAL STATUS CODE MISSING
								AD138	LEGAL STATUS STARTING DATE COMPLETELY MISSING
STONE, FLORA	904800	ADM1	RE	03/03/70	1	04/05	21:30		TRANSACTION REJECTED. CORRECT PROBLEM(S) LISTED BELOW AND RESUBMIT THE FORM
								AD110	SEX MISSING
								AD406	PREVIOUS EPISODE FOR THIS PATIENT NUMBER HAS NOT BEEN TERMINATED

```
**************************************
*  THE ERROR ANALYSIS REPORT PROVIDES  *
*  FOR EACH BUILDING OR SERVICE A LIST  *
*  OF EACH INPUT TRANSACTION AND ITS  *
*  DISPOSITION - ACCEPTED OR REJECTED  *
**************************************
```

Figure 2   Error Analysis Report.

received by the patient. (Where each individual direct service to the patient is recorded on the computer file, this summary may be computer generated.) A computer-produced Patient Termination Note (Figure 7) displaying the information recorded is returned to the facility and may be placed in the patient's chart as part of a summary.

Use for Local or Community Facilities

Available for general use but especially useful in local or community-based facilities are the Admission Form (and a carbon) and the Termination Form (and a carbon) bound together in a four-page packet. The forms in the packet have preprinted serial numbers which insure that the Admission and subsequent Termination Forms for a patient are linked by the same number.

Reports

Various reports derived from the data serve to verify the accuracy of the data submitted, to describe the individual patient, to indicate the status and movement activity of patients in a treatment program, and to delineate the characteristics of the patient population under treatment. Generally, individual patient reports reflect the very latest information stored in the computer. For example, a Patient History (Figure 8) graphically displays, against a time line, the movement history of a patient during an episode within a facility.

Other reports including movement reports, lists of patients in alphabetical order by unit, and a list of patients ordered by case number may also be produced directly from the data base representing the most current information stored in the computer.

A variety of other reports using these data may be produced according to user specifications. Information utilized in these reports is current as of the last day of the preceding month. Tables utilizing the data may be produced to answer questions such as:

What is the median length of stay for inpatients?

What is the readmission rate?

How many patients are being referred to the facility by private clinicians?

To what agencies are patients being referred?

What are the demographic profiles of chronic patients?

From what geographic areas do patients come?

List the patients who have been in the hospital between 21 and 45 days.

Figures 9 and 10 are illustrative of the many tables that are available. One

```
              PATIENT ADMISSION NOTE:  CASE NUMBER  123456

  NAME                                    STEWART,NANCY
  N.Y.STATE ID NUMBER                     1462167
  SOCIAL SECURITY NUMBER                  123-45-6789

                    ***** PERSONAL DATA *****

                       (AS OF: 01/03/72)

  USUAL ADDRESS                           123 QUINN STREET, ORANGEBURG,N.Y.
  HOME RESIDENCE CODE                     987654
  CATCHMENT AREA                          XY
  ENVIRONMENT                             CITY/VILLAGE
  DATE OF BIRTH                           12/01/47
  AGE                                     24
  SEX                                     FEMALE
  ETHNIC GROUP                            WHITE
  CITIZENSHIP                             U.S.
  RELIGION                                PROTESTANT
  MARITAL STATUS                          NEVER MARRIED

  EDUCATIONAL LEVEL                       COMPLETED ONE YEAR COLLEGE
  OCCUPATIONAL CATEGORY                   SEMI-SKILLED
  EMPLOYMENT STATUS                       EMPLOYED
  WEEKLY FAMILY INCOME - NET              $300 OR OVER
  NUMBER OF PERSONS ON INCOME             5
  HOUSEHOLD COMPOSITION                   LIVES WITH PARENTS, WITH SIBLINGS

                    ***** ADMISSION DATA *****

  DATE OF CURRENT ADMISSION               01/03/72
  ACTION CODE ON CURRENT
    ADMISSION FORM (MSIS-5)               ADMISSION
  STATUS ON ADMISSION                     OUTPATIENT-EMERGENCY
  REFERRED BY                             SELF
  LAST SERVICE WAS AS AN                  OTHER THAN INPATIENT
  LAST PSYCHIATRIC OR RETARDATION
    FACILITY OR SERVICE WAS               ROCKLAND COUNTY COMM. M.H.C.
  TIME SINCE LAST SERVICE                 OVER ONE YEAR
  PRIOR PSYCHIATRIC OR RETARDATION
    FACILITY OR SERVICE
      OTHER THAN INPATIENT                MENTAL HEALTH CENTER, PRIVATE
                                          THERAPIST (OTHER THAN PSYCHIATRIST)
```

Figure 3   Admission Note.

consists of a summary of all the variables on the Admission Form (Figure 9). One- or two-dimensional frequency distributions along with their corresponding percentages for all admissions are shown. The tables are useful for identifying patterns and shifts in patient populations over time and for comparing population characteristics across facilities. Thus a hospital administrator can describe the population being served by his facility and use the information as an aid in evaluating and planning programs. Separate tables may be produced summarizing each census tract or aggregate of census tracts, enabling a director to evaluate services rendered to components of the catchment area. Similar summary reports can be generated for terminations.

```
           PATIENT ADMISSION NOTE : CASE NUMBER 123456

    NAME                                  STEWART,NANCY
    N.Y.STATE ID NUMBER                   1462167
    SOCIAL SECURITY NUMBER                123-45-6789



                   ***** PROBLEM APPRAISAL DATA *****
                          (AS OF: 01/03/72)

    INTELLECTUAL DEVELOPMENT               BRIGHT

    PRESENTING PROBLEMS                    SLEEPING
                                           SOCIAL RELATIONS DISTURBANCE WITH FAMILY
                                               OTHER THAN THE IMMEDIATE AND WITH OTHER
                                               PEOPLE
                                           SOCIAL PERFORMANCE DISTURBANCE - JOB
                                           DAILY ROUTINE AND LEISURE TIME
                                               IMPAIRMENT
                                           SUICIDAL THOUGHTS
                                           DEPRESSED MOOD, INFERIORITY
                                         . SOCIAL WITHDRAWAL, ISOLATION
                                           SUSPICION, PERSECUTION
                                           DELUSIONS
                                           HALLUCINATIONS
                                           ANGER,BELIGERENCE,NEGATIVISM
                                           SEXUAL PROBLEMS
                                           DRUG ABUSE
                                           SPEECH DISORGANIZATION, INCOHERENCE
                                           INAPPROP. AFFECT,APPEARANCE,BEHAVIOR

    PROBLEM DURATION                       LESS THAN 1 YEAR

    OVERALL SEVERITY OF CONDITION          SLIGHT
```

Figure 3   (Continued)

The Movement Census Study (Figure 10) illustrates a summary census report for each unit (produced, in this case, monthly). The census at the beginning of the period is given along with the numbers of additions to and removals from the unit during the period. The additions are itemized in terms of admissions, readmissions, and transfers into the unit; removals are itemized in terms of live discharges from the ward, discharges from leave, deaths from the ward, deaths from leave, and transfers out of the unit. This table can be used by an administrator for planning purposes in terms of budget and allocation of staff. A business manager can use the information in this report to purchase adequate supplies for patients. The Medical Records Department is furnished with a monthly census for each unit.

Direct Patient Services

Services rendered to the patient during his treatment program may be recorded on Direct Patient Services Forms (Figure 11) and entered into his computerized record. Recording of direct patient services is usually most useful in outpatient

FORM 6 M.S.I.S. *

CHANGE IN STATUS

FACILITY NAME **R. S. H.**

PATIENT NAME **NANCY STEWART**

CASE/CONSECUTIVE NO. **134456**

BUILDING	WARD/UNIT

CASE/CONSECUTIVE NUMBER

:0: :1: :2: :3: :4: :5: :6: :7: :8: :9: (repeated rows 1 through 6)

ACTION CODE

NEW ■ CORRECT ::: DELETE FORM ::: ONLY :0: :1:

CHANGE IN STATUS

COMPLETE SECTIONS AS APPROPRIATE

HOME VISIT/TEMPORARY LEAVE UP TO 7 DAYS — :C: :1:

LEAVE FOR SPECIFIED PERIOD OVER 7 DAYS — :D: :1:

CONVALESCENT CARE/TRIAL VISIT, INDEFINITE PERIOD (1) — :D: :1:

FOSTER FAMILY CARE — :D: :1:

LEAVE WITHOUT CONSENT

ESCAPE (1)

TEMPORARY TRANSFER TO OUTSIDE FACILITY (2) — :D: :E: :H: :I:

RETURN FROM ANY STATUS ABOVE — :B:

PERMANENT TRANSFER TO OUTSIDE FACILITY (3) — :D: :E: :H: :I:

FACILITY CODE

:0: :1: :2: :3: :4: :5: :6: :7: :8: :9: (multiple rows)

DATE OF CHANGE

MONTH: JAN FEB MAR APR MAY JUNE JULY AUG SEPT OCT NOV DEC

YEAR: 0 1 6

DAY

CHANGE IN TYPE OF CARE (MARK ALL WHICH APPLY)

	BEGIN	DISCONTINUE
DAY CARE	:::	:::
NIGHT CARE	:::	:::
PARTIAL CARE - OTHER OR UNSPECIFIED	:::	:::
FULL TIME CARE	:::	:::
OUTPATIENT	:::	:::

CONDITION ON RELEASE

::::: RECOVERED | ::::: UNIMPROVED | ::::: WITHOUT MENTAL DISORDER

WARD NUMBER AFTER CHANGE

DISCHARGE

DEATH

(E) MUCH IMPROVED
     IMPROVED

NEW WARD ASSIGNMENT

WARD NUMBER BEFORE CHANGE
(A)

WARD NUMBER AFTER CHANGE
(B)

EXPECTED TIME IF LEAVE IS TEMPORARY   DAYS   MONTHS
(C)

OUTSIDE FACILITY CODE
(D)

MEDICARE/MEDICAID ELIGIBILITY   DAYS

TITLE

| | UNDETERMINED | WORSE | MUCH IMPROVED (E) |

REASON FOR RELEASE
(F)
- NO FURTHER CARE BY THIS FACILITY INDICATED
- TYPE SERVICE UNAVAILABLE THIS FACILITY
- CAPACITY TRANSFER
- DISCHARGE AGAINST MEDICAL ADVICE
- OTHER
- OUTPATIENT WITHDREW, FACILITY NOT NOTIFIED
- FACILITY NOTIFIED PATIENT MOVED
- FACILITY NOTIFIED OTHER

RELEASE WITHOUT REFERRAL
(G)
- NO FURTHER CARE INDICATED
- FURTHER CARE INDICATED BUT UNAVAILABLE
- PATIENT UNRESPONSIVE TO REFERRAL

RELEASE WITH REFERRAL (MARK ALL WHICH APPLY)
(H)
- MENTAL HOSPITAL
- MENTAL HEALTH CENTER
- GENERAL HOSPITAL PSYCHIATRIC UNIT
- GENERAL HOSPITAL OTHER UNIT
- VA HOSPITAL
- INSTITUTION FOR RETARDED
- OTHER RETARDATION FACILITY
- HOSTEL/HALFWAY HOUSE
- NURSING HOME
- RESIDENTIAL TREATMENT CENTER
- PARTIAL HOSPITAL, DAY
- PARTIAL HOSPITAL, OTHER
- PSYCHIATRIC CLINIC
- DAY TRAINING CENTER
- SHELTERED WORKSHOP
- VOCATIONAL TRAINING
- PRIVATE PSYCHIATRIST
- OTHER PRIVATE PHYSICIAN
- SCHOOL, SPECIAL CLASS
- COURT OR CORRECTION AGENCY
- PUBLIC HEALTH OR WELFARE AGENCY
- VOLUNTARY AGENCY
- CLERGY
- OTHER

DESTINATION HOUSEHOLD (MARK ALL WHICH APPLY)
(I)
- RETURN TO USUAL HOUSEHOLD
- WILL LIVE ALONE
- WITH SPOUSE
- WITH CHILDREN
- WITH SIBLINGS
- WITH PARENTS
- WITH OTHER RELATIVES
- WITH OTHERS
- INSTITUTION
- UNKNOWN

*Supported in part by NIMH Grant No. 14934, a Multi-State Information System for Psychiatric Patients

Figure 4 Change in Status Form.

83

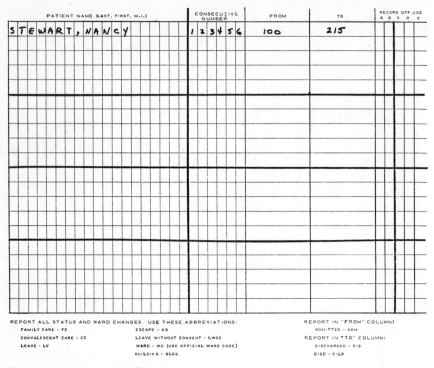

Figure 5 Supervisor's Daily Report.

settings, but in some inpatient environments, such recording may be used to chart participation in particular programs.

Services rendered directly to patients may be recorded on any one of several forms, one or more of which may be appropriate for a particular environment. Designed to capture information on individuals as well as on groups, each of the forms records: the type of direct service, the unit rendering the service, the clinician rendering the service, how much time was involved, and the date the service was rendered. Other details regarding the activity may also be included: the number of other patients and/or nonpatients in the session, the relationship of the persons involved, and the intended disposition of the case.

Two reports that reflect the most current direct patient services data stored in the computer may be generated: the Active Patient Register (Figure 12) and the Patient Summary of Direct Services Received (Figure 13).

The Active Patient Register is an alphabetic listing of patients including the last type of service received by each during a given time period. The listing may be broken down by facility, by building or service, by unit or ward, and by clinician. These reports include the name of the patient, his identifying number, sex, date of last admission, date of last contact, intended disposition of the case, the last type of service, the rendering unit, and the contact clinician. When the intended disposition of the case is a referral, the unit referred to is printed.

The Patient Summary of Direct Services Received is a report on an individual patient which lists all the services he has received during a given time period. The report, particularly useful in billing applications, indicates the date of each contact, the type of service rendered, the amount of time spent, the contact clinician, the unit rendering service, and the intended disposition.

An unlimited variety of other types of reports, statistical analyses, and special purpose listings may be designed and produced through the general report-producing mechanisms of MSIS. Typical of the questions which can be answered using direct patient service information by these means are the following:

Which patients are being served by a particular unit?

Which patients are being served by a particular clinician?

Which patients are receiving a particular type or combination of types of service?

Which patients have not received any service for a given time period?

What proportion of staff time is devoted to the various types of direct patient service?

How is a given clinician spending his time in direct patient service?

How many patients were seen and how much time was spent with patients by a given clinician in a given period?

What types of service is a particular unit rendering?

Data on direct patient services may be combined with data collected on a patient from other forms for special reports. For example, data on direct services may be combined with demographic data collected on the Admission Form so that a user can receive answers to such general questions as:

For a given age, sex, and diagnosis grouping, what percentage of the patients have 10 or more service contacts by this facility?

How many married patients are taking advantage of family counseling services?

Do patients with a particular set of presenting problems get treatment in the appropriate unit?

A table frequently requested by community mental health centers displays for each clinician a summary of the type of service he rendered during a given period (Figure 14). Two entries are shown in each cell of the table: (1) the

FORM MS 5A (3-70)

TERMINATION FORM*

1. ADMISSION OR ACTION				
FIRST ✓	RE	U	C	TERM

2. FACILITY NAME: RSH

3. FAC. CODE: 016   4a. WARD/UNIT: OPC-100   4b. STATUS   5. CONSECUTIVE NO.: 123456

13. NAME: last STEWART   first NANCY   middle initial

6. CASE NUMBER OR ID NUMBER: 1462167

7. SEX: F   8. AGE: 22   9. DATE OF BIRTH (month-day-year): 12-01-49

10. LEGAL STATUS (inpatients only): VOL   11. LEGAL STATUS DATE (month-day-year): 02/06/72   12. ADMISSION DATE (month-day-year): 01-03-72

14a. CATCH AREA: 24

14b. USUAL ADDRESS: no. and street or rd. 23 QUINN STREET   city, town or village ORANGEBURG   state N.Y.   zip code 10962   county ROCK

14c. ADDRESS CODE: ROCK 18765

15. SOCIAL SECURITY NO.: 123-45-6789   16. OCCUPATION: SECRETARY - 061

17. NAME AND LOCATION OF LAST PSYCHIATRIC OR RETARDATION FACILITY OR SERVICE: MENTAL HEALTH CENTER

MARK ONLY ONE CHOICE EXCEPT AS SPECIFIED—USE ONLY NO. 2 PENCIL

18. CONSECUTIVE NUMBER

26. FACILITY CODE: 0 1 6

27. DISPOSITION OF CASE (Mark Either A, B, C, or D)

A. Patient Withdrew: Facility Notified
- No Further Care Indicated
- Moved or Ill
- Died
- Other Reasons

B. Patient Withdrew: Facility Not Notified
- Patient Unresponsive

C. Terminated by Facility: Without Referral
- Further Care Indicated But Unavailable

D. Terminated by Facility: With Referral (Mark All which apply)
- Mental Hospital
- Mental Health Center
- General Hosp.- Psychiatric Unit
- General Hosp.- Other Unit
- V.A. Hospital
- Institution for Retarded
- Other Retardation Facility
- Nursing Home
- Residential Treatment Center
- Partial Hosp.- Day
- Partial Hosp.- Night
- Psychiatric Clinic
- Day Training Center
- Sheltered Workshop
- Private Psychiatrist
- Other Private Physician
- School, Special Class
- Court or Correction Agency
- Public Health or Welfare Agency
- Voluntary Agency
- Clergy

18-1. ACTION CODE: NEW | CORRECT | DELETE TRANSACTION

19. DATE OF TERMINATION

	JAN	FEB	MAR	APR	MAY	JUN	JULY	AUG	SEPT	OCT	NOV	DEC
Month	1											
		69	70	71	72	73	74	75				
Year												
		3	4	5	6	7	8	9	10	11		
Day		13	14	15	16	17	18	19	20	21		
		23	24	25	26	27	28	29	30	31		

20. TIME BETWEEN FIRST INTERVIEW AND SUBSEQUENT TREATMENT OR SERVICE

NO TREAT	NO TIME	1 WK.	2 WKS.	3 WKS.	4 WKS.	2 MOS.	3 MOS.	4 MOS.	5 MOS. & OVER

86

21. TIME BETWEEN DATE OF LAST VISIT AND DATE OF TERMINATION

NO TIME / 1 WK. / 2 WKS. / 3 WKS. / 4 WKS. / 2 MOS. / 3 MOS. / 4 MOS. / 5 MOS. & OVER

22. TYPE OF SERVICE (Mark ALL which apply)

Intake Only / Group Sessions / Electric Shock Therapy

Diagnosis or Evaluation Only / Drug Therapy / Services thru Collateral

Individual Therapy / Rehabilitative Services / Other

Family Group Sessions / Education or Training

23. NUMBER OF VISITS by patient, client, and/or collateral:

	0	1	2	3	4	5-9	10-24	25-49	50-99	100+
To Outpatient Clinic										
To Day Hospital										
To Day Training Center										
To Rehabilitation Center or Sheltered Workshop										
Rec'd. Serv. by Fac. Staff at Other Locations										
Other										

24. MENTAL LEVEL (Mark either A or B)

A. Tested: (IQ)

Profound BELOW 20	Severe 20-35	Mod. 36-51	Mild 52-67	Border 68-85	Aver. 86-109	Bright 110-119	Super. 120 & OVER

Retarded

B. If Not Tested, Enter Impression:

PROFOUNDLY OR SEVERELY RETARDED / MODERATELY OR MILDLY RETARDED / AVERAGE / ABOVE AVERAGE

25. RESPONSIBLE FOR FEE (Mark ALL which apply)

No Fee / Court / Medicare

Self, spouse or parents / Medicaid / Insurance

Other Relative(s) / Other Welfare / Other

8E986H NEI

Hotel or Halfway House / Vocational Training / Other

SPECIFY NAME AND LOCATION OF FACILITY OR THERAPIST

28. CONDITION AT LAST VISIT:

Improved / Unchanged / Worse / Undetermined

29. PRIMARY DIAGNOSIS (Use APA Manual II, 1968)

0 1 2 3 4 5 6 7 8 9 (repeated rows)

SECONDARY DIAGNOSIS (Use APA Manual II, 1968)

0 1 2 3 4 5 6 7 8 9 (repeated rows)

WRITE DIAGNOSIS

Schizophrenia, Paranoid type. Psychosis assoc. w/ drug abuse

COMPLETED BY: *P. Fitch, M.D.*   DATE *6/1/72*

Figure 6 Termination Form.

87

```
           PATIENT TERMINATION NOTE: CASE NUMBER 123456

NAME                                STEWART,NANCY
SOCIAL SECURITY NUMBER              123-45-6789


USUAL ADDRESS                       123 QUINN STREET, ORANGEBURG,N.Y.
DATE OF BIRTH                       12/01/47
AGE                                 24
SEX                                 FEMALE
LEGAL STATUS                        VOLUNTARY
LEGAL STATUS DATE                   02/06/72
DATE OF THIS ADMISSION
  PRIOR TO THIS TERMINATION         01/03/72
TERMINATION DATE                    06/01/72
RESPONSIBLE FOR FEE                 SELF



              **** SERVICE RECEIVED ****

TIME BETWEEN FIRST INTERVIEW AND
  SUBSEQUENT TREATMENT OR SERVICE   NO TIME
TIME BETWEEN DATE OF LAST VISIT
  AND DATE OF TERMINATION           NO TIME

TYPE OF SERVICE RECEIVED            GROUP SESSIONS,DRUG THERAPY,
                                    INDIVIDUAL THERAPY,
                                    CRISIS INTERVENTION

NUMBER OF VISITS BY PATIENT, CLIENT,
   AND/OR COLLATERAL
   TO OUTPATIENT CLINIC             5 VISITS
   TO OUTPATIENT CLINIC             5 VISITS



             **** TERMINATION INFORMATION ****

DISPOSITION OF CASE
  TERMINATED BY FACILITY            NO FURTHER CARE INDICATED
   WITHOUT REFERRAL



             **** DIAGNOSTIC APPRAISAL ****

MENTAL LEVEL
  INPRESSION (NOT TESTED)           ABOVE AVERAGE

CONDITION AT LAST VISIT             IMPROVED

DIAGNOSES
  PRIMARY                           SCHIZOPHRENIA,PARANOID TYPE

SECONDARY                           DRUG DEPENDENCE,HALLUCINOGENS
```

Figure 7   Patient Termination Note.

```
                        **PATIENT HISTORY**

     FROM - 01/03/72    TO - 06/01/72.              OPTION - LOCATION


  CASE NUMBER 123456      STEWART,NANCY    FEMALE    AGE 24


  JAN 1 72  * 1/3 ADMITTED TO FACILITY             *
      8     * 1/3 TO OUTPATIENT CLINIC             *
      15    *                                      *

  FEB 1     * 2/6 ADMITTED AS INPATIENT            *
      8     * 2/6 MOVED TO BLDG 32 WARD 12         *
      15    *                                      *
      22    *                                      *
  MAR 1     *                                      *
      8     * 3/10 HOME VISIT                      *
      15    * 3/15 RETURNED FROM HOME VISIT        *
      22    *                                      *
  APR 1     * 4/1 CHANGED TO OUTPATIENT CLINIC     *
      8     *                                      *
      15    *                                      *
      22    *                                      *
  MAY 1     *                                      *
      8     *                                      *
      15    *                                      *
      22    *                                      *
  JUN 1     * 6/1 TERMINATED                       *
      8     *                                      *
      15    *                                      *
      22    *                                      *
```

Figure 8   Patient History.

number of contacts and (2) the total time spent providing each type of service. The sums shown in the columns represent the total number of contacts and the total time spent for each type of service in the period. Similarly, the row sums represent the total number of direct patient service contacts and the total amount of time spent by each clinician during the period. This table enables a center administrator to monitor both staff and service utilization. For example, a uniformly large entry (in terms of number of contacts and total time) for one type of service may suggest to the administrator the need for more staff to be allocated to that service. A similar table may be produced for each unit of a facility (Figure 15).

The director may be concerned that clinicians are not spending enough time in direct patient service. He may want to monitor the units of his center in terms of how often appointments are not kept. He might want to know if there are any units in which there is an excessive number of appointments which are canceled or not kept and not canceled. A table in which the rows represent the unit rendering the service and the columns represent the cancellation status is useful in answering questions of this type.

```
1972 SEMI-ANNUAL ADMISSIONS FOR  #122      JONES HOS-OPC        FILE DATE 08/12/72

# OF ADMISSIONS:  JAN-FEB = 42   MAR-APR = 50   MAY-JUNE = 61   TOTAL = 153

*********************************PATIENT PROFILE SUMMARY*********************************
```

EDUCATION	#	%		#	%
0 YRS	-	-	10 YRS	11	7
UNGRADED	1	1	11 YRS	4	3
1-2 YRS	-	-	12 YRS	55	36
3 YRS	2	1	VOC/BUS	2	1
4 YRS	1	1	1 YR COLL	4	3
5 YRS	-	-	2 YR COLL	2	1
6 YRS	3	2	3 YR COLL	1	1
7 YRS	1	1	4 YR COLL	1	1
8 YRS	33	22	GRAD SCHL	-	-
9 YRS	9	6	MISSING	2	1
			UNKNOWN	21	14

AGE BY SEX

	MALE	FEM	MSNG	TOTAL	%
<12	-	-	-	-	-
12-15	-	1	-	1	1
16-20	2	1	-	6	4
21-64	59	81	-	140	92
>65	1	5	-	6	4
MSSNG	-	-	-	-	-
TOTAL	65	88	-		
%	42	58	-		

VETERAN

	#	%
YES	23	15
NO	128	84
MISSING	2	1

HOUSEHOLD COMPOSITION BY MARITAL STATUS

	NEV-MARR	MARR/REMAR	DIV/SEPR	WID-OWED	OTHER	TOTAL	%
ALONE	4	2	5	3	-	14	9
CHILDREN	1	9	5	3	-	18	12
SPOUSE	-	41	-	-	-	41	27
SIBLINGS	6	-	2	1	-	9	6
INSTITUTION	-	-	-	-	-	-	-
PARENTS	20	2	3	1	-	26	17
RELATIVES	2	1	2	-	-	5	3
WITH OTHERS	1	-	4	2	-	7	5
UNKNOWN	16	20	8	1	-	45	29
MISSING	-	-	-	1	2	3	2
TOTAL	50	75	29	12	2		
%	33	49	19	8	1		

ETHNIC GROUP

	#	%
WHITE	118	77
NEGRO	23	15
AMER IND	-	-
AFRICAN	10	7
ORIENTAL	-	-
SEE INST	-	-
MISSING	2	1
UNKNOWN	-	-
OTHER	-	-

RELIGION

	#	%
PROTESTNT	55	36
ROM CATHL	80	52
JEWISH	3	2
NONE	3	2
UNKNOWN	-	-
OTHER	10	7
MISSING	2	1

WEEKLY INCOME BY NUMBER ON INCOME

	1	1	3	>3	UNKN	MSNG	TOTAL	%
WELFARE	3	2	-	2	3	-	10	7
<$50	2	-	-	1	-	-	3	2
50-99	4	1	-	1	1	-	7	5
100-149	1	1	1	2	-	-	5	3
150-199	2	3	1	1	1	-	8	5
200-299	-	-	-	-	-	-	-	-
>$299	-	-	-	1	-	-	1	1
UNKNOWN	1	5	2	4	104	-	116	76
MISSING	-	1	-	-	-	2	3	2
TOTAL	13	13	4	12	109	2		
%	8	8	3	8	71	1		

ENVIRONMENT

	#	%
FARM	-	-
CITY VILL	149	97
RURAL	1	1
UNKNOWN	-	-
MISSING	3	2

Figure 9   Admission Summary.

```
1972 SEMI ANNUAL ADMISSIONS FOR   #122      JONIS HCS-OPC        FILE DATE 08/12/72

# OF ADMISSIONS:  JAN-FEB = 42  MAR-APR = 50  MAY-JUNE = 61  TOTAL = 153

*******************************ENTRANCE SUMMARY*******************************

                *EMERGENCY*                        *TYPE OF ADMISSION*
                          #     %                              #     %
          YES             -     -          1ST ADMISSION      66    43
          NO            151    99          RE-ADMISSION       87    57
          MISSING         2     1

                  *SOURCE OF REFERRAL BY ETHNIC GROUP*

               WHITE NEGRO A IND P R ORIEN INSTR MSNG UNKN OTHER TOTAL   %
SELF             4     -    -   -   -    -     -    -    -    -      4     3
MHC              -     -    -   -   -    -     -    -    -    -      -     -
RTRD INST        -     -    -   -   -    -     -    -    -    -      -     -
FAM/FRND         -     -    -   -   -    -     -    -    -    -      -     -
MENT HOSP      110    23    -  10   -    -     -    -    -    -    143    93
OTHR RETRD       -     -    -   -   -    -     -    -    -    -      -     -
CLERGY           -     -    -   -   -    -     -    -    -    -      -     -
GENHSP PSY       1     -    -   -   -    -     -    -    -    -      1     1
COURT/CORR       -     -    -   -   -    -     -    -    -    -      -     -
SCHOOL           -     -    -   -   -    -     -    -    -    -      -     -
GENHSP OTH       -     -    -   -   -    -     -    -    -    -      -     -
PUBHLTH/WF       -     -    -   -   -    -     -    -    -    -      -     -
POLICE           -     -    -   -   -    -     -    -    -    -      -     -
NURSE HOME       -     -    -   -   -    -     -    -    -    -      -     -
DIV/VOC          -     -    -   -   -    -     -    -    -    -      -     -
PVT PSYCH        1     -    -   -   -    -     -    -    -    -      1     1
PSY CLINIC       2     -    -   -   -    -     -    -    -    -      2     1
VOL AGENCY       -     -    -   -   -    -     -    -    -    -      -     -
PVT M.D.         -     -    -   -   -    -     -    -    -    -      -     -
PSY FACLTY       -     -    -   -   -    -     -    -    -    -      -     -
MISSING          -     -    -   -   -    -     -    2    -    -      2     1
OTHER            -     -    -   -   -    -     -    -    -    -      -     -

********************PRIOR PSYCHIATRIC SERVICES********************

  *AS AN INPATIENT*          *ALL OTHER*              *LAST SERVICE WAS*
              #    %                    #    %                          #    %
THIS FCLTY    2    1    THIS FCLTY      86   56    NOT INPATIENT         7    5
MENT HOSP   150   98    PVT PSYCH        -    -    INPATIENT           144   94
MHC           2    1    MHC              -    -    MISSING               2    1
GEN HOSP      -    -    OTHR THERA       -    -
V.A. HOSP     -    -    NURS HOME        -    -
RETRD INST    -    -    N
RETRD INST    -    -    RETRD FAC        -    -      *TIME SINCE LAST SERVICE*
OTHER         -    -    RES TREAT        -    -                          #    %
                       SCHOOL           -    -    WITHIN SAME DAY       -    -
                       PARTL HOSP       -    -    WITHIN   7 DAYS      19   12
NONE          -    -    HOSTEL           1    1    WITHIN  30 DAYS      99   65
UNKNOWN       -    -    PSY CLINIC       1    1    WITHIN   6 MOS       24   16
MISSING       2    1    PENL INST        1    1    WITHIN   1 YEAR       4    3
                       OT PSY FAC       -    -    OVER     1 YEAR       5    3
                       OTHER            -    -    NO PRIOR SERVICE      -    -
                                                  MISSING               2    1

                                                          PAGE 2 OF 3
```

Figure 9   (Continued)

```
1972 SEMI ANNUAL ADMISSICNS FCR  #122      JCNIS HCS-OPC      FILE CATE 08/12/72
# OF ADMISSICNS:  JAN-FEB  =  42  MAR-APR  =  50  MAY-JUNE  =  61  TOTAL  =  153
*****************************SUMMARY OF PSYCHIATRIC IMPRESSIONS***************************

     *DIAGNOSTIC IMPRESSICN*                      *PROBLEM APPRAISAL*
                          #    %                                          #    %
MENTAL RETARD            4    3    PHYSICAL          #    %    OTHER SYMPTOMS      #    %
ORGNC BRAIN SYND         7    5    SLEEPING         19   12    SUICIDL THOUGHT     4    3
NCNPHYS PSYCHCS        121   79    EATING            8    5    SUICIDAL ACTS       4    3
NEUROSES                10    7    ENURESES          1    1    ANXIETY, FEAR      48   31
PERSCNY DISORDER        10    7    SEIZURES          3    2    OBSESSIONS         14    9
PSYCH/PHYSIC DIS         -    -    SPEECH            1    1    DEPRESSION         38   25
SPECIAL SYMPTCM          -    -    CTHER PHYSICAL    3    2    SCMATIC CONCERN     9    6
TRANSIENT SITUAT         1    1                                SOCIAL WITHDRAW    25   16
BEHAVIOR                 -    -    INTELLECTUAL                DEPENDENCY         18   12
SCCIAL MALADJUST         -    -    DEVELCPMENT                 GRANDIOSITY         8    5
NCN-SPECIFIC             -    -    INADEQUATE        5    3    SUSPICION          29   19
NC MENT DISORDER         -    -                                DELUSIONS          23   15
NCT DIAGNOSED            -    -    SOCIAL RELATIONS             HALLUCINATIONS     11    7
MISSING                  -    -    WITH CHILDREN     -    -    ANGER,BELLIGERN    15   10
                                   WITH SPOUSE      12    8    ASSAULTIVE ACTS     5    3
                                   WITH FAMILY      13    8    ALCOHOL ABUSE       9    6
                                   WITH OTHERS      18   12    NARCOTIC, DRUGS     -    -
                                                                ANTISOCIAL ACTS    8    5
                                   SOCIAL PERFORMANCE           SEXUAL PROBLEMS    1    1
                                   SCHCCL            2    1    AGITATION          27   18
                                   JOB              16   10    DISORIENTATION     10    7
                                   HCUSEKEEPING     11    7    SPEECH DISORDER    10    7
                                                                LACK OF EMOTICN   36   24
                                                                INAPPROP AFFECT   21   14
                                                                IMPAIR ROUTINE    12    8
                                                                MISSING            2    1
                     *OVERALL SEVERITY BY PROBLEM DURATICN*
                        WEEK   MCNTH  1-YR  2-YR  >2-YR  MSNG   TOTL    %
SLIGHT                   -     -      2     -     4      -      6       4
MILD                     -     4      12    5     12     -      33      22
MCDERATE                 -     5      17    5     60     1      88      58
SEVERE                   -     2      3     4     14     -      23      15
MISSING                  -     -      -     -     1      2      3       2
NOT ILL                  -     -      -     -     -      -      -       -
TCTAL                    -     11     34    14    91     3
   %                     -     7      22    9     59     2
NOTE:  SUMS CF INDIVICUAL ITEMS MAY NCT EQUAL TCTALS CUE TC INVALID VALUES OR
MULTIPLE ENTRIES.  PERCENTAGES ARE BASED CN TOTAL ADMISSICNS.
PERCENTS ARE RCUNDED TO THE NEAREST INTEGER. A PERCENT OF 0 INDICATES AN
UNROUNDED PERCENT > 0.0 BUT < 0.5.
                                                            PAGE 3 OF 3
```

Figure 9   (Continued)

Recording all Other Staff Activities

The staff of mental health facilities in general, but especially community-based centers and clinics, carry out activities other than those that are directly on behalf of their registered patients. Consultation with community groups and other professional agencies are examples of staff activities relevant to the mental health needs of the community, but not oriented specifically to any identified patient. In addition to service to a community, many members of the staff may be engaged in general administrative duties, in self-evaluation, and in utilization review. A comprehensive understanding of exactly how the staff of a mental health facility spends its time may be derived from examination of data

MOVEMENT
CENSUS
STUDY

3 MAR 1973

ROWS = STATUS   COLUMNS = UNITS

	ADULT CAP UNIT	ADULT EAST UNIT	ADULT REHAB SV	TOTAL ADULT SV	ADOLES CENT SV	GERIAT INTEN-SIVE	GERIAT EXTEN-DED	TOTAL GERIAT SV	DRUG UNIT	ALCOHO UNIT	MED WARD	MED TR WARD	TOTAL MED SV	TOTAL ALL UNITS	KEY
CENSUS BEGIN PERIOD	361	285	246	892	21	64		249	313	56	80	15	19	34	1445	RAW
NEW ADMITS	49	29		78	1	19		19	11	51					168	RAW
RE-ADMITS	35	38	1	74	4	12		12	10	86					205	RAW
PROGRAM GAINS	38	13	11	62		16	4	29	2	9	32	2		34	128	RAW
TOTAL CENSUS GAINS	122	80	12	214	5	47	4	51	23	146	32	2		34	501	RAW
DISCH. FROM WARD	58	32	6	96	1	18	1	19	16	117		2	2		274	RAW
DISCH. FROM LEAVE	19	29	9	57	4	3	2	5	4	4	1		1		81	RAW
DEATH FROM WARD						5		5		1	5		5		11	RAW
DEATH FROM LEAVE																RAW
PROGRAM LOSSES	19	16	35	70	1	8	8	16	4	9	25	1	26		128	RAW
TOTAL CENSUS LOSSES	96	77	50	223	6	34	11	45	24	131	31	3		34	494	RAW
CENSUS END PERIOD	387	288	208	883	20	77	242	319	55	95	16	18		34	1453	RAW

Figure 10   Movement Census Study.

on these "indirect services" in combination with data on services rendered directly to patients. One set of data compliments the other to provide a total accounting of the ways in which a facility is serving its constituency. This information provides input necessary for example, for cost accounting. The MSIS has designed several indirect services forms for recording such nonpatient activities. One of these forms (Figure 16) combines the recording of both direct (top half) and indirect (lower half) services on one sheet.

The procedure for recording indirect services is completely analagous to recording services rendered to a patient already on the books. Before a direct patient service can be recorded, the patient must be admitted to the facility; before an indirect service can be recorded, a recipient agency must be registered so that the services recorded for that agency may be added onto its computer file. The agency is given an identification (or case) number and is categorized by type according to the services it renders, for example, clergy, community action group, general health facility, social and community agency, neighborhood

MS 06* (7/71)

MSIS
DIRECT PATIENT SERVICE FORM

PATIENT NAME: **NANCY STEWART**

CONSECUTIVE NUMBER: **123452**

UNIT RENDERING SERVICE: **OPC/100**

CONTACT CLINICIAN: **M. Brown, MD**

OTHER CLINICIAN: **J. Storm**

CONSECUTIVE NUMBER

	0	1	2	3	4	5	6	7	8	9
	0	1	2	3	4	1				
	0	1	2	3	4					
	0	1	2	3	4					
	0	1	2	3	4					
	0	1	2	3	4					
	0	1	2	3	4					

FACILITY CODE

	0	1	2	3	4	5	6	7	8	9
	0	1	2	3	4	0	6	7	8	9
	0	1	2	3	4	1	6	7	8	9
	0	1	2	3	4	6	6	7	8	9

UNIT RENDERING SERVICE

	0	1	2	3	4	5	6	7	8	9
	0	1	2	3	4	1	6	7	8	9
	0	1	2	3	4	0	6	7	8	9
	0	1	2	3	4	0	6	7	8	9

ACTION CODE

NEW   DELETE

APPOINTMENT TYPE

SCHEDULED   UNSCHEDULED

CANCELLATION

PATIENT CANCELLED   CLINICIAN CANCELLED   NOT KEPT   NOT CANCELLED

DATE OF CONTACT

	JAN	FEB	MAR	APR	MAY	JUN	JUL	AUG	SEPT	OCT
	1	71	72	73	74	75	76	77	9	OCT
	2	3	4	5	6	7	8	9	NOV	DEC
	12	13	14	15	16	17	18	19	20	21
	22	23	24	25	26	27	28	29	30	31

TIME SPENT (minutes)

	0	1	2	3	4	5	6	7	8	9
	0	1	2	3	4	5	6	7	8	9
	0	1	2	3	4	5	6	7	8	9

MANNER OF CONTACT

IN FACILITY   IN FIELD   TELEPHONE

EMERGENCY

TYPE OF SERVICE (1)

GROUP NUMBER

EMERGENCY   NON-EMERGENCY

INTENDED DISPOSITION (mark ALL which apply)

DISCONTINUE SERVICE   REFER   HOLD

TYPE OF SERVICE (2)

UNIT REFERRED TO

PERSON(S) SEEN (mark ALL which apply)

PATIENT   SPOUSE   PARENT

OTHER MEMBER OF PATIENT'S FAMILY   OTHER

CONTACT CLINICIAN

NUMBER OF PATIENTS SEEN

OTHER CLINICIAN

NUMBER OF NON-PATIENTS SEEN

* Supported in part by NIMH Grant No. 14934, a Multi-State Information System for Psychiatric Patients.

IBM M63221

Figure 11   Direct Patient Services Form.

MULTI-STATE INFORMATION SYSTEM

STATE   : JH
FACILITY   : 4 ROCKLAND STATE HOSPITAL
DELIVER TO : TERMINAL DATA CLERK

PROCESSED AT ISD: SEPTEMBER 23,1971 10:38
RECEIVED AT ISD : SEPTEMBER 21, 1971 16:00
BATCH NUMBER:

ACTIVE PATIENT REGISTER
BY FACILITY

FROM: JANUARY 1, 1969   TO: OCTOBER 1, 1971

PATIENT NAME	CASE NUMBER	SEX	DATE OF LATEST ADMISSION	DATE OF LAST CONTACT	INTD.DISP	TYPE OF LAST SERVICE	RENDERING UNIT	CONTACT CLINICIAN
BROWN,BILL	7788	M	08/10/70	06/12/71	DISCONTINUE	(1) 10 CONTACT INTERVIEW	700	141
DROSS,STEVEN	1234567	F	10/02/71	06/02/71	DISCONTINUE	(1) 10 CONTACT INTERVIEW	111	113
GRAY,HAROLD	3344	M	08/10/70	06/05/71	MISSING	(1) 412 ACTIVITY THERAPY	300	127
GREEN,BEN	1122	M	03/15/69	06/05/71	DISCONTINUE	(1) 405 OTHER MEDICAL-SURGICAL SERVICES	200	125

MAJOR,CLIVE	234569	M	06/09/69	07/27/71	MISSING	(I) 391 SOMATIC THERAPY	234	222
						(II) 430 BEHAVIOR THERAPY		
PACE,OLIVIA	123459	F	05/04/69	06/07/71	MISSING	(I) 80 OCCUPATIONAL THERAPY	300	129
RAINER,JIM	8899	M	06/15/68	06/07/71	DISCONTINUE	(I) 103 PSYCHIATRIC EVALUATION	400	132

```
************************************
*                                  *
*  THE ACTIVE REGISTER, AVAILABLE BY  *
*  FACILITY, BUILDING/SERVICE AND WARD/ *
*  UNIT, PROVIDES A LIST OF ALL PATIENTS *
*  RECEIVING SERVICE WITHIN THE     *
*  SPECIFIED TIME PERIOD.           *
*                                  *
************************************
```

Figure 12 Active Patient Register.

```
          PATIENT SUMMARY OF DIRECT SERVICE RECEIVED

          FROM:  JAN. 3,1972            TO:  JUNE 1,1972

PATIENT NAME:  STEWART,NANCY
CASE NUMBER:   123456

                          TIME                UNIT
                          SPENT   CONTACT     RENDERING   INTENDED
DATE OF    TYPE OF        HR:MIN  CLINICIAN   SERVICE     DISPOSITION
CONTACT    SERVICE
-------    ----------------  ------  ---------  ----------  -----------

01/03/72  CRISIS INTERVEN.    2:00   7-M.BROWN  OUTPATIENT  HOLD
                                                CLINIC

01/03/72  MEDICATION           :05   7-M.BROWN  OUTPATIENT  HOLD
          (CHEMOTHERAPY)                        CLINIC

01/10/72  PSYCHIATRIC,        2:30   7-M.BROWM  OUTPATIENT  HOLD
          PSYCHOLOGICAL                         CLINIC
          AND SOCIAL EVAL.

01/15/72  INDIVIDUAL          1:15   7-M BROWN  OUTPATIENT  HOLD
          THERAPY                               CLINIC

02/06/72  CRISIS INTERVEN.    1:00   9-L.PARK   OUTPATIENT  REFER TO INPATIENT
                                                CLINIC      UNIT

02/06/72  MEDICATION           :05   4-G.LORNE  WARD 215    HOLD
          (CHEMOTHERAPY)

02/25/72  INPATIENT CARE             6-F.POUND  WARD 215    HOLD

03/02/72  GROUP THERAPY       1:00   6-F.POUND  WARD 215    HOLD

03/06/72  MEDICATION           :05   4-G.LORNE  WARD 215    HOLD
          (CHEMOTHERAPY)

03/20/72  INDIVIDUAL          1:00   4-G.LORNE  WARD 215    HOLD
          THERAPY

04/01/72  MEDICATION           :05   4-G.LORNE  WARD 215    REFER TO
          (CHEMOTHERAPY)                                    OUTPATIENT CLINIC

04/07/72  INDIVIDUAL          1:00   2-P.FITCH  OUTPATIENT  HOLD
          THERAPY                               CLINIC

04/25/72  MEDICATION           :05   2-P.FITCH  OUTPATIENT  HOLD
          (CHEMOTHERAPY)                        CLINIC

05/15/72  MEDICATION           :10   2-P.FITCH  OUYPATIENT  HOLD
          (CHEMOTHERAPY)                        CLINIC

06/01/72  INDIVIDUAL THERAPY  1:05   2-P.FITCH  OUTPATIENT  DISCONTINUE SERVICE
                                                CLINIC
```

Figure 13   Patient Summary of Direct Service Received.

social and recreational group, private clinician, police and law enforcement agency, or school. The mental health facility itself should be registered since staff members may be rendering administrative service to the facility itself.

After the establishment of a recipient file in the computerized record, all services rendered to that agency may be recorded. For instance, a psychiatrist from the facility may be called upon to speak to the Parent–Teachers Association of a local high school on problems of adolescence. The fact that service was rendered on behalf of the school would be recorded as would the identification

MSIS STARGEN OUTPUT *

NUMBER OF CONTACTS (RAW) AND TOTAL TIME SPENT (WT1) IN EACH TYPE OF
SERVICE RENDERED BY CLINICIAN FROM 1/01/72 - 6/01/72

TOTAL TIME (MINUTES)
SPENT DURING = WT1
CONTACTS ENTRY

ROWS = CMHC CLINICIANS   COLUMNS = CMHC TYPE OF SERVICE

Clinician	Key	INITIAL INTER	PSYCH EVAL	INDIV THERAPY	GROUP THERAPY	FAMILY THERAPY	COUPLE THERAPY	DRUG THERAPY	FAMGRP THERAPY	CCPGRP THERAPY	OTHERS	DB ANOM	ROW SUMS
L.JONES	RAW	6	2	173	326	1	6	8			2	10	534
	WT1	290.00	68.00	8190.00	3825.90	50.00	240.00	160.00			120.00	305.00	13248.9
J.DOE	RAW	5	1	215	124	56	30			1	2	13	447
	WT1	300.00	45.00	11195.0	2325.60	2975.00	1740.00			14.40	90.00	524.40	19209.4
L.SACK	RAW		2	2									4
	WT1		35.00	130.00									165.00
P.POST	RAW	1	1	43	10	2	3						59
	WT1	10.00	10.00	2070.00	98.00	100.00	150.00						2418.00
R.FINK	RAW	4	1	167	94	11	8			14		6	305
	WT1	200.00	40.00	7900.00	1457.50	520.00	390.00			158.40		180.00	10845.9
J.LOGAN	RAW			52	38	1		1					92
	WT1			2575.00	495.00	50.00		15.00					3135.00
H.REED	RAW	2		226	55	3	15		1			4	306
	WT1	100.00		10049.11	557.90	160.00	600.70		16.50			150.00	12034.2
A.SMITH	RAW	5		170	145	6	8					9	343
	WT1	265.00		6955.00	2363.10	360.00	460.00					297.50	10700.6
K.LINK	RAW			50	18	4	2						74
	WT1			2325.00	337.20	200.00	40.00						2902.20
S.ROSS	RAW	1		28	152	13				4	1	2	201
	WT1	60.00		1230.00	1179.80	399.80				60.00	45.00	90.00	3677.60
COLUMN SUMS	RAW	23	7	1126	962	83	86	9	1	19	5	44	2365
	WT1	1215.00	153.00	52619.0	13653.0	4365.00	4070.50	175.00	16.50	232.80	255.00	1546.90	78336.8

Figure 14 Number and types of service rendered by clinician.

99

MSIS STARGEN OUTPUT

TYPE OF SERVICE RENDERED BY UNIT RENDERING SERVICE
FOR APPOINTMENTS THAT WERE KEPT 4/01/72 – 5/01/72

ROWS = CMHC TYPE OF SERVICE
COLUMNS = CMHC SERVICE UNITS

	HOGAN	RYAN	BROOM	BEDFORD	RHODES	LOVELL	ROGERS	BROOKS	PREEN	STEIN	CHARLES	DB ANOM	ROW SUMS	KEY
INITIAL INTER	221		1								3		225	RAW
	98.222		0.444								1.333		100.000	RPR
	64.620		0.140								8.108		9.014	RPC
PSYCH EVAL	107	4	1									2	114	RAW
	93.860	3.509	0.877									1.754	100.000	RPR
	31.287	1.351	0.143									40.000	4.567	RPC
INDIV THERAPY	3	226	504	50	24	31	15	29	168	7		2	1059	RAW
	0.283	21.341	47.592	4.721	2.266	2.927	1.416	2.738	15.864	0.661		0.189	100.000	RPR
	0.877	76.351	72.310	32.258	65.667	63.265	5.119	27.619	43.979	7.071		40.000	42.428	RPC
GROUP THERAPY		42	173	94		9	74	6	178	76		1	653	RAW
		6.432	26.493	14.395		1.378	11.332	0.919	27.259	11.639		0.153	100.000	RPR
		14.189	24.821	60.645		18.367	25.256	5.714	46.597	76.768		20.000	26.162	RPC
FAMILY THERAPY			1		2	9	23	1	16				52	RAW
			1.923		3.846	17.308	44.231	1.923	30.769				100.000	RPR
			0.143		5.556	18.367	7.850	0.952	4.188				2.083	RPC
CCUPLE THERAPY	11	24	13	7	9		12		13				89	RAW
	12.360	26.966	14.607	7.865	10.112		13.483		14.607				100.000	RPR
	3.216	8.108	1.865	4.516	25.000		4.096		3.403				3.566	RPC
DRUG THERAPY			1	4					7	15	34		61	RAW
			1.639	6.557					11.475	24.590	55.738		100.000	RPR
			0.143	2.581					1.832	15.152	91.892		2.444	RPC
FAMILY GROUP THERAPY					1								1	RAW
					100.000								100.000	RPR
					2.778								0.040	RPC
CCLUMN SUMS	342	296	694	155	36	49	124	38	382	98	37	5	2256	RAW
	15.16	13.12	30.76	6.87	1.60	2.17	5.50	1.68	16.93	4.34	1.64	.22	100.000	RPR
	100.00	100.00	100.00	100.00	100.00	100.00	100.00	100.00	100.00	100.00	100.00	100.00	100.000	RPC

Figure 15 Number and types of service rendered by unit.

of the server, the amount of time spent in giving the service, and other pertinent facts about that service.

The full retrieval capabilities may be used to get statistical analyses and listings of the indirect services elements stored in the computer. The data can be used to answer a variety of questions such as:

What proportion of staff time for each category of staff is used in facility administration?

What proportion of staff time for each category of staff is devoted to various types of indirect services?

Which recipients (agencies, facilities, groups, etc.) are being serviced and to what extent by a particular unit, by a particular clinician?

To what extent is a particular type or combination of types of service being rendered?

To whom has no service been rendered over a given time period?

The table in Figure 17, which displays data on indirect services, would indicate to the director of a Community Mental Health Center the types of staff activities not directly related to individual patient care. The columns of the first table entitled "Initiated by" indicate to the director who initiated the service. Such questions as, To what extent do outside agencies initiate contacts with the center? and What is the nature of these contacts? can be answered from this table.

Another table (Figure 18) whose rows indicate the type of service rendered has columns labeled "Time Spent (minutes)." Thus the first entry in each cell indicates the number of contacts of a particular type whose duration falls in a particular time span. This table is both a monitor of staff time in indirect activities and a planning guide for programs involving the community at large.

Patient Progress, Monitoring, and Clinical Management Aids

Clinicians in psychiatric facilities must record a large amount of medical, social, and historical information about their patients. This workup begins immediately upon admission, and, subsequently, notations are made in the file to record changes in the patient's condition at regular intervals during treatment.

Through the efforts of an MSIS advisory group, a series of instruments designed as optically scanned forms have been developed to record clinical appraisals of a patient's psychiatric condition. In developing these forms, consideration was given to the construction of medically sound instruments that meet the needs of the clinician and that are suited to automation: each instrument was designed to substitute for a specific portion of the traditional medical

MULTI-STATE
INFORMATION
SYSTEM

DIRECT SERVICES

DATE OF SERVICE	UNIT/CLINIC RENDERING SERVICE	CONTACT MODE 1= IN FACILITY 2= IN FIELD 3= TELEPHONE	PATIENTS CONSECUTIVE NUMBER	PATIENTS NAME	SCHEDULED 1= APPOINTMENT 2= NON-SCHEDULED	1= EMERGENCY 2= NON-EMERGENCY	CANCELLATION 1= BY PATIENT 2= BY CLINICAN 3= NO SHOW/ NO CANCEL.
DATE OF SERVICE	UNIT/CLINIC RENDERING SERVICE	CONTACT MODE 1= IN FACILITY 2= IN FIELD 3= TELEPHONE	RECIPIENTS ID NUMBER	RECIPIENTS NAME	MEETING TIME 1= AFTER HOURS 2= DURING HOURS	1= EMERGENCY 2= NON-EMERGENCY	INITIATED 1= THIS FACILITY 2= OTHER AGENCY 3= JOINT

INDIRECT SERVICES

Figure 16   Direct/Indirect Combined Services Form.

DIRECT/INDIRECT COMBINED SERVICES FORM

FACILITY CODE _____

TYPE OF SERVICE I	TYPE OF SERVICE II	GROUP NUMBER	PERSONS SEEN 1= PATIENT 2= SPOUSE 3= PARENT 4= OTHER FAMILY 5= OTHERS	NUMBER OF PATIENTS SEEN	NUMBER OF NON-PATIENTS SEEN	TIME SPENT (min)	INTENDED DISPOSITION 1= DISCONTINUE 2= REFER 3= HOLD	UNIT REFERRED TO	CONTACT CLINICAN	OTHER CLINICAN	ACTION CODE	INSERT 'D'

TYPE OF SERVICE I	TYPE OF SERVICE II	CONSULTEE CATEGORY	FREE FIELD I	FREE FIELD II	NUMBER OF STAFF INVOLVED	TIME SPENT (min)	CONTACT TYPE 1= ON GOING 2= SINGLE 3= SPECIAL	CLINICAN OR TEAM NUMBER	NUMBER OF CASES DISCUSSED	NUMBER OF RECIPIENTS OF SERVICE	ACTION CODE	INSERT 'I'

103

record. Other relevant information specific to a particular individual must be added manually by the physician into the patient's chart and is not added to the computer record; thus the patient's record is a combination of computer-produced and manually recorded information. To foster uniformity in the data collected, the definitions of all terms have been printed on the reverse side of the forms, and, whenever possible, the same terms were used from form to form.

The MSIS forms are:

Psychiatric Diagnosis Recording Form (PDRF): Data on psychiatric diagnosis is collected on forms which enable a rater to record a provisional, an admission, a reevaluation, or a final official diagnosis. Up to three diagnoses (primary, secondary, and tertiary) including qualifying phrases from the official nomenclature of the American Psychiatric Association may be submitted. This form (Figure 19) is also available in a key-punch version.

Mental Status Examination Record (MSER) (Figure 20): This form enables a rater to record the results of a mental status examination. The recorded in-

```
MSIS STARGEN OUTPUT                                           TABLE       1
       INDIRECT SERVICE REPORT
                                                              PAGE   1-  1
                                                              16 MAR 1973
ROWS = TYPE OF SERVICE(1)    COLUMNS = INITIATED BY-
       RENDERED
                THIS    RECPNT                    ROW
                FACILTY AGENCY  JCINT   MISSING   SUMS    KEY
           I--------I--------I--------I--------I
CASE      I    33I      8I      5I      2I     48    RAW
ORIENTDI 68.750I 16.667I 10.417I 491671100.000     RPR
SRVCES I 12.692I 12.903I  7.813I 14.286I 12.000     RPC
           I--------I--------I--------I--------I
PROGRAMI   67I     19I     17I      4I    107    RAW
ORIENTDI 62.617I 17.757I 15.888I  3.738I100.000     RPR
SRVCES I 25.769I 30.645I 26.563I 28.571I 26.750     RPC
           I--------I--------I--------I--------I
PUBLIC I   18I     17I      9I      3I     47    RAW
INFO & I 38.298I 36.170I 19.149I  6.383I100.000     RPR
EDUCATNI  6.923I 27.419I 14.063I 21.429I 11.750     RPC
           I--------I--------I--------I--------I
OTHER  I   13I      3I     1I      1I     18    RAW
COMMRCLI 72.222I 16.667I  5.556I  5.556I100.000     RPR
SRVCES I  5.000I  4.839I  1.563I  7.143I  4.500     RPC
           I--------I--------I--------I--------I
SEMINARI   63I      2I    11I      1I     77    RAW
WORKSHPI 81.818I  2.597I 14.286I  1.299I100.000     RPR
LECTUREI 24.231I  3.226I 17.188I  7.143I 19.250     RPC
           I--------I--------I--------I--------I
CLINICNI   45I      I     5I      2I     52    RAW
CASE   I 86.538I      I  9.615I  3.846I100.000     RPR
CONFRNCI 17.308I      I  7.813I 14.286I 13.000     RPC
           I--------I--------I--------I--------I
PROGRAMI   21I     13I    16I      1I     51    RAW
PLNING I 41.176I 25.490I 31.373I  1.961I100.000     RPR
     •   I  8.077I 20.968I 25.000I  7.143I 12.750     RPC
           I--------I--------I--------I--------I
COLUMN    260     62      64      14     400    RAW
  SUMS   65.000  15.500  16.000   3.500 100.000     RPR
         100.000 100.000 100.000 100.000 100.000    RPC
```

Figure 17   Indirect Service Report.

```
MSIS STARGEN OUTPUT                                              TABLE      1
     INDIRECT SERVICE REPORT

                                                             PAGE   1-  1
                                                             16 MAR 1973
ROWS = TYPE OF SERVICE(1)   COLUMNS = TIME SPENT (MINUTES)
       RENDERED
                                                             ROW
          11-20   21-30   41-50   51-60   71-80   81-90    91+   SUMS  KEY
       I-------I-------I-------I-------I-------I-------I-------I
CASE   I       I       I       I     6I       I     11I    31I    48  RAW
ORIENTOI       I       I       I 12.500I       I 22.917I 64.583I100.000 RPR
SRVCES I       I       I       I  8.955I       I 14.103I 13.420I 12.000 RPC
       I-------I-------I-------I-------I-------I-------I-------I
PROGRAMI     -       3I      2I    20I      2I    24I    56I   107  RAW
ORIENTOI  2.804I  1.869I 18.692I  1.869I 22.430I 52.336I100.000 RPR
SRVCES I 60.000I 28.571I 29.851I 20.000I 30.769I 24.242I 26.750 RPC
       I-------I-------I-------I-------I-------I-------I-------I
PUBLIC I     2I       I     3I      1I      2I    39I    47  RAW
INFO & I  4.255I       I  6.363I  2.128I  4.255I 82.979I100.000 RPR
EDUCATNI100.000I       I  4.478I 10.000I  2.564I 16.883I 11.750 RPC
       I-------I-------I-------I-------I-------I-------I-------I
OTHER  I       I     1I       I     4I       I     1I    12I    18  RAW
COMMRCLI  5.556I       I 22.222I       I  5.556I 66.667I100.000 RPR
SRVCES I 20.000I       I  5.970I       I  1.282I  5.195I  4.500 RPC
       I-------I-------I-------I-------I-------I-------I-------I
SEMINARI       I       I       I     5I      1I    24I    46I    77  RAW
WORKSHPI       I       I  1.299I  6.494I  1.299I 31.169I 59.740I100.000 RPR
LECTUREI       I       I 14.286I  7.463I 10.000I 30.769I 19.913I 19.250 RPC
       I-------I-------I-------I-------I-------I-------I-------I
CLINICNI       I       I       I    24I      6I     8I    14I    52  RAW
CASE   I       I       I       I 46.154I 11.538I 15.385I 26.923I100.000 RPR
CONFRNCI       I       I       I 35.821I 60.000I 10.256I  6.061I 13.000 RPC
       I-------I-------I-------I-------I-------I-------I-------I
PROGRAMI-------I     1I      4I     5I       I     8I    33I    51  RAW
PLNING I       I  1.961I  7.843I  9.804I       I 15.686I 64.706I100.000 RPR
       I       I 20.000I 57.143I  7.463I       I 10.256I 14.286I 12.750 RPC
       I-------I-------I-------I-------I-------I-------I-------I
COLUMN        2       5       7      67      10      78     231     400  RAW
SUMS      0.500   1.250   1.750  16.750   2.500  19.500  57.750 100.000 RPR
        100.000 100.000 100.000 100.000 100.000 100.000 100.000 100.000 RPC
```

Figure 18   Indirect Service Report.

formation is used by the computer to produce a narrative description of the results of the examination (Figure 21).

Periodic Evaluation Record (PER) (Figure 22): On this form a rater can record clinical judgments of a patient's condition at frequent intervals. Items on this report (Figure 23) are a subset of the data collected on the MSER. This form is designed for use in an inpatient environment.

Periodic Evaluation Record—Community Version (PER-C) (Figure 24): This form enables a rater to record periodically his judgments of the condition of a patient who is living in the community. The items on the PER-C with the exception of the information dealing with the patient's life in the community are identical to those on the Periodic Evaluation Record and are a subset of the Mental Status Examination Record. Output is in cryptic phrases rather than narrative (Figure 25).

Problem Appraisal Scales (PAS) (Figure 26): With this form a rater can make a scaled appraisal of the patient's problems. All or any of 38 problems referring to a 2-week evaluation period can be marked. In addition, the rater can note the overall severity of the condition and the duration of the condition. The

PSYCHIATRIC DIAGNOSIS
RECORDING FORM (PDRF)*

Form MS 01 (11–71)

Read instructions on reverse side.

Patient's last name: STEWART
First name: NANCY
M.I.

Facility: R.S.H.
Ward: 100

Case or consecutive number	0	1	2	3	4	5	6	7	8	9
		1								
			2							
				3						
					4					
					5					
						6				

Facility code	0	1	2	3	4	5	6	7	8	9

Date	Jan	Feb	Mar	Apr	May	Jun	Jul	Aug	Sep	Oct	Nov	Dec
Month												
	1											
	2	3	4	5	6	7	8	9	10	11		
	12	13	14	15	16	17	18	19	20	21		
	22	23	24	25	26	27	28	29	30	31		

| Year | 69 | 70 | 71 | 72 | 73 | 74 | 75 | | | |
| Day | | | | | | | | | | |

Transaction	provisional admission	reevaluation	final official	correction	deletion

	0	1	2	3	4	5	6	7	8	9
	0									
										9
		1								
										9
			2							
										9

Rater code	0	1	2	3	4	5	6	7	8	9

I MENTAL RETARDATION
310. Borderline
311. Mild
312. Moderate
313. Severe
314. Profound
315. Unspecified

With each. Following or associated with
.0 Infection or intoxication
.1 Trauma or physical agent
.2 Disorders of metabolism, growth or nutrition
.3 Gross brain disease (postnatal)
.4 Unknown prenatal influence
.5 Chromosomal abnormality
.6 Prematurity
.7 Major psychiatric disorder
.8 Psycho-social (environmental) deprivation
.9 Other condition

II ORGANIC BRAIN SYNDROMES (OBS)
A PSYCHOSES
Senile and pre-senile dementia
290.0 Senile dementia
290.1 Pre-senile dementia
Alcoholic psychosis
291.0 Delirium tremens
291.1 Korsakov's psychosis

B NON-PSYCHOTIC
309.0 Intracranial infection
309.13 Alcohol (simple drunkenness)
309.14 Other drug, poison or systemic intoxication
309.2 Brain trauma
309.3 Circulatory disturbance
309.4 Epilepsy
309.5 Disturbance of metabolism, growth, or nutrition
309.6 Senile or pre-senile brain disease
309.7 Intracranial neoplasm
309.8 Degenerative disease of the CNS
309.9 Other physical condition

III PSYCHOSES NOT ATTRIBUTED TO PHYSICAL CONDITIONS LISTED PREVIOUSLY
Schizophrenia
295.0 Simple
295.1 Hebephrenic
295.2 Catatonic
295.23 Catatonic type, excited
295.24 Catatonic type, withdrawn
295.3 Paranoid
295.4 Acute schizophrenic episode
295.5 Latent
295.6 Residual
295.7 Schizo-affective
295.73 Schizo-affective, excited

V PERSONALITY DISORDERS AND CERTAIN OTHER NON-PSYCHOTIC MENTAL DISORDERS
Personality disorders
301.0 Paranoid
301.1 Cyclothymic
301.2 Schizoid
301.3 Explosive
301.4 Obsessive compulsive
301.5 Hysterical
301.6 Asthenic
301.7 Antisocial
301.81 Passive-aggressive
301.82 Inadequate
301.89 Other specified types
Sexual deviation
302.0 Homosexuality
302.1 Fetishism
302.2 Pedophilia
302.3 Transvestitism
302.4 Exhibitionism
302.5 Voyeurism
302.6 Sadism
302.7 Masochism
302.8 Other sexual deviation
Alcoholism
303.0 Episodic excessive drinking
303.1 Habitual excessive drinking
303.2 Alcohol addiction
303.9 Other alcoholism

VII SPECIAL SYMPTOMS (continued)
306.5 Feeding disturbance
306.6 Enuresis
306.7 Encopresis
306.8 Cephalalgia
306.9 Other special symptom

VIII TRANSIENT SITUATIONAL DISTURBANCES
307.0 Adjustment reaction of infancy
307.1 Adjustment reaction of childhood
307.2 Adjustment reaction of adolescence
307.3 Adjustment reaction of adult life
307.4 Adjustment reaction of late life

IX BEHAVIOR DISORDERS OF CHILDHOOD AND ADOLESCENCE
308.0 Hyperkinetic reaction
308.1 Withdrawing reaction
308.2 Overanxious reaction
308.3 Runaway reaction
308.4 Unsocialized aggressive reaction
308.5 Group delinquent reaction
308.9 Other reaction

X CONDITIONS WITHOUT MANIFEST PSYCHIATRIC DISORDER AND NON-SPECIFIC CONDITIONS
Social maladjustment without manifest

Figure 19 Psychiatric Diagnosis Recording Form.

291.2 Other alcoholic hallucinosis
291.3 Alcohol paranoid state
291.4 Acute alcohol intoxication
291.5 Alcoholic deterioration
291.6 Pathological intoxication
291.9 Other alcoholic psychosis
Psychosis associated with intracranial infection
292.0 General paralysis
292.1 Syphilis of central nervous system
292.2 Epidemic encephalitis
292.3 Other and unspecified encephalitis
292.9 Other intracranial infection
Psychosis associated with other cerebral condition
293.0 Cerebral arteriosclerosis
293.1 Other cerebrovascular disturbance
293.2 Epilepsy
293.3 Intracranial neoplasm
293.4 Degenerative disease of the CNS
293.5 Brain trauma
293.9 Other cerebral condition
Psychosis associated with other physical condition
294.0 Endocrine disorder
294.1 Metabolic and nutritional disorder
294.2 Systemic infection
294.3 Drug or poison intoxication (other than alcohol)
294.4 Childbirth
294.8 Other and unspecified physical condition

295.74 Schizo-affective, depressed
295.8 Childhood
295.90 Chronic undifferentiated
295.99 Other schizophrenia
Major affective disorders
296.0 Involutional melancholia
296.1 Manic-depressive illness, manic
296.2 Manic-depressive illness, depressed
296.3 Manic-depressive illness, circular
296.33 Manic-depressive, circular, manic
296.34 Manic-depressive, circular, depressed
296.8 Other major affective disorder
Paranoid states
297.0 Paranoia
297.1 Involutional paranoid state
297.9 Other paranoid state
Other psychosis
298.0 Psychotic depressive reaction
IV NEUROSES
300.0 Anxiety
300.1 Hysterical
300.13 Hysterical, conversion type
300.14 Hysterical, dissociative type
300.2 Phobic
300.3 Obsessive compulsive
300.4 Depressive
300.5 Neurasthenic
300.6 Depersonalization
300.7 Hypochondriacal
300.8 Other neurosis

Drug dependence
304.0 Opium, opium alkaloids and their derivatives
304.1 Synthetic analgesics with morphine-like effects
304.2 Barbiturates
304.3 Other hypnotics and sedatives or "tranquilizers"
304.4 Cocaine
304.5 Cannabis sativa (hashish, marihuana)
304.6 Other psycho-stimulants
304.7 Hallucinogens
304.8 Other drug dependence
VI PSYCHOPHYSIOLOGIC DISORDERS
305.0 Skin
305.1 Musculoskeletal
305.2 Respiratory
305.3 Cardiovascular
305.4 Hemic and lymphatic
305.5 Gastro-intestinal
305.6 Genito-urinary
305.7 Endocrine
305.8 Organ of special sense
305.9 Other type
VII SPECIAL SYMPTOMS
306.0 Speech disturbance
306.1 Specific learning disturbance
306.2 Tic
306.3 Other psychomotor disorder
306.4 Disorders of sleep

psychiatric disorder
316.0 Marital maladjustment
316.1 Social maladjustment
316.2 Occupational maladjustment
316.3 Dyssocial behavior
316.9 Other social maladjustment
Non-specific conditions
317 Non-specific conditions
No Mental Disorder
318 No mental disorder
XI NON-DIAGNOSTIC TERMS FOR ADMINISTRATIVE USE
319.0 Diagnosis deferred
319.1 Boarder
319.2 Experiment only
319.9 Other
FIFTH DIGIT QUALIFYING PHRASES
Section II
X1 Acute
X2 Chronic
Section III
X6 Not psychotic now
Section IV through IX
X6 Mild
X7 Moderate
X8 Severe
All disorders
X5 In remission

I First diagnosis
II Second diagnosis
III Third diagnosis

Signature P. Fifth, M.D.   Date 6/1/7-

*Developed by Robert L. Spitzer, M.D. and Jean Endicott, Ph.D. Biometrics Research, N.Y.S. Department of Mental Hygiene, with the assistance of the Multi-State Information System for Psychiatric Patients Project. Supported by N.Y.S. Department of Mental Hygiene, C29820 and NIMH Grant 14934.

IBM M634118

Form MS9 (9/70)

MENTAL STATUS EXAMINATION RECORD (MSER)*

Patient's last name	First name	M.I.
STEWART	NANCY	

* Read instructions on reverse side.

Facility	Ward
PSH	215

IDENTIFICATION

Case or consecutive number: 1 2 3 4 5 6

Facility code: 0 1 6

Rater code: 0 0 7

Last day of week being evaluated

Jan Feb Mar Apr May Month: Jun Jul Aug Sep Oct Nov Dec

69 70 71 72 Year: 73 74 75

APPEARANCE

Patient looks — his age / older / younger / good looking

Apparent physical health — very good / good / only fair / poor / very poor

Physical deformity — slight / mild / mod / mark

Weight — underweight / average / overweight — gaining / losing

Height — very short / short / average / tall / very tall

Ambulation disturbance — walks with assistance / must use wheel chair / bed-ridden

Dress and grooming:
Unkempt — slight / mild / mod / mark
Inappropriate
Seductive
Neat and appropriate for occasion

Posture:
Stooped — slight / mild / mod / mark
Stiff
Bizarre

Face:
Impassive — slight / mild / mod / mark
Tense
Perplexed

108

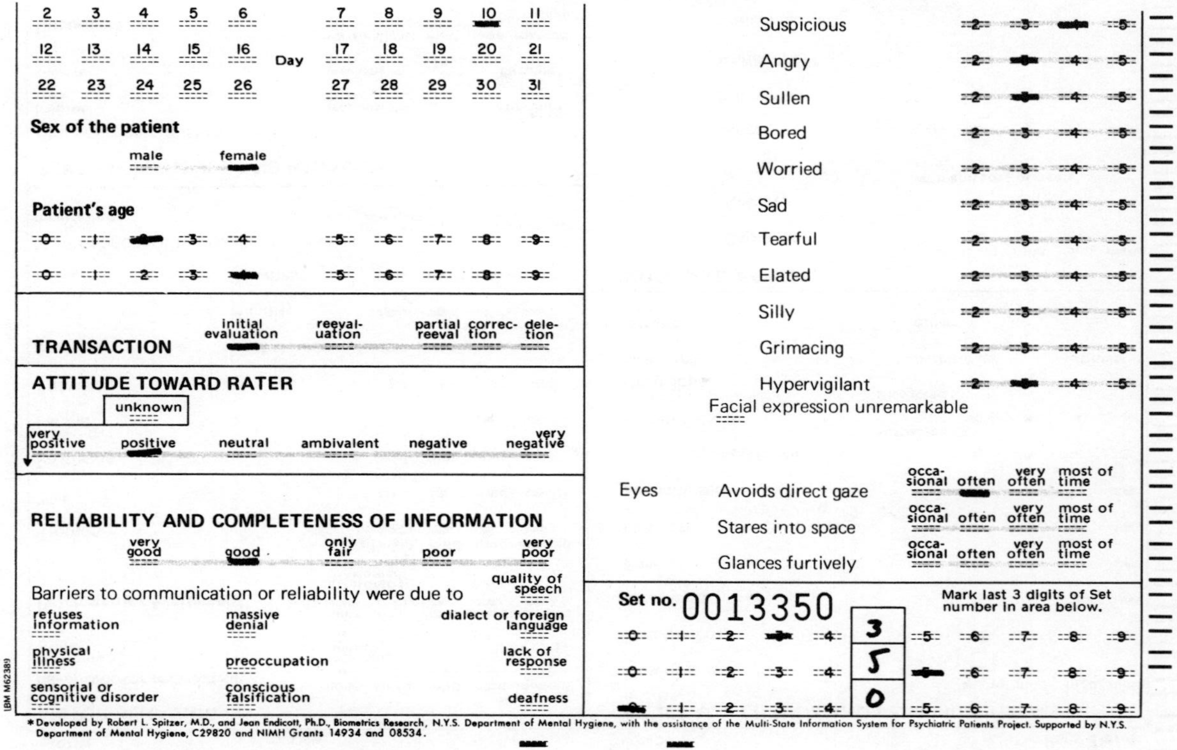

Mental Status Examination Record

Sex of the patient: male / female

Patient's age

Day: 2 3 4 5 6 7 8 9 10 11 / 12 13 14 15 16 17 18 19 20 21 / 22 23 24 25 26 27 28 29 30 31

TRANSACTION: initial evaluation | reevaluation | partial reeval | correction | deletion

ATTITUDE TOWARD RATER: unknown | very positive | positive | neutral | ambivalent | negative | very negative

RELIABILITY AND COMPLETENESS OF INFORMATION: very good | good | only fair | poor | very poor — quality of speech

Barriers to communication or reliability were due to:
- refuses information | massive denial
- physical illness | preoccupation
- sensorial or cognitive disorder | conscious falsification
- dialect or foreign language
- lack of response
- deafness

Suspicious
Angry
Sullen
Bored
Worried
Sad
Tearful
Elated
Silly
Grimacing
Hypervigilant
Facial expression unremarkable

Eyes: (occasional | often | very often | most of time)
- Avoids direct gaze
- Stares into space
- Glances furtively

Set no. 0013350

Mark last 3 digits of Set number in area below.

3 5 0

* Developed by Robert L. Spitzer, M.D., and Jean Endicott, Ph.D., Biometrics Research, N.Y.S. Department of Mental Hygiene, with the assistance of the Multi-State Information System for Psychiatric Patients Project. Supported by N.Y.S. Department of Mental Hygiene, C29820 and NIMH Grants 14934 and 08534.

IBM M62389

Figure 20 Mental Status Examination Record.

109

Form MS9 (9/70)

MSER

MOTOR BEHAVIOR

Psychomotor retardation — none (1), slight (2), mild (3), mod (4), marked (5)
- catatonic stupor
- catatonic rigidity / waxy flexibility

Psychomotor excitement — none (1), slight (2), mild (3), mod (4), marked (5)
- catatonic excitement — slight (2), mild (3), mod (4), marked (5)

	none	slight	mild	mod	marked
Tremor	1	2	3	4	5
Tics	1	2	3	4	5
Posturing	1	2	3	4	5
Pacing	1	2	3	4	5
Fidgeting	1	2	3	4	5
Gait — Unsteadiness	1	2	3	4	5
Gait — Rigidity	1	2	3	4	5
Gait — Slowness	1	2	3	4	5

Motor abnormality possibly because of:
- orthopedic problem
- neurological disorder
- medication

GENERAL ATTITUDE AND BEHAVIOR

Positive characteristics:
- responsible
- helpful
- good sense of humor
- pleasant
- cheerful
- likeable

	none	slight	mild	mod	marked
Uncooperative	1	2	3	4	5

GENERAL ATTITUDE AND BEHAVIOR (continued)

	slight	mild	mod	mark
Obsequious	2	3	4	5
Despondent	2	3	4	5
Apathetic	2	3	4	5
Fearful	2	3	4	5
Dramatic	2	3	4	5
Sexually seductive	2	3	4	5
Homosexual behavior	2	3	4	5
Alcohol abuse — suspected	2	3	4	5
Drug abuse — suspected	2	3	4	5

hallucinogen / barbiturate / stimulant
narcotic / other

MOOD AND AFFECT

	none	slight	mild	mod	mark
Depression	1	2	3	4	5
Anxiety	1	2	3	4	5

with episodes of panic

	none	slight	mild	mod	mark
Anger	1	2	3	4	5
Euphoria	1	2	3	4	5
Anhedonia	1	2	3	4	5
Loneliness	1	2	3	4	5

110

Quality of mood and affect

	none (1)	slight (2)	mild (3)	mod (4)	mark (5)
Withdrawn	1	2	3	4	5
Inappropriate	1	2	3	4	5
Impaired functioning in goal directed activities	1	2	3	4	5
Suspicious	1	2	3	4	5

Flatness — none 1, slight 2, mild 3, mod 4, mark 5
Inappropriate — 1 2 3 4 5
Lability — 1 2 3 4 5
Diurnal mood variation — worse in morning ... worse in evening

Anger (overt)

sarcastic		critical (3)	argumentative (4)	
sullen		assaultive (3)	physically destructive (5)	
irritable		threatens violence		
Provokes anger				

Suicidal behavior

none		at least threats (2)	at least gesture(s) (3)	mod	attempt(s) (5)
Self mutilation (degree of disfiguring)		slight (2)	mild (3)	mod (4)	marked (5)

	slight (2)	mild (3)	mod (4)	marked (5)
Antisocial	2	3	4	5
Impulsive	2	3	4	5
Passive	2	3	4	5
Dependent	2	3	4	5
Domineering	2	3	4	5
Guarded	2	3	4	5
Complaining	2	3	4	5
Ritualistic	2	3	4	5

QUALITY OF SPEECH AND THOUGHT

Voice
- very loud | shouts | screams
- whining | monotonous | overly dramatic
- very soft

	none (1)	slight (2)	mild (3)	mod (4)	mark (5)
Rate	very slow	slow	average	fast	very fast
Productivity	markedly reduced	reduced	average	increased	markedly increased
Incoherence	1	2	3	4	5
Irrelevance	1	2	3	4	5
Evasiveness	1	2	3	4	5
Blocking		2	3	4	5

Set no. 0001819

Mark last 3 digits of Set number in area below.

0	1	2	3	4	5	6	7	8	9
0	1	2	3	4	5	6	7	8	9
0	1	2	3	4	5	6	7	8	9

IBM M62391

Figure 20 (*Continued*)

111

Form MS 9 (9/70)
MSER

QUALITY OF SPEECH AND THOUGHT (continued)

	slight 2	mild 3	mod 4	marked 5
Circumstantiality				
Loosening of associations	2	3	4	5
Obscurity	2	3	4	5
Concreteness	2	3	4	5
Other				

echolalia	clang associations	neologisms
flight of ideas	excessive profanity	plays on words
perseveration	unintelligible muttering	suggestive of neurological disorder

CONTENT OF SPEECH AND THOUGHT

	unknown	none 1	slight 2	mild 3	mod 4	marked 5
Grandiosity	?	1	2	3	4	5
Suicidal ideation	?	1	2	3	4	5
Ideas of reference	?	1	2	3	4	5
Bizarre thoughts	?	1	2	3	4	5
Phobia(s)	?	1	2	3	4	5
Compulsion(s)	?	1	2	3	4	5
Obsession(s)	?	1	2	3	4	5
Guilt	?	1	2	3	4	5
Alienation	?	1	2	3	4	5
Pessimism	?	1	2	3	4	5

CONTENT OF SPEECH AND THOUGHT (continued)

	slight 2	mild 3	mod 4	mark 5
Religious delusions	2	3	4	5
Delusions of guilt	2	3	4	5
Delusions of influence				
Nihilistic delusions	2	3	4	5
Influence of delusion on behavior	very little	considerable	marked	

SOMATIC FUNCTIONING AND CONCERN

Appetite	very poor	poor	normal	excessive	very excessive
	requires urging to eat		requires help to eat		

Energy level	very easily fatigued	easily fatigued	normal	very energetic	extremely energetic

Change in sexual interest or activity	sleeps excessively	marked decrease	slight decrease	slight increase	marked increase
					feels little need for sleep

Insomnia (overall severity any type): none 1, slight 2, mild 3, mod 4, mark 5
difficulty falling asleep
early morning awakening
awakening during night

Incontinence	occasionally	often	very often	most of time

Seizures (this week)	one	several	daily	several per day

Severe sensory impairment (organic)	visual	hearing	likely hysterical	likely organic

Conversion reaction	hearing loss	visual	suspected	likely	definite
Type				hearing	visual defect

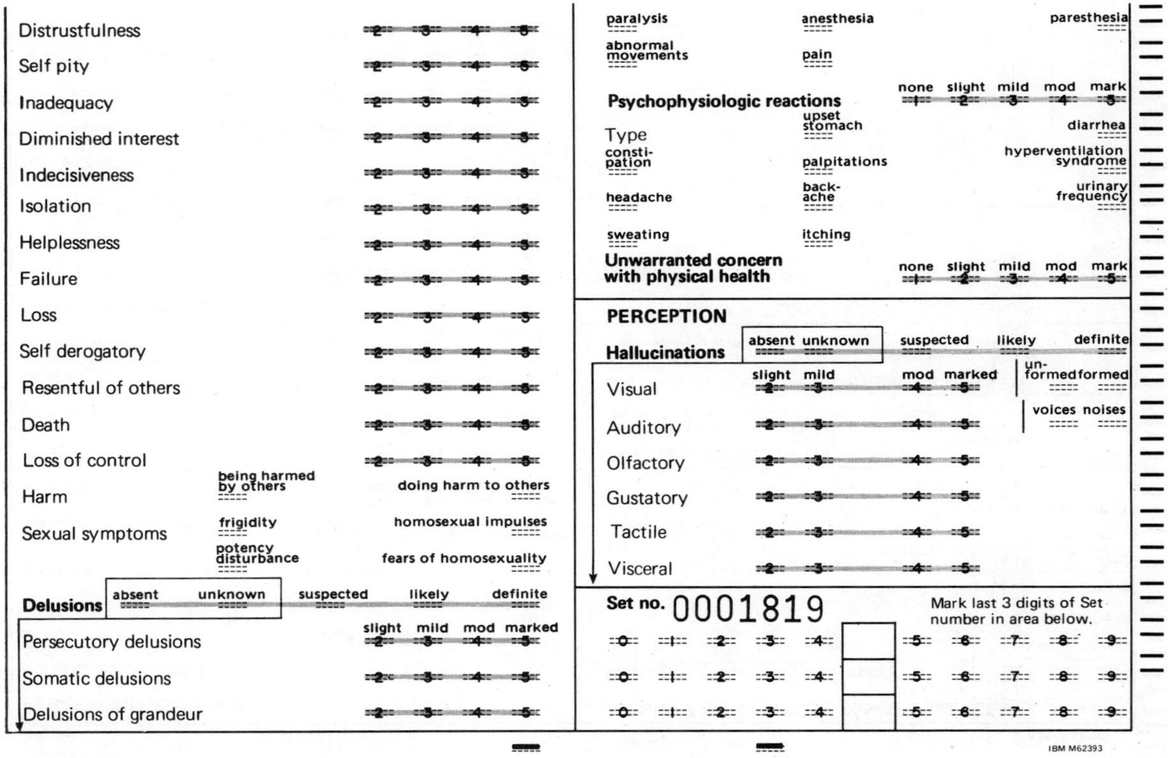

	2	3	4	5
Distrustfulness	2	3	4	5
Self pity	2	3	4	5
Inadequacy	2	3	4	5
Diminished interest	2	3	4	5
Indecisiveness	2	3	4	5
Isolation	2	3	4	5
Helplessness	2	3	4	5
Failure	2	3	4	5
Loss	2	3	4	5
Self derogatory	2	3	4	5
Resentful of others	2	3	4	5
Death	2	3	4	5
Loss of control	2	3	4	5

Harm — being harmed by others; doing harm to others

Sexual symptoms — frigidity; homosexual impulses; potency disturbance; fears of homosexuality

Delusions — absent, unknown, suspected, likely, definite

	slight	mild	mod	marked
Persecutory delusions	2	3	4	5
Somatic delusions	2	3	4	5
Delusions of grandeur	2	3	4	5

paralysis; anesthesia; paresthesia; abnormal movements; pain

Psychophysiologic reactions — none 1, slight 2, mild 3, mod 4, mark 5

Type: upset stomach; diarrhea; constipation; palpitations; hyperventilation syndrome; headache; backache; urinary frequency; sweating; itching

Unwarranted concern with physical health — none 1, slight 2, mild 3, mod 4, mark 5

PERCEPTION

Hallucinations — absent, unknown, suspected, likely, definite

	slight	mild	mod	marked
Visual	2	3	4	5
Auditory	2	3	4	5
Olfactory	2	3	4	5
Gustatory	2	3	4	5
Tactile	2	3	4	5
Visceral	2	3	4	5

Visual: unformed; formed

Auditory: voices; noises

Set no. 0001819

Mark last 3 digits of Set number in area below.

0 1 2 3 4 5 6 7 8 9

0 1 2 3 4 5 6 7 8 9

0 1 2 3 4 5 6 7 8 9

IBM M62393

Figure 20 (Continued)

Form MS 9 (9/70)

MSER

PERCEPTION (continued)

Content of hallucinations

threatening — accusatory — flattering

benign — religious — self derogatory

grandiose — reassuring — sexual

Conviction hallucinations real: knows unreal — unsure — convinced

Illusions: slight mild mod marked

Depersonalization

Derealization

Deja vu

SENSORIUM

Orientation disturbance — too disturbed to test

Time: unknown none slight mild mod marked

Place

Person (self and others)

Memory disturbance — too disturbed to test — confabulation

Recent: unknown none slight mild mod marked

Remote

Clouding of consciousness: fluctuating — continuous

INSIGHT AND ATTITUDE TOWARD ILLNESS (continued)

Motivation for working on problem

not applicable   unknown

very good   good   only fair   little   none   desires   refuses   treatment offered

Awareness of his contribution to difficulties

not applicable   unknown

very good   good   only fair   little   none   blames circumstances   others

OVERALL SEVERITY OF ILLNESS

not ill   slight   mild   mod   marked   severe   among most extreme

CHANGE IN CONDITION DURING PAST WEEK

marked improv   impr   stable   variable   worse

RATER HAS WRITTEN COMMENTS ELSEWHERE

Signature _____   Date _____

114

Dissociation

trance ||||
hysterical attack ||||

amnesia ||||
other ||||

fugue ||||

COGNITIVE FUNCTIONS

	slight	mild	mod	marked
Attention disturbance				
Distractability				

Intelligence (estimate)

unknown	superior	bright	average	borderline	retarded

JUDGMENT

	very good	good	only fair	poor	very poor
Family relations					
Other social relations					
Employment					
Future plans	no plans (or)	very good	good	only fair	poor	very poor

POTENTIAL FOR SUICIDE OR VIOLENCE

	unsure	not significant	low	mod	high	very high
Suicide						
Physical violence						

INSIGHT AND ATTITUDE TOWARD ILLNESS

not applicable unknown

says physically ill only

Recognition that he is ill

very good	good	only fair	little	none

Set no. 0013350

Mark last 3 digits of Set number in area below.

	-0-	-1-	-2-	-3-	-4-	-5-	-6-	-7-	-8-	-9-
	-0-	-1-	-2-	-3-	-4-	-5-	-6-	-7-	-8-	-9-
	-0-	-1-	-2-	-3-	-4-	-5-	-6-	-7-	-8-	-9-

IBM M62394

Figure 20   (Continued)

115

PATIENT: STEWART, NANCY
CASE NUMBER: 123456

DATE OF EXAM: JANUARY 10, 1972
FACILITY NO.   16
RATER NO.   7

INTRODUCTION

THIS IS A REPORT OF AN INITIAL EVALUATION FOR THIS ADMISSION OF
A 24 YEAR OLD FEMALE PATIENT BASED ON INFORMATION COLLECTED USING THE
MENTAL STATUS EXAMINATION RECORD. HER ATTITUDE TOWARD THE EXAMINER WAS
POSITIVE. THE RELIABILITY AND COMPLETENESS OF THE MATERIAL IN THIS
REPORT ARE CONSIDERED GOOD.

APPEARANCE

THE PATIENT LOOKS HER AGE. SHE APPEARS TO BE IN VERY GOOD
PHYSICAL HEALTH. SHE IS OF AVERAGE HEIGHT AND WEIGHT. IN HER DRESS AND
GROOMING SHE IS SLIGHTLY UNKEMPT AND MARKEDLY SEDUCTIVE. HER POSTURE IS
SLIGHTLY STIFF. HER FACIAL EXPRESSION IS MODERATELY SUSPICIOUS, MILDLY
PERPLEXED, ANGRY, SULLEN, AND HYPERVIGILANT, AND SLIGHTLY TENSE. OFTEN
SHE AVOIDS DIRECT GAZE.

GENERAL ATTITUDE AND BEHAVIOR
-------- --------- --- ---------

HER BEHAVIOR IS MODERATELY WITHDRAWN, AND SLIGHTLY
UNCOOPERATIVE. SHE SHOWS MODERATE IMPAIRMENT IN FUNCTIONING IN GOAL
DIRECTED ACTIVITIES. SHE SEEMS SLIGHTLY SUSPICIOUS. SHE SHOWS MILD
OVERT ANGER. SHE HAS BEEN CRITICAL OF OTHERS AND SULLEN. SHE HAS MADE
AT LEAST ONE SUICIDAL THREAT. SHE IS MILDLY GUARDED AND COMPLAINING.
THE PATIENT HAS A HISTORY OF MILD DRUG ABUSE INVOLVING HALLUCINOGENS.
SHE IS SEXUALLY SEDUCTIVE.

Figure 21   Mental Status Examination Report.

116

PATIENT: STEWART,NANCY
CASE NUMBER: 123456
RATER: NUMBER 7

MOTOR BEHAVIOR AND GAIT
----- --------- --- ----

        THE PATIENT SHOWS PSYCHOMOTOR EXCITEMENT TO A SLIGHT DEGREE. AN
UNUSUAL MOTOR FEATURE PRESENT IS MILD FIDGETING.

        THE PATIENT EXHIBITS NO PSYCHOMOTOR RETARDATION.

MOOD AND AFFECT
---- --- ------

        THE PATIENT IS MILDLY DEPRESSED. ANGER IS PRESENT TO A MILD
DEGREE. OTHER AFFECTIVE DISTURBANCES INCLUDE SLIGHT ANHEDONIA.
QUALITATIVELY, HER AFFECT IS SLIGHTLY FLAT.

QUALITY OF SPEECH AND THOUGHT
------- -- ------ --- -------

        SHE SPEAKS WITH A VERY LOUD VOICE. HER RATE OF SPEECH IS FAST
AND PRODUCTIVITY IS INCREASED. SHE IS MODERATELY EVASIVE, AND SLIGHTLY
INCOHERENT AND IRRELEVANT. MODERATE LOOSENING OF ASSOCIATIONS, AND
SLIGHT BLOCKING AND CIRCUMSTANTIALITY ARE ALSO NOTED. EXCESSIVE
PROFANITY IS ALSO PRESENT.

CONTENT OF SPEECH AND THOUGHT
------- -- ------ --- -------

        THIS PATIENT HAS MODERATE IDEAS OF REFERENCE, AND MILD SUICIDAL
IDEATION AND BIZARRE THOUGHTS. SHE MANIFESTS MARKED RESENTMENT TOWARDS
OTHERS, MODERATE DISTRUSTFULNESS, DIMINISHED INTEREST, FEELINGS OF
ISOLATION, AND LOSS OF CONTROL, AND MILD PESSIMISM AND CONCERN ABOUT
DEATH. DELUSIONS ARE DEFINITELY PRESENT, INCLUDING MODERATE
PERSECUTORY DELUSIONS AND MILD DELUSIONS OF INFLUENCE. IN THE
EXAMINER'S JUDGMENT, THE PATIENT'S DELUSIONS HAVE CONSIDERABLE INFLUENCE
ON HER BEHAVIOR.

        THERE IS NO EVIDENCE OF GRANDIOSITY, PHOBIAS, COMPULSIONS, OR
OBSESSIONS.

```
PATIENT: STEWART,NANCY
CASE NUMBER: 123456
RATER:      NUMBER 7



    SOMATIC FUNCTIONING AND CONCERN
    ------- ----------- --- -------

          HER APPETITE IS POOR AND SHE IS NORMAL IN REGARD TO ENERGY LEVEL.
    SHE HAS MILD INSOMNIA WITH DIFFICULTY FALLING ASLEEP.

          THIS PATIENT HAS NO PSYCHOPHYSIOLOGIC REACTIONS OR UNWARRANTED
    CONCERN WITH HER PHYSICAL HEALTH.


    PERCEPTION
    ----------

          HALLUCINATIONS ARE DEFINITELY PRESENT.  THESE INCLUDE MARKED
    AUDITORY (VOICES), AND MILD TACTILE HALLUCINATIONS.  THE CONTENT OF THE
    PATIENT'S HALLUCINATIONS IS THREATENING AND ACCUSATORY.  THE PATIENT IS
    CONVINCED THAT HER HALLUCINATIONS ARE REAL.  SHE EXPERIENCES MILD
    DEPERSONALIZATION.


    SENSORIUM
    ---------

          THIS PATIENT IS SLIGHTLY DISORIENTED IN REMOTE MEMORY.  THIS
    PATIENT IS ORIENTED AS TO TIME, PLACE, AND PERSON.  RECENT MEMORY IS
    INTACT.


    COGNITIVE FUNCTIONS
    --------- ---------

          HER INTELLIGENCE IS ESTIMATED TO BE WITHIN THE BRIGHT RANGE.
    MILD ATTENTION DISTURBANCE AND MILD DISTRACTIBILITY ARE OBSERVED.


    JUDGMENT
    --------

          THE PATIENT HAS NO PLANS FOR THE FUTURE.  HER JUDGMENT
    CONCERNING FAMILY RELATIONS AND NON-FAMILIAL SOCIAL RELATIONS IS POOR,
    AND HER JUDGMENT CONCERNING EMPLOYMENT IS VERY POOR.
```

Figure 21   (Continued)

118

PATIENT: STEWART,NANCY
CASE NUMBER: 123456
RATER: NUMBER 7

POTENTIAL FOR SUICIDE OR VIOLENCE
---------- --- ------- -- ---------

        IN THE EXAMINER'S JUDGMENT, THIS PATIENT'S POTENTIAL FOR SUICIDE
IS MODERATE, AND POTENTIAL FOR PHYSICAL VIOLENCE IS LOW.

INSIGHT AND ATTITUDE TOWARD ILLNESS
------- --- -------- ------ -------

        THIS PATIENT HAS LITTLE RECOGNITION THAT SHE IS ILL. SHE HAS
LITTLE MOTIVATION FOR WORKING ON HER PROBLEMS. SHE HAS LITTLE AWARENESS
OF HER OWN CONTRIBUTION TO HER DIFFICULTIES. SHE TENDS TO BLAME OTHERS
FOR HER DIFFICULTIES.

OVERALL SEVERITY OF ILLNESS
------- -------- -- -------

        THE OVERALL SEVERITY OF THIS PATIENT'S ILLNESS IS JUDGED TO BE
SEVERE. DURING THE PERIOD UNDER STUDY, HER CONDITION HAS BEEN
VARIABLE.

* SIGNATURE: ------------------------- TITLE: -----------------

DATE: ----------

* THE SIGNATURE ON THIS REPORT MEANS THAT THIS MATERIAL HAS BEEN READ
AND APPROVED. CORRECTIONS OR DELETIONS MUST BE MADE IN INK OR BALL
POINT PEN.

Form MS 8 (7/69)

PERIODIC EVALUATION RECORD (PER) *

Patient's last name: **STEWART** First name: **NANCY** M.I.

Facility: **R.S.H** Ward: **215**

Read instructions on reverse side.

IDENTIFICATION

Case or consecutive no.

:0:	:1:	:2:	:3:	:4:	:5:	:6:	:7:	:8:	:9:

(Boxed values reading down: 1, 2, 3, 4, 5, 6, 0, 1, 6, 0, 0, 4)

Facility code

Rater code

Last day of week being evaluated

Month: Jan Feb Mar Apr May Jun Jul Aug Sep Oct Nov Dec

Year: 69 70 71 72 73 74 75

Day: 1–31

Sex: male / female

SOMATIC FUNCTIONING AND CONCERN

Physical health — very good / good / poor / very poor

Appetite — normal / mild / mod / marked / excessive / sleeps excessively / eat requires urging help

Insomnia — none / slight / mild / mod / marked

Severe sensory impairment (organic) — visual / hearing

Other symptoms — physiological / psycho-physiological / incontinence / seizures

Unwarranted concern with physical health — none / slight / mild / mod / marked

HALLUCINATIONS — none / slight / mild / mod / marked / auditory / visual

ORIENTATION DISTURBANCE

Time — unknown / none / slight / mild / mod / marked

Place — unknown / none / slight / mild / mod / marked

Person — unknown / none / slight / mild / mod / marked

MEMORY DISTURBANCE

Recent — unknown / none / slight / mild / mod / marked

Remote — unknown / none / slight / mild / mod / marked

JUDGMENT ABOUT FUTURE PLANS

no plans (or) — very good / good / only fair / poor / very poor

POTENTIAL FOR

Suicide — unsure / not significant / low / mod / high / very high

Physical violence — unsure / not significant / low / mod / high / very high

MANAGEMENT

Staff attention required — almost none / very little / fair amount / considerable / unauthorized leave / because of behavior / phys viol / suicide / violence

Special observations

TRANSACTION — initial evaluation / reevaluation / partial reevaluation / correction / deletion

APPEARANCE
under-weight — average — over-weight
Unkempt — (neat) none — slight — mild — mod — marked
Weight — gaining — losing
Ambulation disturbance — walks with assistance — must use wheel chair — bed-ridden

PSYCHOMOTOR ACTIVITY
very retarded — retarded — aver-age — accel-erated — very accel

GENERAL ATTITUDE, BEHAVIOR
Uncooperative — none — slight — mild — mod — marked
Withdrawn
Inappropriate
Impaired functioning in goal directed activities
Suspicious
Anger (overt) — none — slight — mild — mod — marked — physically destructive — assaul-tive

MOOD AND AFFECT
Depression — none — slight — mild — mod — marked — inappro-priate — euphoric
Anxiety — flat — labile
Quality — mark reduc — reduc-ed — aver-age — incr-eased — marked increase

QUALITY OF SPEECH, THOUGHT
Productivity — none — slight — mild — mod — mark — evasive — blocking
Incoherence — loosening of associations
Irrelevance — none — slight — mild — mod — marked

CONTENT OF SPEECH AND THOUGHT
obsessions — compulsions — inade-quacy — pho-bia — suicidal ideation
distrustfulness — bizarre thoughts — ideas of reference
Delusions — none — slight — mild — mod — marked — grandi-osity — perse-cutory — somatic

---

Permitted to leave (by himself) — neither ward or facility / ward / facility
Permitted to leave (with escort) — neither ward or facility / ward / facility

ACTIVITIES
Social conversation — pract never — rarely — occa-sional — often — very often
Family contact — no family available (or) — pract never — rarely — occa-sional — often — very often
Has visitors at facility — pract never — rarely — occa-sional — often — very often
Sees people outside facility — pract never — rarely — occa-sional — often — very often
Works (hours/week) — 1-5 — 6-10 — 11-20 — 21-30 — 31+ — for pay — no pay
Interest in voluntary leisure time activities — none — little — only fair — aver-age — consider-able
organized recreation — writes letters — reads
games with other people — religious activities — watches TV
organized patient groups — hobbies

OVERALL SEVERITY OF ILLNESS

CHANGE IN CONDITION — marked impr — im-proved — not ill — slight — mild — mod — mark — stable — vari-able — worse — during past week/month — elsewhere — below

RATER HAS WRITTEN COMMENTS

Signature — *L. Lowe* — Date — 3/6/7-

COMMENTS

*Developed by Robert L. Spitzer, M.D., and Jean Endicott, Ph.D. Biometrics Research, N.Y.S. Department of Mental Hygiene, with the assistance of the Multi-State Information System for Psychiatric Patients Project. Supported by N.Y.S. Department of Mental Hygiene, C39920 and NIMH Grant 14934.

M6H1053

Figure 22   Periodic Evaluation Record.

121

PERIODIC EVALUATION REPORT

THE FOLLOWING COMPUTER GENERATED REPORT IS BASED
ON INFORMATION NOTED ON A PERIODIC EVALUATION
RECORD (PER). THE NUMBER IN PARENTHESES FOLLOW-
ING CERTAIN TERMS INDICATES THE LEVEL OF SEVER-
ITY NOTED BY THE RATER: (2) SLIGHT, (3) MILD,
(4) MODERATE, (5) MARKED.   WHEN THE RATER CHECKS
A "NONE" CATEGORY, IT IS NOTED IN WORDS RATHER
THAN NUMBERS.

IDENTIFICATION

PATIENT CASE NUMBER 123456
EVALUATION PERIOD ENDING MARCH 6, 1972
FACILITY CODE 16
FEMALE   RATER CODE 4

TRANSACTION

INITIAL EVALUATION FOR THIS ADMISSION.

APPEARANCE

THE PATIENT IS NEAT. SHE IS OF AVERAGE WEIGHT.

PSYCHOMOTOR ACTIVITY

THE RATER DID NOT NOTE THE LEVEL OF PSYCHOMOTOR ACTIVITY.

GENERAL ATTITUDE AND BEHAVIOR

THE PATIENT IS WITHDRAWN (2). SHE IS NOT UNCOOPERATIVE. HER BEHAVIOR
IS NOT INAPPROPRIATE. SHE SHOWS NO IMPAIRMENT IN HER ABILITY TO
FUNCTION IN GOAL DIRECTED ACTIVITIES. SHE IS SUSPICIOUS (2). SHE SHOWS
OVERT ANGER (2).

MOOD AND AFFECT

HER MOOD IS ONE OF DEPRESSION (2). THERE ARE NO SIGNS OF ANXIETY.
AFFECT IS FLAT.

QUALITY OF SPEECH AND THOUGHT

PRODUCTIVITY OF SPEECH IS AVERAGE. SHE IS INCOHERENT (2). IN ADDITION.
THERE IS LOOSENING OF ASSOCIATIONS. SHE IS NOT IRRELEVANT.

Figure 23   Periodic Evaluation Report.

CONTENT OF SPEECH AND THOUGHT

THE CONTENT OF HER SPEECH INDICATES SUICIDAL THOUGHTS. DELUSIONS ARE
PRESENT (2), NAMELY, PERSECUTORY DELUSIONS.

SOMATIC FUNCTIONING AND CONCERN

SHE IS IN GOOD PHYSICAL HEALTH. HER APPETITE IS NORMAL. THERE IS NO
REPORT OF INSOMNIA. SHE DOES NOT EXHIBIT ANY UNWARRANTED CONCERN WITH
HER PHYSICAL HEALTH.

PERCEPTION AND SENSORIUM

THERE IS NO EVIDENCE OF HALLUCINATIONS. THERE IS NO DISTURBANCE AS TO
TIME, PLACE, OR PERSON. RECENT AND REMOTE MEMORY ARE INTACT.

JUDGMENT

SHE HAS ONLY FAIR JUDGMENT REGARDING FUTURE PLANS.

POTENTIAL FOR SUICIDE OR VIOLENCE

THE PATIENT IS JUDGED TO HAVE NO SIGNIFICANT POTENTIAL FOR SUICIDE OR
PHYSICAL VIOLENCE.

MANAGEMENT

VERY LITTLE STAFF ATTENTION IS REQUIRED FOR THE MANAGEMENT OF THIS
PATIENT. SHE IS PERMITTED TO LEAVE THE WARD AND THE FACILITY BY
HERSELF.

ACTIVITIES

THE PATIENT OFTEN ENGAGES IN SOCIAL CONVERSATION. THE PATIENT OFTEN
HAS CONTACT WITH HER FAMILY. SHE OFTEN HAS VISITORS AT THE FACILITY.
SHE OCCASIONALLY SEES PEOPLE OUTSIDE OF THE FACILITY. SHE WORKS FOR PAY.
THE RATER NOTED THE NUMBER OF HOURS PER WEEK BY CHECKING A CATEGORY
WHICH HAS THE RANGE OF 6-10 HOURS PER WEEK. SHE HAS LITTLE INTEREST IN
VOLUNTARY LEISURE TIME ACTIVITIES. SHE WRITES LETTERS, READS, WATCHES
TV, AND PARTICIPATES IN ORGANIZED PATIENT GROUPS.

OVERALL SEVERITY AND CHANGE IN CONDITION

THE RATER NOTED HER OVERALL SEVERITY OF ILLNESS AS MODERATE. HER
CONDITION HAS IMPROVED DURING THE PAST MONTH.

SIGNATURE: DATE:

Form MS 03 (9/69)
PERIODIC EVALUATION RECORD – Community Version (PER-C)*

Read instructions on reverse side.

Patient's last name: STEWART
First name: NANCY
M.I.
Facility: RSH
Ward: 100

IDENTIFICATION

Case or consecutive no.

Facility Code

Rater code

Last day of week being evaluated

	Jan	Feb	Mar	Apr	May	Jun	Jul	Aug	Sep	Oct	Nov	Dec
Month	1											
Year	69	70	71	72	73	74	75					
Day		3	4	5	6		7	8	9	10	11	
	12	13	14	15	16	17	18	19	20	21		

CONTENT OF SPEECH AND THOUGHT

- grandiosity — inadequacy — phobia
- obsessions — compulsions — suicidal ideation
- distrustfulness — bizarre thoughts — ideas of reference
- Delusions: none / slight / mild / mod / marked / perse-cutory / so-matic

SOMATIC FUNCTIONING AND CONCERN

- Physical health: very good / good / only fair / poor / very poor
- Appetite: poor / normal / exces-sive / very exces / to eat requires urging / help
- Insomnia: none / slight / mild / mod / marked / sleeps excessively
- Severe sensory impairment (organic): visual / hearing
- Other symptoms (psycho-physiological): incon-tinence / sei-zures
- Unwarranted concern with physical health: none / slight / mild / mod / mark
- HALLUCI-NATIONS: none / slight / mild / mod / marked / audi-tory / visual
- ORIENTATION DISTURBANCE: ? / none / slight / mild / mod / mark
- MEMORY DISTURBANCE: ? / none / slight / mild / mod / mark
- JUDGMENT ABOUT FUTURE PLANS: no plans (or) / very good / good / only fair / poor / very poor
- POTENTIAL FOR Suicide: unsure / not sig-nificant / low / mod / high / very high
- Physical violence: unsure / not sig-nificant / low / mod / high / very high

*Developed by Robert L. Spitzer, M.D. and Jean Endicott, Ph.D., Biometrics Research, N.Y.S. Department of Mental Hygiene, with the assistance of the Multi-State Information System for Psychiatric Patients Project. Supported by N.Y.S. Department of Mental Hygiene, C29820 and NIMH Grants 14934 and 08534.

Left panel (columns 22 23 24 25 26 27 28 29 30 31):

Sex: male | female

TRANSACTION: initial evaluation | reeval-uation | partial reeval | correc-tion | dele-tion

APPEARANCE: Unkempt — (neat) none | slight | mild | mod | marked

Weight: under-weight | average | over-weight | gaining | losing

PSYCHOMOTOR ACTIVITY: very retarded | retard-ed | aver-age | accel-erated | very accel

GENERAL ATTITUDE, BEHAVIOR: cheerful | pleas-ant | like-able

Uncooperative: none | slight | mild | mod | marked

Withdrawn

Inappropriate

Impaired functioning in goal directed activities

Suspicious

Antisocial: suspected

Alcohol abuse: suspected

Drug abuse: suspected | physically destructive | assaul-tive

Anger (overt): none | slight | mild | mod | marked | inappro-priate | euphoric

MOOD AND AFFECT

Depression: none | slight | mild | mod | marked | flat | labile

Anxiety: mark reduc-ed | reduc-ed | aver-age | incr-eased | marked increase

QUALITY OF SPEECH, THOUGHT

Productivity: none | slight | mild | mod | mark | evasive | blocking

Incoherence: loosening of associations

Irrelevance

IBM M62005

Right panel:

ACTIVITIES

Works (hours/week): 1-5 | 6-10 | 11-20 | 21-30 | 31+ | goes to school | keeps house for pay | no pay

Work performance (if working): very good | good | only fair | poor | very poor — Amount of time working limited by

Doesn't work at all because of (or): physical illness | psychopathology | going to school | looking for work | household responsibilities | his retirement

Involvement in voluntary leisure time activities: consid erable | mod erate | only fair | little | none

Good friends: many | several | a few | only one | none | prefers being alone

Heterosexual adjustment: very good | good | only fair | poor | very poor | homosexual behavior

frigidity | potency disturbance

Marital adjustment (if married): very good | good | only fair | poor | very poor

Pleasure out of life: a great deal | consid erable | mod erate | little | none

ADEQUACY OF HOUSING: ? | very good | good | only fair | poor | very poor

FINANCIAL PROBLEMS: ? | none | slight | mild | mod | mark

OVERALL SEVERITY: not ill | slight | mild | mod | mark | severe | among most extreme

CHANGE IN CONDITION: marked im-proved | marked impr-oved | stable | vari-able | worse | during past week month

RATER HAS WRITTEN COMMENTS ELSEWHERE

Signature: *P. Fitch, M.D.*   Date: 4/25/72

Figure 24   Periodic Evaluation Record—Community Version.

PERIODIC EVALUATION RECORD
COMMUNITY VERSION

THE FOLLOWING COMPUTER GENERATED REPORT IS BASED
ON INFORMATION NOTED ON A PERIODIC EVALUATION
RECORD - COMMUNITY VERSION (PER-C). (STATEMENTS
NOTING MISSING INFORMATION THAT THE RATER WAS
EXPECTED TO PROVIDE, OR INCONSISTENCIES BETWEEN
RATINGS, ARE ENCLOSED IN PARENTHESES).

IDENTIFICATION:
    PATIENT'S CASE NUMBER 123456
    FACILITY CODE 16
    RATER CODE 7
    LAST DAY OF WEEK BEING EVALUATED MAY 25, 1972
    SEX FEMALE

TRANSACTION:
    INITIAL EVALUATION.

APPEARANCE:
    NEAT. AVERAGE WEIGHT.

PSYCHOMOTOR ACTIVITY:
    AVERAGE.

GENERAL ATTITUDE AND BEHAVIOR:
    SLIGHTLY UNCOOPERATIVE.
    SLIGHTLY IMPAIRED FUNCTIONING IN GOAL DIRECTED ACTIVITIES.
    SLIGHTLY SUSPICIOUS.

    NOT WITHDRAWN OR INAPPROPRIATE. NO OVERT ANGER. NOT
    ANTISOCIAL. NO ALCOHOL OR DRUG ABUSE.

MOOD AND AFFECT:
    SLIGHT DEPRESSION.

    NO ANXIETY.

QUALITY OF SPEECH AND THOUGHT:
    AVERAGE PRODUCTIVITY. NO INCOHERENCE OR IRRELEVANCE.

CONTENT OF SPEECH AND THOUGHT:
    NO DELUSIONS.

Figure 25   Periodic Evaluation Report.

SOMATIC FUNCTIONING AND CONCERN:
    GOOD PHYSICAL HEALTH. NORMAL APPETITE. NO INSOMNIA. NO
    UNWARRANTED CONCERN WITH PHYSICAL HEALTH.

HALLUCINATIONS: NONE.

ORIENTATION DISTURBANCE: NONE.

MEMORY DISTURBANCE: NONE.

JUDGMENT ABOUT FUTURE PLANS:
    POOR JUDGMENT ABOUT FUTURE PLANS.

POTENTIAL FOR SUICIDE, PHYSICAL VIOLENCE:
    LOW POTENTIAL FOR SUICIDE.

    POTENTIAL FOR PHYSICAL VIOLENCE NOT SIGNIFICANT.

ACTIVITIES:
    ONLY FAIR INVOLVEMENT IN VOLUNTARY LEISURE TIME ACTIVITIES.
    HAS ONLY ONE GOOD FRIEND.
    SEXUALLY PROMISCUOUS
    LITTLE PLEASURE OUT OF LIFE.

    WORKS 31+ HOURS PER WEEK FOR PAY. GOOD WORK PERFORMANCE.

ADEQUACY OF HOUSING:
    GOOD HOUSING.

FINANCIAL PROBLEMS: NONE.

OVERALL SEVERITY OF ILLNESS:
    MILDLY ILL.

CHANGE IN CONDITION:
    IMPROVED.

SIGNATURE: DATE:

Form MS 02 (7/70)

PROBLEM APPRAISAL SCALES (PAS)*

Patient's last name	First name	M.I.	Facility	Unit
STEWART	NANCY		R.S.H.	100

INSTRUCTIONS: Rate the patient's condition during the last two weeks. When no information is available on a dimension or when a dimension is not applicable (e.g. Social Relations With Children), the scale should be left blank. 1=none, 2=slight, 3=mild, 4=moderate, 5=marked

Case or consecutive number

Facility code

Last day of two weeks being evaluated

Month: Jan Feb Mar Apr May Jun Jul Aug Sep Oct Nov Dec

Year: 69 70 71 72 73 74 75

Day

TRANSACTION — initial evaluation, reevaluation, partial reeval, correction, deletion

SOCIAL PERFORMANCE

12 School
Impairment in performance as a student. Consider grades, work habits, missed classes. If not going to school because of psychopathology, rate 5.

13 Job
Impairment in performance of job. Include missing work, need for supervision. If not working because of psychopathology, rate 5. If retired leave blank.

14 Housekeeping
Impairment in the performance of duties associated with caring for home and family. Consider shopping, cleaning, cooking.

PHYSICAL FUNCTION

01 Sleep problems
Too much or too little.

02 Eating problems
Too much or too little.

03 Enuresis, soiling

04 Seizures, convulsions

05 Speech articulation problem

06 Other physical problems

07 INTELLECTUAL DEVELOP.
Estimate if IQ score unavailable.

| 120+ | 110-119 | 86-109 | 68-85 | below 68 |

22 Dependency, clinging
Feelings of being unable to cope without assistance, praise, or reassurance from others; clings to other people in order to get them to take care of him.

23 Grandiosity
Inflated appraisal of his worth, contacts, power or knowledge.

24 Suspicion, persecution
From mild suspiciousness to belief that he is being persecuted. Examples: distrustfulness; feels mistreated or taken advantage of; feels people stare at him.

25 Delusions
Conviction(s) in some important personal belief which is almost cer-

31 Antisocial attitudes, acts
Lying; stealing; swindling; "conning" encouraging breaking of rules; minor or serious illegal acts.

32 Sexual problems
Impairment in performance or satisfaction in sexual activities, homosexual or other perverse impulses or behavior.

33 Agitation, hyperactivity
Overt tension, agitation or hyperactivity. Examples: fidgeting, inability to sit still; pacing, fast speech. Do not include mere subjective restlessness or tension.

128

super bright average dull retard

SOCIAL RELATIONS

08 With children
Impairment of expected parental role with his child(ren). Consider performance of expected tasks, comfort and satisfaction.

09 With mate, spouse
Impairment in satisfaction, comfort and performance of expected social and sexual activities with his mate or spouse (include common-law).

10 With other family
Impairment in satisfaction, comfort and performance of expected social activities with other family members (sibs, parents, cousins, in-laws).

11 With other people
Impairment in satisfaction, comfort and performance of expected social activities with other people (not in family).

Primary problem (Number of scale. 01 to 38. Leave blank if unknown.)

Overall severity of condition or impairment
not slight mild moderate marked severe among most extreme

Duration of condition or impairment less than
Present or most recent episode showing continuous evidence of disturbance; if chronic, when a noticeable change in intensity or nature occurs.
1wk 2wk 1mo 3mo 6mo 1yr 2yr+

* Developed by Robert L. Spitzer, M.D. and Jean Endicott, Ph.D. Biometrics Research, N.Y.S. Department of Mental Hygiene, with the assistance of the Multi-State Information System for Psychiatric Patients Project Supported by N.Y.S. Department of Mental Hygiene, C29820 and NIMH Grant 14934

IBM M6222B

OTHER SIGNS AND SYMPTOMS

15 Suicidal thoughts
Suicidal thoughts or preoccupation.

16 Suicidal acts, gestures
Suicidal acts, attempts or gestures. Consider threat to life.

17 Anxiety, fears, phobias
Feelings of apprehension, worry, anxiety, nervousness, tension, fear and phobia(s).

18 Obsessions, compulsions
Unwanted recurrent thoughts, acts, or routines, the content or purpose of which he regards as senseless.

19 Depressed mood, inferiority
Feelings of sadness, depression, worthlessness, inadequacy, remorse, guilt, failure or loss.

20 Somatic concerns, hypochond.
Excessive concerns with bodily functions; preoccupation with one or more real or imagined physical complaints or disabilities.

21 Social withdrawal, isolation
Avoidance of contact or involvement with people; preference for being alone; feelings of isolation, rejection or discomfort with people.

personal belief which is almost certainly not true.

26 Hallucinations
Hears voices or sounds; sees, feels, smells, or tastes something with no external source.

27 Anger, belligerence, negativism
Overt anger, belligerence, or negativism. Examples: evasive, argumentative, sarcastic, acts or threats of violence.

28 Assaultive acts
Actual physical violence or assault against some person.

29 Alcohol abuse
Excessive use of alcohol, causing physical symptoms, alteration in mood or behavior, or interfering with routine or duties.

30 Narcotics, other drugs
Excessive self medication, unprescribed use of narcotics, barbiturates, stimulants, or consciousness expanding substances.

34 Disorientation, memory
Signs that he does not know where he is, the date or time of day, or who he is; impairment in memory of recent or past events.

35 Speech disorg., incoherence
Impairment in the form of speech which makes it difficult to follow or understand. Examples: speech aimless, too detailed, phrases or thoughts have little logical connection, makes no sense, rapid changes of topic so ideas are not completed.

36 Slowed up, lack of emotion
Slowing down or lack of speech or movements; lack of emotional expression or response in face, speech or gestures.

37 Daily routine, leisure time
Inability or refusal to do usual daily activities or to carry through tasks which he or others expect him to do; impairment in pleasure or ability in leisure time activities.

38 Inapprop. affect., appear., behav.
Inappropriate, odd, or strange affect, appearance or behavior.

Rater code   0   0   7

Signature   M. Brown, MD

Date   1/5/72

Figure 26   Problem Appraisal Scales.

```
                    PROBLEM APPRAISAL SCALES (PAS) REPORT


      THE FOLLOWING COMPUTER GENERATED REPORT IS BASED ON INFORMATION NOTED ON
   THE PROBLEM APPRAISAL SCALES (PAS).  THE RATINGS DESCRIBE THE PATIENT'S
   CONDITION DURING THE LAST TWO WEEKS.  WHEN NO INFORMATION WAS AVAILABLE ON A
   DIMENSION, OR WHEN A DIMENSION IS NOT APPLICABLE, THE SCALE WAS LEFT BLANK.
   1=NONE, 2=SLIGHT, 3=MILD, 4=MODERATE, AND 5=SEVERE.


                             IDENTIFICATION

   PATIENT'S NAME    NANCY STEWART
   PATIENT'S CASE OF CONSECUTIVE NUMBER      123456
   FACILITY CODE 111
   RATER CODE   333
   LAST DAY OF TWO WEEKS BEING EVALUATED   JANUARY 2, 1973
   INITIAL TRANSACTION

        SCALE                              IMPAIRMENT SCALE LEVEL
                          PHYSICAL FUNCTION
   01 SLEEP PROBLEMS . . . . . . . . . . . . . . NONE     1
   02 EATING PROBLEMS. . . . . . . . . . . . . . NO RATING
   03 ENURESIS, SOILING. . . . . . . . . . . . . SLIGHT      2
   04 SEIZURES, CONVULSIONS. . . . . . . . . . . SLIGHT      2
   05 SPEECH ARTICULATION PROBLEM. . . . . . . . SLIGHT      2
   06 OTHER PHYSICAL PROBLEMS. . . . . . . . . . SEVERE             5
   07 INTELLECTUAL DEVELOPMENT . . . . . . . . . BRIGHT          4

                          SOCIAL RELATIONS

   08 WITH CHILDREN. . . . . . . . . . . . . . . NONE     1
   09 WITH MATE, SPOUSE. . . . . . . . . . . . . NONE     1
   10 WITH OTHER FAMILY. . . . . . . . . . . . . SLIGHT      2
   11 WITH OTHER PEOPLE. . . . . . . . . . . . . MODERATE        4

                          SOCIAL PERFORMANCE

   12 SCHOOL . . . . . . . . . . . . . . . . . . MILD        3
   13 JOB. . . . . . . . . . . . . . . . . . . . NONE     1
   14 HOUSEKEEPING . . . . . . . . . . . . . . . MILD        3

                          OTHER SIGNS AND SYMPTOMS

   15 SUICIDAL THOUGHTS. . . . . . . . . . . . . SLIGHT      2
   16 SUICIDAL ACTS, GESTURES. . . . . . . . . . NO RATING
   17 ANXIETY, FEARS, PHOBIAS. . . . . . . . . . NONE     1
   18 OBSESSIONS, COMPULSIONS. . . . . . . . . . SEVERE             5
   19 DEPRESSED MOOD, INFERIORITY. . . . . . . . SLIGHT      2
   20 SOMATIC CONCERNS, HYPOCHONDRIACAL. . . . . MILD        3
   21 SOCIAL WITHDRAWAL, ISOLATION . . . . . . . SLIGHT      2
   22 DEPENDENCY, CLINGING . . . . . . . . . . . MILD        3
```

Figure 27   Problem Appraisal Scales Report.

report produced by the computer is a tabular display of all the information that the rater has noted (Figure 27).

Psychiatric Anamnestic Record (PAR) (Figure 28): This form enables a rater to record background information pertinent to a patient's psychiatric history. The recorded information is used by the computer to produce a narrative account (Figure 29).

```
PATIENT NAME:   NANCY STEWART                                          PAGE  2 OF 2
CASE NUMBER:    123456


    SCALE                                   IMPAIRMENT    SCALE LEVEL

23 GRANDIOSITY. . . . . . . . . . . . . . . NO RATING
24 SUSPICION, PERSECUTION . . . . . . . . . NO RATING
25 DELUSIONS. . . . . . . . . . . . . . . . MILD            3
26 HALLUCINATIONS . . . . . . . . . . . . . NO RATING
27 ANGER, BELLIGERENCE, NEGATIVISM. . . . . NO RATING
28 ASSAULTIVE ACTS. . . . . . . . . . . . . MILD            3
29 ALCOHOL ABUSE. . . . . . . . . . . . . . NO RATING
30 NARCOTICS, OTHER DRUGS . . . . . . . . . MILD            3
31 ANTISOCIAL ATTITUDES, ACTS . . . . . . . NO RATING
32 SEXUAL PROBLEMS. . . . . . . . . . . . . NO RATING
33 AGITATION, HYPERACTIVITY . . . . . . . . MILD            3
34 DISORIENTATION, MEMORY . . . . . . . . . NONE         1
35 SPEECH DISORGANIZATION, INCOHERENCE. . . SLIGHT       2
36 SLOWED UP, LACK OF EMOTION . . . . . . . NO RATING
37 DAILY ROUTINE, LEISURE TIME. . . . . . . MODERATE          4
38 INAPPROPRIATE AFFECT, APPEARANCE,. . . . NO RATING
      BEHAVIOR

    IN THE RATER'S JUDGEMENT, THE PRIMARY PROBLEM IS IN THE AREA OF OBSESSIONS.
THE RATER NOTED THE PATIENT'S OVERALL SEVERITY OF CONDITION OR IMPAIRMENT AS
MILDLY ILL AND THE DURATION OF THIS CONDITION OR IMPAIRMENT AS LESS THAN
SIX MONTHS.

SIGNATURE:                              DATE:
```

Figure 27   (Continued)

SCALED SCORES FROM THE MENTAL STATUS EXAMINATION RECORD

To enhance the usefulness of the data, MSIS has provided scaled scores derived from mental status data. Using data from 2000 Mental Status Examination Records, a principal component factor analysis was performed. Resulting from this analysis were 20 scores from each Mental Status Examination Record submitted. These scores are plotted on an individual profile report called MSER GRAPH (Figure 30) which indicates the patient's relative standing in the norm group of 2000 cases. For example, a factor score at the 70th percentile means that the patient's score on the factor was greater than the scores of 70% of the patients in the norm group. In addition, a graph depicts "clinical equivalent scores" along an axis with scales more nearly matching those of the clinician's assessment of severity. The scale used has six points (none, minimal, mild, moderate, severe, extreme) for most of the factors.

The display format of the MSER GRAPH report enables the clinician to identify rapidly the most severely affected domain of the patient's behavior in relation to the norm population.

Form MS 04
PSYCHIATRIC ANAMNESTIC RECORD (PAR)*

Read instructions on reverse side.

Patient's last name	First name	M.I.	Facility	Ward
STEWART	NANCY		RSH	OPC /110

IDENTIFICATION

Case or consecutive number

Facility code

Rater code

Date of admission to facility

Month: Jan Feb Mar Apr May Jun Jul Aug Sep Oct

RELIABILITY AND COMPLETENESS OF INFORMATION

? · very good · good · only fair · poor · very poor

CHARACTERISTICS OF CURRENT CONDITION

exacerbation of chronic condition

recurrence of similar previous condition

significant change from any previous condition

indistinguishable from past

Onset of current condition: sudden · gradual · very gradual

Duration of current condition
Unit: days · weeks · months · years

Precipitating stress

? · none · slight · mild · mod · mark

drug reaction — traumatic incident — someone's death

financial — physical illness in family — physical illness in patient

sexual problems — family problems — nonfamily inter-personal problems

school problems — occupational problems — other change in life circumstances

→ Course since onset of current condition
worsened greatly · worsened somewhat · remained stable · variable · improved somewhat · improved greatly

PSYCHIATRIC DISTURBANCE IN FAMILY

functional psych illness · organic brain syndrome

Psychiatric Admission Form

Mother [?] [none] — mild severe / mild severe — ? 1 2 3 4+

Father [?] [none] — mild severe / mild severe — ? 1 2 3 4+ → next section (none)

Siblings at least mildly ill

PREVIOUS TREATMENT FOR PSYCHIATRIC DISTURBANCE

Age when first treated (any treatment)
:0: :1: :2: :3: :4: :5: :6: :7: :8: :9:

Treated at (all occasions) educat special / special partial
residential treatment — rehabilitation facility — educat classes — outpatient partial Rx hosp
:0: :1: :2: :3: :4: :5: :6: :7: :8: :9:

psychiatric hospitalization (not including this one)
:0: :1: :2: :3: :4: :5: :6: :7: :8: 8+

→ number   1 2 3 4 5 6 7 8+

Age at first hospitalization (not including this one)
:0: :1: :2: :3: :4: :5: :6: :7: :8: :9:

:0: :1: :2: :3: :4: :5: :6: :7: :8: :9:

Total time of psychiatric hospitalizations (not including this one)
Unit   days   weeks   months   years
:0: :1: :2: :3: :4: :5: :6: :7: :8: :9:
:0: :1: :2: :3: :4: :5: :6: :7: :8: :9:

Set no. 0058260   Mark last 3 digits of Set number in area below

2 6 0

:0: :1: :2: :3: :4: :5: :6: :7: :8: :9:
:0: :1: :2: :3: :4: :5: :6: :7: :8: :9:
:0: :1: :2: :3: :4: :5: :6: :7: :8: :9:

	69	70	71	72	73	74	75	Nov	Dec
I				Year				Nov	Dec
2	3	4	5	6	7	8	9	10	11
12	13	14	15	16	Day 17	18	19	20	21
22	23	24	25	26	27	28	29	30	31

Status on admission: inpatient day night OPD other

TRANSACTION
first admission / re-admission / correction / deletion

DESCRIPTION

Sex   male   female

Ethnic group   ?   White   Negro   Puerto Rican   Oriental   Amer Indian   Other
:0: :1: :2: :3: :4: :5: :6: :7: :8: :9:

Age
:0: :1: :2: :3: :4: :5: :6: :7: :8: :9:
:0: :1: :2: :3: :4: :5: :6: :7: :8: :9:

Marital status
married   divorced   widowed   separated   annulled   never married

Siblings (living or dead)   is a twin   other multiple births
0 1 2 3 4 5 6 7 8 9+

ATTITUDE TOWARDS ADMISSION
?   positive   neutral   ambivalent   negative   very negative

INFORMANTS
physician   nonmedical therapist   school
patient   family member   friend
associate   other facility or agency   police

*Developed by Robert L. Spitzer, M.D. and Jean Endicott, Ph.D., Biometrics Research, N.Y.S. Department of Mental Hygiene, with the assistance of the Multi-State Information System for Psychiatric Patients Project. Supported by N.Y.S. Department of Mental Hygiene, C29820 and NIMH Grants 14934 and 08534.

IBM M61997

133

PREVIOUS TREATMENT (continued)

Treatments received (as outpatient or inpatient)

drugs	counseling	indiv supportive psychotherapy
indiv dynamic psychotherapy	group psychotherapy	behavior therapy
ECT	brain surgery	insulin coma
family psychotherapy	vocational rehabilitation	hypnosis

Most likely diagnosis of condition(s) treated previously   ?

mental retardation	organic brain syndrome	schizophrenia
psychotic affective disorder	neurosis	antisocial personality
other personality disorder	sexual deviation	alcoholism
	psychophysiologic disorder	transient sit disorder
drug dependence		
behavior disorder of childhood & adolescence	condition without manifest psychiatric disorder	non-specific condition

CHILDHOOD (prior to age 12)

Problems	?	no apparent problems
withdrawn	hallucinations	bizarre behavior
enuresis	school phobia	excessive fears
temper tantrums	stuttering	extreme shyness
excessive agression	destructiveness	fire setting
stealing	sadism	chronic lying
no friends	school truancy	hyperactivity

OCCUPATIONAL HISTORY

Highest occupational level ever attained

	never worked	higher executive	major professional
business manager	proprietor medium business	proprietor large business	owner small business
administrative personnel	large farm owner	lesser professional	clerical worker
sales worker	technician	semi-professional	farm owner
small farm owner	skilled manual employee	owner little business	unskilled employee
		semiskilled employee	

During last 5 years was employed (for pay)

?	virtually all time	almost all time	most of time	about half less than half	only briefly	not at all
at (predominantly)			full time job	half time job		less than half time

Amount of time employed during last 5 years limited by

physical illness	psycho-pathology
household responsibilities	type of work
	retire-ment
	going to school
	job market

Work performance last 5 years (if worked at all)

?	superior	very good	good	aver-age	only fair	poor	very poor

Change in occupational status or responsibility last 5 years (if worked)

?	marked elevation	some elevation	no change	some decline	marked decline

ADOLESCENT HETEROSEXUAL ADJUSTMENT

	?	excel-lent	very good	good	average	fair	poor	very poor
Overall								

Sexual activity	none	little	Sexual curiosity	little	none
Dated	rarely	occa-sionally	often	average	excessive
Promiscuous		occa-sionally	often		

134

Raised by (all that apply)
both natural parents | one natural parent | other relatives
foster parents | adoptive parents | institution
?

Adequacy of environment for personality development
? | very good | good | fair | poor | very poor

ADOLESCENT FRIENDSHIP PATTERN (12-18)
Relationship with friends: ? | no friends or | very good | good | only fair | poor | very poor
Good friends: many | several | a few | only one | none | preferred being alone
avoided groups | enjoyed group activities | was a leader

ADULT FRIENDSHIP PATTERN (last 5 years) [not adult → skip section]
Relationship with friends: ? | no friends or | very good | good | only fair | poor | very poor
Good friends: many | several | a few | only one | none | preferred being alone
avoided groups | enjoyed group activities | was a leader

EDUCATION AND INTELLECTUAL CAPACITY
Education (level completed)
completed grade: ? | none | 1-5 | 6 | 7 | 8 | 9 | 10 | 11 | 12 high school
college or business school: less 1yr | 2yr | 3yr | 4yr | some graduate school | graduate school | degree

Overall academic performance (junior high and beyond)
? | superior | very good | average | only fair | very poor | variable | consistent

Estimate of intellectual capacity
? | superior | bright | average | borderline | retarded

IBM H99414

HIGHEST LEVEL ADULT HETEROSEXUAL ADJUSTMENT OVER A SUSTAINED PERIOD [not adult → skip sect]
? | excellent | very good | good | fair | poor | very poor
Overall
Sexual activity: none | little | average | excessive
Impotent: often | usually | occasionally | Premature ejaculation | usually
Promiscuous: occasionally often | Frigid | usually often

SEXUAL DEVIATIONS
relation to partners
Homosexual activity
Adolescent: ? | none | rare | occasional | frequent | very freq | casual friends | usual friends
Adult: ? | none | rare | occasional | frequent | very freq | casual friends | usual friends
Other deviations as adult: exhibitionism | voyeurism | transvestism

MARRIAGE [never married → skip section]
If married more than once, number: 1 | 2 | 3 | 4 | 5+
reason(s): divorced | annulled
death | bigamy

Set no. Mark last 3 digits of Set number from page 1.
0 1 2 3 4 5 6 7 8 9
0 1 2 3 4 5 6 7 8 9
0 1 2 3 4 5 6 7 8 9

Figure 28 (Continued)

135

PAR

MARRIAGE (continued)

Age when first married: ? 0 1 2 3 4 5 6 7 8 9

Marital adjustment (if currently married): 0 1 2 3 4 — very good / good / only fair / poor / very poor

NUMBER OF OWN CHILDREN

Alive: 0 1 2 3 4 5 6 7+

Dead: 0 1 2 3 4 5 6 7+

PHYSICAL HEALTH

Up to age 12: ? — very good / good / only fair / poor / very poor

After age 12: ? — very good / good / only fair / poor / very poor

Permanent brain damage: suspected / likely / definite

beginning at: prenatal period / birth / prior to age 12 / childhood / adolescence / adulthood / age 12 to last month / last month

Seizures occurred

SIGNS AND SYMPTOMS SINCE AGE 12

	age 12 to last month				last month	reason for admission
	slight	mild	mod	mark	LM	RA
Impaired relations with: parents						
associates						
boyfriend(s)						
girlfriend(s)						
spouse						

SIGNS AND SYMPTOMS SINCE AGE 12 (continued)

	age 12 to last month				last month	reason for admission
	slight	mild	mod	mark	LM	RA
Depressed mood						
Anxiety						
Poor appetite						
Insomnia						
Phobia(s)						
Obsession(s)						
Compulsion(s)						
Guilt						
Broods excessively						
Excessive anger						
Antisocial behavior						
Autistic thinking						
Grandiosity						
Assaultive						
Suspiciousness						
Unwarranted concern with physical health						
Psychophysiologic reactions						
Easily fatigued						

children	2	3	4	5	LM	RA
Impaired performance at: school	(covered previously)				LM	RA
job	(covered previously)				LM	RA
housekeeping	2	3	4	5	LM	RA
Delusions ?	absent	sus-pected	like-ly	defi-nite	LM	RA
persecutory	slight 2	mild 3	mod 4	mark 5	LM	RA
somatic	2	3	4	5	LM	RA
grandeur	2	3	4	5	LM	RA
guilt	2	3	4	5	LM	RA
religious	2	3	4	5	LM	RA
influence	2	3	4	5	LM	RA
nihilistic	2	3	4	5	LM	RA
Hallucinations ?	absent	sus-pected	like-ly	defi-nite	LM	RA
auditory	slight 2	mild 3	mod 4	mark 5	LM	RA
visual	2	3	4	5	LM	RA
olfactory	2	3	4	5	LM	RA
gustatory	2	3	4	5	LM	RA
tactile	2	3	4	5	LM	RA
visceral	2	3	4	5	LM	RA

Homosexual fears	2	3	4	5	LM	RA
Sexual deviations	(covered previously)				LM	RA
Impaired sexual functioning	2	3	4	5	LM	RA
Withdrawal	2	3	4	5	LM	RA
Disorientation	2	3	4	5	LM	RA
Inappropriate behavior	2	3	4	5	LM	RA
Apathy	2	3	4	5	LM	RA
Dissociative symptoms	2	3	4	5	LM	RA
Depersonalization	2	3	4	5	LM	RA
Conversion reactions	2	3	4	5	LM	RA
Impaired memory	2	3	4	5	LM	RA
Disorganized speech	2	3	4	5	LM	RA
Psychomotor retardation	2	3	4	5	LM	RA
Psychomotor excitement	2	3	4	5	LM	RA
Impaired functioning goal directed activities	2	3	4	5	LM	RA

Set no. Mark last 3 digits of Set number from page 1.

0	1	2	3	4		5	6	7	8	9
0	1	2	3	4		5	6	7	8	9
0	1	2	3	4		5	6	7	8	9

IBM M62001

Figure 28 (Continued)

SIGNS AND SYMPTOMS SINCE AGE 12 (continued)

	Age 12 to last month			last month	reason for admission
Excessive use of	slight / mild / mod / mark				
alcohol	2 3 4 5			M	A
narcotics	2 3 4 5			M	A
barbiturates	2 3 4 5			M	A
stimulants	2 3 4 5			M	A
hallucinogens	2 3 4 5			M	A
cannabis	2 3 4 5			M	A
other substances	2 3 4 5			M	A
Suicidal preoccupation	? 2 3 4 5			M	A
Suicidal gestures	? never / once / several / many			M	A
Suicidal attempts	? never / once / several / many			M	A

PERSONALITY TRAITS (not limited to episodes of illness)

	slight	mild	mod	mark
Rigid	2	3	4	5
Inhibited	2	3	4	5
Unable to relax	2	3	4	5
Overly conscientious	2	3	4	5
Emotionally distant	2	3	4	5
Emotionally unstable	2	3	4	5

PERSONALITY TRAITS (continued)

	very irresponsible	somewhat irresponsible	generally responsible	responsible	very responsible
Responsible					
Concern for others	pract none	little	only fair	aver- age	consid- erable
Ability to cope with stress	very poor	poor	only fair	aver- age	very consid- erable
Judgment	very poor	poor	only fair	good	very good
Ambitious	pract none	little	mod- erate	good	a great deal
Perseverance	pract none	little	mod- erate	good	a great deal

ARRESTS

never

	?	1	2	3	4	5	6	7+
Number								
For disorderly conduct			assault				fraud	theft
			sexual offense				reckless driving	
murder			drug possession				illegal gambling	
Convictions		1	2	3	4	5	6	7+
Punishments			suspended sentence				prison	fine

PREVIOUS EPISODES

no episodes

Number (all kinds) of previous episodes (best guess)

?	1	2	3	4	5	6	7	8	9+

Number of previous episodes lasting more than one week where depression or elation of at least moderate intensity was predominant.

?	1	2	3	4	5	6	7	8	9+

OVERALL SEVERITY OF ILLNESS

Episodes   all elated   all depressed   depressed and elated

Prior to age 12
? not ill   slight mild mod   mark severe   among most extre | was overtly psychotic

Age 12 to last month
? not ill   slight mild mod   mark severe   among most extre | was overtly psychotic

Last month
? not ill   slight mild mod   mark severe   among most extre | was overtly psychotic

Age when first demonstrated significant impairment because of psychopathology   ? never

==== RATER HAS WRITTEN COMMENTS ELSEWHERE

Signature _____   Date

Set no.   Mark last 3 digits of Set number from page 1.

Excitable
Histrionic
Cyclothymic (mood swings)
Impulsive
Stubborn-
Passive-aggressive
Self-defeating
Dependent
Aimless
Hostile (overt)
Suspicious
Domineering
Eccentric
Hypersensitive (to others)
Tending to blame others

Traits which may be positive or negative

Pleasure out of life   ?   pract none   little   only fair   mod-erate   consid-erable
Involvement in voluntary leisure time activities   pract none   little   only fair   mod-erate   consid-erable
Sense of humor   very poor   poor   only fair   good   very good

Figure 28 (Continued)

139

```
                  PSYCHIATRIC ANAMNESTIC RECORD


        THE FOLLOWING COMPUTER GENERATED REPORT IS BASED
        ON INFORMATION NOTED ON A PSYCHIATRIC ANAMNESTIC
        RECORD (PAR).  THE NUMBER IN PARENTHESES FOLLOW-
        ING CERTAIN TERMS INDICATES THE LEVEL OF SEVERITY
        AS NOTED BY THE RATER:   (2) SLIGHT,   (3) MILD,
        (4) MODERATE,   (5) MARKED.   (STATEMENTS NOTING
        MISSING INFORMATION THAT THE RATER WAS EXPECTED
        TO PROVIDE, OR INCONSISTENCIES BETWEEN RATINGS,
        ARE ENCLOSED IN PARENTHESES.)


                      INDENTIFICATION

PATIENT CASE NUMBER: 123456
PATIENT'S NAME: STEWART,NANCY
FACILITY CODE: 16
RATER CODE: 7
RATER'S NAME: DR. JAMES JONES
DATE OF PATIENT'S ADMISSION TO FACILITY: JANUARY 3, 1972
PATIENT'S STATUS ON ADMISSION: OUTPATIENT


                       TRANSACTION

THIS IS THE FIRST ADMISSION FOR THE PATIENT TO THIS FACILITY.

                       DESCRIPTION

THE PATIENT IS A 24 YEAR OLD, SINGLE (NEVER MARRIED), WHITE FEMALE.  SHE
HAS TWO SIBLINGS.  HER ATTITUDE TOWARD THIS ADMISSION IS AMBIVALENT.
INFORMATION FOR THIS REPORT HAS BEEN OBTAINED FROM A PHYSICIAN, THE
PATIENT, AND A FAMILY MEMBER.  IN THE RATER'S JUDGMENT, THE RELIABILITY
OF THE INFORMATION IN THIS REPORT IS GOOD.


             CHARACTERISTICS OF CURRENT CONDITION

THE PATIENT'S CURRENT CONDITION REPRESENTS A SIGNIFICANT CHANGE FROM
ANY PREVIOUS CONDITION.  HER CURRENT CONDITION DEVELOPED GRADUALLY AND
HAS BEEN EVIDENT FOR 3 MONTHS.  THE ONSET OF HER CURRENT CONDITION WAS
APPARENTLY ASSOCIATED WITH A MILDLY STRESSFUL SITUATION INVOLVING A
DRUG REACTION AND FAMILY PROBLEMS.  HER CURRENT CONDITION HAS BEEN
VARIABLE SINCE ITS ONSET.


             PSYCHIATRIC DISTURBANCE IN FAMILY

THE PATIENT'S MOTHER HAS A HISTORY OF A MILD FUNCTIONAL PSYCHIATRIC
ILLNESS.  HER FATHER HAS A HISTORY OF A SEVERE FUNCTIONAL PSYCHIATRIC
ILLNESS.  THE PATIENT HAS 1 SIBLING WHO HAS BEEN AT LEAST MILDLY ILL.
```

Figure 29   Psychiatric Anamnestic Report.

PREVIOUS TREATMENT FOR PSYCHIATRIC DISTURBANCE

THE PATIENT WAS FIRST TREATED FOR A PSYCHIATRIC DISTURBANCE AT AGE 23.
SHE HAS HAD OUTPATIENT TREATMENT. SHE HAS BEEN TREATED WITH INDIVIDUAL
SUPPORTIVE PSYCHOTHERAPY. THE MOST LIKELY DIAGNOSIS OF THE CONDITION
FOR WHICH THE PATIENT WAS TREATED PREVIOUSLY IS SCHIZOPHRENIA.

CHILDHOOD

THE PATIENT'S PROBLEMS AS A CHILD (PRIOR TO AGE 12) INCLUDED
WITHDRAWAL, EXTREME SHYNESS, AND NO FRIENDS. SHE WAS RAISED BY BOTH HER
NATURAL PARENTS. HER CHILDHOOD ENVIRONMENT IS JUDGED TO HAVE BEEN POOR
FOR PERSONALITY DEVELOPMENT.

ADOLESCENT AND ADULT FRIENDSHIP PATTERNS

DURING ADOLESCENCE (AGE 12-18) THE PATIENT GENERALLY HAD ONLY FAIR
RELATIONSHIPS WITH FRIENDS. SHE HAD ONLY ONE GOOD FRIEND, PREFERRED
BEING ALONE AND AVOIDED GROUPS. AS AN ADULT (DURING THE PAST 5 YEARS),
THE PATIENT HAS GENERALLY HAD ONLY FAIR RELATIONSHIPS WITH FRIENDS. SHE
HAS HAD ONLY ONE GOOD FRIEND, HAS PREFERRED BEING ALONE AND HAS AVOIDED
GROUPS.

EDUCATION AND INTELLECTUAL CAPACITY

THE PATIENT HAS COMPLETED ONE YEAR OF COLLEGE OR BUSINESS SCHOOL. HER
OVERALL ACADEMIC PERFORMANCE (JUNIOR HIGH SCHOOL AND BEYOND) WAS
AVERAGE. HER INTELLECTUAL CAPACITY IS WITHIN THE BRIGHT RANGE.

OCCUPATIONAL HISTORY

AT HER HIGHEST OCCUPATIONAL LEVEL, THE PATIENT WORKED AS A SEMI-SKILLED
EMPLOYEE. DURING THE PAST 5 YEARS, SHE HAS BEEN EMPLOYED MOST OF THE
TIME AND HAS WORKED PREDOMINANTLY FULL-TIME. THE AMOUNT OF TIME SHE HAS
WORKED HAS BEEN LIMITED BY HER PSYCHOPATHOLOGY. THE PATIENT'S WORK
PERFORMANCE DURING THE PAST 5 YEARS HAS BEEN ONLY FAIR. THERE HAS BEEN
NO CHANGE IN HER OCCUPATIONAL STATUS OR RESPONSIBILITY DURING THIS
PERIOD.

ADOLESCENT HETEROSEXUAL ADJUSTMENT

THE PATIENT'S OVERALL HETEROSEXUAL ADJUSTMENT AS AN ADOLESCENT WAS
FAIR. SHE DATED RARELY. SHE HAD LITTLE SEXUAL CURIOSITY.

HIGHEST LEVEL ADULT HETEROSEXUAL
ADJUSTMENT OVER A SUSTAINED PERIOD

THE HIGHEST LEVEL OF THE PATIENT'S ADULT HETEROSEXUAL ADJUSTMENT (OVER
A SUSTAINED PERIOD) HAS BEEN FAIR. DURING THIS PERIOD, SHE WAS SEXUALLY
PROMISCUOUS.

```
                         SEXUAL DEVIATIONS

THE PATIENT HAS NOT ENGAGED IN HOMOSEXUAL ACTIVITY AS AN ADOLESCENT OR
AS AN ADULT.


                      MARRIAGE AND CHILDREN

THE PATIENT HAS NEVER BEEN MARRIED.  SHE HAS HAD NO CHILDREN.


                       PHYSICAL HEALTH

AS A CHILD (PRIOR TO AGE 12) THE PATIENT WAS IN ONLY FAIR HEALTH.
SINCE THEN HER HEALTH HAS BEEN GOOD.


                    REASON FOR ADMISSION

IMPAIRED RELATIONS WITH HER ASSOCIATES, IMPAIRED PERFORMANCE ON THE
JOB, PERSECUTORY DELUSIONS, AND EXCESSIVE USE OF HALLUCINOGENS ARE THE
MAJOR REASONS FOR THE PATIENT'S CURRENT ADMISSION.

             SIGNS AND SYMPTOMS DURING THE PAST MONTH

DURING THE PAST MONTH, THE PATIENT'S PERFORMANCE ON THE JOB HAS BEEN
IMPAIRED.  THERE HAS BEEN EVIDENCE OF PERSECUTORY DELUSIONS AND
DELUSIONS OF INFLUENCE.  THE PATIENT HAS BEEN DEPRESSED.  SHE HAS HAD A
POOR APPETITE. SHE HAS TENDED TO BROOD EXCESSIVELY. SHE HAS EXHIBITED
EXCESSIVE ANGER.  SHE HAS MANIFESTED AUTISTIC THINKING AND
SUSPICIOUSNESS.  DISORGANIZED SPEECH HAS BEEN EVIDENT.  HER FUNCTIONING
IN GOAL DIRECTED ACTIVITIES HAS BEEN IMPAIRED.  SHE HAS EXHIBITED
EXCESSIVE USE OF HALLUCINOGENS.  SHE HAS BEEN PREOCCUPIED WITH SUICIDAL
THOUGHTS DURING THE PAST MONTH.


             SIGNS AND SYMPTOMS-AGE 12 TO LAST MONTH

DURING THIS PERIOD, THE PATIENT'S RELATIONSHIPS WITH HER PARENTS (4) AND
ASSOCIATES (5) WERE IMPAIRED.  DELUSIONS WERE DEFINITELY PRESENT,
SPECIFICALLY, PERSECUTORY DELUSIONS (3).  HALLUCINATIONS WERE LIKELY,
SPECIFICALLY, AUDITORY (2) HALLUCINATIONS.  THE PATIENT WAS DEPRESSED
(3).  SHE HAD OBSESSIONS (3).  SHE TENDED TO BROOD EXCESSIVELY (4). SHE
EXHIBITED EXCESSIVE ANGER (4). SHE MANIFESTED AUTISTIC THINKING (5) AND
SUSPICIOUSNESS (4).   SHE WAS WITHDRAWN (4) AND APATHETIC (3).
DEPERSONALIZATION (4) WAS ALSO EVIDENT.  THE PATIENT'S FUNCTIONING IN GOAL
DIRECTED ACTIVITIES WAS IMPAIRED (4).  SHE EXHIBITED EXCESSIVE USE OF
HALLUCINOGENS (4).   DURING THIS PERIOD THE PATIENT WAS PREOCCUPIED WITH
SUICIDAL THOUGHTS (3), BUT SHE NEVER MADE ANY SUICIDAL GESTURES OR ATTEMPTS.
```

Figure 29   (Continued)

Automated Diagnosis Suggestion

Upon receipt of a Mental Status Examination Record, the computer automatically returns a suggested diagnosis for consideration by the clinician
(Figure 31). Two different methods are used to arrive at the diagnostic suggestions: one based on responses to the Mental Status Examination Record alone
and one based on responses to both the Mental Status Examination Record and
the Psychiatric Anamnestic Record.

```
        PERSONALITY TRAITS (NOT LIMITED TO EPISODES OF ILLNESS)

THE PATIENT IS CHARACTERISTICALLY INHIBITED (3), UNABLE TO RELAX (3),
AND EMOTIONALLY DISTANT (4). SHE IS STUBBORN (3). SHE TENDS TO BE
SELF-DEFEATING (3). SHE IS SUSPICIOUS (3). SHE TENDS TO BLAME OTHERS
FOR HER DIFFICULTIES (4). SHE GETS LITTLE PLEASURE OUT OF LIFE. SHE HAS
ALMOST NO INVOLVEMENT IN VOLUNTARY LEISURE TIME ACTIVITIES.
HER SENSE OF HUMOR IS POOR. SHE SHOWS POOR ABILITY TO COPE WITH STRESS.
SHE EXERCISES POOR JUDGMENT.  SHE HAS PRACTICALLY NO AMBITION AND
DEMONSTRATES LITTLE PERSEVERANCE.


                             ARRESTS

THE PATIENT HAS NEVER BEEN ARRESTED.


                        PREVIOUS EPISODES

THE PATIENT HAS HAD NO PREVIOUS EPISODES OF PSYCHOPATHOLOGY.


                   OVERALL SEVERITY OF ILLNESS

DURING CHILDHOOD AND ADOLESCENCE, SHE EXHIBITED NO MANIFEST PSYCHOPATHOLOGY.
SHE HAS BEEN SEVERELY ILL DURING THE PAST MONTH AND HAS BEEN OVERTLY
PSYCHOTIC AT SOME TIME DURING THIS PERIOD.  THE PATIENT FIRST DEMONSTRATED
SIGNIFICANT IMPAIRMENT BECAUSE OF PSYCHOPATHOLOGY AT AGE 23.



    SIGNATURE:                                   DATE:
```

Figure 29   (Continued)

A rational, branching logic method of arriving at a differential diagnosis is used to classify each individual patient into one or more suggested diagnostic categories as specified by the American Psychiatric Association. The logic of the analysis is based on abstractions of text book classification rules and on the clinical experience of the developers. When the diagnosis is made from a combination of the Mental Status Examination data and the Psychiatric Anamnestic Record data, 92 diagnoses, including one of "no mental illness," are possible. When the process is performed using Mental Status Examination data only, a more limited set of 42 categories is possible as the analysis is restricted because of limited case history information.

Diagnoses are made at two levels of confidence: diagnoses called "definite" appear in the report preceded by the statement, "The most likely diagnosis is . . . ," and diagnoses referred to as "possible" appear in the report preceded by the statement "However the following condition(s) should also be considered. . . ." If no diagnosis is considered by the computer as definite (including "no mental illness"), and if there is evidence suggesting any specific diagnosis, then this is noted on the report as "There is no condition for which

```
                             ** MSER GRAPH **

PATIENT NAME   STEWART,NANCY
PATIENT NO. 123456        2/6/72          FACILITY NO. 16          RATER NO. 7


      SUMMARY SCALES                   CLINICAL EQUIVALENTS        PER-
                                                                  CEN-
                                 NONE MIN  MILD MOD  SEV  EXTRM  TILE  T

ANGER-NEGATIVISM. . . . . . . .  XXXXXXXXXXXXXXXXXXXXXX            91   65
DEPRESSIVE IDEATION AND MOOD. .  XXXXXXXXXXXXXXXX                  67   50
DISORIENTATION-MEMORY . . . . .  XXXXXX                           72   47
HALLUCINATIONS. . . . . . . . .  XXXXXXXXXXXXXXXXXXXXXXXX          98   78
EXCITEMENT. . . . . . . . . . .  XXXXXXXXXXXXXXXX                 89   59
RETARDATION-EMOTIONAL WITHDRAWL  XXXXXX                           60   48
SLEEP-APPETITE DISTURBANCE. . .  XXXXXXXXXXXXXXXX                 86   60
SUICIDE . . . . . . . . . . . .  XXXXXXXXXXXXXXXX                 92   66
VIOLENCE IDEATION . . . . . . .  XXXXXXXXXXXXXXXX                 89   59
COGNITIVE DISORGANIZATION . . .  XXXXXXXXXXXXXXXX                 80   55
UNUSUAL THOUGHTS-DELUSIONS. . .  XXXXXXXXXXXXXXXXXXXXXX            92   67
ANXIETY . . . . . . . . . . . .  XXXXXXXXXXXXXXXX                 63   50
SUSPICIOUSNESS. . . . . . . . .  XXXXXXXXXXXXXXXXXXXXXX            95   70
SOMATIC CONCERN . . . . . . . .  X                                71   45
DENIAL OF ILLNESS . . . . . . .  XXXXXXXXXXXXXXXXXXXXXX            77   56
INAPPROPRIATE APPEARANCE. . . .  XXXXXX                           73   49

                                       SUSP SLI-
                                 NONE  ECTD GHT  MILD MOD  MARK
ALCOHOL ABUSE . . . . . . . . .  X                                80   45
DRUG ABUSE. . . . . . . . . . .  XXXXXXXXXXXXXXXX                 94   71

                                 VERY       ONLY      VERY EXTRM
                                 GOOD  GOOD FAIR POOR POOR POOR
JUDGMENT. . . . . . . . . . . .  XXXXXXXXXXXXXXXXXXXXXX            94   64

                                 UNRE AVER QUI-          UNUS EXTRE
                                 MARK AGE  TE   VERY     UALY MELY
LIKEABLE. . . . . . . . . . . .  X                                48   42
```

Figure 30   MSER GRAPH.

there is strong evidence, however, the following condition(s) should be considered."

Certain diagnostic conventions are followed. Only one functional psychosis and one neurosis can be made for a subject as a definite diagnosis. In contrast, a subject may be diagnosed as having more than one organic brain syndrome, sexual deviation, drug dependence, or psychophysiologic disorder. In the presence of a definite organic brain syndrome or functional psychosis, a definite diagnosis of neuroses will not be made.

Because little historical information is available for analysis when the analysis is performed using only the mental status examination, some diagnoses cannot be made (e.g., personality disorder). Also all brain syndromes are called "acute." In addition, some schizophrenic subtypes are classified as

```
                    MSER COMPUTERIZED DIAGNOSIS
THE INFORMATION CONTAINED ON THE MENTAL STATUS EXAMINATION RECORD WAS
ANALYZED BY MEANS OF A COMPUTER PROGRAM, DIAGNOIII-MSER, VERSION 2,
NOVEMBER 1972. THE RESULTS OF THIS ANALYSIS ARE GIVEN BELOW AND ARE
INTENDED TO SERVE AS AN AID IN THE DIFFERENTIAL DIAGNOSTIC PROCESS.
BECAUSE THIS PROGRAM DOES NOT HAVE HISTORICAL INFORMATION, SOME
DIAGNOSES CANNOT BE MADE (E.G. PERSONALITY DISORDERS). ALSO, ALL BRAIN
SYNDROMES ARE CALLED ACUTE. IN ADDITION, SOME SCHIZOPHRENIC SUBTYPES
ARE CLASSIFIED AS 'SCHIZOPHRENIA, UNSPECIFIED TYPE' AND SOME SPECIFIC
AFFECTIVE ILLNESSES ARE CLASSIFIED AS 'PSYCHOTIC DEPRESSIVE MOOD
DISORDER'. A MORE DETAILED AND ACCURATE DIAGNOSTIC EVALUATION IS
POSSIBLE BY SUBMITTING A PSYCHIATRIC ANAMNESTIC RECORD ON THIS PATIENT
WITHIN TWO WEEKS, PROVIDING THIS MSER IS STORED ON THE DATA BASE.

PATIENT IDENTIFICATION NUMBER- 123456
FACILITY CODE- 016
RATER CODE-    3
DATE OF MSER EVALUATION- JANUARY 5, 1972

THE MOST LIKELY DIAGNOSIS IS-
    295.3   SCHIZOPHRENIA, PARANOID TYPE

HOWEVER, THE FOLLOWING CONDITION(S) SHOULD ALSO BE CONSIDERED-
    294.8   PSYCHOSIS WITH OTHER AND UNSPECIFIED PHYSICAL CONDITION
    296.1   MANIC-DEPRESSIVE ILLNESS, MANIC TYPE

SUMMARY OF BASIS FOR COMPUTERIZED MAIN DIAGNOSIS BASED ON MSER RATINGS

A MAIN DIAGNOSIS OF SCHIZOPHRENIA IS MADE BECAUSE
ALTHOUGH THERE IS EVIDENCE OF AN ORGANIC BRAIN SYNDROME, (SEE BELOW),
THE PRESENCE OF DELUSIONS OR HALLUCINATIONS IN A PERSON AGE 50 OR
YOUNGER MAKES A FUNCTIONAL PSYCHOSIS MORE LIKELY AS A PRIMARY
DIAGNOSIS
NO DEFINITE DIAGNOSIS OF AN ORGANIC BRAIN SYNDROME COULD BE MADE,
HOWEVER AN ORGANIC BRAIN SYNDROME SHOULD BE CONSIDERED BECAUSE OF
RATINGS OF - DISTURBANCE IN ORIENTATION AND/OR MEMORY.
FUNCTIONAL PSYCHOSIS IS STRONGLY SUGGESTED BY RATINGS OF
    -DELUSIONS,  -AT LEAST MILD INCOHERENCE
AN AFFECTIVE DISORDER IS RULED OUT BECAUSE SCORES ON INDICES OF THE
DEPRESSIVE AND MANIC SYNDROMES ARE TOO LOW.
PARANOID TYPE BECAUSE OF RATINGS OF -DELUSIONS OF GRANDIOSITY
```

Figure 31   MSER computerized diagnosis.

"schizophrenia, unspecified type" and some specific affective illnesses are classified as "psychotic depressive mood disorder." The computer program prints the rationale as to why a particular diagnosis was suggested (see Figure 31).

Monitoring Drug Prescriptions

Since one of the principal methods utilized in the treatment of the mentally ill is psychotropic medication, MSIS has provided an automated procedure for recording drug prescriptions. Each time a drug is ordered, discontinued, or changed, a form, a structured prescription blank (Figure 32), is completed. While this form is specifically designed for use in an inpatient environment, it can with minor modifications serve in other locations.

The drug order captures the essential facts of a prescription and may be used, when properly signed, as a legal record in the patient's chart. The same form (utilizing carbon copies in various ways) is used to order a drug, to order a continuation of an existing drug after a specified elapsed period of time, to discontinue a drug order, and to report the number of "PRN" administrations. On the form are recorded the essential data about the prescription: patient name, drug name, dosage, frequency, form and route, and start and discontinue dates. The original signed copy remains in the patient chart (Figure 33) while a carbon copy is sent for computer processing. A third copy is temporarily kept with the original record to be sent for computer processing when the drug order is discontinued.

When a drug order is discontinued, the right-hand portion of the original drug order form is completed with the reason for discontinuance, the number of PRN administrations, and the date. The physician then signs the order, and the third copy is detached and sent for computer processing.

A special error analysis, the Drug Transaction Verification Report (Figure 36), is produced and returned to the facility. The report contains the entire prescription ordered as well as notations as to the disposition of each drug transaction.

Several reports are routinely available using the drug data:

Doctor's Report: The Doctor's Report (Figure 34) is a listing of each patient in a building or service and all the currently active drug orders for a given point in time. It serves as a concise review of the drug regimen of the patients of a given clinician, and it provides a check of the accuracy of the data in the files since the clinician can readily catch and correct errors.

Psychotropic Drug History: A capsule history of the psychotropic drugs ordered for a particular patient during his stay at a facility, the Psychotropic Drug History (Figure 35), provides a graphic description of concurrent medication as well as a detailed report on each drug ordered.

Problem Oriented Psychiatric Record

To satisfy a need for more specific detailed information on the care and the rationale for the care given to patients, many mental health facilities are considering the use of a Problem Oriented Psychiatric Record (POPR), which is a way of organizing both the key problems presented by a patient and the interventions of the treating team.

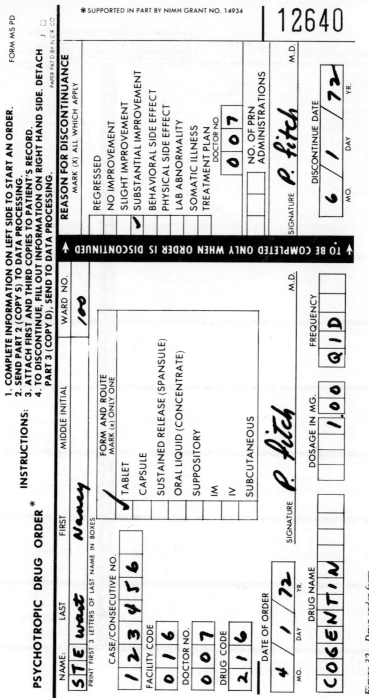

Figure 32 Drug order form.

147

INSTRUCTIONS:
1. COMPLETE INFORMATION ON LEFT SIDE TO START AN ORDER.
2. SEND PART 2 (COPY S) TO DATA PROCESSING.
3. ATTACH FIRST AND THIRD COPIES TO PATIENT'S RECORD.
4. TO DISCONTINUE, FILL OUT INFORMATION ON RIGHT HAND SIDE. DETACH PART 3 (COPY D), SEND TO DATA PROCESSING.

PSYCHOTROPIC DRUG ORDER *

NAME: LAST   FIRST   MIDDLE INITIAL   WARD NO.

PRINT FIRST 3 LETTERS OF LAST NAME IN BOXES

CASE/CONSECUTIVE NO.

FORM AND ROUTE
MARK (x) ONLY ONE

- TABLET
- CAPSULE
- SUSTAINED RELEASE (SPANSULE)
- ORAL LIQUID (CONCENTRATE)
- SUPPOSITORY
- IM
- IV
- SUBCUTANEOUS

FACILITY CODE

DOCTOR NO.

DRUG CODE

REASON FOR DISCONTINUANCE
MARK (X) ALL WHICH APPLY

- REGRESSED
- NO IMPROVEMENT
- SLIGHT IMPROVEMENT
- SUBSTANTIAL IMPROVEMENT
- BEHAVIORAL SIDE EFFECT
- PHYSICAL SIDE EFFECT
- LAB ABNORMALITY
- SOMATIC ILLNESS
- TREATMENT PLAN

DOCTOR NO.

NO. OF PRN ADMINISTRATIONS

→ TO BE COMPLETED ONLY WHEN ORDER IS DISCONTINUED

* SUPPORTED IN PART BY NIMH GRANT NO. 14934

DATE OF ORDER
MO DAY YR
SIGNATURE   M.D.
DRUG NAME   DOSAGE IN MG.   FREQUENCY

SIGNATURE   M.D.
DISCONTINUE DATE
MO DAY YR

11112

DATE OF ORDER
MO DAY YR
SIGNATURE   M.D.
DRUG NAME   DOSAGE IN MG.   FREQUENCY

SIGNATURE   M.D.
DISCONTINUE DATE
MO DAY YR

11111

→ TO BE COMPLETE

DATE OF ORDER
MO DAY YR
SIGNATURE   M.D.
DRUG NAME   DOSAGE IN MG.   FREQUENCY

SIGNATURE   M.D.
DISCONTINUE DATE
MO DAY YR

11110

→ TO BE COMPLETE

DATE OF ORDER
MO DAY YR
SIGNATURE   M.D.
DRUG NAME   DOSAGE IN MG.   FREQUENCY

SIGNATURE   M.D.
DISCONTINUE DATE
MO DAY YR

11108

→ TO BE COMPLETE

DATE OF ORDER
MO DAY YR
SIGNATURE   M.D.
DRUG NAME   DOSAGE IN MG.   FREQUENCY

SIGNATURE   M.D.
DISCONTINUE DATE
MO DAY YR

11107

→ TO BE COMPLETE

DATE OF ORDER
MO DAY YR
SIGNATURE   M.D.
DRUG NAME   DOSAGE IN MG.   FREQUENCY

SIGNATURE   M.D.
DISCONTINUE DATE
MO DAY YR

11106

→ TO BE COMPLETE

DATE OF ORDER
MO DAY YR
SIGNATURE   M.D.
DRUG NAME   DOSAGE IN MG.   FREQUENCY

SIGNATURE   M.D.
DISCONTINUE DATE
MO DAY YR

11105

→ TO BE COMPLETE

Figure 33   Drug order forms.

An Admission Form is completed and, if desired, a Mental Status Examination Record and the Psychiatric Anamnestic Record. Also in the patient's chart are a narrative history of the present episode and a physical examination, if appropriate. These data serve as a basis for the development of a Problem List (Figure 37), a list of problems that are unique to this particular patient. The identified problems are coded, submitted on MSIS Problem Oriented Psychiatric Record forms (Figure 38), and stored in the computer. All subsequent entries to the record, such as progress notes and treatment orders are keyed to one of the coded problems. The Problem List may be revised as the patient changes: new problems may be added, old ones may be dropped, and one problem may be subsumed by another. Notes may be added to the record by any member of the treatment team. Output reports identify the source of each note but do not segregate them into separate sections, for example, nurses' notes, social service notes, and occupational therapy notes, but display them either chronologically (Figure 39) or chronologically within each problem (Figure 40). The treatments prescribed are also coded, and each treatment may be associated with one or more problems. In addition to the problem notation, the Problem Oriented Psychiatric Record Form has space for brief comments by the clinician and for other comments which are not entered into the computer but which remain in the patient's chart. These other comments may be organized as follows:

SUBJECTIVE   What the patient reports about this problem.

OBJECTIVE   Staff observations or lab reports relevant to this problem.

ASSESSMENT   Evaluation of current problems and plans for additional observations or tests needed for understanding this problem.

PLAN   Long-term and/or immediate plans for treatment.

With progress notes and treatments keyed to problems, reports can easily convey what the clinician had in mind; the comments serve to clarify the case further, and the approach of the treatment team to each problem can readily be followed. Treatment plans (Figure 41) are explicitly organized, and the reader can be kept up-to-date on all aspects of the case.

MSIS has developed detailed code lists for the uniform recording of both problems and treatments. Every MSIS code may be qualified where needed to facilitate the coding of highly idiosyncratic problems or treatments. The use of free text to elaborate on the codes permits clinical staff the freedom of detailing patient-specific data within the disciplined context of the uniform coding structures.

The current severity of a problem may be rated at arbitrary intervals of time in a separate area of the form. Thus, on a fixed scale, the patient may progress

STATE   : N.Y.
FACILITY : RSH
DELIVER TO : MISS ANNA JACKSON

MULTI-STATE INFORMATION SYSTEM   PROCESSED AT ISD :   APRIL 13, 1972 4:57
                                     RECEIVED AT ISD :   APRIL 10, 1972 12:00

BUILDING NO.- 2   D O C T O R S   R E P O R T
                       WARD NO.- 4   PERIOD COVERED- 03/01/72 THRU 03/31/72

PATIENT NAME DIAGNOSIS CODE	CASE NUMBER	DOCTR NO.	ORDER NUMBER	DRUG NAME	DOSE IN MG	FREQ.	FORM & RT	DATE OF ORDER	DATE OF DISC.	TOTAL MG CONSUMED IN BLDG.	* = ORDER AGE OVER 90 DAYS
SMITH, JANE 296.0	78663	318	14527	THORAZINE	100.00	PRN	TAB	03/30/72	OPEN		
		318	14528	MELLARIL	50.00	BID	TAB	03/22/72	OPEN	200.00	
		318	14537	THORAZINE	100.00	HS	TAB	03/22/72	03/30/72	900.00	
		318	14538	MELLARIL	50.00	TID	TAB	03/22/72	03/30/72	1350.00	
		318	14550	MELLARIL	25.00	STAT	TAB	03/22/72	03/22/72	25.00	
SYMONDS, ELAINE 295.90	17663	327	14001	STELAZINE	30.00	BID	TAB	02/01/71	OPEN	1860.00	*
		327	14002	MELLARIL	100.00	HS	TAB	02/01/72	OPEN	3100.00	
TALBERT, JOANNE 295.74	78634	333	14019	THORAZINE	100.00	PRN	TAB	03/22/72	OPEN		
		333	14020	THORAZINE	50.00	PRN	IM	03/22/72	OPEN	8000.00	
		333	14022	THORAZINE	400.00	BID	TAB	03/22/72	OPEN		
		333	14015	THORAZINE	600.00	HS	TAB	03/20/72	OPEN	7200.00	
		333	14014	STELAZINE	20.00	BID	TAB	03/16/72	OPEN	640.00	

150

Name	ID		Code	Drug	Dose	Freq	Form	Start	End	Amount
TYLER, ELIZABETH (ACNE)	17742	333	14021	THORAZINE	200.00	OD	TAB	03/20/72	03/22/72	600.00
		333	14010	THORAZINE	200.00	HS	TAB	03/15/72	03/20/72	1200.00
		333	14009	STELAZINE	10.00	BID	TAB	03/15/72	03/16/72	40.00
TYLER, ELIZABETH (ACNE)	17742	333	14004	STELAZINE	10.00	OD	TAB	02/25/72	OPEN	310.00
		333	14005	STELAZINE	5.00	ON	TAB	02/25/72	03/01/72	5.00
VERNON, SYLVIA 295.3	78547	332	14026	MELLARIL	100.00	BID	TAB	03/20/72	OPEN	2400.00
		332	14024	THORAZINE	50.00	OD	TAB	03/15/72	03/20/72	300.00
		332	14025	THORAZINE	50.00	HS	TAB	03/15/72	03/20/72	300.00

Name	ID	Status
ADAMS, SHIRLEY	78321	PATIENT NOT CURRENTLY ON MEDICATION.
ALTMAN, LOIS	30268	PATIENT NOT CURRENTLY ON MEDICATION.
BROWN, SARAH	77749	PATIENT NOT CURRENTLY ON MEDICATION.
BYRON, LENORE	78728	PATIENT NOT CURRENTLY ON MEDICATION.
CALDER, JUDY	77910	PATIENT NOT CURRENTLY ON MEDICATION.
DATON, PEARL	78525	PATIENT NOT CURRENTLY ON MEDICATION.
DRUE, ALICE	78646	PATIENT NOT CURRENTLY ON MEDICATION.
ELKIN, FLORENCE	27397	PATIENT NOT CURRENTLY ON MEDICATION.
FRIED, PHYLLIS	78257	PATIENT NOT CURRENTLY ON MEDICATION.
MAY, IDA	78342	PATIENT NOT CURRENTLY ON MEDICATION.
NORRIS, LOUISE	17311	PATIENT NOT CURRENTLY ON MEDICATION.

BUILDING TOTALS

1 TOTAL PATIENTS — 16
2 TOTAL PATIENTS ON DRUGS — 5
3 TOTAL NUMBER OF OPEN DRUG ORDERS — 11

Figure 34 *Doctor's Report.*

151

```
                         PSYCHOTROPIC DRUG HISTORY                    AS OF 6/03/72
                         CONCURRENT THERAPY


CASE NUMBER 123456    STEWART,NANCY    SEX F    AGE 24    DIAGNOSIS 295.3

                     DRUG NAME         DOSE IN FREQ FORM PRN   START DISC DOC REAS FOR DISC
                                       MG                ADM  DATE  DATE  NO  *=FAVORABLE
  JAN  1  A  B
       8  A  B    A-CHLORPROMAZINE   50.00 QID  TAB        1/3/72 2/6/72 7 REGRESSED
      15  A  B                       75.00 QID  TAB        2/6/72 3/1/72 7 NO IMPROV.
      22  A  B                      100.00 QID  TAB        3/2/72 3/9/72 7 NO IMPROV.
  FEB  1  A  B                       75.00 QID  TAB        3/9/72 4/1/72 7 *SUBSTANT IMP
       8  A  B                       50.00 QID  TAB        4/1/72 6/1/72 9 *SUBSTANT IMP
      15  A  B
      22  A  B    B-COGENTIN          1.00 BID  TAB        1/3/72 3/2/72 7 NO IMPROV
  MAR  1  A  B                        1.00 TID  TAB        3/2/72 4/1/72 7 NO IMPROV
       8  A  B                        1.00 QID  TAB        4/1/72 6/1/72 9 *SUBSTANT IMP
      15  A  B
      22  A  B
  APR  1  A  B
       8  A  B
      15  A  B
      22  A  B
  MAY  1  A  B
       8  A  B
      15  A  B
      22  A  B
  JUN  1  A  B
```

Figure 35   Patient Drug History.

with regard to a particular problem from severe to moderate or mild, and this course can be traced through the notes. In addition, the treating team may set a progress goal with regard to the particular problem. For instance, perhaps the goal of treatment for a given problem is reduction of the severity of the condition to mild. This technique allows monitoring of treatment outcomes in terms of the specific known goals which have been set for the individual patient.

Special output reports include:

The Problem List (a master list of problems coded and recorded for the patient)

Treatment Plan Report (treatments keyed to problem numbers)

Problem-Oriented Chronological Report (organized by problem and by date within problem)

Chronological Problem-Oriented Report (organized by date)

Automated Goal-Oriented Medical Records For the Mentally Retarded

Lack of precision and uniformity in the identification of client needs, deficits, assets, and goals and in the specification of habilitative service plans are representative of some of the major deficiencies in the present manual record-keeping procedures in mental health and mental retardation. Sheer bulk of the

```
MULTI-STATE INFORMATION SYSTEM          PROCESSED AT ISD:  DECEMBER 1, 1969  21:00
                                                 STARTED AT ISD:  DECEMBER 1, 1969  19:00
STATE    : NY
FACILITY : 16
DELIVER TO : BUILDING 15 M. SMITH

WARD 10                          DRUG TRANSACTION VERIFICATION REPORT

              CASE     ACTN  TRANS     DOCTOR  ORDER
PATIENT NAME  NUMBER   CODE  DATE      NUMBER  NUMBER        ERROR/DISPOSITION
------------  ------   ----  -----     ------  ------        -----------------

ABRAMSON, JOES  12346    C   11/31/69   123    12679         TRANSACTION ACCEPTED AS RECORDED
                                                 DG703       PATIENT OFF LIBRIUM 20MG T.I.D. TABLET

BLUMENTAHL, JOHN  12347  R   11/31/69   123    12680         TRANSACTION ACCEPTED AS RECORDED
                                                 DG705       AN ACTIVE ORDER FOR LIBRIUM 20MG
                                                             TID CONCENTRATE HAS BEEN REMOVED

LAPINYATA, JOSEPH  12345  S  11/31/69   123    12678         TRANSACTION ACCEPTED AS RECORDED
                                                 DG701       PATIENT STARTED ON LIBRIUM 10MG
                                                             QID TABLET

RAPP, JEROME  12348      A   11/31/69   127    12943         TRANSACTION ACCEPTED AS RECORDED
                                                 DG707       A DISCONTINUED ORDER FOR 10MG
                                                             QID CA
                                                             PSULE HAS BEEN ACTIVATED
SMITH, PETER  12395      S   11/31/69   127    12689         TRANSACTION REJECTED
                                                 DG401       CASE NUMBER NOT ON FILE

                      ***************************************
                      *  THE DRUG TRANSACTION VERIFICATION  *
                      *  REPORT PROVIDES A VERIFICATION THAT *
                      *  THE PROPER PRESCRIPTION RECORD WAS  *
                      *  PLACED IN THE PATIENT'S FILE.       *
                      *                                      *
                      ***************************************
```

Figure 36 Drug Transaction Verification Report.

153

MULTI - STATE INFORMATION SYSTEM

PROBLEM LIST

NY016 PATIENT: STEWART,NANCY,#1234567   PRPL   -FEB 22 1972-

12/10/71 PROBLEM: 1   MARIJUANA ABUSE.
                                RESOLVED 12/28/71

         PROBLEM: 2   SLEEP PROBLEMS
                                SUBSUMED BY PROBLEM 4

01/01/72 PROBLEM: 3   AGITATION, POSSIBLY SECONDARY TO DRUG
                        ABUSE.
                                SUBSUMED BY PROBLEM 4

01/05/72 PROBLEM: 4   HALLUCINOGEN ABUSE
                                RESOLVED 02/10/72

         PROBLEM: 5   SUSPICIOUS OF OTHERS, ESP. CO-WORKERS AND
                        FAMILY MEMBERS.

         PROBLEM: 6   HEARS VOICES; CONTENT IS THREATENING AND
                        ACCUSATORY.

Figure 37   Problem List.

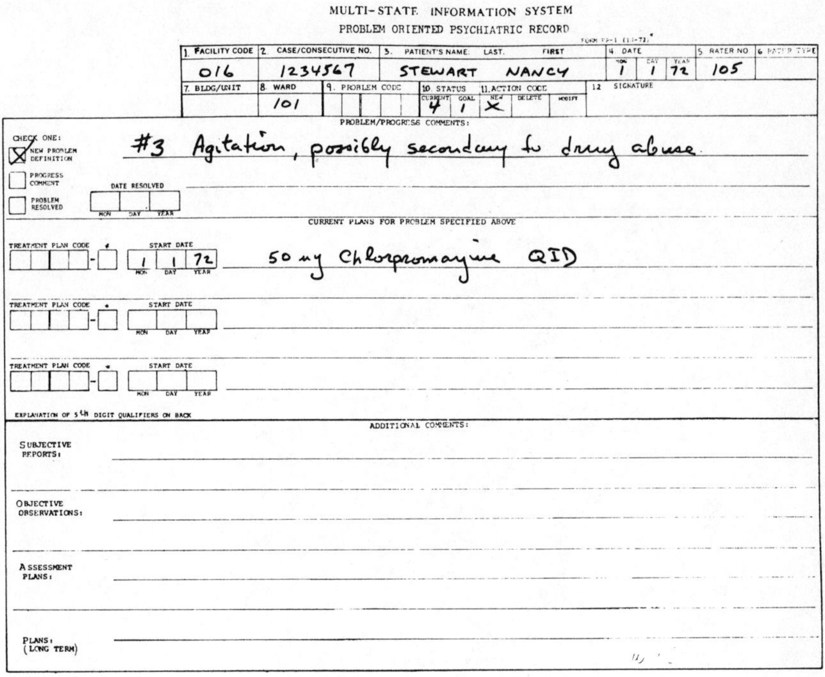

MULTI-STATE INFORMATION SYSTEM
PROBLEM ORIENTED PSYCHIATRIC RECORD

1. FACILITY CODE	2. CASE/CONSECUTIVE NO.	3. PATIENT'S NAME: LAST. FIRST	4. DATE (MON DAY YEAR)	5. RATER NO	6. RATER TYPE
016	1234567	STEWART NANCY	1 1 72	105	
7. BLDG/UNIT	8. WARD	9. PROBLEM CODE	10. STATUS (CURRENT GOAL) / 11. ACTION CODE (NEW DELETE MODIFY)	12. SIGNATURE	
	101		4 1 X		

PROBLEM/PROGRESS COMMENTS:

CHECK ONE: [X] NEW PROBLEM DEFINITION — #3 Agitation, possibly secondary to drug abuse

[ ] PROGRESS COMMENT

[ ] PROBLEM RESOLVED — DATE RESOLVED (MON DAY YEAR)

CURRENT PLANS FOR PROBLEM SPECIFIED ABOVE

TREATMENT PLAN CODE * START DATE (MON DAY YEAR) 1 1 72 — 50 mg Chlorpromazine QID

TREATMENT PLAN CODE * START DATE (MON DAY YEAR)

TREATMENT PLAN CODE * START DATE (MON DAY YEAR)

EXPLANATION OF 5th DIGIT QUALIFIERS ON BACK

ADDITIONAL COMMENTS:

SUBJECTIVE REPORTS:

OBJECTIVE OBSERVATIONS:

ASSESSMENT PLANS:

PLANS: (LONG TERM)

Figure 38 Problem Oriented Psychiatric Record.

manual record, as well as the manner in which information is traditionally stored in the record have made it virtually impossible for clinical managers to monitor the delivery of service, to evaluate individual outcome, and to assess the efficiency and the cost effectiveness of different service modalities.

With these problems in mind, a large-scale project was designed to develop and implement a manual and computerized information system which will (*a*) provide clinical and management aids for the delivery of habilitative services to mentally retarded individuals, (*b*) introduce individual goal planning as a formal clinical framework within which such habilitative services can be delivered, (*c*) establish comprehensive assessment procedures for each client, and (*d*) establish a data base and data-retrieval capabilities for research in the field of mental retardation. A 3-year, $2.5 million federal grant was awarded to the State Department of Mental Hygiene to work with the Information Science Division on development of the system, which will be implemented at Willowbrook Developmental Center.

```
        M U L T I - S T A T E    I N F O R M A T I O N    S Y S T E M
                      C H R O N O L O G I C A L    R E P O R T

NY016 PATIENT: STEWART,NANCY,#1234567        PRTL            -FEB 22 1972-

12/10/71 PROBLEM: 1    MARIJUANA ABUSE.
                       **RESOLVED 12/29/71**

12/10/71 PROBLEM: 2    SLEEP PROBLEMS.
                       **SUBSUMED BY PROBLEM 4**

12/28/71 PROBLEM: 1    **RESOLVED**

01/01/72 PROBLEM: 3    AGITATION, POSSIBLY SECONDARY TO DRUG
                       ABUSE.
                       **SUBSUMED BY PROBLEM 4**

        3              -50MG CHLORPROMAZINE QID.          (PSY: I. SMITH)

01/02/72 COMMENT: 3    MARKED IMPROVEMENT, PATIENT RESTED, QUIET.
                                                   (NUR: JANE JOHNSON)

        3              -75MG CHLORPROMAZINE QID, 1MG COGENTIN
                        BID.                             (PSY: I. SMITH)
```

156

```
         3          -PLACE PATIENT ON OUTPATIENT STATUS.
                     SET UP APPOINTMENTS FOR SW FOLLOW UP.
                                                   (PSY: T. SMITH)

01/05/72 PROBLEM: 4   HALLUCINOGEN ABUSE
                      **RESOLVED 02/10/72**

         PROBLEM: 5   SUSPICIOUS OF OTHERS, ESP. CO-WORKERS AND
                      FAMILY MEMBERS.

         PROBLEM: 6   HEARS VOICES; CONTENT IS THREATENING AND
                      ACCUSATORY.

         COMMENT: 4   USE OF LSD CONFIRMED. PATIENT EMOTIONALLY
                      DISTANT. POSSIBLE RECENT LSD USE.  (SOURCE UNKNOWN)

01/07/72 COMMENT: 4   PATIENT UNABLE TO RELAX. DOESN'T KEEP
         COMMENT:     SCHEDULED APPOINTMENTS.              (SW : OKO KTM)
                      GENERAL PROGNOSIS SEEMS POOR. NO IMPROVEMENT
                      SEEN. INCREASE IN HOSTILITY.         (PSY: T. SMITH)

         4,5,6       -SCHEDULE INDIVIDUAL THERAPY SESSIONS
                      WITH DR. BROWN.                      (PSY: T. SMITH)
         6          -PSYCHIATRIC ANAMNESIS TO BE DONE TO
                     EXPLORE HISTORY OF HALLUCINATIONS.     (PSY: T. SMITH)
         5          -MENTAL STATUS EXAM TO BE DONE.        (SOURCE UNKNOWN)

01/08/72 COMMENT: 6   PATIENT BABBLES PROFUSELY AND INCOHERENTLY
                      APPARENTLY IN RESPONSE TO HEARD VOICES.
                                                   (PSY: ROBERT BROWN)
```

Figure 39 Chronological Report.

```
                    C H R O N O L O G I C A L   R E P O R T

MY016 PATIENT: STEWART,NANCY,#1234567          PPTL                    -FEB 22 1972-D

01/10/72 COMMENT: 4    SUSPECT PATIENT IS MOONLIGHTING AS
                       PROSTITUTE TO SUPPORT DRUG HABIT.        (PSY: ROBERT BROWN)
         COMMENT: 6    EMPLOYER AND FAMILY CONFIRM PATIENT OFTEN (PSY: ROBERT BROWN)
                       NOTED TALKING TO HERSELF.
         COMMENT: 5    CONDITION AT WORK BECOMING WORSE. EMPLOYER (PSY: ROBERT BROWN)
                       REPORTS UNSATISFACTORY PERFORMANCE AS
                       SUSPICIOUSNESS INCREASES.
              4        -DO LAB STUDIES RE: DRUG USE        (SW : OKO KIM)
              5        -MEET WITH EMPLOYER                 (PSY: ROBERT BROWN)
              5        -MEETING WITH FAMILY SCHEDULED      (SW : OKO KIM)
                       -SCHEDULE NEUROLOGICAL STUDY.       (SW : OKO KIM)
                        REVIEW WITH DR. SMITH              (PSY: ROBERT BROWN)
                       -REVIEW SCHOOL RECORDS. SEE TEACHERS. (SW : OKO KIM)

01/15/72 COMMENT: 4    LAB RESULTS INDICATE PATIENT NOT TAKING
                       PRESCRIBED MED. DRUG TESTS POSITIVE. (PSY: ROBERT BROWN)
         COMMENT:      CONSIDER FOR INPATIENT STATUS. PATIENT WOULD
                       NOT WELCOME THIS. ANGER EXPRESSED AT MENTION (PSY: I. SMITH)
                       OF TRANSFER TO INPATIENT.
         COMMENT:      EEG NORMAL.                         (PSY: I. SMITH)

01/17/72 COMMENT: 5    EMPLOYER REPORTS THAT PATIENT HASN'T BEEN TO
                       WORK FOR 5 DAYS. HAVE BEEN UNABLE TO CONTACT
                       FOR MEETINGS.                       (SW : OKO KIM)

01/23/72 COMMENT: 4    FRIENDS SAY PATIENT BACK ON HEAVY DRUG USE. (SW : OKO KIM)
         COMMENT: 5    FAMILY REPORTS GETTING BELLIGERENT PHONE (SOURCE UNKNOWN)
                       CALLS FROM PATIENT.

01/26/72 COMMENT: 4    POLICE PICK-UP; NO ARREST.-RETURNED TO (PSY: ROBERT BROWN)
                       FAMILY.
         COMMENT: 6    PATIENT STATES VOICES SUGGEST SUICIDE, (PSY: ROBERT BROWN)
                       CONVINCED VOICES ARE REAL.
              6        -INCREASE TO 100MG CHLORPROMAZINE CID, (PSY: I. SMITH)
                       1MG COGENTIN TID.
                       -TRANSFER TO INPATIENT STATUS.      (PSY: I. SMITH)

02/10/72 PROBLEM: 4    **RESOLVED**
```

Figure 39 (Continued)

158

```
                MULTI-STATE INFORMATION SYSTEM

            PROBLEM ORIENTED PSYCHIATRIC REPORT
       ---------------------------------------------------
       NY016 PATIENT: STEWART,NANCY,#1234567      POPR      -FEB 22 1972-

       12/10/71 PROBLEM: 1    MARIJUANA ABUSE.
                                **RESOLVED 12/28/71**
       -----------------
       12/10/71 PROBLEM: 2    SLEEP PROBLEMS
                                **SUBSUMED BY PROBLEM 4**
       -----------------
       01/01/72 PROBLEM: 3    AGITATION, POSSIBLY SECONDARY TO DRUG
                              ABUSE.
                                **SUBSUMED BY PROBLEM 4**
       -----------------
                              -50MG CHLORPROMAZINE QID.         (PSY: I. SMITH)

       01/02/72 COMMENT:      MARKED IMPROVEMENT, PATIENT RESTED, QUIET.
                                                           (NUR: JANE JOHNSON)
                              -75MG CHLORPROMAZINE QID, 1MG COGENTIN
                               BID.                             (PSY: I. SMITH)
                              -PLACE PATIENT ON OUTPATIENT STATUS.
```

Figure 40   Problem Oriented Psychiatric Report.

```
                                              -PLACE PATIENT ON OUTPATIENT STATUS.
                                               SET UP APPOINTMENTS FOR SW FOLLOW UP

--------------------------------------
01/05/72 PROBLEM: 4    HALLUCINOGEN ABUSE
--------------------        **RESOLVED 02/10/72**

         COMMENT:    USE OF LSD CONFIRMED. PATIENT EMOTIONALLY
                     DISTANT. POSSIBLE RECENT LSD USE.        (SOURCE UNKNOWN)

01/07/72 COMMENT:    PATIENT UNABLE TO RELAX. DOESN'T KEEP
                     SCHEDULED APPOINTMENTS.                  (SW : OKO KIM)
                        -SCHEDULE INDIVIDUAL THERAPY SESSIONS
                         WITH DR. BROWN.                     (PSY: I. SMITH)

01/10/72 COMMENT:    SUSPECT PATIENT IS MOONLIGHTING AS
                     PROSTITUTE TO SUPPORT DRUG HABIT.        (PSY: ROBERT BROWN)
                        -DO LAB STUDIES RE: DRUG USE          (PSY: ROBERT BROWN)

01/15/72 COMMENT:    LAB RESULTS INDICATE PATIENT NOT TAKING
                     PRESCRIBED MED. DRUG TESTS POSITIVE. (PSY: ROBERT BROWN)

01/23/72 COMMENT:    FRIENDS SAY PATIENT BACK ON HEAVY DRUG USE.(SW : OKO KIM)

01/26/72 COMMENT:    POLICE PICK-UP; NO ARREST. RETURNED TO
                     FAMILY.                              (PSY: ROBERT BROWN)
                        -TRANSFER TO INPATIENT STATUS.        (PSY: I. SMITH)
```

160

```
***** INFORMATION SCIENCES DIVISION, RSH *****          DATE 08/27/1974                    PAGE NO. 0005

              PROBLEM  ORIENTED  PSYCHIATRIC  REPORT
   -----------------------------------------------------------------------
   NY016 PATIENT: STEWART,NANCY,#1234567        PDPR              -FEB 22 1972-P
   -----------------------------------------------------------------------

   01/05/72 PROBLEM: 5    SUSPICIOUS OF OTHERS, ESP. CO-WORKERS AND
   -----------------      FAMILY MEMBERS.

   01/07/72               -SCHEDULE INDIVIDUAL THERAPY SESSIONS
                           WITH DR. BROWN.                    (PSY: T. SMITH)
                          -MENTAL STATUS EXAM TO BE DONE.     (SOURCE UNKNOWN)

   01/10/72 COMMENT:      CONDITION AT WORK BECOMING WORSE. EMPLOYER
                          REPORTS UNSATISFACTORY PERFORMANCE AS
                          SUSPICIOUSNESS INCREASES.                 (SW : OKO KIM)
                          -MEET WITH EMPLOYER                       (SW : OKO KIM)
                          -MEETING WITH FAMILY SCHEDULED            (SW : OKO KIM)

   01/17/72 COMMENT:      EMPLOYER REPORTS THAT PATIENT HASN'T BEEN TO
                          WORK FOR 5 DAYS. HAVE BEEN UNABLE TO CONTACT
                          FOR MEETINGS.                             (SW : OKO KIM)

   01/23/72 COMMENT:      FAMILY REPORTS GETTING BELLIGERENT PHONE
                          CALLS FROM PATIENT.                 (SOURCE UNKNOWN)
```

Figure 40 (*Continued*)

161

```
01/05/72  PROBLEM: 6      HEARS VOICES: CONTENT IS THREATENING AND
                          ACCUSATORY.

01/07/72                  -SCHEDULE INDIVIDUAL THERAPY SESSIONS
                           WITH DR. BROWN.                       (PSY: I. SMITH)
                          -PSYCHIATRIC ANAMNESIS TO BE DONE TO
                           EXPLORE HISTORY OF HALLUCINATIONS.    (PSY: I. SMITH)

01/08/72  COMMENT:        PATIENT BABBLES PROFUSELY AND INCOHERENTLY
                          APPARENTLY IN RESPONSE TO HEARD VOICES.
                                                             (PSY: ROBERT BROWN)

01/10/72  COMMENT:        EMPLOYER AND FAMILY CONFIRM PATIENT OFTEN
                          NOTED TALKING TO HERSELF.          (PSY: ROBERT BROWN)

01/26/72  COMMENT:        PATIENT STATES VOICES SUGGEST SUICIDE.
                          CONVINCED VOICES ARE REAL.          (PSY: ROBERT BROWN)
                          -INCREASE TO 100MG CHLORPROMAZINE QID.
                                                               (PSY: I. SMITH)
                          1MG COGENTIN TID.                    (PSY: I. SMITH)
                          -TRANSFER TO INPATIENT STATUS.

NON-SPECIFIC PROGRESS/TREATMENT PLAN COMMENTS
--------------------------------------------------------------
01/07/72  COMMENT:        GENERAL PROGNOSIS SEEMS POOR. NO IMPROVEMENT
                          SEEN. INCREASE IN HOSTILITY.         (PSY: I. SMITH)



*****  INFORMATION SCIENCES DIVISION, PSH  *****                 DATE 08/27/1974             PAGE NO.  0006


           P R O B L E M   O R I E N T E D   P S Y C H I A T R I C   R E P O R T

        NY016  PATIENT: STEWART,NANCY,#1234567          PGPR          -FEB 22 1972-P

                          -SCHEDULE NEUROLOGICAL STUDY.
                          REVIEW WITH DR. SMITH                (PSY: ROBERT BROWN)
                          -REVIEW SCHOOL RECORDS. SEE TEACHERS. (SW : OKO KIM)

        01/15/72  COMMENT:   CONSIDER FOR INPATIENT STATUS. PATIENT WOULD
                             NOT WELCOME THIS. ANGER EXPRESSED AT MENTION
                             OF TRANSFER TO INPATIENT.           (PSY: I. SMITH)
                  COMMENT:   EEG NORMAL.                          (PSY: I. SMITH)
```

***** INFORMATION SCIENCES DIVISION, RSH *****   DATE 08/27/1974

            M U L T I - S T A T E   I N F O R M A T I O N   S Y S T E M

                    T R E A T M E N T   P L A N   R E P O R T

NY016 PATIENT: STEWART,NANCY,#1234567   -FEB 22 1972-

DATE	PROBLEM	TREATMENT PLANS	SOURCE
01/01/72	3	-50MG CHLORPROMAZINE QIC.	(PSY: I. SMITH)
01/02/72	3	-75MG CHLORPROMAZINE QID, 1MG COGENTIN BID.	(PSY: I. SMITH)
	3	-PLACE PATIENT ON OUTPATIENT STATUS. SET UP APPOINTMENTS FOR SW FOLLOW UP.	(PSY: I. SMITH)
01/07/72	4,5,6	-SCHEDULE INDIVIDUAL THERAPY SESSIONS WITH DR. BROWN.	(PSY: I. SMITH)
	6	-PSYCHIATRIC ANAMNESIS TO BE DONE TO EXPLORE HISTORY OF HALLUCINATIONS.	(PSY: I. SMITH)
	5	-MENTAL STATUS EXAM TO BE DONE.	(SOURCE UNKNOWN)
01/10/72	4	-DO LAB STUDIES RE: DRUG USE	(PSY: ROBERT BROWN)
	5	-MEET WITH EMPLOYER	(SW : OKG KIM)
	5	-MEETING WITH FAMILY SCHEDULED	(SW : OKG KIM)
		-SCHEDULE NEUROLOGICAL STUDY. REVIEW EEG WITH DR. SMITH	(PSY: ROBERT BROWN)
		-REVIEW SCHOOL RECORDS. SEE TEACHERS.	(SW : OKG KIM)
01/26/72	6	-INCREASE TO 100MG CHLORPROMAZINE QID, 1MG COGENTIN TID.	(PSY: I. SMITH)
	4,6	-TRANSFER TO INPATIENT STATUS	(PSY: I. SMITH)

Figure 41   Treatment Plan Report.

163

Among the specific goals of the project are the following:

1.   A computer-based system that will provide timely clinical and management information and feedback to habilitation workers as well as administrators of a mental retardation facility.

2.   A comprehensive medical record system that will reflect the medical, psychosocial, and educational plans and objectives for each client, and attest to the execution of these plans.

3.   A structure for insuring accountability for planning and implementation of habilitative action.

4.   Procedures that will facilitate case reviews by peers.

5.   A framework within which cost finding and resource allocation will be facilitated.

6.   A system that will allow for cost and benefits reporting by client.

The reporting of physically observable, functional assets and deficits within a uniform conceptual framework, the precise specification of services and goals for each problem, the recording of time frames for goals, and the clear identification of staff members primarily responsible for delivering these services will supply both the clinical team and supervisory personnel with precise information about the care planned and the consequences of such care. With such information stored and readily accessible in a computer system, clinical management can make more informed decisions and monitor more closely the services delivered to individuals in their care. The accumulation and subsequent analysis of such data should facilitate the identification of successful, efficient, and cost-effective service modalities for specific problems.

Information on clients will be recorded in a structured format and processed by the computer to produce narrative, tabular, and graphic summaries. The Admission Form and a Change in Status Form will keep the identity, location, and status of each client up to date, thereby maintaining a complete and accurate census of the population being served.

The entire gamut of services rendered to a client, ranging from training in self-help skills to occupational therapy to classroom activities will be recorded for each client and stored in the computer. All these data will be available for retrieval, making it possible to know at all times what is being done, by whom, and how often for each client. Other components of the existing MSIS system including those which facilitate cost finding will be installed.

Each individual admitted for service at Willowbrook will undergo a thorough diagnostic assessment of his functional assets and deficiencies. Neurological, pediatric, social, and psychological assessments will also be conducted, and the results will be stored in the computer. Computer-generated reports of these data will be used by the clinician to build a list of needs for each client; goals will then be set and habilitation services will be specified in direct response to individual needs. The computer will be used to monitor delivery of services and will generate periodic reminders of the goals and milestones set and the time frames specified for each goal. These will facilitate the timely evaluation of the progress made by each individual. Computer-generated charts and graphs will help keep staff informed of the progress of each client, so that goals can be modofied as necessary. As goals set for an individual are attained, additional goals will be specified until the overall objectives for which that client was admitted are met. Thus the computer will function as a record-keeping tool and as an aid to the clinical staff by facilitating ongoing evaluation of each client's progress.

The information system will initially be implemented in a pilot unit at Willowbrook designated by the Director of the School. This unit will include all residents of a single building, and the population will range from 100 to 150. A one-to-one staffing ratio will be maintained in this unit.

The staff of the pilot unit is responsible for assessing each resident and for formulating and recording the goals, milestones, and time frames set. This staff will, as usual, administer the treatments and interventions they prescribe for achieving the milestones and goals their specify. The project staff will assist clinical personnel in articulating goals and treatments and in entering and retrieving data from the computerized, goal-oriented files; the project staff will therefore be an active and integral part of the clinical team.

Design and implementation of an automated goal-oriented record system in mental retardation is an effort undertaken with the hope and expectation that it will lead ultimately to improvements in habilitation. To assess the impact of the information system, evaluation studies will be carried out along a number of dimensions. An independent evaluator or contractor will design the studies, collect the data, and interpret the results. The work of the evaluator will begin soon after the start date of the project so that base-line and formative evaluation data can be collected.

It is anticipated that the evaluative effort will have three parts. The first part will be a "process evaluation," with emphasis on measuring the extent to which project staff have met the timetable for the design and implementation of the automated system. Parameters will include the level and pace of the effort, and quality of training and documentation.

The thrust of the second phase, "impact evaluation," will be directed at two objectives of the project: improvement of management practices and improvement in clinical and habilitative service delivery.

The final phase, "outcome evaluation," will focus on the extent to which the institution has improved in terms of its management and its residents have improved in terms of client outcome as a result of the information system.

Cost Finding and Rate Setting System (COFARS)

As previously noted in Part I, cost finding and rate setting are accounting techniques that enable a facility to estimate the costs of providing different types of services and to set rates equitably for billing clients or third-party payors. Even when costs are not recovered by billing, cost finding may be used to justify budget requirements to funding agencies and other external groups and for internal management cost controls. Cost finding involves establishing cost centers within a facility and allocating direct and indirect costs. The MSIS system provides for both the "step-down" and the "simultaneous equations" methods of allocation. It may also be used as a general system for posting expenses to a file and comparing them to the amount of funds budgeted for a time period. Rate setting is a means of establishing equitable rates based on the actual costs of services delivered. Computer processing enhances the procedure by automating data collection and storage and expediting the complicated methods of allocating funds.

There are five input forms into the MSIS cost-finding system. The Cost Center Registration Form (Figure 42) is a list of cost centers and their characteristics. The Budget Recording Form (Figure 43) is a listing of budgeted amounts by cost centers within established dates (the budget information is optional). Additional forms provide for direct expense (Figure 44), these being the direct cost of running a cost center exclusive of professional personnel; indirect expenses (Figure 45), the costs attributable to a final revenue-producing center by a support center; and personnel expenses (Figure 46) listing the costs of professional service-giving personnel.

For the purposes of rate setting, the output divides costs into two categories; the "facillites and support" expense and the "professional personnel" expense. These two types of costs are used to generate an equitable cost to the consumer based on services actually received rather than an inclusive per diem rate. Table 1 in Figure 47 is a sample of output data showing professional personnel expenses by individual staff member, hours worked, total cost, and cost per hour.

As an illustration of the applications of this system, for example, output from the cost-finding system might show that the facilities and support cost (the combined direct and allocated indirect expenses) of operating the inpatient unit for a month amounted to $30,000. Data from the MSIS patient data indicate that there were 600 patient days in the inpatient unit for the month. Therefore the facilities and expense charge for the inpatient unit would be $50 per day. To this must be added the costs for professional personnel who gave service to the client. This can be done in a variety of ways. Table 1 in Figure 47 shows sample data for individual workers and displays the number of hours worked (WT3), the total cost for those hours (WT2), and the cost per hour (ME1). MSIS patient data indicate that the client under consideration took part in 1-

| M S I S | | | FACILITY NAME AND CODE |
| COST CENTER REGISTRATION FORM | | | |

COST CENTER NO.	COST CENTER CATEGORY	COST CENTER ACTIVE DATE MM DD YY	COST CENTER NAME
| | | | | |	| |	| | | | |	
| | | | | |	| |	| | | | |	
| | | | | |	| |	| | | | |	
| | | | | |	| |	| | | | /	
| | | | | |	| |	| | | | |	
| | | | | |	| |	| | | | |	
| | | | | |	| |	| | | | |	
| | | | | |	| |	| | | | |	
| | | | | |	| |	| | | | |	
| | | | | |	| |	| | | | |	
| | | | | |	| |	| | | | |	
| | | | | |	| |	| | | | |	
| | | | | |	| |	| | | | |	
| | | | | |	| |	| | | | |	
| | | | | |	| |	| | | | |	
| | | | | |	| |	| | | | |	
| | | | | |	| |	| | | | |	

Figure 42   Cost Center Registration Form.

167

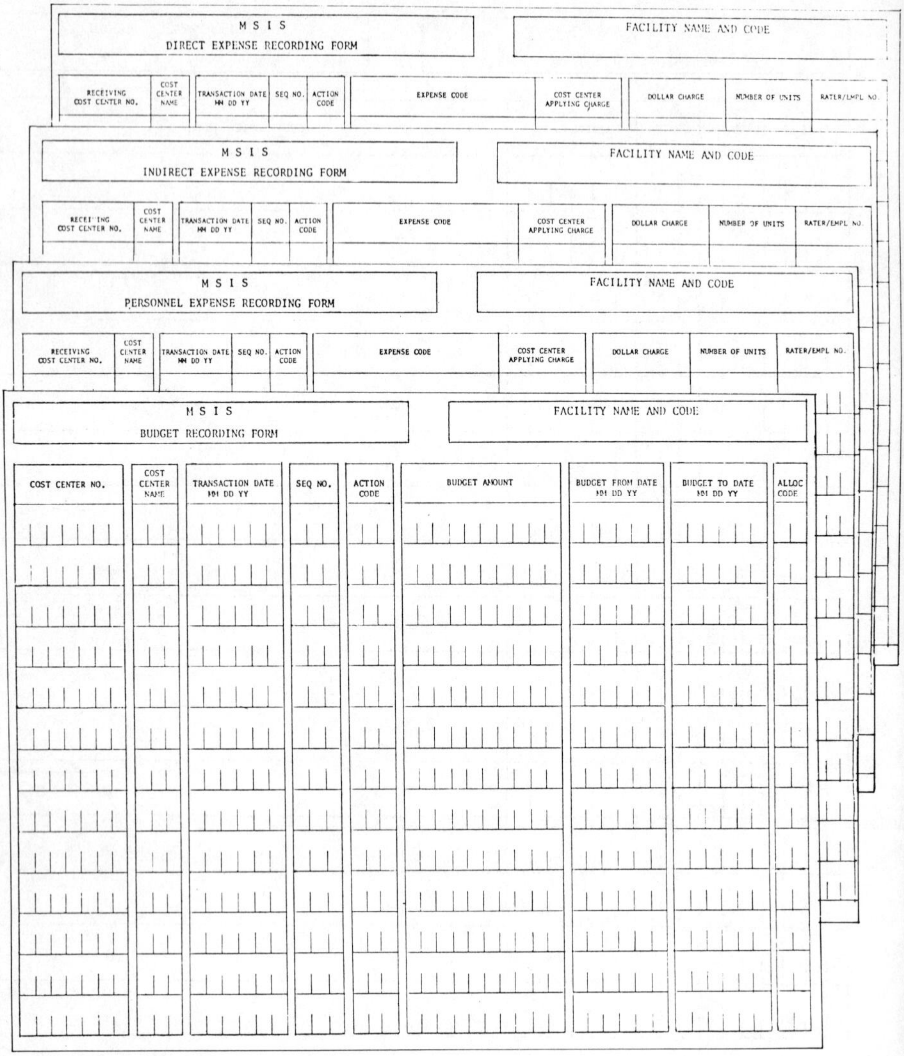

Figure 43   Budget Recording Form.
Figure 44   Direct Expense Recording Form.
Figure 45   Indirect Expense Recording Form.
Figure 46   Personnel Expense Recording Form.

```
NSIS STARGEN OUTPUT


                                                    TABLE 1

                                                                          WT2 = TOTAL DOLLARS
  ROWS = .RATER                        COLUMNS = TOTAL HOURS AND          WT3 = TOTAL HOURS
                                            COSTS FOR RATERS             ME1 = RATE PER HOUR


                              ROW
                TOTALS        SUMS   KEY
            I------------I
PSYCHI-I      20000I       20000   WT2
ATRIST I       2000I        2000   WT3
A      I    10.00000I    10.00000  ME1
            I------------I
PSYCHI-I      20000I       20000   WT2
ATRIST I       2000I        2000   WT3
B      I    10.00000I    10.00000  ME1
            I------------I
PSYCHI-I      20000I       20000   WT2
ATRIST I       2000I        2000   WT3
C      I    10.00000I    10.00000  ME1
            I------------I
PSYCHO-I      16000I       16000   WT2
LOGIST I       2000I        2000   WT3
A      I     8.00000I     8.00000  ME1
            I------------I
PSYCHO-I      16000I       16000   WT2
LOGIST I       2000I        2000   WT3
B      I     8.00000I     8.00000  ME1
            I------------I
PSYCHO-I      16000I       16000   WT2
LOGIST I       2000I        2000   WT3
C      I     8.00000I     8.00000  ME1
            I------------I
SOCIAL I      12000I       12000   WT2
WORKER I       2000I        2000   WT3
A      I     6.00000I     6.00000  ME1
            I------------I
SOCIAL I      12000I       12000   WT2
WORKER I       2000I        2000   WT3
B      I     6.00000I     6.00000  ME1
            I------------I
SOCIAL I      12000I       12000   WT2
WORKER I       2000I        2000   WT3
C      I     6.00000I     6.00000  ME1
            I------------I
MENTAL I      10000I       10000   WT2
HEALTH I       2000I        2000   WT3
WORKR AI     5.00000I     5.00000  ME1
            I------------I
MENTAL I      10000I       10000   WT2
HEALTH I       2000I        2000   WT3
WORKR BI     5.00000I     5.00000  ME1
            I------------I
COLUMN        164000       164000  WT2
  SUMS         22000        22000  WT3
             7.57143      7.57143  ME1
```

Figure 47   Personnel Cost.

hour session with Psychologist A. Using the data from Table 1, the individual setting rates may choose to add to the $50 facilites and support expense one of the following:

- A charge for 1 hour of psychologist A's time—$8.00.
- A charge for 1 hour of an "average" psychologist's time—still $8.00.
- A charge for 1 hour of a "composite" professional's time—in this case $7.57.

When rates are set, it is possible to begin to look at the cost effectiveness of various types of treatment modalities.

OBTAINING OUTPUT REPORTS—STATISTICAL AND LIST RETRIEVAL CAPABILITIES OF MSIS

Report Types

To make the data stored on patients and staff activities readily usable, MSIS has provided three report-producing mechanisms.

First, most data forms submitted with information about a patient result in a report automatically produced by the computer. For example, when the Admission Form is submitted, the computer produces an Admission Note. When a Mental Status Examination Record is submitted, the computer produces a narrative report reflecting the items recorded on the form. No special action is required for receipt of these reports; once the computer has accepted the data as being valid, the report is automatically produced.

Second, several commonly used reports have been specially programmed. For example, the Patient History Report provides a compact mechanism for examining the series of movements and status changes that a patient has experienced during his course of treatment in the facility. A Summary of Direct Services Received lists in chronological order the services which a patient has received. To receive such a report, an MSIS participant simply requests it by identifying the patient involved and the time period in which he is interested.

Third, to supplement these standard reports MSIS has designed two simple techniques that allow a user to design and request reports tailored to his own needs: the Generalized Alphabetic Listor (GALS), which is used to produce lists of patients who satisfy specified criteria, and the Statistical Report Generator (STARGEN), which is used to produce cross-tabulations. (These two techniques are described below.) Once the content of a report has been determined by the requester, a simple set of statements informs the computer which data items to select and how to organize the needed report. Thus a variety of reports and lists can be generated to satisfy the wide requirements of different disciplines and different facilities.

Variables

In one report it is possible to request data items that were collected from a variety of different forms. For example, a table that would answer the question "What is the age distribution of patients who have received group therapy in this facility in the last month?" would require demographic information such as age and sex which was gathered on the Admission Form and data on the types of service rendered which were gathered on the Direct Patient Services Form.

In addition to the data items (or variables) available directly as they are recorded on the MSIS forms, new variables are derived from combinations of data items. For example, to answer the question above, the patient's date of birth (recorded on the Admission Form) and today's date are used to derive the variable "the patient's current age." This derived variable would be used in determining the age distribution of the patients in question.

A wide collection of such variables may be utilized in producing reports. To assist the user in the design of reports, MSIS has developed a Glossary which contains a list of all the variables available to GALS and STARGEN. Each entry in the Glossary describes the variable giving the information needed for its use in the report including a description of the source document from which the variable comes, the technical name, and the number of the variable.

GALS

The General Alphabetic Listor (GALS) is a simple language used to produce lists of data from selected patient records.

Components of a GALS List

A sample listing might look something like Figure 48. The report displays the patients who were admitted during a given time period (June 20, 1971 to July 31, 1971), who are of a certain age (between 25 and 45) and who are not married or remarried. Further, the list is sorted by religion, and the number of patients falling into each category is indicated. In addition, the report lists each patient's case number, name, admission date, birth date, sex, household composition, action code on admission, diagnosis, and religion.

There are four items that may be specified in a GALS listing. Each of these is a "statement" in the GALS language:

1. At the top of the page, a specified heading is printed (Heading Statement).
2. The variables on the page are laid out according to a user-specified ordering—in this case, case number, patient name, and so on (List Statement).
3. The list of patients selected is ordered in a specified way—in this case, alphabetically, within religion (Sort Statement).
4. Only patients who meet specified criteria appear in the listing—in this case, a patient is included in the list if he was admitted in a particular time period (June 20, 1971 to July 31, 1971), is between the ages of 25 and 45, and is either not married or remarried (If Statement).

PATIENTS ADMITTED IN THE PERIOD BEGINING 6/20/71 AND ENDING 7/31/71 WHO ARE BETWEEN THE AGES 25-45, AND NOT MARRIED OR REMARRIED (SORTED AND COUNTED BY RELIGION)

CASE NUMBER	PATIENT NAME	ADMIT DATE	BIRTHDATE	PATIENT SEX	HOUSEHOLD COMPOSITION	ACTION CODE	DIAGNOSIS	RELIGION
0080153	ARDEN, HELEN	710708	301112	FEMALE	CHILDREN	READMIT	29520	PROTESTANT
0080111	CISTER, PAUL	710629	360909	MALE	ALONE	READMIT	29530	PROTESTANT
0080146	CONRAD, ELLEN	710707	400113	FEMALE	PARENTS	FIRST	29530	PROTESTANT
0080132	GILBERT, EDWARD	710704	251116	MALE	ALONE	READMIT	00000	PROTESTANT
0080139	GRAND, PETER	710707	340822	MALE	OTHER REL	READMIT	30310	PROTESTANT
0080160	GRIMES, PETER	710711	330630	MALE	ALONE	FIRST	30310	PROTESTANT
0080096	HOLDER, KAREN	710624	300423	FEMALE	ALONE	FIRST	29574	PROTESTANT
0080131	HUNTER, ELLEN	710703	430821	FEMALE	PARENTS	READMIT	29510	PROTESTANT
0080159	NADER, EVELYN	710709	450607	FEMALE	PARENTS	READMIT	29590	PROTESTANT
0080086	PARKER, PHILIP	710621	280324	MALE	SIBLING	READMIT	29530	PROTESTANT
0080183	POTEA, GEORGE	710716	270330	MALE	ALONE	READMIT	29150	PROTESTANT
0080100	SASTON, ROBERT	710624	270217	MALE	ALONE	FIRST	30300	PROTESTANT
0080192	SOLEN, GRACE	710719	270722	FEMALE	PARENTS	FIRST	29590	PROTESTANT
0080130	TORDE, JUNE	710702	300201	FEMALE	PARENTS	FIRST	29530	PROTESTANT

14

CASE NUMBER	PATIENT NAME	ADMIT DATE	BIRTHDATE	PATIENT SEX	HOUSEHOLD COMPOSITION	ACTION CODE	DIAGNOSIS	RELIGION
0080089	CANTOR, ALBERT	710621	261220	MALE	PARENTS	FIRST	29590	JEWISH
0080201	CONLEY, MARGARET	710721	271111	FEMALE	ALONE	FIRST	29590	JEWISH
0080189	FASTEN, MARK	710718	320808	MALE	SIBLING	READMIT	00000	JEWISH
0080172	GORDON, NANCY	710714	360531	FEMALE	OTHERS	READMIT	29530	JEWISH
0080085	GREEN, ALAN	710621	300704	MALE	SIBLING	FIRST	29590	JEWISH
0080107	MARK, JOSEPH	710627	331207	MALE	ALONE	FIRST	30327	JEWISH
0080186	O'NEIL, BERTRUM	710717	360205	MALE	ALONE	READMIT	00000	JEWISH
0080129	PUOEL, ANNA	710702	331110	FEMALE	CHILDREN	FIRST	30040	JEWISH
0080102	SAX, JOHN	710625	290512	MALE	PARENTS	FIRST	29530	JEWISH
0080169	SWINTON, BRUCE	710713	330120	MALE	PARENTS	READMIT	30310	JEWISH

10

Figure 48   GALS list.

STAtistical Report GENerator (STARGEN)

When cross-tabulations (counts of the number of times in which specific values of two or more variables simultaneously occur, for example, ethnic group and current age) are required, the STARGEN language is used. Each STARGEN-produced report* is a table in which the entries in the columns give the categories of one variable (e.g., "ethnic group") and the entries in the rows given the categories of a second (e.g., "current age"). Specification of more than two variables is possible and results in the generation of several tables.

The request for a STARGEN report specifies which variables chosen from the Glossary are to be displayed. For example, the table in Figure 49 is a sample STARGEN report.

The table displays the age and ethnic group distribution of patients in residence in January, 1973. The columns of the table are the categories of the variable "ethnic group" (White, Negro, American Indian, Puerto Rican, Oriental, missing, unknown, other). The rows of the table are the categories of the variable "current age" (0 to 11, 12 to 15, 16 to 20, 21 to 64, 65 and over, missing).

Each cell in the table gives the counts of the patients in residence during the specified time falling into the corresponding specific combination of categories of each of the two variables. For example, in the first cell are the number of patients in residence in January 1973 who are both white and under 12 years of age.

Each cell in a STARGEN table can contain many separate entries. Normally the first entry is the "raw" count or number of patients who fall into the cell, labeled "RAW" in the last column (KEY) of the table.

Usually two other entires appear in each cell, the first of which represents the percent of the row total accounted for by the cell (raw per cent of the row—RPR). The second represents the percent of the column total accounted for by the cell (raw per cent of the column—RPC). In addition to the raw frequencies, row totals, column totals, and overall table totals appear on the right and across the bottom of each report under the heading "SUMS."

Thus in the table illustrated, 71 patients (RAW) who are both white and under 12 represent 1.042% of all the white patients (RPR) and 47.651% of all patients under 12 (RPC).

Under user-specified conditions, the types of entries in each cell may be changed or eliminated (Figure 50). Other types of entries for a cell and instructions on exercising these options are explained in the user manual.

---

* STARGEN is basically a program developed by the Multi-State Information system to allow MSIS users without extensive data processing training to use a proprietary software package, CROSSTABS II. Technically trained users who wish to utilize additional capabilities (for example, chi-square tests) may do so.

Group	Key	0-11	12-15	16-20	21-64	65 AND OVER	MISSING	ROW SUMS
WHITE	RAW	71	126	315	4261	2025	15	6913
	RPR	1.042	1.849	4.624	62.542	29.723	0.220	100.000
	RPC	47.651	37.389	57.587	67.421	79.756	13.889	68.130
NEGRO	RAW	57	124	136	1355	376	7	2055
	RPR	2.774	6.034	6.618	65.937	18.297	0.341	100.000
	RPC	38.255	36.795	24.863	21.440	14.809	6.481	20.550
AMERICAN INDIAN	RAW		2		15			17
	RPR		11.765		88.235			100.000
	RPC		0.593		0.237			0.170
PUERTO RICAN	RAW	16	59	34	239	8	4	360
	RPR	4.444	16.389	9.444	66.389	2.222	1.111	100.000
	RPC	10.738	17.507	6.216	3.782	0.315	3.704	3.600
ORIENTL	RAW		1	1	23	3		28
	RPR		3.571	3.571	82.143	10.714		100.000
	RPC		0.297	0.183	0.364	0.118		0.280
MISSING	RAW	5	20	56	412	122	82	697
	RPR	0.717	2.869	8.034	59.110	17.504	11.765	100.000
	RPC	3.356	5.935	10.238	6.519	4.805	75.926	6.970
UNKNOWN	RAW			1	1	1		3
	RPR			33.333	33.333	33.333		100.000
	RPC			0.183	0.016	0.039		0.030
OTHER	RAW		5	4	14	4		27
	RPR		18.519	14.815	51.852	14.815		100.000
	RPC		1.484	0.731	0.222	0.158		0.270
COLUMN SUMS	RAW	149	337	547	6320	2539	108	10000
	RPR	1.490	3.370	5.470	63.200	25.390	1.080	100.000
	RPC	100.000	100.000	100.000	100.000	100.000	100.000	100.000

MSIS STARGEN OUTPUT — PATIENTS IN RESIDENCE - JAN. 1, 1973 — ROWS = ETHNIC GROUP — COLUMNS = CURRENT AGE — TABLE 1 — PAGE 1- 1 — 21 MAR 1973

Figure 49   STARGEN report.

These then are the items that may be specified when requesting a STARGEN report:

1. *A Report Title.* The title, which should be fully descriptive of the report, may be a maximum of 216 characters in length (including blanks).

2. *Patients to be included in the tabulation.* The requester must specify which subset of the patient population he wishes to include in the requested cross-tabulation. Four options are provided:

- Patients admitted during a specified period (the user supplies the dates of the period).

- Patients terminated during a specific period (the user supplies the dates of the period).

```
MSIS STARGEN OUTPUT                                    TABLE     1
PATIENTS IN RESIDENCE JAN 1973
                                                       PAGE  1-  1
                                                       30 MAR 1973

                                      CURRENT AGE
ROWS = ETHNIC GROUP          COLUMNS = OUTPATIENT
                                      GROUPING

                                      65 AND            ROW
          0-11    12-15   16-20   21-64  OVER   MISSING  SUMS  KEY
        I-------I-------I-------I-------I-------I-------I
WHITE   I    71I   126I   315I   4261I  2025I     15I   6813  RAW
        I-------I-------I-------I-------I-------I-------I
NEGRO   I    57I   124I   136I   1355I   376I      7I   2055  RAW
        I-------I-------I-------I-------I-------I-------I
AMRICANI I         2I          I    15I        I        I     17  RAW
INDIAN  I        I       I       I       I       I       I
        I-------I-------I-------I-------I-------I-------I
PUERTO  I    16I    59I    34I    239I     8I      4I    360  RAW
RICAN   I        I       I       I       I       I       I
        I-------I-------I-------I-------I-------I-------I
ORIENTLI         1I     1I    23I     3I        I     28  RAW
        I-------I-------I-------I-------I-------I-------I
MISSINGI     5I    20I    56I    412I   122I     82I    697  RAW
        I-------I-------I-------I-------I-------I-------I
UNKNOWNI        I       I     1I     1I     1I        I      3  RAW
        I-------I-------I-------I-------I-------I-------I
OTHER   I        I     5I     4I    14I     4I        I     27  RAW
        I-------I-------I-------I-------I-------I-------I
COLUMN      149    337    547   6320   2539    108   10000  RAW
SUMS
```

Figure 50   STARGEN report.

- Patients born during a specified period (the user supplies the dates of the period).
- All patients in the MSIS file for that facility.

The specifications of the selected patients automatically appear under the title of the report.

3. *Column Variable.* The column variable determines the set of categories which comprise the headings to appear on the top of each column of the report. (The categories included in each variable are those described in the Glossary entry for that variable.)

4. *Row Variable.* The row variable determines the set of categories comprising the row headings which appear vertically on the left side of the report.

5. *Additional Variables.* A table broken down by more than two variables may be specified, causing a separate table to be produced for each category within the third variable. For example, if the table in Figure 50 were requested further broken down into two diagnostic categories, those with or-

ganic brain syndromes and those with all other diagnoses, then two tables would be produced, one which showed ethnic group by age for those with organic brain syndromes and one which showed ethnic group by age for patients with all other diagnoses.

Using GALS to Amplify STARGEN Tables

An important use of GALS is the identification of the individuals who appear in a particular cell in a STARGEN report. For example, a researcher might become interested in studying the mental illness of adult American Indians in his facility and might therefore request a list of the 15 patients who fell into the cell American Indian/21-64 from a STARGEN table. Using GALS, he could request additional data on the patients, for example, marital status and education, and have the list sorted alphabetically by ward within building for ease in locating the patients.

EXTRACT File

The MSIS data base is composed of all the information accumulated about each patient. Individual patient record reports are generally produced on the basis of the most current data in the data base. Generally, however, neither GALS nor STARGEN reports are produced directly from the "current" data base; a "snaphot" of the file as it exists on the last day of the preceding month is taken. This separate file, the Extract File, is used in running the GALS and STARGEN reports. This file contains a subset of the information in the data base and is created for each facility within MSIS. Of course Extract Files can be created more frequently, and also many reports can be run against the data base directly. The program that scans the MSIS data files creates on the Extract File one record for each episode for each patient. An episode is defined as all the information about a patient starting with the date of admission and ending either with a termination data (indicating that the episode is complete) or with the date the Extract File was created.

In addition to the data items found on the forms such as age and sex, some derived variables are calculated by the Extract program and are included in the Extract File. Other derived variables are calculated by STARGEN during the creation of a report.

SERVICES TO PARTICIPANTS

One of the chief responsibilities of MSIS personnel is to insure that MSIS participants are aware of the capabilities of the system and are able to utilize them fully. Liaison personnel assigned to mental health programs visit locations and consult with administrators and clinicians to ascertain their needs and to insure that the capabilities of the system are utilized whenever possible in meeting these needs. They help introduce new forms and procedures into facilities and advise the management of both the MSIS and the facility on educational program needs.

Classes, seminars, and orientation sessions are conducted by MSIS personnel. In addition, MSIS prepares manuals describing how each component of the system is used. (At the end of this chapter, manuals containing further details are referenced.) Users are kept informed of changes and extensions to the sytem through periodically issued information bulletins.

Technical assistance is provided to users who may encounter problems in processing the data; staff assistance is provided in developing and in interpreting special reports; and the programming staff advises users on programming problems and lends assistance in developing special data-collection applications.

MSIS forms are printed in bulk, stored at Rockland, and may be purchased by system users.

Legal Protection of the Data

Because of the great concern over the issues of privacy and confidentiality of the data stored in the computers at MSIS, safeguards have been instituted to limit access to the records. Technical precautions have been taken within the system to prevent unauthorized access to files: internal programming checks and the use of identifying codes insure to the greatest extent possible the integrity of the data. Physical security measures have been taken at MSIS and are in effect at terminal locations.

A special enabling statute (Section 79j) of the Civil Rights Law of New York State directly declares that the MSIS records collected on patients from other states and stored at Rockland Research Institute are confidential. The bill provides that the records and information stored in the system by facilities located outside New York are not open to inspection by an agency or individual other than the agency or facility submitting them and are not subject to subpoena in any court, tribunal, or administrative agency. (See Part IV for fuller discussion of confidentiality and legal safeguards.)

BIBLIOGRAPHY

E. Laska, E. Varga, J. Wanderling, G. Simpson, G. Logemann, and B. K. Shah, *Diseases of the Nervous System,* **34,** (Aug./Sept., 1973), 294–305.

E. Laska, G. Logemann, G. Honigfeld, A. Weinstein, and R. Bank, *Evaluation,* **1,** (Fall 1972), 66–71.

E. Laska, A. Weinstein, G. Logemann, and R. Bank, *Intern. J. Psychiatr.,* **9,** (1969), 637–460.

E. Laska, G. Simpson, and R. Bank, *Compr. Psychiatr.,* **10,** (1968), 136–146.

E. Laska, A. Weinstein, G. Logemann, R. Bank, and F. Breuer, *Compr. Psychiatr.,* **8,** 476–490 (December 1967).

MSIS Manual #21.100, "The Admission System," 1971.

MSIS Manual #21.200, "Movement/Status System," 1971.

MSIS Manual #22.000, "The Patient Progress Sub-System," 1971.

MSIS Manual #23.000, "The Psychotropic Drug Sub-System," 1972.

MSIS Manual #23.500, "Direct Patient Services System," 1972.

MSIS Manual #23.600, "The Indirect Services System," 1973.

MSIS Manual #46.100, "GALS," 1973.

MSIS Manual #31.000, "STARGEN," 1971.

R. L. Spitzer and J. Endicott: *Am. J. Psychiatr.,* **131,** (1974), 5.

R. L. Spitzer, J. Endicott, J. Cohen, and J. L. Fleiss, *Arch. Gen. Psychiatr.,* **31,** 197–203. (1974).

R. L. Spitzer and J. Endicott, *Arch. Gen. Psychiatr.,* **24,** (1971), 540–547.

R. L. Spitzer and J. Endicott, *Intern. J. Psychiat.,* **9,** (1969), 604–620.

R. L. Spitzer, J. Endicott, and J. L. Fleiss, *Comp. Psych.* (1975), in press.

Technical Overview

MSIS is a modular and flexible computerized information system. The technical aspects reviewed here include brief descriptions of the software that allow the data to be input, processed, stored, secured, and retrieved and of the hardware needed to run the system. Detailed documentation is, of course, available to users of MSIS.

DATA FLOW

The pattern of data flow is illustrated in Figure 1.

Data Gathering.   Many forms are completed by psychiatric care givers during the various phases of the patient's course of treatment. These documents are gathered at a central location. Optical mark page readers and/or key punches are used to prepare data in computer-readable form for submission to the MSIS computers (Figure 2).

Data Analyzed, Processed, and Stored.   The interrelationships given in Figure 1 are the subject of this chapter and are discussed more fully below. The data base is patient oriented and historically complete: once an item is recorded in the files, it is kept until the patient is no longer receiving service, at which point the record is "archived." Processing is batch oriented: groups of similar

179

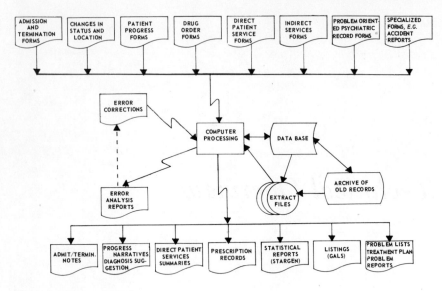

Figure 1   Pattern of data flow.

transactions are processed in several job streams. Jobs are entered into the job stream either from the in-house card reader or from card readers located at terminals.

Data Retrieved.   Output reports derived from the data submitted and generated by the jobs are either printed at Rockland or transmitted to line printers at the terminals.

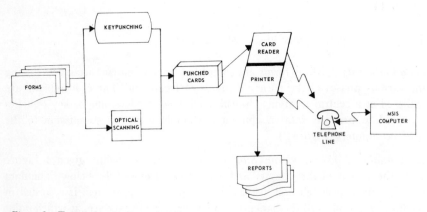

Figure 2   Terminal to computer data flow.

HARDWARE REQUIREMENTS

The MSIS can operate on any IBM 360 or 370 model with a minimum of 150K user region. In its current version, it may be operated under MVT or MFT, with or without HASP. All programs are written in PL/1 and BAL. At the Information Sciences Division, processing is presently accomplished on a 1.5 megabyte 360/67 under OS MVT with HASP.

MSIS is terminal oriented as well as batch oriented. The most frequently used terminal is currently an IBM 2780 MODEL 1 equipped with a card reader (400 cards per minute maximum) and line printer (200 lines per minute maximum). The card reader can handle all valid EBCDIC codes and has an RPQ (special feature designed for MSIS) to substitute a "$" for non-EBCDIC codes; thus the card reader never stops on a data check. The line printer has the 63-character set. Terminals other than the 2780 are readily supported under HASP Dial-In.

To prepare input, a terminal facility may use an IBM 1232 optical mark page reader linked to an IBM 534 Model 3 key punch. MSIS conventions utilize scan forms with 80 segments, and the scanner converts these to 80 punched columns. However the optical scanner is not an essential piece of equipment, since MSIS data may be key punched as well. The usual terminal configuration employs an IBM 029A stand-alone key punch. MSIS forms design standards assure that the bottom two segments on a form, always found in card columns 79 and 80, uniquely identify each input type.

MSIS SOFTWARE

MSIS software was designed to accept the data from the forms, group similar types of data for efficient processing, store relevant information in patient files, return a variety of standard output reports (Figure 3), and allow the user to request specific information about individual patients or groups of patients.

Data Input. MSIS FRONTEND (Figure 4) is a series of programs designed to receive data transactions and route them to appropriate processing programs. Data can be submitted by users with no knowledge of the Operating System Job Control Language. The FRONTEND consists of three programs that operate together to facilitate the submission of data and to optimize execution while guaranteeing security of the data. All data-base transactions are saved and are processed as a batch one or more times a day; retrieval transactions are immediately submitted for processing.

Each of the three programs of the FRONTEND performs security checks to

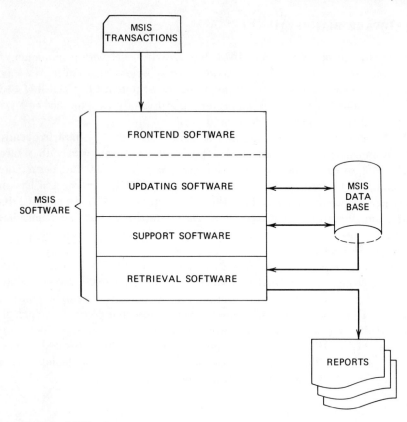

Figure 3   MSIS software.

protect the data bases from unauthorized access. In addition, all three provide restart capability in case of system failure at any point; data are never lost. The Data Collector program expedites the collection of data transactions, keeps track of data submissions, and controls priorities among transactions. The Batcher then groups all like transactions which access the data base for execution and creates one job for each type for each data base. The Batcher operates as an OS batch job and generates a history of all jobs and a summary of jobs by number and type. The Queue Manager program allows the computer operator to control the job queues.

MSIS FILES

Data sets kept within MSIS include the patient record files, information regarding data transmission, backup of data bases, retrieval files, reference tables, and program libraries (Figure 5).

Data Bases.   Each facility is allocated a distinct group of data sets to hold its patient record files. Because the data areas are physically distinct, the data from each facility are protected from unwarranted access and accidental damage while the computer system processes files from another facility. The data are kept in direct access format to facilitate the updating of individual patient record files and for retrieval.

Data bases are accessed using the DL/1 (Data Language 1) Data Base Management of the IBM Information Management System (IMS). DL/1 supports hierarchical data structures on either direct-access or serial-access devices and may be obtained without utilizing IMS. Briefly, the DL/1 file contains a

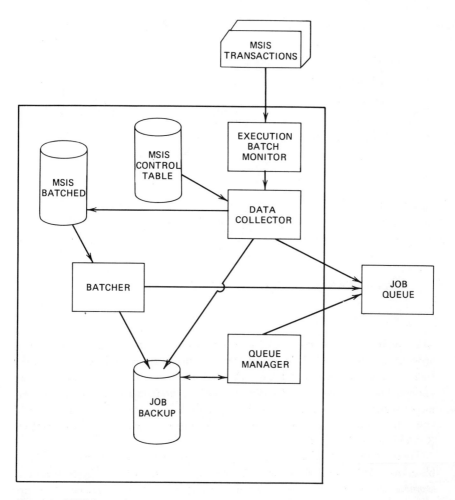

Figure 4   MSIS frontend.

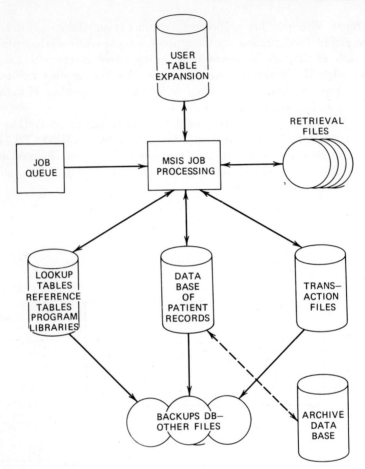

Figure 5   MSIS job processing.

tree structure of small records or segments, each identified by a key. The file is ordered on the key of the apex of the tree, the root segment. DL/1 uses the Index Sequential Access Method (ISAM) to store data physically on disk; various DL/1 subroutines handle the packing and unpacking of logical segments within the physical record. DL/1 extends the length of the initial ISAM entry by chaining records within an Overflow Sequential Access Method (OSAM) area (Figure 6).

There is generally a one to one correspondence between segments of the data base and MSIS input systems, although some systems create more than one segment and some segments can be accessed by more than one system. Data are

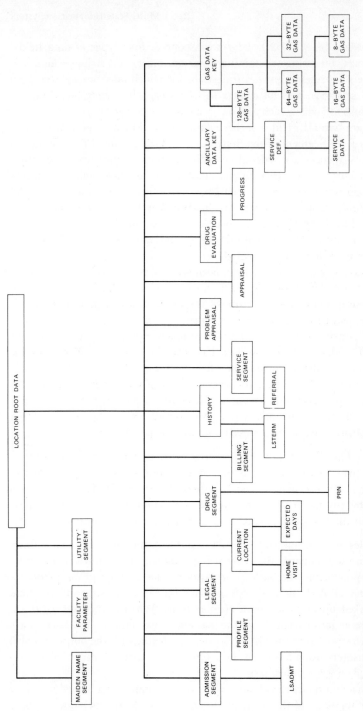

Figure 6   MSIS master file—hierarchical data structure.

185

stored in the data base in packed format as one of four types of data fields: character strings; bit strings containing binary numbers; bit strings containing binary numbers representing codes (questions for which only one answer from a list may be selected); and bit strings in which each list represents a yes/no choice (questions for which each answer in a list may be selected).

MSIS utilizes two DL/1 files of three data sets each to store patient records. The Location Root Segment of the first DL/1 file; the Master File, is designed so that patients' records are ordered according to their administrative locations within the facility. A two-level facility structure is assumed and records are ordered first on building/service, then on ward/unit, and then alphabetically within ward/unit. Duplicate names are further ordered by case number. The second DL/1 file is the Case Index ordered on case number. The Case Root Segments each contain the patient's building and ward and an indication of where the Master File record is located.

Unique processing options that have been selected by particular facilities are indicated in a Facility Profile in each data base. The Facility Profile also contains a description of the structure of the facility including, if desired, the names of administrative units and of personnel.

An archive system stores records on tape of inactive patients terminated prior to a prespecified date. The active data base (on-line) contains all records for patients admitted, active or terminated after the prespecified date. The archive system can return to the active data base a record of a readmitted patient. An exception list is produced during an archive run if a patient is found to have been readmitted and is currently active. An archive Extract is created so that cumulative statistics requiring archived data may be performed.

Other Files. The Transaction File records every update transaction and includes a statement of each error discovered and the disposition of the transaction (whether it was accepted, rejected, or partially accepted). The Transaction File created by any particular updating job is the input to the Error Analysis Program. This file is usually purged after a reasonable period of time.

Backup Files are maintained to show the status of the file at particular times in the past, in the event that the current file is damaged and must be restored. To facilitate processing, the backup program creates a direct physical copy of the ISAM and OSAM files. A cycle of back-up tapes is used, and the data bases are backed up by group on a regular basis. When it is necessary to restore a data base, jobs executed against that data base since the last backup are automatically respooled to the HASP queues and rerun with the output spooled to in-house printers using a feature of the Queue Manager. Library backups are also performed on a scheduled basis.

Retrievals from a hierarchical data base involve complicated logical decisions regarding the topology of the segments to be selected. MSIS includes mapping programs to generate, from the hierarchical file, unit record files suitable for processing. The principal unit record file of patient information is the Extract File, which contains one record for each episode for each patient in a data base; a number of individual Spinoff Files exist and the Merge System collates the files.

Look-up tables which specify processing parameters are needed by many of the MSIS programs. For example, the Drug System requires the Formulary of the facility and a Doctor/Rater Table indicating the physicians who are allowed to write drug orders. The Expansion File is an Indexed Sequential Access Method (ISAM) data set used as a look-up table for converting codes to texts. Coded texts including message formats can thus be modified without the necessity for recompiling the programs. Also, keeping the expansions on one general file guarantees that the various programs using the same fields in the data base generate the same texts.

Dictionary files are used by the two retrieval systems, the Statistical Report Generator and the General Alphabetic Listor (described below).

The Report Monitor System utilizes a table indicating the mnemonics of reports that can be requested and the module names of the system within the program libraries needed to generate those reports.

PROGRAM STRUCTURE

To maintain program consistency and to insure uniform input transactions and output reports, a series of general subsystems was developed. MSIS software interacts with these general systems (see Figures 7 and 8).

ONE STEP Procedure Supervisor.   All updating subsystems (e.g., Census, Progress) are executed under the ONE STEP Procedure Supervisor, a BAL program. Executing the equivalent of an OS Proc in a single OS step, ONE STEP thereby reduces the OS overhead involved in step initiation and termination. ONE STEP passes OS parameters to the programs, handles completion codes and conditional execution, updates the Operator's Display Active Tables, and stops the job if one of the programs ends prematurely.

Scanfins.   All data recorded on mark sense forms are interpreted through Scanfins, which allows a programmer to specify the fields to be read from the form, the locations of the response within each field, and how the response is to be translated. The output of the translation process is a PL/1 array containing binary fixed and bit string variables filled with the values read from the form.

Error Analysis and Message System.   Each time data are entered, a record of the transaction and the disposition of the transaction are written to the trans-

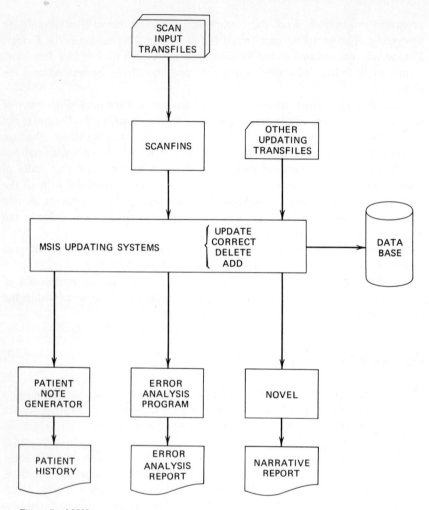

Figure 7   MSIS program structure.

action file. Using this file as input, the Error Analysis Program produces a uniform series of messages to the user describing what happened to the data.

NOVEL.   NOVEL is a high-level programming language developed at ISD to facilitate the generation of narratives from coded responses such as those appearing on a questionnaire. It is used, for example, to generate narrative reports from responses on clinical forms such as the Mental Status Examination Record and the Psychiatric Anamnestic Record. NOVEL has been used widely outside of the MSIS system.

Patient Note Generator (REPGEN).   This system facilitates the programming of notes and reports for individual patients. The system consists of a PL/1 precompiler and a series of subroutines and modules of PL/1 code. The report is assumed to have the format of an itemized list of a series of columns. The notes and reports which can be generated using the system are composed of many instances of one basic syntactic element, consisting of column number, a translation indicator, and a datum to be printed.

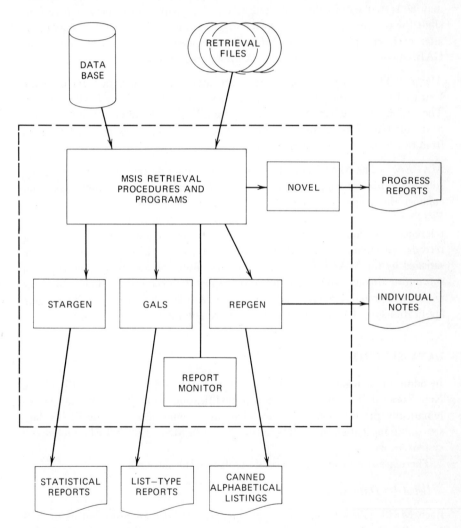

Figure 8   Retrieval software.

STARGEN.   The Statistical Report Generator (STARGEN) generates cross-tabulations. STARGEN is a supervisory function added to CROSSTABS, a proprietary software package purchased from Cambridge Computer Associates. A predefined dictionary of MSIS variables allows the user to request relatively sophisticated statistical reports with a minimum of programming effort.

GALS.   The Generalized Alphabetical Listing System (GALS) provides the ability to display lists of information. The information is displayed in columns, the entries within a selected column may be sorted, entries in another column may be sorted within the first, and so on. The display of information can include the counts of entries thus sorted together, and/or a page break may occur after each group. Information may be expanded into text, according to the GALS dictionary, and appropriate headings may be specified.

Merge.   The Merge System permits the user to include data from both the Extract File and other Spinoff Files in the same STARGEN or GALS request. The system takes effect at the point where STARGEN or GALS requests the next unit record to be considered for the report. Merge presents records taken from two or more files as a single record.

MAVEN.   The MAVEN system consists of a data description language and a subroutine library supporting a variety of application-programming tasks that enhance the preparation and verification of character data and that streamline FRONTEND data-base operations. Application programs that use MAVEN reference a dictionary for descriptions of the structure and content of incoming records. Auxiliary tasks such as error analysis and message formatting are satisfied by the MAVEN subroutine library. Both the dictionary language and subroutine linkages can be extended to support the processing of fields that cannot be adequately described and processed with standard routines. The major applications of MAVEN allow users to store and retrieve idiosyncratic data.

DATA SECURITY

In addition to legal safeguards that protect MSIS data [section 79(j) of the New York Civil Rights Law], several modifications of both HASP and OS automatically protect against accidental or intentional access to any MSIS data set containing patient data. These together with MSIS FRONTEND make the system secure.

There are several levels of security built into the software.

Level 1   Data Set Level

Each MSIS data set containing patient data is password protected in the OS sense. Standard OS password protection routines have been modified so that the password is automatically checked and does not require operator intervention.

Level 2   Job Execution Level

Before a job accessing MSIS data can be properly executed, the OS password protection routine performs a match between the JOBNAME and the Data Set Name being accessed. The proper combination of Remote Number and Facility Number must be present.

Level 3   Date Entry Level

MSIS users do not submit jobs; rather they submit data headed by a ..F card. The MSIS FRONTEND cuts the actual jobs thereby controlling the generation of JOBNAMES. It performs a check between the facility code submitted on the ..F card and the remote number of the terminal submitting the job. HASP has been modified to stamp the Remote Number on the ..F card along with the date and time.

Level 4   RJE Level

The user trying to access MSIS data must conform to the JOBNAME conventions. A further HASP modification prevents a user at one remote from accessing the data from another remote. HASP matches the remote number in the JOBNAME field (which is required) against the remote number of the terminal submitting the job. Access is only permitted if they match.

Level 5   SIGNON Level

A required PASSWORD field has been added to the standard HASP SIGNON card.

3 Applications of MSIS in Existing Mental Health Programs

The true value of a computerized psychiatric information system is not in the use of the computer as a mere repository of information, but in the use of the computer as an analytical tool in the scrutiny of the stored data. Rather than returning information in an approximation of the form in which it was entered, the computer can prepare data in a variety of formats, for example, comparisons, lists, juxtapositions, and counts, to play a more viable role in such areas as planning, forecasting trends, and reviewing treatment.

An information system so used can meet important needs in administrative and clinical modes. Administrative uses of data from an automated system can be as diverse as internal program management, accountability reporting to funding bodies, fiscal control, and everyday housekeeping, accounting, and business functions. Clinically, the computer enables the professional to communicate with himself and/or his peers through structured records and offers assistance in diagnostic evaluation of patients. Supervisors, administrators, and external review groups may utilize the data for monitoring functions such as assessing patient progress and goal attainments, tracing patient movement through a treatment program, establishing the efficacy of particular forms of

193

treatment, tabulating cost of treatment, and assuring equity of service patterns throughout a catchment area.

In Part 3 a series of papers are presented to illustrate some applications of the Multi-State Information System and to demonstrate how information gathered from routinely used MSIS input forms is used for a variety of purposes. On the administrative level, Levine describes a support system that enables a facility to track patient flow and monitor treatments rendered. Astrachan describes the utility of data in administrative decision making by offering feedback on task accomplishments and by providing an information base useful for planning and program development, distributing resources among service components of a facility, and determining areas of unmet need. The use of MSIS data as an evaluative tool is described by Tischler who scrutinizes such factors as admission and treatment data by demographic variables. Siegel and Goodman analyze data across four mental health centers to evaluate the attainment of process objectives.

Clinical uses are described in several papers: Weiner shows how data can be used for utilization review; Endicott and Spitzer show the use of two MSIS forms for history gathering and for making diagnostic assessments; and Simpson describes a drug-monitoring system and its potential. A new form of psychiatric record keeping oriented toward problem descriptions and their resolutions is described by Pulier who also proposes a broadened form of program and treatment evaluation.

The MSIS system is used not only by individual facilities but as part of State and National Programs. Cobb describes the uses of data for state-level planning. The adaptation of the MSIS system to Indonesia and to Israel are also discussed.

ADMINISTRATION

Support System for the Multi-State Information System

MICHAEL S. LEVINE

The greater utilization of mental health facilities, a phenomenon spurred by the increased availability of services through community mental health centers and the greater variety of treatment modalities, has been responsible for growing demands for accountability to insure effective and efficient service delivery. Automated patient information systems have been designed that assist mental health facilities in carrying out mandates for accountability reporting, evaluating programs, and monitoring patient flow.

The success of any such computerized system is dependent, in large measure, upon the effectiveness of a support system. A support system is the set of uniform procedures and guidelines an institution develops to assist staff in effectively handling the flow of patients from intake to termination and the associated data needed for clinical and administrative purposes.

The implementation of automation and computer-based processes is preceded by a feasibility study, a systems study, and analysis and a programming design, as has been detailed in Part 1. An effective support system is a by-product of the complete systems study of a facility's total organizational structure and prerequisite to computerization. The systems study must provide an understanding of how patients enter and move through the system with the possible treatment alternatives delineated. Administrative and clinical data requirements of the institution need to be clearly identified and documented. During the design of the support system, there must be communication between data and systems design staff, and staff who will be assisted (or supported) by the system being established. In this way, the system can be implemented and priorities set for the gradual introduction of different components of the support system.

CONNECTICUT MENTAL HEALTH CENTER SUPPORT SYSTEM

The Connecticut Mental Health Center (CMHC), a joint venture of the State of Connecticut and Yale University, is a community mental health center in New Haven, Connecticut, meeting federal funding criteria by offering inpatient and outpatient care, full and partial hospitalization, emergency services, and consultation and education. The Center was linked to the Multi-State Information System (MSIS), a computerized system, on July 1, 1969. Implementation of MSIS was preceded by a systems study in order to establish various patient flow and data needs.

The systems study indicated the need for establishing uniform administrative–clinical procedures in handling individuals seeking services at CMHC and also for reducing the number of forms then being used to collect patient information. It also found that there were many portals of entry into CMHC and each entry point had different procedures for admitting patients for service. In addition, the study determined that once an individual was placed into a program, there was no uniform way in which the patient's activity was monitored.

As a result of these findings, a "support system" was developed to establish uniform admission procedures and to develop methods of monitoring patient activity. Furthermore, in order to implement the MSIS effectively and to insure the utilization and effectiveness of the support system, responsibility was placed in a centralized unit, the CMHC Statistics Center.

CMHC ADMISSION SYSTEM

As an outgrowth of the findings of the systems study, the CMHC admission system was designed (Figure 1).

The admission system covers three basic steps: intake, clinical evaluation, and disposition. This system was designed to facilitate the evaluation of individuals seeking services at CMHC, to reduce the possibility of duplication of

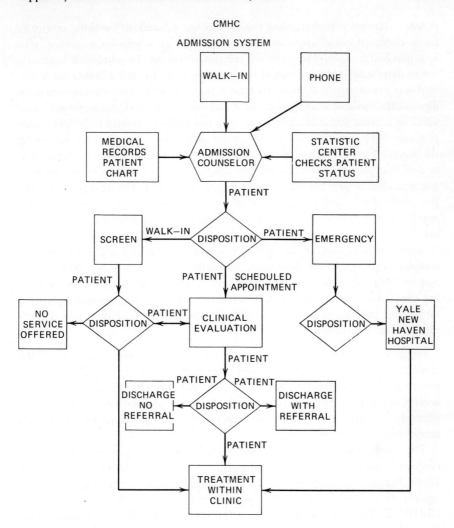

Figure 1   CMHC Admission System.

admission procedures, and to insure that the utilization of the MSIS is effective.

The number of portals of entry into CMHC was reduced and an Evaluation Unit was established for the most used portal. While the description of the admission system (below) is of the Evaluation Unit at the main building of CMHC, other portals of entry, such as the satellite field stations have established similar procedures.

Intake.   An individual entering the CMHC as a "walk-in" seeking service or for a scheduled initial appointment is directed to an admission counselor, who is a psychiatric aide. The primary responsibilities of the admission counselor are to determine if the individual needs emergency care and whether the applicant was previously or is currently known to the facility. If emergency care is indicated, the medical officer of the day is immediately alerted. An applicant's previous or present status is ascertained by a counselor manually searching an alphabetic master index for a CHMC identification number and then telephoning the Statistics Center for an immediate report of the patient's present status, a 2- to 3-minute procedure. Active patients are then referred to their clinicians or, if not available, to another clinician serving as a screener. For new patients, and previously discharged patients, the admission counselor completes MSIS Admission Form to item 33, and a CMHC Supplemental Admission Form (Figure 2).

After this brief contact, the applicant is usually seen by a staff clinician for a complete evaluation. All forms are forwarded to an admission clerk who is responsible for establishing new charts and obtaining old charts for the evaluating clinicians. The admission clerk also places the noncomputerized admission forms into the patient's chart and attaches the partially completed MSIS Admission Form to the outside cover.

Clinical Evaluation and Disposition.   During the evaluation session, the clinician's primary responsibility is to determine the patient's needs and to arrive at a clinical decision on how to help the patient. The clinician may choose among requiring the patient to return for further evaluation, discharge without referral, discharge with referral to another resource, or transfer to a CMHC service unit.

The data needs connected with the evaluation are provided for by the clinician completing the MSIS Admission Form, Items 34 to 37, the MSIS Direct Patient Service Form, and CMHC Initial Contact Form (Figure 3). The clinical disposition is recorded by completing the MSIS PER-C form and a CMHC Transfer or Discharge Form (Figure 4). The CMHC Transfer/Discharge Form is then forwarded to the evaluation unit system clerk, who in turn completes the MSIS Change in Status Form. All MSIS forms are forwarded daily to the Statistics Center for processing. The noncomputerized forms are incorporated into the patient's chart by the unit system clerk.

In the event that a patient is admitted directly to a unit, other than the Evaluation Unit, within the main building, the admitting clinician is responsible for having the patient seen by the admitting counselor to be registered. If the patient is confined to an inpatient unit and is unable to be formally registered, then the system clerk of the unit calls the admitting clerk to obtain a CMHC number. The admitting clerk issues a CMHC number, or uses the

```
CMHC SUPPLEMENTAL ADMISSION FORM                    UNIT:                        C2-4
Patient's Last Name C5-7          First              M   CMHC # C8-13

                                                  Transaction: C20
Date:(C14-15) Mo:         (C16-17) Day:    (C18-19) Yr:  1= 1st Adm.      2= Readm.

1.  CHIEF COMPLAINT:




2.  Did alcohol lead to Pt's. adm.?(C21):  1= Yes        2= No
3.  Did Drug Problem Exist? (C22):  No     0= Unknown     1= Heroin, Opiates

    2= Hallucinogenics   3= Amphetamines   4= Barbituates   5= Mixed drug problem   6=Other
                                                                                      Drug
4.  Present Employment Status of Pt: (C23)
    1=Employed full time                       4=Unemployed 1 - 12 mos.
    2=Employed part time                       5=Unemployed more than 12 mos.
    3=Unemployed less than 1 month             6=Not in Labor Force
5.  Is Pt. Head of Household?.(C24):  1= YES     2= NO
    a)  If no, who is the Head of Household? Name:
           Relation to Pt: (C25) 1=Spouse   2-Father   3=Mother   4=Sibling   5=Relative   6=Other
    b)  Usual occupation of Head of Household? (C26-28)
    c)  Highest Greade Completed: (C29-30)
6.  Have any principal relatives received previous psychiatric care? (C31)   1= YES     2=NO

7.  How many children does Pt have living with him?(C32-33)
8.  When did applicant move into present house or apartment(Check last move only) (C34)
    1=Less than 1 yr      2=More than 1 yr but less than 5 yrs
        3=More than 5 yrs but not always                4=Always lived in this house
9.  If moved less than 5 yrs ago where did applicant live  5 yrs ago(C=35)
    1=Same city     2=Other city,       3=Other State          4=Foreign Country
                     this State
10. Is Pt. sensitive to any drugs? (C38)  1= YES     2= NO
                    If YES specify which drug(s) (C39-74)

11. Is Pt. being assisted by a Federal,State,City or Community Agency?  Yes____   No____
                    If YES specify which one(s):
12. Pt's Family Physician:  None____   Don't know ____
        Name:                                  Address:

13. Who to contact in case of emergency?
    Name:                                     Relationship:

    Address:                                  Phone:
```

Figure 2   CMHC Supplemental Admission Form.

CMHC INITIAL CONTACT

INTERVIEWER:_____   NAME:_____

DATE:____/____/____   CMHC#_____
        mo.   day   yr.

_____

REASON FOR VISIT:

PERTINENT PSYCHIATRIC AND MEDICAL HISTORY:

TREATMENT PLAN:

DISPOSITION:

DATE:_____

                              (1)   Internal Referral:
                                    Transfer to Unit #_____

                              (2)   Discharged with Referral to:_____

                              (3)   Discharged no Referral

                                    _____
                                    Supervisor's Signature
(Use blank sheet of paper for additional comments - must indicate date, patient's CMHC #
and supervisor's signature)

MR 11/73

Figure 3   CMHC Initial Contact.

previous CMHC number of the patient if he is a readmission, and indicates in
the admission log book that the patient has not been registered. This enables the
admission counselor to follow up to insure that the patient eventually is
registered.

TRANSFER OR DISCHARGE FORM

C.M.H.C. NO. ☐☐☐☐☐☐   DATE ___/___/___

PATIENTS NAME _____   TEL. _____

STREET _____   CITY _____

FROM   TRANSFER WITHIN UNIT   TO

GCD ☐ HWH ☐ DRUG ☐ DEP. ☐ RESEARCH ☐   GCD ☐ HWH ☐ DRUG ☐ DEP. ☐ RESEARCH ☐

UNIT _____

CLINICIAN _____   UNIT _____ CLINICIAN _____

FROM   TRANSFER OUT OF UNIT   TO

GCD ☐ HWH ☐ DRUG ☐ DEP. ☐ RESEARCH ☐   GCD ☐ HWH ☐ DRUG ☐ DEP. ☐ RESEARCH ☐

UNIT _____

CLINICIAN _____   UNIT _____ CLINICIAN _____

FROM   DISCHARGE FROM C.M.H.C.   TO

GCD ☐ HWH ☐ DRUG ☐ DEP. ☐ RESEARCH ☐   GCD ☐ HWH ☐ DRUG ☐ DEP. ☐ RESEARCH ☐

UNIT _____   CLINICIAN OR AGENCY _____ (IF REFERRAL MADE)

CLINICIAN _____

APA DIAGNOSIS _____

CONDITION ON DISCHARGE

(E) ☐ RECOVERED   ☐ UNIMPROVED   ☐ WITHOUT MENTAL DISORDER

☐ MUCH IMPROVED   ☐ WORSE   ☐ UNDETERMINED

☐ IMPROVED

REASON FOR DISCHARGE OR TRANSFER

(F) ☐ NO FURTHER CARE BY THIS FACILITY INDICATED   ☐ CAPACITY TRANSFER   ☐ OUTPATIENT WITHDREW: FACILITY NOT NOTIFIED

☐ TYPE SERVICE UNAVAILABLE THIS FACILITY   ☐ DISCHARGE AGAINST MEDICAL ADVICE   ☐ FACILITY NOTIFIED PATIENT MOVED

☐ OTHER   ☐ FACILITY NOTIFIED OTHER

DISCHARGE WITHOUT REFERRAL

(G) ☐ NO FURTHER CARE INDICATED   ☐ FURTHER CARE INDICATED BUT UNAVAILABLE   ☐ PATIENT UNRESPONSIVE TO REFERRAL

DISCHARGE WITH REFERRAL (MARK ALL WHICH APPLY)

(H) ☐ MENTAL HOSPITAL   ☐ NURSING HOME   ☐ PRIVATE PSYCHIATRIST

☐ MENTAL HEALTH CENTER   ☐ RESIDENTIAL TREATMENT CENTER   ☐ OTHER PRIVATE PHYSICIAN

☐ GENERAL HOSPITAL PSYCHIATRIC UNIT   ☐ PARTIAL HOSPITAL DAY   ☐ SCHOOL, SPECIAL CLASS

☐ GENERAL HOSPITAL OTHER UNIT   ☐ PARTIAL HOSPITAL OTHER   ☐ COURT OR CORRECTION AGENCY

☐ VA HOSPITAL   ☐ PSYCHIATRIC CLINIC   ☐ PUBLIC HEALTH OR WELFARE AGENCY

☐ INSTITUTION FOR RETARDED   ☐ DAY TRAINING CENTER   ☐ VOLUNTARY AGENCY

☐ OTHER RETARDATION FACILITY   ☐ SHELTERED WORKSHOP   ☐ CLERGY

☐ HOSTEL/HALFWAY HOUSE   ☐ VOCATIONAL TRAINING   ☐ OTHER

DESTINATION HOUSEHOLD (MARK ALL WHICH APPLY)

(I) ☐ RETURN TO USUAL HOUSEHOLD   ☐ WITH CHILDREN   ☐ WITH OTHER RELATIVE

☐ WILL LIVE ALONE   ☐ WITH SIBLINGS   ☐ WITH OTHER

☐ WITH SPOUSE   ☐ WITH PARENT   ☐ INSTITUTION

☐ UNKNOWN

Figure 4   Transfer or Discharge Form.

201

TREATMENT-MONITORING SYSTEM

The other component of the CMHC support system is the monitoring of patients in treatment (see Figure 5). The monitoring of active patients while in treatment at CMHC is performed by system clerks. They aid the clinical staff not only in obtaining patients' charts but also in completing the necessary forms that are required by CMHC. Each major service component has at least one system clerk whose functions are to complete the MSIS Change in Status Form as indicated by the clinician, maintain an active patient card file, assist clinicians in completing the Direct Patient Service Form, when necessary, and route all MSIS forms to the Statistics Center.

The system clerks are assigned to a unit and are supervised by a service manager. The service manager is responsible to the unit chief who is a senior clinician.

CMHC STATISTICS AND RECORD CENTER

The CMHC support system is a uniform set of procedures carried out by support and clinical staff, as assisted by the Statistics and Record Center. Prior to

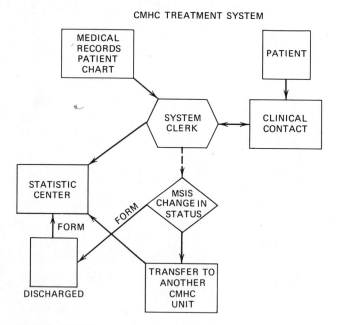

Figure 5   CMHC treatment system.

the implementation of MSIS, the Statistics and Record Center functioned as a single entity. The systems study pointed out the necessity for a concentrated effort to coordinate the implementation and utilization of MSIS, and the two components were physically separated, although they are still considered one department with a single chief.

Record Center. The Record Center is staffed by the Medical Record Librarian, a typist, and a clerk. The Record Center's primary responsibility is the monitoring, review, and storage of CMHC patient charts. In addition, this area is responsible for handling all patient correspondence and related manual matters.

Statistics Center. The Statistics Center is located in its own quarters and houses the terminal that links CMHC with the MSIS. This area is staffed by the Chief of Statistics and Record Center, a stenographer, clerk, terminal operator, and key punch operator. The staff's primary functions are to process all MSIS forms used at CMHC, encourage and facilitate the utilization of MSIS, monitor all patient activity and status, design standard administrative–management reports using the MSIS, and fulfill all statistical requests that utilize the CMHC data base at the MSIS.

The Statistics Center acts as the focal point for both the total operation of the MSIS and the support system at CMHC. In these dual roles, its tasks are accomplished through automated, semiautomated, and manual processes. The integration of the support system and MSIS has expedited agency functioning and enhanced utilization of MSIS, as the support system and MSIS operate in-coordination with each other.

A variety of computer-produced output reports generated by MSIS have been utilized by the facility. A Direct Patient Service Listing is produced at the beginning of each month giving all direct service contacts (kept or canceled) from the beginning of the fiscal year to the present (Figure 6). The listing is presented in CMHC case number order, sorted by date of contact, indicating type of service rendered, unit rendering service, clinician, and present status. The report is useful as part of the patient-monitoring system in conjunction with the Patient Log Book (described below).

The system clerks are aided by the Statistics Center in monitoring their caseloads via several kinds of MSIS reports. One example of this is the 90-Day No Show Listing (see Figure 7) which indicates all patients who have not been seen in 90 days, lists the date of the last contact, the unit the patient is presently in, and the clinician who last saw the patient. Through this mechanism, the system clerk can then check with the clinician, if available, to find out his plans with regard to the case. This listing maintains a continuity in the overall management of cases within any given CMHC ambulatory unit.

Case Number	Patient Name	Contact Date YrMoDay	Cancel- lation	Service #1	Unit	Terminated Date or Active	Contact Clinician
000210	XYZ	730705	-	101	100	Active	012
"	"	730801	-	310	130	"	"
"	"	730808	-	310	130	"	"
"	"	731009	-	310	130	73/10/09	"
001535	ROE	730803	-	101	100	Active	432
"	"	730910	-	310	131	"	"
"	"	731012	-	310	131	"	"
"	"	731212	By Pt	310	131	"	"
017532	DOE	731203	-	101	100	"	304
"	"	731218	-	101	100	"	"
"	"	731229	By Clinician	101	100	"	"

Figure 6   Listing of CMHC patients and direct patient service information for July 1 to December 31, 1973.

The Statistics Center is also involved in obtaining output reports from MSIS that satisfy internal administrative needs and reports submitted to groups outside the center.

The CMHC Patient Log Book (Figure 8) is produced through the Statistics Center and is maintained manually with information obtained from MSIS forms. It was implemented simultaneously with the MSIS at CMHC and has proven in many respects to work very effectively with this system. In particular, the Patient Log Book prevents duplication of admitting procedures which could be a costly process. The Patient Log Book is a record of all CMHC patient ad-

CONTACT CLINICIAN	CASE NUMBER	Patient NAME	Most Recent Contact Date	Move Date	Unit Number
001	14321	QST	Sept. 1, 1973	730703	130
001	12305	RSV	Sept. 4, 1973	730501	130
001	10534	HRM	Oct. 1, 1973	730203	130

Figure 7   Active patients in Unit XYZ without a contact in 90+ days.

Page 1a

CMHC #	Pt's Initials	Date Admitted	Date Re-Admitted	To Unit Admitted	Clinician	Date Terminated

Page 1b   PAGE__

Date Transf.	Date Readm.	Unit	Clinician	Date Termi-nated	Date Transf.	Date Readm.	Unit	Clinician	Date Termi-nated	Date Transf.	CMHC #

Figure 8   Sample page of Patient Log Book.

missions, readmissions, internal transfers, and discharges by patient case number. The information that goes into the Patient Log Book comes directly from the MSIS Admission and Change in Status Forms. The data are entered daily by a clerk in the Statistics Center. The Patient Log Book has been able to establish a cohesiveness to the entire system in such a way that the data fed into the MSIS is virtually error free. Thus the Patient Log Book not only provides patient status but acts as a quality control mechanisms that weeds out errors prior to processing via the MSIS. One basic advantage of this procedure is confidence in the reliability of data stored on the MSIS computers, thus resulting in a more assured utilization of the output.

A major role for the Chief of Statistics and Record Center is as an in-house consultant to CMHC staff. Through formal educational seminars and consultation activities, the potentials of MSIS and the possible utilizations of output reports are discussed. All new employees, especially trainees or residents who will become the major source of MSIS input information, participate in a formal training seminar to discuss their roles in the total system. The seminars focus on why and how CMHC participates in MSIS and on ways clinicians can make use of the system for research and administrative management needs. These seminars provide a jumping-off point from which future discussions will develop.

The Chief of Statistics and Record Center also provides consultation services through participation in a number of ongoing task forces at CHMC. He acts in an advisory capacity aiding the task forces in understanding what kinds of data are available through MSIS, helping obtain the necessary information to complete the assignment of the task force, and assisting in the interpretation of the output. This analysis of the data depends greatly on understanding how both the CMHC Support System and the MSIS operate. This type of involvement is critical not only because the task forces cover a variety of institutional concerns from utilization review to designing better management techniques to monitoring patient and clinician activities within one particular clinical unit, but also because of the diversified membership of these groups from clinical supervisors to support staff. This approach provides a wide and active exposure to MSIS.

All CMHC staff are encouraged to participate in utilizing the MSIS both from a research point of view and from an administrative-support point of view. The prevailing philosophy of the Statistics Center has been that usage begets usage; the more staff understand and use MSIS, the more they and other colleagues will use the system.

CONCLUSION

CMHC maintains an effective support system based on a uniform design that is successfully utilized because of its comprehensive approach and strong administrative backing. The support system has integrated MSIS as an important means of storing and processing data and as a source for a number of output reports that provide for admissions, patient monitoring, and administrative needs.

The general concepts of this support system can be applied to any other institutions of similar size which have similar service objectives. The system that has been presented is flexible—should any new programs be implemented or shift in pattern of service occur, the entire support of the system does not have to be redesigned but in essence only modified to incorporate changes.

A well-designed support system protects the investment of time, energy, and money expended to implement a computerized information system.

BIBLIOGRAPHY

Computers in Psychiatry, supplement to the *Am. J. Psychiatr.*, **125**, (1969), 7.

Information Sciences Division, Research Center, Rockland State Hospital, *The Multi-State Information System: An Overview*, The Research Foundation for Mental Hygiene, 1973.

M. S. Levine, "*Utilization of MSIS at CMHC*," paper presented at the Southern Regional Conference on Mental Health Statistics, New Orleans, October 1973.

United States Department of Health, Education and Welfare, Public Health Service, Health Services and Mental Health Administration, *Health Resources Statistics*, Washington, D.C., 1970.

ADMINISTRATION

MSIS Input
to Administrative Decision
Making

BORIS M. ASTRACHAN

The tasks of administration are to direct the work of the organization to the attainment of its ends, to maintain and modify organizational structure to accomplish tasks, to allocate resources in response to organizational needs and to the changing relationship of organization to environment, and to anticipate and plan for the future. To do this work the administrator needs data. The psychiatric administrator should know who is being served, how served, by whom served, with what efficiency, with what result, and at what cost? The administrator requires base-line data: data that help monitor the work of the organization and data that can be utilized as part of a feedback mechanism within the organization to change expectations and move the organization toward better accomplishment of its defined tasks or toward new tasks as they arise. The administrator must continually evaluate the organization, its inputs, resources, processes, and outcomes.

To evaluate, one must measure. Those who work in areas which are being studied must accumulate the data to make meaningful the process of evaluation. Initially all individuals and sectors within the organization need to be educated as to the value of self-examination and to understand that the major goal of

207

such work is to assist the organization in attaining its articulated goals, not to enable "big brother" to spy better on individuals and groups.

The act of measuring begins to change the organization. The commitment of the organization to the process of evaluation is a major administrative decision with wide-ranging ramifications. The most significant administrative uses of data are (1) to provide feedback to sectors of the organization to help them accomplish their tasks and (2) to provide an information base for planning and program development. Data are utilized to maintain institutional focus on tasks and to continually clarify and refine organizational goals.

Brenner (1) identifies four levels of informational systems. The first is an institutional information system that provides data on (1) the characteristics of the populations served, (2) the services provided, (3) costs, and (4) progress of the clients within the system, and which enables one to examine the relationship between these areas.

The next level allows for the comparison of data gathered about clients in level 1 to relatively stable demographic characteristics of the population so that rates about those served may be calculated (e.g., number of patients per unit population, number black, white, male, female patients per unit population, age characteristics of patient group compared to age characteristics of population, etc.).

The third level examines posttreatment characteristics of the population served and thus provides information about outcome (symptomatic improvements, social improvements,) and about outcomes in relation to the population served (as above).

The final level relates the population served and outcomes to economic indicators and also permits examination of the interaction of institutional services with services provided in other community systems (including industry, courts, rehabilitation services, etc.). Thus the institution and its services can be examined in relation to the changing socioeconomic characteristics of the community.

The Multi-State Information System provides many of the characteristics of a first-level informational system. Base-line demographic data on people who are served is easily available. The system also collects information about clinical issues, although such material currently remains less useful because of continuing difficulty in identifying which information is most relevant to clinical practice and to clinicians and patients in decision making. Information on services provided is available through the system (type and modalities of service, medication, etc.) as are patterns of utilization (via collection of data about contacts). A cost system has not yet been incorporated into the Multi-State Information System, but experimental work in this area continues. Progress of patients through the system is currently monitored by counting, but not yet by measuring meaningful change. The utilization of cross-tabulations and various computer programs allows for the examination of the relationship among patient demographic characteristics, some patient clinical data, services provided, and patterns of utilization.

The system can easily accept data about population demographic characteristics so that meaningful rates may be obtained. The data within the system can be utilized for the development of patient outcome studies (e.g., to identify patient groups, examine entry characteristics, count episodes of treatment, etc.) and the system could relate to larger-scale ecological studies.

Data are available and easily retrievable for transmission throughout the organization to help sectors accomplish their defined tasks.

The Multi-State Information System is a system in process. Currently it provides the administrator with increased power to study his organization and to examine the relationship of some patient characteristics to various treatment interventions and to some community characteristics. More importantly, it awakens the organization to issues of measurement, to beginning the practice of articulating individual and institutional goals, and to examining process and progress.

One must always be aware that the Multi-State Information System or any information system is of value only so long as it enables individuals and the institution to monitor and enhance work and to ask those questions that improve service. Its value is limited if no questions are asked. Its value is problematic if the information is collected solely to please funders and only answers the questions others pose. It is detrimental if staff reify data, if they believe that what is collected and transmitted substitutes for careful and continual examination and questioning.

ADMINISTRATIVE USES OF DATA AT THE CONNECTICUT MENTAL HEALTH CENTER

Pre-Multi-State Information System

The Connecticut Mental Health Center is a vastly different organization today than when it first opened. It's structure is dramatically changed. The clinical organization has gone through several modifications so that it hardly resembles what it was at the opening 8 years ago. In all of this painful work of restructuring and reordering priorities and services, the collection and utilization of data has been of fundamental importance.

When the Connecticut Mental Health Center first opened in July of 1966, it was expected that approximately 1200 patients per year would be served. In the first year 1800 patients were served and by March 1967, extensive waiting lists developed. For the period 1967 to 1968, the waiting list was already being utilized by February of 1968 and 2400 patients were served. Staff insisted that new personnel were required and felt harassed, overworked, and burdened by what they experienced as pressing clinical needs. However new resources were not forthcoming and a committee of the staff was charged with examining existing organizational structures and recommending appropriate changes.

The available data base was limited. Information had been painfully accumulated by hand and was, with even greater difficulty, retrieved and collected in order to give some portrait of who was being served by the Center and how individuals were being served. It became obvious that the Center was structured so that it might effectively function as a specialty hospital for referrals from professionals while it was required to accommodate increasing numbers of individuals seeking services who directly applied for such services (2). In 1968 the modal social class of patients was class 3, that is, lower middle class patients who often had referring physicians. Poor patients and black and Puerto Rican patients were underrepresented.

During the year of deliberations, the Connecticut Mental Health Center began to put people on the waiting list in January (1969) and once again 2400 patients were served by the Center.

The committee recommended that an intake system be developed for the Connecticut Mental Health Center. The system should immediately have the capacity to evaluate *all* new applicants for service, provide brief treatment for large numbers of these applicants, and, when appropriate, refer applicants for service to other treatment units within the Mental Health Center. Since it was understood that no new resources would be available for this reorganization, all ongoing programs were examined to determine how staff might be redeployed for such an intake service.

At that time the Day Hospital was the only resource available for the continuing treatment of chronic psychiatric patients within the Mental Health Center. This unit treated approximately 100 patients a year in an intensive group-oriented program. After careful evaluation the decision was made to take half of the personnel of the Day Hospital as a nucleus for an intake service and to utilize the remaining staff for a continuing-care service that would be able to deal flexibly with a chronic patient population through medication clinics, socialization and rehabilitation activities, and a variety of group therapies. It was estimated that approximately 80% of the patients who had previously been treated in the Day Hospital could be managed within the community by this new service.

Following this re-organization and the addition of a drug-dependency program the number of patients served by the Center rose dramatically to 3600 in the year 1969 to 1970. The number of chronic patients maintained in the Continuing Care Service rose to the approximately 250.

Multi-State Information System Use at the Connecticut Mental Health Center

The introduction of the Multi-State Information System within the Center almost exactly coincided with these changes in organizational structure. The cumbersome data collection system (a data collection system that proved to be of limited use because information could not be easily retrieved) was modified and a simplified computerized system adopted.

The continuing development of the intake system has been intimately interwined with the ability to utilize data generated by the Multi-State Information System. Since addresses by census tract are coded, the capacity to compare utilization data with census tract data exists (Table 1). Even a cursory examination of data indicates reasonably high service utilization rates within New Haven and the town of West Haven (Figure 1). Communities at a greater distance from the Center and its satellite clinics demonstrate significantly less utilization of services. Data were also analyzed comparing Center utilization patterns to state hospital utilization patterns, specifically in regard to the more chronic patients in treatment. We demonstrated that service utilization by discharged state hospital patients mirrored over all center utilization patterns. Thus the more chronic patients from more distant communities were being engaged in treatment at lower rates. These findings led directly to the development of a closer affiliation of the Center's programs with the state hospital which serves our patient population, including joint discharge planning for these patients. They have also led to proposals in conjunction with community groups and planning organizations for the development of direct service delivery programs at several additional community sites.

To be of value, data must be used by the administrator. This simple information comparing population served with population in one's service area emphasizes to the administrator and staff that a facility, any facility, has a consumer population and that the consumer population comes from some region, lives there, returns there. Such data may sensitize the administrator to community. Where it is? How are communities bounded, served by transportation? What are their characteristics, what other institutions serve them, and so on. At the grossest level, the ability to generate data comparing population served to population in the service area and to make it available to Unit Chiefs alerts them to the tasks of the organization and to the questions, whom do we serve, how well do we serve, and whom are we *not* serving?

Several years ago both available data and information from Spanish-speaking staff and Spanish-speaking community leaders made it quite clear that the Center was not serving its area's Puerto Rican population. Some of the staff insisted that Spanish-speaking individuals underutilized traditional medical

Table 1 CMHC Admissions by Place of Residence (Town) Compared to 1970 Census Population Figures (Utilization Rate)

Town	CMHC 1972–1973 Admissions	(1970 Census) Population	Rate per 1000	White No.	White Rate per 1000	Black No.	Black Rate per 1000	Other No.	Other Rate per 1000
Bethany	14	3,857	3.6	11	2.9	3	0	3	0
Branford	136	20,444	6.6	133	6.5	0	0	3	47.6
East Haven	176	25,120	7.0	174	6.9	2	42.5	0	—
Guilford	53	12,033	4.4	52	4.3	0	—	1	31.2
Hamden	222	49,357	4.4	207	4.3	15	9.3	0	—
Madison	41	9,768	4.1	41	4.2	0	—	0	—
Milford	170	50,858	3.3	164	3.2	3	6.7	3	23.0
New Haven	1939	137,707	14.0	1189	11.8	654	18.0	96	61.4
North Branford	45	10,778	4.1	44	4.0	0	—	1	66.6
North Haven	89	22,194	4.0	85	3.8	4	16.7	0	—
Orange	43	13,524	3.1	43	3.2	0	—	0	—
West Haven	624	52,851	11.8	581	11.6	33	12.1	10	55.5
Woodbridge	37	7,673	4.8	35	4.6	1	10.4	1	18.8
Ansonia	2	21,160	0.02	2	0.1	0	—	0	—
Derby	3	12,599	0.04	3	0.2	0	—	0	—
Seymour	7	12,776	0.5	6	0.4	1	24.3	0	—
Shelton	3	27,165	0.1	2	0.02	1	9.0	0	—
Other Connecticut	60	—	—	53	—	6	—	1	—
Out-of-State	4	—	—	3	—	1	—	0	—
Unknown	9	—	—	9	—	0	—	0	—
Total	3677			2837		724		116	

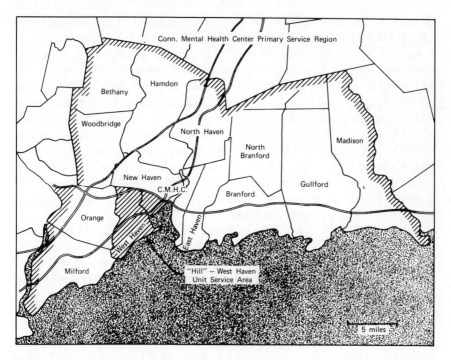

Figure 1   Connecticut Mental Health Center Primary Service Region.

and psychiatric resources, preferring "native healers." At that time the Connecticut Mental Health Center had the opportunity to examine data generated by the Hill Health Center as to the utilization of their medical resources. The Spanish-speaking population quite actively utilized medical services and even psychiatric resources when they were available within the context of a health center and when they were delivered by Spanish-speaking professionals and allied health professionals. Connecticut Mental Health Center data indicated limited use of its services while others were able to reach this important population group with relative ease. In collaboration with community groups, a Spanish Clinic within the Mental Health Center was developed. The establishment of this clinic has significantly increased the numbers of Spanish-speaking individuals served. Community requests for service were reinforced by data. Data sensitized staff to need, undercut resistance to change, and provided a rational framework from which to plan the reallocation of personnel.

Data collection leads to new questions and the need to examine data. If utilization rates seem acceptable, does that relax the manager? Hopefully not! Pies can be sliced in many ways and populations must be examined and reexamined. Age, sex, social class and diagnostic category are all important indicators in identifying those whom the institution served (e.g., the Connecticut Mental Health Center tends to serve young adults and underserves the aged.)

Rice (3, 4), an important student of organizational behavior, noted that when organizations have limited control of their boundaries (e.g., whom they will accept or reject for services; and who may be hired) there is a tendency to rebuild organizational boundaries deeper within the matrix of the organization. Thus colleges with open admissions often make the transition between first and second year an important boundary; state hospitals whose boundaries are controlled by tickets of admission (e.g., commitment papers) reserve scarce treatment resources to select populations and construct boundaries about them.

Equality of access may not guarantee equal utilization of institutional programs and data are needed that indicate the ways in which individuals are served once they get into the institution.

Illustrated in Table 2 are some important differences in regard to utilization of services in specific units by race. Data always raise questions. Are differential rates indicative of bias for or against a population group or do such rates indicate that in one area use is proportional to population, while in other areas overutilization occurs on the basis of special need?

Shortly after becoming Director of the Mental Health Center, I requested information about patterns of service within the Center. Material similar to this was generated (of course, we did not have the cross-tabulation capacity of the Multi-State Information System available then). The data indicated that one of the inpatient units was functioning as a remarkably restricted setting servicing primarily middle-class white individuals. Such data were made available to leadership and to staff on the unit with the insistence that the unit develop a structure that could accommodate poor patients, minority patients, and patients without resources and which would enable the unit to serve as a backup for other Center programs. We were able to accomplish these changes within 1 year, and the data indicate that inpatient service utilization now reflects overall center utilization patterns (see Table 2). We are currently examining utilization patterns in our psychotherapies section to try to understand why the rates of utilization are so different from overall utilization rates.

Thus at the grossest level the ability to generate and retrieve data enables an administrator to monitor programs and to examine whether targeted populations are being served and whether organizational tasks are being accomplished. The process of continual monitoring further allows the organization to examine whether agreed upon changes do in fact occur, whether innovations do indeed take place.

The use of the Multi-State Information System not only allows for the evaluation of a system and system changes, but also, in a limited way, for the monitoring of care. With the introduction of the contact form (Direct Patient

Table 2 *Utilization of Center Services by Race by Sex 1972–1973 Service Units*[a]

Race/Sex	Assessment	Psycho-therapies	Medication Clinics	Inpatient	Field Services	Drug Unit	All Other	Total	
								No.	%
White/male	902	457	254	307	159	438	67	2584	33.2
Nonwhite/male	157	60	58	85	59	475	58	952	12.3
White/female	1412	696	432	431	198	138	122	3429	43.9
Nonwhite/female	242	64	121	135	60	121	90	833	10.6
Total No.	2713	1277	865	958	476	1172	337	7798	—
Total %	34.8	16.4	11.1	12.3	6.1	15.0	4.3	—	100

[a] This table includes patients who were active on July 1, 1972 plus additions during 1972–1973 and patients who were active on June 30, 1973.

Service Form), individuals and groups of patients can be tracked through the system (Tables 3 and 4).

The high number of contacts in the Psychotherapy Sections represents both intensive contact and limited access. Note that if the intakes in brief therapy continue to rise without concommitant discharges, the Unit may become oversubscribed. It is possible to determine whether patients may move relatively freely between units and, if bottlenecks exist, where they exist. Thus, with this relatively simple data base, some examination can be made as to whether the institution is achieving its articulated goals of serving the community, whether patients are being served in the various units of the institution, and whether the units are accomplishing their tasks. It has been established that a major determinant of length of stay in any unit is the pressure to admit new patients; and one needs to consider whether length of stay reflects patient need or clinician or organizational need. Statistical issues must be examined in the light of service philosophy. Data point to areas which need study and do not provide all the answers.

The Multi-State Information System also has the capacity to monitor individual staff member performance and, even more importantly, to examine performance by type of group. Who serves patients, to what extent are various staff members interchangeable? Are egalitarian ideas about interchangeability of clinicians true or merely biased statements?

We have been carefully examining data about cancellation rates for various groupings of clinicians over the past year. Initially our data indicated wide differences between groups, with Master's and Doctoral level professionals having cancellation rates between 10 and 12%; nurses had cancellation rates of about 16% and psychiatric aids had rates up to 25%. More recent data indicate that professionals with Master's or Doctoral degrees have cancellation rates of 10 to 12%, whereas nurses and psychiatric aids have cancellation rates of 14 to 16%.

Table 3 CMHC Direct Patient Services by Selected Unit for July 1, 1973 to September 30, 1973. Number of Kept Appointments for Primary Service by Administrative Unit

Unit	No. of Contacts	No. of Patients[a]	No. of Contacts per Patients
Intake Assessment Evaluation[b]	1952	737	2.6
Brief Treatment	591	157	3.8
Individual Psychotherapy	2731	437	6.2
Group Psychotherapy	843	115	7.3

[a] Number of individual patients seen (unduplicated count) within each unit.

[b] Includes intake contacts with patients not registered.

Table 4 CMHC Movement/Census Report for Selected Units October 1 to October 31, 1973

CMHC Clinical Units	Last Patient Census	Adjust-ments[a]	New Admissions	Readmissions	Transfers In	Transfers Out	Dis-charges	Oct. 31, 1973 Patient Census
Intake assessment evaluation	365	−4	154	108	2	74	101	450
Brief treatment	91	+1	0	0	31	2	3	118
Individual psycho-therapy	325	+1	1	1	17	8	12	325
Group psycho-therapy	133	−1	0	0	4	1	10	125

[a] Adjustments due to reporting factors after last census is completed and distributed.

The Connecticut Mental Health Center is very dependent upon the utilization of psychiatric nurses and psychiatric aids in work with chroniclly psychotic patients. Do they treat the more regressed patients and the more recalcitrant patients? Is attendance and cancellation status in clinics serving the more chronic patients related to competency of clinician or to the status of the clinician? Are our patients perhaps being overtreated? Preliminary data from the pharmacy which has been studying issues of drug compliance and noncompliance indicate that approximately 10% of all prescriptions are never even picked up (5, 6). A preliminary breakdown of data for the chronic patient populations indicates that those patients that visit only once a month have a greater likelihood of picking up their medication than those who visit the Center more frequently (although over a period of time approximately one-third of the patients fail to pick up prescriptions).

It is extraordinarily important for the administrator to understand that data produce as many questions as are answered and that the planning process involves the analysis of data and not simply their collection and retrieval.

The ability to monitor clinical care can be extended to monitoring individual clinician performance. The spector of Big Brother is not only appalling to staff within an institution, but also causes concern to the administrator. The administrator must know how resources are utilized within the institution and must insist that guidelines be established for evaluating individual staff performance. However the administrator of health or mental health institutions must also be aware of the deleterious impact of an excessively bureaucratic structure on professional performance. Engel (7) described bureaucracy's effect on the autonomy of the physician. In her paper she empirically demonstrated that it is not bureaucracy per se, but the degree of bureaucracy that limits professional autonomy. Well-organized and well-run institutions can enhance professional competence by providing resources and organizational structures that enable professionals to attain their goals of providing excellent service. The excessively bureaucratized organization *often acts as though data were unavailable.* More and more rules and regulations are promulgated which cover increasingly specific areas of the professionals' work domain. The development of an effective data system can modulate this tendency toward excessive bureaucratization by providing information to the professionals that they need to carry out their tasks effectively. Thus, instead of the administrator's putting forth rules and regulations, it is possible to utilize data to compare staff behaviors with articulated goals. It is appropriate to share information to make the organization more open and more responsive. This use of information can assist staff to achieve their goals rather than lock staff into patterns of rule-defined behavior which may well be counterproductive. The administrator must help to define the work and then must create the conditions in which competent staff can do their work. The purpose of monitoring individual, group, and organizational behavior is not to punish deviance from defined norms or rules but rather to provide information so that organizational practice and organizational goals may become more congruent.

The organization, in order to survive, must justify its activities, not only to the community it serves, but to those who fund the services. This justification must be based upon meaningful information. To facilitate this work, administrators need to instruct staff that unless significant information is generated, programs cannot be defended and services will suffer. Thus data are of political value in justifying the activities of the intuition. Far more importantly, data are of value in the ongoing life of the institution because the need for justification increasingly requires staff members to examine programs, to monitor them, to measure their impact, and finally, when they are clearly enough defined, to begin to consider cost benefit analyses of programs based upon the identification of meaningful alternatives.

Within the Center, the Multi-State Information System helps in administrative activities. It provides a base for the development of the utilization review policies. It is of importance in evaluative research and in examining structure, organizational processes, and outcomes. The examination of outcome is still in a primitive stage, and it is not clear that the data most easily collected are the data that are most relevant. As yet, there are very limited tools to help evaluate indirect services. The Center has only begun to count them. Although systems for cost benefit analyses are being developed, such work demands clear definition of program and program goals as well as clear definition of meaningful alternatives. Initially the work in this area will be limited to examining (1) whether programs do indeed achieve stated aims and (2) the cost of such work.

Most importantly, data are of value to the administrator in assisting individuals throughout the organization to being thinking in terms of their goals and the processes utilized to accomplish those goals. Within the Center, data are currently utilized on a routine basis by senior administrators, by Unit Chiefs, by individuals involved in utilization review, by pharmacists, and increasingly by individual clinicians as they too become involved in monitoring ongoing programs and developing new programs to meet changing needs.

REFERENCES

1. M. H. Brenner, "Economics and Behavioral Perspectives," paper presented at Johns Hopkins University Symposium on Operations Research in Mental Health Service, January 17–19, 1974.

2. B. M. Astrachan, "Many Modest Goals: the Pragmatics of Health Delivery," *Conn. Med.,* **37,** (1973), 174–180.

3. A. K. Rice, *The Enterprise and the Environment,* Tavistock Publications, London, England, 1964.

4. E. Miller and A. K. Rice, *Systems of Organization*, Tavistock Publications, London, England, 1967.

5. A. J. Kubica and G. C. Gousse, "The Effects of an Outpatient Medication Compliance System on Improving Patient Services and Expansion of Pharmacy Activities in Community Mental Health Center," paper presented at Annual Mid-year Clinical Meeting of American Society of Hospitals and Pharmacists, 8th, New Orleans, La., December 10, 1973.

6. T. Swedenburg, "An analysis of Non-Compliance at a Community Mental Health Center," Hospital Pharmacy Residency Project Proposal, 1974.

7. G. V. Engel, "The Effect of Bureaucracy on the Professional Autonomy of Physicians," *J. Health Soc. Behav.*, **10**, 30–41 (1969).

EVALUATION

The Use of MSIS in Program Evaluation*

GARY L. TISCHLER, M.D.

There is currently a program-evaluation movement afoot in this country. In scope and magnitude, it threatens to outstrip "Women's Lib" and leave providers naked in the snows of primal accountability.

If the imagery is offensive one could go back in time to the temperate years of the mid-sixties when wealth abounded and programs sprouted from godheads—with hardly a Professional Standards Review Organization or utilization review requirement in sight. Something else was going on, however, which some may have experienced in the form of "confrontation." People had begun to believe in the premise set forth by Aristotle in *Politics*:

> Health of mind and body is so fundamental to the good life that if we believe that
> men have any personal rights at all as human beings, then they have an absolute
> moral right to such a measure of good health as society alone is able to give them.

This health rights movement, tempered by the emergence of a strong drive towards consumerism, was catalyzed by the recognition that health care had come to absorb over 7% of the gross national product. A corollary was the

* Preparation of this report was completed as a subsection to a study conducted in fulfillment of NIMH Contract Number: HSM-42-72-212.

realization that issues in regard to the delivery, organization, financing, and control of health have important political components. As a result, the self-regulation practiced in the past is giving way to more pluralistic systems of accountability that include the consumer, third-party agents, and the body politic.

Within this broader context, program evaluation emerges as a major vehicle for generating information needed to determine whether we the people are, indeed, "getting our monies' worth" from a considerable investment.

PROGRAM AND PROGRAM EVALUATION—SOME DEFINITIONS

Perhaps it would be useful to begin by attempting to define "program." In managerial science, the term is frequently used to describe an enterprise having inputs of both resources and conditions; technologic, managerial, and psychosocial processes for organizing inputs and relating them one to another; and outputs with standards for evaluating them. Of course the definition can be set forth somewhat less cryptically:

   I. A "program" is an organized *response* to reduce or eliminate one or more problems.
      A. The "response" involves *specifying* one or more *objectives*.
          1. "Objectives" are situations or conditions which are considered desirable. They may be either *ultimate* or *programmatic*.
              a. "Ultimate Objectives" are objectives desired in and of themselves according to the dominant value system.
              b. Programmatic Objectives" are statements of that particular situation or condition intended to result from the sum of the programs efforts.
          2. "Specifying includes a clear statement of:
              a. What the program objectives are
              b. When the desired condition is to be achieved
              c. In relation to the objectives, how much does one anticipate achieving
              d. Who is to benefit if and when the objectives are achieved
              e. Where is the program locus to be.
      B. The "response" involves the selection and performance of one or more activities.
          1. "Activities" are work performed by program personnel in the service of an objective.
      C. The "response" involves the acquisition and use of *resources*.
          1. "Resources" are personnel, funds, materials, and facilities available to support the performance of activities.

Programs generally come into being because of the identification of some needs. Goals are then promulgated by the agency responsible for meeting the defined needs. Management develops a program and an evaluation group is assigned to determine whether the stated goals are being met. This final stage brings us to the subject of the present discourse—program evaluation.

A number of organizational rationales have been offered in support of the evaluative endeavor. The most common includes the following:

1.   The determination of whether a program is meeting the needs for which it was designed.

2.   The comparison of different types of programs, program methods, and program approaches in terms of impact.

3.   The determination of program cost both in terms of money and human effort.

4.   The demonstration to others of a program's "worth".

5.   The need to satisfy someone demanding evidence of effect.

6.   The justification of past or projected expenditures.

7.   The generation of support for program expansion.

These, in turn, can be reduced to two basic elements of the human condition which may, at times, be interchangeable: virtue and survival.

Program evaluation itself may be defined as a process for determining the value or the amount of success achieved in attaining a predetermined objective. This involves: (1) formulating the objective, (2) identifying proper criteria to be used in measuring success, (3) determining the explaining the program's degree of success, and (4) recommending further program activity. The utility of the definition lies in the inclusion of feedback and program modification as core elements of an evaluative enterprise. The definition assumes that: (1) by nature, programs are evolutionary, (2) modification of the program is likely to be required in order to facilitate the attainment of predetermined objectives, and (3) the objectives themselves require periodic review and, at times, will have to be explicated or even reformulated. Thus the worth of the evaluative endeavor derives from a capacity to both measure achievement and yield information useful in decision making.

AN APPROACH TO EVALUATING A PATIENT-CARE PROGRAM

With this in mind, let us move to a consideration of the approach to patient-care evaluation currently evolving at the Connecticut Mental Health Center. The patient-care program is viewed as a complex social system in constant interaction with its environment. Within a given population, individuals-at-risk are either referred to or seek out the services of the program. Entry is through an evaluation subsystem from which individuals may be discharged back into the community, referred to another mental health treatment program, returned to the referring agent or agency, or transferred to the program's treatment subsystem. At the time of discharge from treatment, the patient reenters the community and, indeed, may represent an important part of the population-at-risk, with a likelihood of subsequent reentry either into the evaluation subsystem or directly into the treatment subsystem (Figure 1).

Adopting a modified systems perspective such as the one briefly outlined above to conceptualize a patient-care program has the additional benefit of providing a fulcrum for organizing the evaluative endeavor. Attention is drawn to issues related to the program's input, throughput, and output. The issues themselves can then be approached by the use of a variety of analytic techniques including the appraisal of structure, outcome, and process.

The appraisal of structure focuses upon organizational aspects that have impact upon patient care. These include personnel, facilities, equipment, information and record systems, formal organization, and financing. Two basic assumptions underlie the use of a structural approach: (1) it is possible to identify what is good in terms of staff, physical structure, and formal organization; and (2) better care is more likely to be provided when better qualified staff, improved physical facilities, and sounder fiscal and administrative procedures are applied. Such assumptions make it possible to frame evaluative questions in terms of organizational as well as clinical objectives.

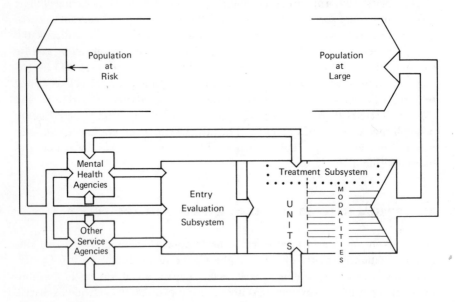

Figure 1   A patient care program as a complex social system.

The appraisal of process makes use of criteria-oriented approaches and special studies to focus on the activities of care givers in the management of patients. In the appraisal of process, the question asked is: Does the care rendered meet currently accepted standards? In essence, the appraisal provides feedback to ensure that patient-care activity does what it claims.

In the appraisal of outcome, some direct measure of results is related to the treatment given. Within this framework, the qualifications of those rendering care, the structure of their organization, and the extent to which they use acceptable methods can theoretically be disregarded in favor of appraising whether or not the desired results are achieved. In the evaluation of outcome, it is assumed that there is a strong concordance between societal and professional views of what end results are deemed advisable, good results are brought about to a significant degree by good care, and those good results can be translated into indices of success that reflect the effectiveness of the care-giving process. Thus outcome-evaluation provides the final evidence of whether care is good or bad.

Basically, structural approaches facilitate asking questions about a patient-care program from an organizational as well as clinical perspective, process approaches allow for a detailed examination of the degree to which clinical activities conform to the standards of excellence within the field, and outcome approaches encourage the scrutiny of program performance in terms of benefits accrued to the population served.

The Center's attempt to link various analytic techniques to a service delivery model was made in an effort to facilitate the framing of evaluative questions in terms of both program objectives and program dimensions. For example, input assumes a variety of forms (i.e., personnel, time, money, information, and actual and potential program users) (Figure 2) that invite questions related to the allocation of resources and the utilization of services. Throughput (Figure 3) includes programs and subprograms structured to fulfill task requirements. Since throughput involves both technologic and managerial dimensions of organizational processes, it generates questions related to the quality of the care provided. Finally, systems output (Figure 4) takes on a variety of forms such as products, profits, and satisfactions that are best addressed through questions concerning comparative cost, efficiency, cost benefit, as well as measures of change in the client population served.

AN APPLICATION OF THE EVALUATIVE APPROACH

Let us now move to a more concrete consideration of the use of Multi-State Information Systems in the evaluative approach outlined above.

The settling for the evaluative study was the Hill-West Haven Division of the Connecticut Mental Health Center. The Division is a federally funded

---

INPUT

Personnel, facilities, equipment,
financing, information, potential and
actual applicants for service

STRUCTURAL APPROACHES IN INPUT ASSESSMENT

Epidemiologic and ecologic
study of primary service regions

Comparative study of differential
utilization of service facilities

Effect of change in reimbursement
system on help-seeking behaviors

MD/Non-MD therapist ratios and
applicancy

Figure 2   The assessment of input.

community mental health center offering a comprehensive range of services to a
defined catchment (1–4). Major program elements include: (1) decentralized
satellites in the community offering outreach, emergency, child/family care,
and community development services; (2) centralized outpatient, day hospital,
and 24-hour inpatient services; and (3) through affiliation with the Drug Dependence Unit of the parent organization, services for substance abusers, ranging from methadone maintenance through residential treatment.

THROUGHPUT

Managerial and technologic organizational processes

STRUCTURAL AND PROCESS APPROACHES IN ASSESSING THROUGHPUT

Study of the continuity of care

Differential allocation of services by
MD and Non-MD clinicians

Appropriate use of medication in sattelite
versus clinic-based programs

Analysis of patterns of care
criterion-oriented case review

The relationship between problem recognition,
diagnosis, and patient management

Figure 3   The assessment of throughput.

OUTPUT

Products, profits, satisfactions,
change in population served

STRUCTURAL AND OUTCOME APPROACHES TO ASSESS OUTPUT

Cost benefit analysis

Effect of unit size and
staffing on readmission

Characteristics of productive versus unproductive units

Followup study of treated and untreated
applicants for service measuring
psychological functioning,
role performance, satisfaction
reentry into service network

Figure 4   The assessment of output.

The catchment consists of an inner city section of 21,628, the Hill neighborhood of New Haven, and a more stable industrial town of 52,851, the city of West Haven. There are 35,669 males and 38,810 females residing in the area. Of the residents 62,698 are white and 11,781 are nonwhite. There are 15,340 catchment residents living in block groups classified as SES (upper class); 23,652 in SES II (upper middle class) block groups; 18,118 in areas classified as SES III (lower middle class); and 17,369 in block groups classified as SES IV (lower class). The SES breakdowns were made on the basis of census data according to a social area analytic technique described elsewhere by Deshaies, Korper, and Siker (5). The patient sample included all individuals on the books as of July 1, 1972, plus first admissions and readmissions between July 1, 1972 and June 30, 1973. Z score and chi-square tests were used to determine the significance of observed differences.

Overall Center Admissions (Table 1).   A basic objective of the Division's clinical program was to insure the availability of mental health services to the socially disadvantaged. Using race and socioeconomic status as indices, the inquiry began by considering the pattern of overall center admissions. Data was obtained from the MSIS Admission Form. Utilization by nonwhites and individuals from lower and lower-middle-class areas of the catchment is considerably higher than that by either whites or individuals from upper and upper middle class areas. This finding, expressed as a rate per 1000, indicates that the performance of the overall program is consistent with the stated objective.

Table 1   *Overall Admission and Readmission Rates*

	Race			Socioeconomic Status		
	White	Non-white				
First admissions	7.4	14.3	6.1	6.0	9.3	11.7
Readmissions	5.0	12.5	3.5	3.7	6.0	11.1
Total admissions	12.4	26.8	9.6	9.7	15.3	22.8
Z score	12.8			-0.29	-5.0	-5.0
Significance	0.002			NS	0.002	0.002

Admission by Service Elements (Figure 5). In the next comparisons involving the center's major service elements, the bias favoring nonwhites was characteristic of all except the satellite program. Differential utilization by race, however, was considerably higher for the drug-dependence (DDU) and the inpatient/partial hospitalization (INPT/PART HOSP) services. The performance of all service elements with the exception of the satellite program was biased in favor of residents from lower social status areas.

The analysis indicates that trends initially noted in overall facility use reflect a selective utilization of discrete service elements by subpopulations within the catchment. For instance, the dominance of nonwhites as consumers of mental health services is strongly influenced by the differential utilization of drug-dependence and inpatient/partial hospitalization services. Seventy-seven per cent of all white patients admitted are enrolled in the ambulatory care programs as opposed to 45% of the nonwhites. A similar trend exists in relation to socioeconomic status where minimal differentiation is noted in the use of either the outpatient or satellite programs. When the utilization of these ambulatory services is compared with the drug dependence and inpatient/partial hospitalization programs, 57% of the admissions from SES I to SES III areas are to the ambulatory services as opposed to only 37% from the lowest socioeconomic status areas.

The Utilization Profile (Figure 6). Because of the differential accessibility noted in relation to the Division's major service elements the analysis was expanded to include an inquiry as to whether the character of care provided varied as a function of race or SES. To explore this issue, a Utilization Profile was developed. The profile consists of three indices constructed on the basis of data derived from the MSIS Admission and Change in Status Forms.

	OUTPATIENT			SATELLITE			INPATIENT PART. HOSP.			DDU		
	rate/1000	Z Score	Sig Level	rate/1000	Z Score	Sig Level	rate/1000	Z Score	Sig Level	rate/1000	Z Score	Sig Level
RACE												
White	6.5	2.0	.05	3.0	0.0	NS	1.8	11.4	.002	1.0	13.6	.002
Non-white	9.1			3.0			7.4			7.2		
SES												
I	5.1	.69	NS	2.0	-1.9	.05	1.4	-.25	NS	1.2	1.8	.05
II	4.6	-3.5	.002	3.0	-1.8	.05	1.5	-2.7	.005	0.6	-3.0	.005
III	6.5	-3.1	.002	4.1	4.6	.002	2.7	-3.4	.002	1.4	-6.0	.002
IV	10.4			2.2			5.0			5.2		

Figure 5   Admissions by locus of care.

229

$$\underline{\text{The Overall Use Factor (OUF)}} = \begin{array}{l}\text{patients on books} \\ \text{at the start of the} \\ \text{fiscal year}\end{array} + \begin{array}{l}\text{first admissions, readmissions} \\ \text{and transfers in during the} \\ \text{course of the fiscal year}\end{array}$$

$$\underline{\text{The Discharge Index (DI)}} \quad = \quad \frac{\text{discharges during the fiscal year}}{\text{OUF}} \quad \text{X } 100$$

$$\underline{\text{The Retention Index (RI)}} \quad = \quad \frac{\text{patients on books at end of fiscal year}}{\text{OUF}} \quad \text{X } 100$$

$$\underline{\text{The Absorption Index (AI)}} \quad = \quad \frac{\text{transfers in during the fiscal year}}{\text{OUF}} \quad \text{X } 100$$

Figure 6   The utilization indices.

The Absorption Index addresses questions related to differential referral patterns within the institution and facilitates the exploration of whether distributive biases favoring particular population subgroups are operative. The Discharge and Retention Indices, on the other hand, serve as gross measures of differences in the character of care provided subpopulations. The Discharge Index reflects the proportion of users terminated from treatment during a 12-month period. The higher the index, the more the unit acts as a final path in the patient's treatment career. The Retention Index serves as a rough measure of length of treatment stated as that proportion of the overall user pool who enter and remain on service during the 12-month period. A high-retention and low-discharge index for a particular group of patients suggests the differential receptivity on the part of the service towards that group. For this analysis the partial and full hospitalization programs were separated and the outpatient program divided into its component parts (evaluation/brief treatment, psychotherapies, and medication/resocialization).

Two examples illustrate the use of the Utilization Profile:

Example 1.   Utilization Profile

Medication Maintenance by Race

	White	Nonwhite
DI	17	36
RI	70	52
AI	35	36

The Medication Maintenance/Resocialization Unit is primarily an aftercare program serving a population of chronic psychotics who have experienced multiple hospitalizations. As can be seen, no differential in referral as measured by the Absorption Index is noted. The character of care as reflected in the Discharge and Retention Indices, however, does differ as a function of race: Nonwhite patients are more likely to be discharged and less likely to be retained on service during a given 12-month period.

Example 2.   Utilization Profile

Inpatient Care by Race

	White	Nonwhite
DI	33	39
RI	06	06
AI	42	20

On the inpatient service, the bias favoring nonwhites noted earlier in relation to overall admissions is countered, to a certain extent, by a trend towards the referral of proportionally more whites than nonwhites. Thus there exists a distributive bias favoring the white population that runs counter to the entry bias which favors the nonwhite population. The character of care as measured by the Discharge and Retention Indices, however, does not differ significantly as a function of race.

This analytic process was then applied in relation to each of the Division's service units (Figure 7).

The only significant differences noted in internal referral processes as reflected by the Absorption Index are both a function of race. Nonwhites are more likely to be referred to the drug-dependence program and whites to inpatient care. In terms of the character of care (1) nonwhites are more likely to be discharged and less likely to remain in continued care within the medication maintenance/resocialization program; (2) nonwhites are more likely to be discharged directly into the community from partial hospitalization; and conversely, (3) nonwhites are more likely to continue and less likely to be discharged from treatment in the satellite programs. Socioeconomic status differences were noted in the psychotherapy and the satellite programs. In the former, fewer individuals from the lowest socioeconomic status areas were discharged during the 12-month period; in the latter, not only were fewer discharged, but a significantly greater number were still in treatment at the end of the fiscal year. While the majority of all inpatients were referred for aftercare, significantly fewer individuals from lower middle as opposed to upper, upper middle and the lowest socioeconomic status areas were discharged directly into the community.

		RACE		SOCIOECONOMIC STATUS		
		White	Non-white	I-II	III	IV
Evaluation						
	D I	46	53	50	52	49
	R I	11	8	12	11	10
	A I	1	0	1	0	1
Psychotherapy						
	D I	38	45	53	57	38
	R I	25	18	24	20	24
	A I	65	53	61	67	56
Med Main/Resoc						
	D I	17	36	24	37	24
	R I	70	52	66	59	54
	A I	35	36	52	44	43
Satellite						
	D I	50	32	54	55	21
	R I	45	55	43	49	76
	A I	5	11	4	8	10
Drug Dep						
	D I	49	40	56	46	40
	R I	23	24	20	26	28
	A I	28	44	24	35	37
Part Hosp						
	D I	29	45	28	45	30
	R I	6	10	6	9	7
	A I	92	99	92	99	99
Inpatient						
	D I	33	39	46	21	38
	R I	6	6	5	6	5
	A I	42	20	30	33	36

Figure 7   Utilization profiles for CMHC service units.

Summary

A three-step analytic sequence was employed to evaluate a community mental health center's success at ensuring accessibility of care and the equitable distribution of services to catchment residents. Race and socioeconomic status were selected as target variables. Socially disadvantaged groups were strongly represented in terms of overall center admissions, indicating a high degree of accessibility for these populations previously denied service in the community. When controls were introduced to explore admissions to discrete service elements, however, the distribution of admissions was skewed. A distributive bias existed. The magnitude of the original differences noted in overall admission patterns emerged clearly as a function of the performance of two service elements.

Subsequent analyses revealed that allocative and service biases also existed. The allocative biases became apparent when exploring referral processes. Race was shown to be a significant corollary of clinical decisions related to the internal referral of individuals to inpatient and drug-dependence units. The character of care provided individuals on certain services also varied significantly as a function of race and socioeconomic status. While the service biases generally, but not always, favored the disadvantaged, their existence suggests that attention must be paid to distributive and allocative process as well as entry phenomenon in the assessment of issues related to accessibility of care and the equitable distribution of service. Clearly, the success of the program studied in terms of the target variables must be regarded as conditional rather than absolute.

Concepts of accessibility and equity are central to contemporary thinking concerning health delivery systems. The analyses presented suggest that it is possible to structure a service system so as to maximize accessibility, while simultaneously developing treatment subsystems that deal selectively with certain problems and population subgroups. Such treatment subsystems may operate differentially either to counter or to support program objectives. Indeed, they may be constructed so that barriers to service which formerly operated at an entry level are moved deeper into the organization's intrastructure, where they are less visible.

While the presentation has been limited to two target variables, the analytic procedure could be applied to a host of clinical, social, economic, and cultural indices. It represents a mechanism for identifying biases in a delivery system. These may be entry, distributive, allocative, or service biases. Their presence merely indicates that differentials exist in terms of who is served or the character of care provided. Even where bias conforms with program objectives, as was the case in the present study, further investigation should be undertaken to determine whether observed differentials are consistent with "good" as opposed to "bad" clinical practice.

To answer this question, CMHC is in the process of applying the criterion-oriented method described by Goldblatt et al. and Tischler and Reidel to analyze the adequacy and appropriateness of the care-giving process and to comment upon whether observed biases are justifiable in terms of norms of clinical practice (6, 7). The basic dimensions of the method are shown in Figure 8. It has been only since the implementation of the utilization Review Program that the feasibility of this method has become apparent. After selecting a sample of white and nonwhite patients admitted, CMHC Staff will match groups in terms of age, sex, and clinical diagnosis. Each case will then be reviewed. The adequacy of care as a function of race will be expressed quantitatively as the percentage of cases reviewed where care conformed to institutional standards of excellence. Additionally, the data from the review process will be used to identify and explicate the reasons for deviation from institutional norms.

While the use of the criterion method will allow comment upon whether the distributive bias or differences in the character of care can be justified in terms of norms of clinical practice, follow-up studies measuring end results in terms of symptom amelioration, enhanced social functioning, or other indices of change and improvement are required to answer the question of whether extant biases influence the potential benefit derived from participation in a particular clinical program.

Currently data of a follow-up study in relation to the Evaluation and Brief Treatment Unit is being analyzed. Outcome was measured in terms of change in symptomatology and instrumental and social role performance, as well as postdischarge treatment status. Preliminary results suggest that the more complex instrumentation used in this study can be replaced by the MSIS Admission Form, Change in Status Form, Direct Patient Service Form, Psychiatric Diagnosis Recording Form, and Periodic Evaluation Record—Community Version. With this in mind, a follow-up study is being contemplated that will directly address the question of whether the observed biases influence the potential benefits of involvement in a treatment program. Two services will be selected for study—one in which distributive, allocative, and service biases run counter to the program objective and one where performance is consistent with the objective. Twenty-five white and 25 nonwhite patients will be randomly assigned to the study group from each unit. Data will be collected at time of admission, time of discharge, and 6 months postdischarge. Benefit accrued will be measured in terms of symptomatology, social and instrumental role performance, and postdischarge treatment status. Once complete, CMHC will then have gone full cycle in applying the evaluative approach outlined at the beginning of this Chapter (see Figure 4).

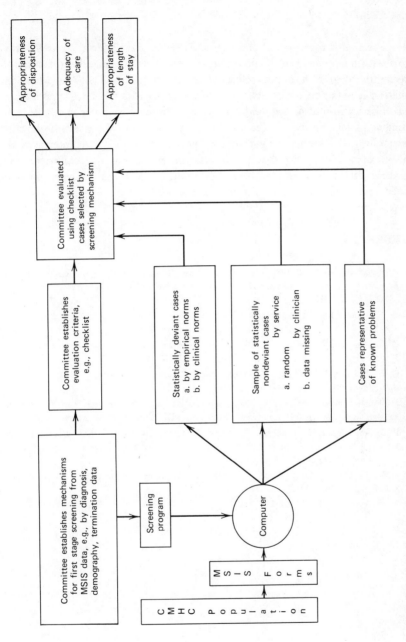

Figure 8 *BURP as modified for psychiatric utilization review.*

235

CONCLUSION

The scope and dimensions of the evaluative endeavor undertaken at CMHC begins with a statement of the objective and proceeds in a sequential fashion to measure the degree of success achieved in meeting it. At each step, new information is obtained which generates further questions related to the objecive itself. This open-ended, sequential process of inquiry is intended not only to document variance in relation to an objective, but also to allow for an objective assessment as to whether the variance is "good" or "bad." Thus interest is not only in measuring compliance, but also in evaluating the objective. The evaluative endeavor itself has been structured to maximize reliance on data derived from the Multi-State Information System.

REFERENCES

1. P. B. Goldblatt, R. M., Berberian, B. Goldberg, G. L. Klerman, G. L. Tischler and H. Zonane, "Catchmenting and the Delivery of Mental Health Services, *Arch. Gen. Psychiatr.,* **28,** (1973), 478–482.

2. G. Klerman, "Mental Health and the Urban Crisis," *Am. J. Orthopsychiatr.,* **39,** (1969), 818–826.

3. G. L. Tischler, J. Henisz, J. K. Myers, and V. Garrison, "Catchmenting and the Use of Mental Health Services," *Arch. Gen. Psychiatr.,* **27,** (1972), 389–392.

4. G. L. Tischler, J. Henisz, J. K., Myers, and V. Garrison, "The Impact of Catchmenting," *Adm. Ment. Health,* 22–29 (Winter 1972).

5. J. Deshaies, S. Korper, and E. Siker, *Census Use Study,* Health Information System II, Report No. 12, Bureau of the Census, United States Department of Commerce, 1971.

6. P. B. Goldblatt, L. D. Brauer, V. Garrison, J. Henisz, and M. Malcolm-Lawes, "A Chart Review Checklist for Utilization Review in a Community Mental Health Center," *Hosp. Community Psychiatr.,* **24,** (1973), 753–756.

7. G. L. Tischler and D. C. Riedel, "A Criterion Approach to Patient Care Evaluation," *Am. J. Psychiatr.,* **130,** (1973), 913–916.

EVALUATION

Evaluating the Attainment of Process Objectives of Community Mental Health Centers Using MSIS*

CAROLE SIEGEL, Ph.D., and ANN GOODMAN, M.A., M.S.

BACKGROUND

In order to plan programs adequately and more effectively utilize manpower and funds in the delivery of community mental health services, information is required on who is served, both in terms of patients and population-at-large, what kinds of services are received, and in what manner they are delivered. This information relates to the *process* of care delivery. Process-related objectives have been explicitly delineated by the National Institute of Mental Health (NIMH) in the federal guidelines for the operation of federally funded com-

* This work was supported in part by NIMH Contract Number: HSM-42-72-212.

munity mental health centers as typified by the following:

1.   The community mental health centers (CMHC) shall be equally accessible to all residents of the populations they serve according to relative need.
2.   Equal quantity and quality of service appropriate for the patient's problems shall be given to all center clients regardless of the client's ethnic group or socioeconomic level.
3.   Community mental health centers shall insure that care provided residents of the population is continuous regardless of the setting in which the patient is being treated.

Evaluation efforts ideally should go beyond monitoring the numbers of clients and types and amounts of service delivered and seek to analyze the effects that service delivery has had on the status of the population in need. However this is a complicated and difficult task. Although rate indices measuring recidivism, infant mortality, juvenile delinquency, alcoholism, suicide, and mental hospital admissions may be used to delineate populations in need, the direct effect of mental health service interventions is not easily measured. Changes in the mental health status of the population in need may only tangentially or very indirectly be attributed to the provision of such services. Studies and measurement tools must be carefully designed to capture outcome information which can serve as evaluative aids. Such outcome evaluation efforts are being carried on by others, but these efforts fall outside the scope of the present study, which directs itself only to process evaluation.

Although there are limitations in adequately developing evaluative criteria that depict change in mental health status, measures related to the evaluation of process objectives can be developed and superimposed onto already existing ongoing information systems. Such measures are useful descriptive tools for categorizing and defining populations served in terms of variables which have been shown to directly influence mental health status. High-risk groups can be targeted, service utilization and delivery can be examined, and concomitant administrative and clinical decisions can be made on an informed basis.

A report is given here of a study conducted for NIMH whose purpose was to develop methodology and measures of the attainment of process objectives utilizing data collected routinely by community mental health centers using an automated patient-management system. Four community mental health centers participating in the MSIS—such an automated system collecting detailed demographic, clinical and other patient information—collaborated with MSIS in an analysis of their data. Following a description of the methodology, measures, and potential uses of such an approach, the kinds of results obtained for the centers are summarized. The four participating centers with their study periods indicated are:

- Connecticut Mental Health Center in New Haven, Connecticut, September 1, 1972 to July 31, 1973
- Erich Lindemann Mental Health Center in Boston, Massachusetts, October 1, 1972 to February 28, 1973
- Rockland Community Mental Health Center in Pomona, New York, September 1, 1972 to July 31, 1973
- Area B Community Mental Health Center in Washington, D.C., September 1, 1972 to July 31, 1973

METHODOLOGY

The aims of this study were to provide focused formulations of some of the NIMH "process" objectives and to develop specific procedures for methodology and evaluative measurement based on available MSIS data.

Forming Homogeneous Social Groups within the Catchment

The first step in developing a methodology for an assessment of equity of process within a catchment population was the disaggregation of the catchment population into "homogeneous" subgroups with respect to ethnicity and socioeconomic levels. This was done by aggregating census tracts based on social-area analysis.

The specific social-area analysis model used in the present study followed that of Redick, Goldsmith, and Unger (1) and Goldsmith and Unger (2). Both of these publications are specifically concerned with the application of 1970 United States population census data to the study of mental health center catchment area populations. Redick, Goldsmith, and Unger state that "Social area analysis encompasses the theory that much of residence-related behavior can be understood and accounted for in terms of three types of society-wide population characteristics or dimensions: social rank, life style or urbanization and ethnicity" (1). The definitions of these indices were taken from the work of Greer (3). He suggested that "social rank" includes such social class factors as occupation, age, and stage of family rearing for the population; and "ethnicity" refers to the differentiation of the population by racial background. Goldsmith and Unger (2) indicate specifically those census variables that can be used to define each of these factors.

In this study several specific census variables were chosen to characterize the socioeconomic status of the tract. These variables were:

1. Percent of the population that is nonwhite
2. Median house value
3. Median rent
4. Percent of dwellings rented
5. Percent of persons in overcrowded housing

The variables follow the recommendations given by Goldsmith and Unger (2) for forming social area aggregates in that they capture social rank, lifestyle, and ethnicity. A numerical score obtained from median house value and median rent (using a weighting factor of percent of rented dwellings) was used to describe the social rank of the tract. The variable percent of persons in overcrowded housing was chosen to reflect lifestyle or urbanization and the per cent of nonwhites in the population was the variable chosen to characterize ethnicity.

Following the identification of the characteristics of the tracts of a catchment area, a statistical method for grouping them was developed. Low, medium, and high ranges were determined for the two variables, percent nonwhites in the population and percent of persons in overcrowded housing. The boundaries separating low and medium, and medium and high were determined by using a nearest neighbor clustering computer program. A score of low, medium, or high for each of these variables was then associated with each tract.

Using the same clustering program, median house value and median rent values of the tracts were classified into low, medium, and high ranges. A single social rank score was then derived on the basis of these in combination with the percent of dwellings which are owned and classified into low, medium, and high.

In this manner each tract in the catchment area had associated with it a three-dimensional vector whose entries were high, medium, or low scores representing the clustered range values of the social area variables. Tracts with the same vector scores or close scores were subsequently grouped to form at most five different tract aggregations (Figure 1).

Data Collection Instruments

The data used in this study were obtained from forms utilized routinely by the participating centers. These forms capture descriptive data relevant to the sociodemographic characteristics of the patients served by the centers, as well as the services provided to the patients. These standard data-collection instruments of MSIS are described in Part 2.

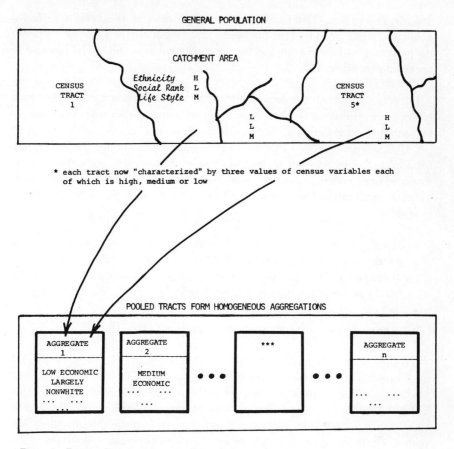

GENERAL POPULATION

CATCHMENT AREA

CENSUS
TRACT
1

Ethnicity   H
Social Rank   L
Life Style   M

L
L
M

CENSUS
TRACT
5*

H
L
M

* each tract now "characterized" by three values of census variables each
of which is high, medium or low

POOLED TRACTS FORM HOMOGENEOUS AGGREGATIONS

| AGGREGATE 1 | AGGREGATE 2 | *** | AGGREGATE n |

LOW ECONOMIC
LARGELY
NONWHITE

MEDIUM
ECONOMIC

Figure 1   Forming homogeneous general population groups.

The patient populations considered in this analysis consisted of distinct patients who were admitted to the center during the specified study periods and were unduplicated in count. If a patient was readmitted to the center during the study period, the patient was counted only once, although service data were collected for his multiple admissions.

Process Objectives and Evaluative Measures Used

The formulation of the first process objective and the procedure followed was:

1. *Process Objective.* The CMHC should admit all residents of the population which it serves without regard to ethnicity or socioeconomic level, in accordance with the needs of that population.

Specific Procedure. Determine the admission rates of the various socioeconomic and ethnic groups of the catchment area. What are the variations between the percentages of these groups in the general population and the percentages in the client population?

In order to establish the demographic character of the population which each center serves (in terms of whether or not specific population segments were being admitted in differential fashions) sex/ethnic/age specific admission rates per 10,000 were tabulated for each of the aggregations and for the total catchment areas. Along with an analysis of these admission rates, comparisons were made between census population and center population distributions. Further, for each aggregation three summary rates were computed. These are shown below:

- Total (sex/ethnic/age) adjusted admission rate (a rate which to some extent eliminates the effect of differences in the sex, ethnic, and age distributions in the aggregation populations by standardization against the total catchment population distributions).
- White (sex/age) adjusted admission rate.
- Nonwhite (sex/age) adjusted admission rate (Table 1).

To further characterize the population that a center is serving, MSIS "admission summaries" were created for each aggregation as well as for the total catchment. These summaries are part of the packaged capability of the MSIS and tabulate not only the univariate distribution of admissions of all variables appearing on the MSIS admission form: age, sex, ethnic group, education, source of referral, diagnosis, and so on, but several bivariate distributions as well (Figure 2).

The second objective formulated and the procedure followed are as follows:

2. *Process Objective.* The various socioeconomic and ethnic groups should receive treatment according to their needs.

Specific Procedure. Determine the variations among groups of patients in type and quantity of treatment received as evidenced by their (1) modality on admission, and (2) by the number and type of direct patient services rendered.

This objective was much more difficult to specify, for the question of what is appropriate treatment for different patients clearly has no simple answer. Working within the confines of the MSIS data collected, the approach taken was to examine whether there were differential service-delivery patterns for homogeneous patient groups as examined across the census tract aggregations.

```
                ADMISSION SUMMARY FOR  CT CHMNT                      FILE DATE 01/24/74

 # OF ADMISSIONS: CT010   = 883                                      TOTAL = 883

 *********************PATIENT PROFILE SUMMARY***************************************

                      *EDUCATION*                            *AGE BY SEX*

            #    %                #    %              MALE  FEM  MSNG  TOTAL    %
 0 YRS      7    1   10 YRS       99   11             25    15    -    40       5
 UNGRADED   4    0   11 YRS       83   9      <12     25    15    -    40       5
 1-2 YRS    21   2   12 YRS       239  27     12-15   21    17    -    38       4
 3 YRS      11   1   VOC/BUS      21   2      16-20   67    74    -    141      16
 4 YRS      12   1   1 YR COLL    39   4      21-64   272   378   -    650      74
 5 YRS      8    1   2 YR COLL    36   4      >65     6     8     -    14       2
 6 YRS      17   2   3 YR COLL    18   2      MSSNG   -     -     -    -        -
 7 YRS      26   3   4 YR COLL    22   2
 8 YRS      66   7   GRAD SCHL    23   3      TOTAL   391   492   -
 9 YRS      73   8   MISSING      -    -        %     44    56    -
                     UNKNOWN      58   7

         *VETERAN*                   *HOUSEHOLD COMPOSITION BY MARITAL STATUS*
            #    %
 YES       83   9                  NEV-  MARR/  DIV/  WID-  OTHER  TOTAL    %
 NO        800  91                 MARR  REMAR  SEPR  OWED
 MISSING   -    -     ALONE        40    5      37    10    -      92      10
                      CHILDREN     24    195    85    11    -      315     36
                      SPOUSE       3     268    2     -     -      273     31
      *ETHNIC GROUP*  SIBLINGS     63    1      4     -     1      69      8
            #    %    INSTITUTION  4     1      1     -     -      6       1
 WHITE     628  71    PARENTS      212   10     32    -     -      254     29
 NEGRO     200  23    RELATIVES    21    7      11    4     1      44      5
 AMER IND  -    -     WITH OTHERS  69    4      22    2     -      97      11
 P RICAN   46   5     UNKNOWN      8     3      9     -     -      20      2
 ORIENTAL  -    -     MISSING      -     -      -     -     -      -       -
 SEE INST  -    -
 MISSING   -    -     TOTAL        371   302    183   26    1
 UNKNOWN   4    0       %          42    34     21    3     0
 OTHER     5    1

        *RELIGION*              *WEEKLY INCOME BY NUMBER ON INCOME*
            #    %
 PROTESTNT 215  24             1    2    3    >3   UNKN  MSNG  TOTAL    %
 ROM CATHL 454  51   WELFARE   57   22   44   57   11    -     191     22
 JEWISH    25   3    <$50      36   8    5    5    1     -     55      6
 NONE      54   6    50-99     44   17   16   19   1     -     97      11
 UNKNOWN   40   5    100-149   21   14   36   45   2     -     118     13
 OTHER     95   11   150-199   7    14   8    33   -     -     62      7
 MISSING   -    -    200-299   3    2    3    25   -     -     33      4
                     >$299     -    -    -    1    -     -     1       0
      *ENVIRONMENT*  UNKNOWN   68   32   24   64   136   -     324     37
            #    %   MISSING   -    -    1    1    -     -     2       0
 FARM      -    -
 CITY VILL 882  100  TOTAL     236  109  137  250  151   -
 RURAL     -    -      %       27   12   16   28   17
 UNKNOWN   -    -
 MISSING   1    0
                                                              PAGE 1 OF 3
```

Figure 2   Admission Summary for Catchment.

But what is a homogeneous patient group? One may argue that patients are so unique in their problems and background that no two patients may be grouped. On the other hand, if patients are grouped in some manner and if gross differential patterns are unearthed by an analysis of these groups, administrators can use their own judgments as to the extent to which these represent legitimate variations in individual care as opposed to service inequities.

```
        ADMISSION SUMMARY FOR   CTCHMNT                        FILE DATE 01/24/74

# OF ADMISSIONS: CT010    =  883                                      TOTAL =  883

*****************************ENTRANCE SUMMARY*****************************************
        *EMERGENCY*                             *TYPE OF ADMISSION*
               #      %                                  #     %
        YES    122    14          1ST ADMISSION         552    63
        NO     761    86          RE- ADMISSION         331    37
        MISSING  -     -


                *SOURCE OF REFERRAL BY ETHNIC GROUP*

            WHITE NEGRO A.IND P.R. ORIEN INSTR MSNG UNKN OTHER TOTAL    %
SELF          304   91    -    20    -     -     -    3     1   419    47
MHC             8    1    -     -    -     -     -    -     -     9     1
RTRD INST       -    -    -     -    -     -     -    -     -     -     -
FAM/FRND       91   22    -     6    -     -     -    1     -   120    14
MENT HOSP       5    -    -     1    -     -     -    -     -     6     1
OTHR RETRD      -    -    -     -    -     -     -    -     -     -     -
CLERGY          5    -    -     -    -     -     -    -     -     5     1
GENHSP PSY     15    5    -     2    -     -     -    -     -    22     2
COURT/CORR     26   40    -     1    -     -     -    -     -    67     8
SCHOOL         26    8    -     -    -     -     -    -     3    37     4
GENHSP OTH     17    5    -     2    -     -     -    -     -    24     3
PUBHLTH/WF     11    3    -     2    -     -     -    -     -    16     2
POLICE          8    -    -     -    -     -     -    -     -     8     1
NURSE HOME      -    -    -     -    -     -     -    -     -     -     -
DIV/VOC         -    -    -     -    -     -     -    -     -     -     -
PVT PSYCH      10    -    -     -    -     -     -    -     1    11     1
PSY CLINIC      3    2    -     -    -     -     -    -     -     5     1
VOL AGENCY      1    -    -     -    -     -     -    -     -     1     0
PVT M.D.       35    2    -     2    -     -     -    -     -    39     4
PSY FACLTY      5    2    -     -    -     -     -    -     -     7     1
MISSING         -    -    -     -    -     -     -    -     -     -     -
OTHER          58   19    -    10    -     -     -    -     -    87    10

****************PRIOR PSYCHIATRIC SERVICES************************************

   *AS AN INPATIENT*            *ALL OTHER*                   *LAST SERVICE WAS*
             #    %                        #    %                          #    %
THIS FCLTY   98   11    THIS FCLTY   298   34    NOT INPATENT            379   43
MENT HOSP    87   10    PVT PSYCH     42    5    INPATIENT                95   11
MHC          38    4    MHC           68    8    MISSING                 409   46
GEN HOSP     17    2    OTHR THERA     8    1
V.A. HOSP     7    1    NURS HCME      -    -
RETRD INST    -    -    RETRD FAC      -    -       *TIME SINCE LAST SERVICE*
OTHER        30    3    RES. TREAT     3    0                            #    %
                       SCHOOL         2    0    WITHIN SAME DAY          18    2
                       PARTL HOSP     7    1    WITHIN   7 DAYS          37    4
NONE        369   42    HOSTEL         4    0    WITHIN  30 DAYS          35    4
UNKNOWN      37    4    PSY CINIC     35    4    WITHIN   6 MOS.          65    7
MISSING       -    -    PENL INST      3    0    WITHIN   1 YEAR          79    9
                       OT PSY FAC     6    1    OVER     1 YEAR         241   27
                       OTHER         92   10    NO PRIOR SERVICE        202   23
                                                MISSING                 206   23

                                                                  PAGE 2 OF 3
```

Figure 2   (Continued)

The approach taken was to group patients based on their diagnosis on admission for specific sex/ethnic/age categories. The total client population from the catchment area was examined and the diagnosis accounting for the most patients in a sex/ethnic/age group was used to delineate a homogeneous grouping; thus all patients of a particular sex/ethnic/age category with the same "most prevalent diagnosis" (MPD) were grouped for purposes of further

```
              ADMISSION SUMMARY FOR  CTCHMNT                        FILE DATE 01/24/74

 # OF ADMISSIONS: CTO10     =  883                                         TOTAL =   883


 ***************************************SUMMARY OF PSYCHIATRIC IMPRESSIONS**************************

    *DIAGNOSTIC IMPRESSION*                        *PROBLEM APPRAISAL*
                     #     %                                            %
 MENTAL RETARD       3     0     PHYSICAL            #       OTHER SYMPTOMS       #     %
 ORGNC BRAIN SYND    9     1     SLEEPING          251   28  SUICIDL THOUGHT    102    12
 NONPHYS PSYCHOS    58     7     EATING            158   18  SUICIDAL ACTS       38     4
 NEUROSES          146    17     ENURESES            7    1  ANXIETY, FEAR      214    24
 PERSONY DISORDER  132    15     SEIZURES            9    1  OBSESSIONS          35     4
 PSYCH/PHYSIO DIS    2     0     SPEECH              7    1  DEPRESSION         370    42
 SPECIAL SYMPTOM     1     0     OTHER PHYSICAL     90   10  SOMATIC CONCERN     59     7
 TRANSIENT SITUAT   88    10                                SOCIAL WITHDRAW    145    16
 BEHAVIOR            -     -     INTELLECTUAL                DEPENDENCY         106    12
 SOCIAL MALADJUST   41     5     DEVELOPMENT                 GRANDIOSITY         14     2
 NON-SPECIFIC        2     0     INADEQUATE         38    4  SUSPICION           67     8
 NO MENT DISORDER   51     6                                DELUSIONS           25     3
 NOT DIAGNOSED     109    12     SOCIAL RELATIONS            HALLUCINATIONS      37     4
 MISSING           241    27     WITH CHILDREN     127   14  ANGER,BELLIGERN    113    13
                                 WITH SPOUSE       271   31  ASSAULTIVE ACTS     35     4
                                 WITH FAMILY       200   23  ALCOHOL ABUSE      102    12
                                 WITH OTHERS       164   19  NARCOTIC, DRUGS    169    19
                                                                ANTISOCIAL ACTS   39     4
                                 SOCIAL PERFORMANCE          SEXUAL PROBLEMS     74     8
                                 SCHOOL             81    9  AGITATION           45     5
                                 JOB               120   14  DISORIENTATION      29     3
                                 HOUSEKEEPING       69    8  SPEECH DISORDER     11     1
                                                                LACK OF EMOTION   61     7
                                                                INAPPROP AFFECT   49     6
                                                                IMPAIR ROUTINE   113    13
                                                                MISSING           67     8


               *OVERALL SEVERITY BY PROBLEM DURATION*

                    WEEK  MONTH   1-YR   2-YR  >2-YR   MSNG    TOTL     %
         SLIGHT       2     15     28     16     26      -      87     10
         MILD         3     30     55     29     57      2     176     20
         MODERATE     5     25     67     53    127      1     278     31
         SEVERE       1      4     16     23     77      -     121     14
         MISSING      -      2      9     17     34     76     138     16
         NOT ILL      9     17     19      7     19     12      83      9

         TOTAL       20     93    194    145    340     91
            %         2     11     22     16     39     10


 NOTE: SUMS OF INDIVIDUAL ITEMS MAY NOT EQUAL TOTALS DUE TO INVALID VALUES OR
       MULTIPLE ENTRIES. PERCENTAGES ARE BASED ON TOTAL ADMISSIONS.
       PERCENTS ARE ROUNDED TO THE NEAREST INTEGER. A PERCENT OF 0 INDICATES
       AN UNROUNDED PERCENT > 0.0 BUT < 0.5.
                                                                PAGE 3 OF 3
```

Figure 2   (Continued)

analysis. Comparisons of type and quantity of treatment across aggregations were made first for sex/ethnic/age groups (or sex/age groups if ethnicity did not play a role) and second, in order to homogenize the client population, for sex/ethnic/age MPD groups (or sex/age MPD groups) (Figure 3).

To examine whether ethnicity played a role with respect to service delivery within an aggregate, first sex/age groups of whites were compared with non-

Table 1 Population Distribution, Admission Distribution, and Admission Rates by Sex/Ethnicity/Age[a]

AGGREGATE II

Total Population = 14148
Total Admission = 148

Adjusted Admission Rates per 10,000
Total   141
White   100
Nonwhite 373

	Total			0–14			15–24		
	Pop. (%)	Adm. (%)	Adm./10,000	Pop. (%)	Adm. (%)	Adm./10,000	Pop. (%)	Adm. (%)	Adm./10,000
Total	100.00	100.00	105	23.12	7.43	34	15.68	35.14	234
White male	44.26	31.76	75	10.91	2.70	26	6.91	11.49	174
White female	51.54	52.02	106	10.40	2.70	27	7.82	18.92	253
White total	95.80	83.78	91	21.31	5.40	27	14.73	30.41	216
Nonwhite male	2.05	6.76	344	0.89	1.35	159	0.38	1.35	370
Nonwhite female	2.51	9.47	395	0.92	0.68	77	0.57	3.38	625
Nonwhite total	4.56	16.23	372	1.81	2.03	117	0.95	4.73	522
Male total	46.31	38.52	87	11.80	4.05	36	7.29	12.84	184
Female total	54.05	61.49	119	11.32	3.38	51	8.39	22.30	278

	25–44			45–64			Over 64		
	Pop. (%)	Adm. (%)	Adm./ 10,000	Pop. (%)	Adm. (%)	Adm./ 10,000	Pop. (%)	Adm. (%)	Adm./ 10,000
Total	21.17	41.90	207	25.20	13.51	56	15.19	2.03	9
White male	9.87	12.84	136	10.78	4.05	39	5.99	0.68	12
White female	10.08	20.27	210	13.99	8.78	66	9.25	1.35	15
White total	19.95	33.11	174	24.77	12.83	54	15.04	2.03	14
Nonwhite male	0.56	3.38	633	0.18	0.68	385	0.04	0	0
Nonwhite female	0.66	5.41	860	0.25	0	0	0.11	0	0
Nonwhite total	1.22	8.79	756	0.43	0.68	164	0.15	0	0
Male total	10.43	16.22	163	10.96	4.73	45	5.83	0.68	12
Female total	10.74	25.68	250	14.24	8.78	65	9.36	1.35	15

[a] All calculations were performed to six decimal places, but only four are exhibited. Thus recalculations based on figures reported in this table (i.e., using only four decimal places) would produce incorrect results due to round off.

A'. Only those sex/ethnic/age patients with MPD of sex/ethnic/age group

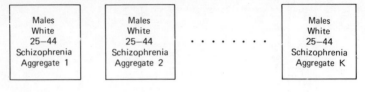

B'. Only those sex/age patients with MPD of sex/age group

C'. All sex/ethnic/age patients without regard to diagnosis

D'. All sex/age patients without regard to diagnosis

Figure 3   Equity comparisons among aggregates (across social areas). S/E/A, sex/ethnic/age; S/A, sex/age.

whites, and then sex/age/MPD groups were compared for whites versus nonwhites using (*a*) the MPD of whites and (*b*) the MPD of nonwhites (Figure 4).

(1) Modality of Admission.   Data pertaining to modality on admission were analyzed. If certain subgroups were showing excessive entry to the center by one specific entry unit (i.e., inpatient or emergency), an assessment could be made whether such a pattern was in accord with center policy, and programs planned either to modify admission patterns or to allocate staff more knowledgeably in line with the existing admission trends.

Unit on Admission on the Admission Form (MS 5) was classified into the center's modality structure. Comparisons of patient subgroups as outlined above were made with standard Chi square analysis used to test for dependency of either social area aggregation or ethnicity on modality on admission.

(2) Number and Type of Direct Patient Services Rendered.   The number of service units of a given type rendered to a client was examined. One of the data collection instruments of the MSIS system is the Direct Patient Service (DPS) Form which captures service data. Part of the information collected on this form is the occurrence of a patient contact with a clinician characterized in terms of the type of service. These data were examined for all services combined and for the individual service types for "homogeneous" groups of patients exposed to treat-

A. Only those sex/age patients with MPD of whites of sex/age group

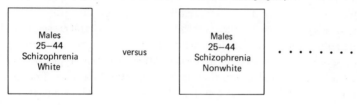

B. Only those sex/age patients with MPD of nonwhites of sex/age group

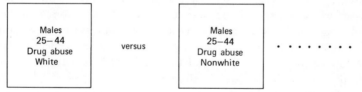

C. All sex/age patients without regard to diagnosis

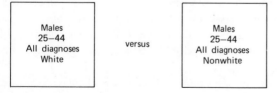

Figure 4   Equity comparisons within aggregates (whites and nonwhites). S/A, sex/age.

ment for the same length of time; those who received service for at least 30 days, and those who received service for at least 90 days. The total group which included any patient receiving service within the study period also was analyzed. For the "at least 30 day" group, service received only within the first 30 days after admission was examined, while for the "at least 90 day" group, service only within the first 90 days after admission was examined. For the total group, services rendered at any time in the period were included in the analyses.

There are many possible types of services that a center may provide. Each center was asked to characterize its service codes in terms of individual therapy, group therapy, medication, rehabilitation–restoration–habilitation services, client-related activities, residential-care services, and hospitalization–partial hospitalization. Only these seven broad categories of service were considered.

To describe these data, several measures and analyses were developed and outputs were produced:

The "client service rate" for sex/ethnic/age groups (total contacts/total patients) was defined as the average number of contacts received by each patient within the group (some of whom may not have received any service). A "client service rate" was also defined for the particular types of service (e.g., group therapy) as total group therapy contacts/total patients. For the total period for each sex/ethnic/age group a "population service delivery rate" (total contacts/total population) was calculated. Further, an "adjusted population service delivery rate" was obtained for the total population of each aggregate, enabling comparisons to be made of this rate among the aggregates.

The client service rate describes the process by which care is allocated or utilized by patient subgroups already seeking care at the center. The population service rate describes the rate at which care is delivered to the overall population, regardless of who within the population seeks or receives care.

Variations in population service rates may be more dependent on factors related to characteristics of the population itself, such as perception of need for care, tolerance of deviant social behavior, extent of high risk, and numbers of high-need persons within the area. Variations in client service rates may be more dependent upon factors that are directly related to the manner in which care is delivered within the center, such as clinical determinations of severity of illness and administrative/clinical decisions as to types and amounts of care to be rendered to the client population.

A statistical analysis of client service rates was developed to test the hypothesis that the service-specific client service rates are the same for subgroups of the patient population. Table 2 illustrates the type of tables analyzed to test for differential service patterns across aggregates and within aggregates.

For a given "homogeneous" group of clients, the client service rate can be viewed as a summary measure. Although the measure conveys a great deal of

Table 2 Client Service Rate for Overall Patient Population and for Major Therapy Classifications by Ethnicity and Aggregate

Population Patient Subgroup	Number of Patients		Number of Services		Overall Client Service Rate	Direct Service						Tests for Differences		
						IND		GRP		MED				
	N	%	N	%		N	Rate	N	Rate	N	Rate	$-2 \log \lambda$	Degrees of Freedom	Level of Significance
White	101	80	653	84	6.47	391	3.87	190	1.88	57	0.56	55.58	4	0.01
Nonwhite	25	20	129	16	5.16	106	4.24	5	0.20	12	0.48			
Total	126	100	782	100	6.21	497	3.94	195	1.55	69	0.55			
								Among Population Groups				5.76	1	0.05
								Among Direct Service Types				49.82	3	0.01
Aggregate														
1	40	32	242	31	6.05	174	4.35	41	1.02	18	0.45	124.98	12	0.01
2	22	17	177	23	8.05	124	5.64	37	1.68	16	0.73			
3	34	27	144	18	4.24	109	3.21	21	0.62	8	0.24			
4	30	24	219	28	7.30	90	3.00	96	3.20	27	0.90			
Total	126	100	782	100	6.21	497	3.94	195	1.55	69	0.55			
								Among Population Groups				40.56	3	0.01
								Among Direct Service Types				84.42	9	0.01

information, it does not describe possible disparities in receipt of the number of contacts among the clients in the group. Thus in one group each of 10 patients may receive 10 services and in another group each of 9 patients may receive 1 service while a tenth patient receives 91. Both groups received a total of 100 services for a client service rate of 10 and therefore none of the measures described above would distinguish between them. However the distribution of the number of contacts, that is, the number of distinct patients receiving no contacts, the number receiving one contact, the number receiving two contacts, and so on can be used to describe these disparities. In lieu of the distribution of contacts, a graphical representation, referred to as a Lorenz curve, of the distribution of service was presented, as demonstrated by Siegel, Meisner, and Laska (4). From these curves, disparities in the receipt of number of contacts among clients becomes more visually apparent.

To form Lorenz curves, first clients are "ordered" (listed) according to increasing number of contacts. The graph displays for each point on the X axis the percent of total contacts accounted for by the xth percentile of the clients. Using this curve the reader may ascertain such relationships as "90% of the clients received 9% of the contacts." A typical Lorenz curve is shown in Figure 5. (The proportion of patients receiving no contacts is marked on the X axis of each graph by the symbol *.)

If each xth percentile of clients would receive x% of the service, the curve that would represent this situation is the 45-degree line. For a given Lorenz curve, the area between the Lorenz curve and the 45-degree line (multiplied by 2) is referred to as the Gini coefficient. The value of the Gini coefficient varies between a lower bound, depending on the data, which is greater than 0 to a maximal value of 1. A large Gini coefficient corresponds to large disparities among numbers of contacts received by members of the group.

The third objective and the procedures addressed to this directive were as follows:

3. *Process Objective.*   The client should receive continuous care that is non-disruptive as long as it is therapeutically necessary.

Specific Procedure.

a.   What proportion of clients scheduled for appointments are "no shows" (that is, at least one appointment was neither kept nor canceled)? Determine the variations of these proportions among groups of patients. Compare service delivery to "no shows" with that of "never no shows."

b.   Among terminated patients, determine the proportions lost to the program in terms of those who withdrew from treatment without notifying the center and those who are unresponsive to referral or for whom further care is indicated but unavailable.

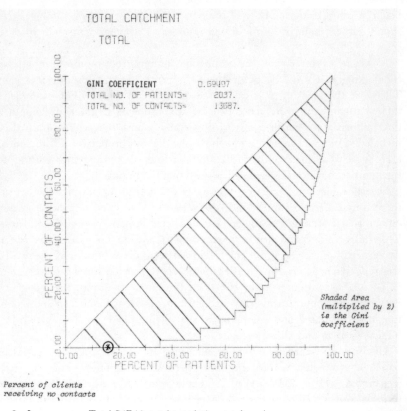

TOTAL CATCHMENT

. TOTAL

GINI COEFFICIENT   0.69497
TOTAL NO. OF PATIENTS=   2037.
TOTAL NO. OF CONTACTS=   13687.

*Shaded Area
(multiplied by 2)
is the Gini
coefficient*

PERCENT OF CONTACTS

PERCENT OF PATIENTS

(*) *Percent of clients
receiving no contacts*

Figure 5   Lorenz curve. Total S/E/A, total population, total service.

Evaluating the degree to which an individual who requires treatment continues to receive care without disruption within the community mental health center's jurisdiction involves a multitude of issues. The issues considered in this analysis were of three types: (1) disruption of care while the individual is a client of the center in active treatment, (2) loss of contact with individuals requiring further service from the center, for example, clients who prematurely and inappropriately drop out of treatment, and (3) ensuring adequate and appropriate care for individuals terminated from the center who require further service.

Centers utilizing the Direct Patient Services system fill out the form if a scheduled appointment is not kept, indicating whether the patient or clinician canceled, or if the appointment was neither kept nor canceled (no show).

The first measure of the disruption of care to be considered in the analysis was the proportion of the total number of patients scheduled for service in some period who were no shows for one or more appointments. The proportion was taken in terms of the number of patients who, at one time or another, were no shows rather than in terms of the number of appointments which were no show.

It is to be expected that this proportion changes from month to month as the client participates in the program of the center and as his attitudes change. Therefore the measure was calculated on a monthly basis. For example, only those patients who were scheduled for appointments in the third month after their admission, regardless of which calendar month they were admitted, were included. For each center, a graph displaying the proportion of no shows for each aggregation by month since admission was plotted together with a plot of the number of contacts scheduled in each month (Figure 6).

Several tables and statistical tests were developed to examine whether or not there were differences in the measure between whites and nonwhites as well as among social area aggregations. A Chi square statistic was utilized to test the hypothesis of independence between ethnicity and the no show measure within an aggregation as well as for the total catchment area. Similarly, the procedure was repeated to determine whether there were differences among aggregations.

To further evaluate center efforts to the no show group, the *client service rate* for kept appointments (or not kept but canceled) for the no show population was calculated and compared to that of the never no show group for the total catchment and all aggregates.

Disruption of care was further examined by considering the disposition of patients terminated within the study period. The centers either utilized the Termination Form (MS 5A) or the Change in Status Form (MS 6) to record terminations. Only the most recent termination data of clients terminated during the study period were examined, as it was felt that if there were a disruption of care, it would be most evident in the data of the client's last termination in the period.

To measure loss of contact with individuals requiring further service, a *Notification Index* was created, which is defined as the proportion of the total number of patients withdrawing from treatment who withdraw without notifying the center.

To measure whether clients receive adequate and appropriate care in other mental health facilities outside the center is obviously beyond the scope of the MSIS data base unless the other agencies are utilizing the system. However the referral status for patients terminated from the center requiring further care can be examined. This could indicate the degree to which centers are successful in pointing patients in the direction of agencies that could provide adequate and appropriate care and in getting the patient to respond to such referrals.

A *Referral Index* was defined as the proportion of the total number of patients terminated by the facility (excluding self-terminations) who were terminated without referral for either one of two reasons: (1) further care indi-

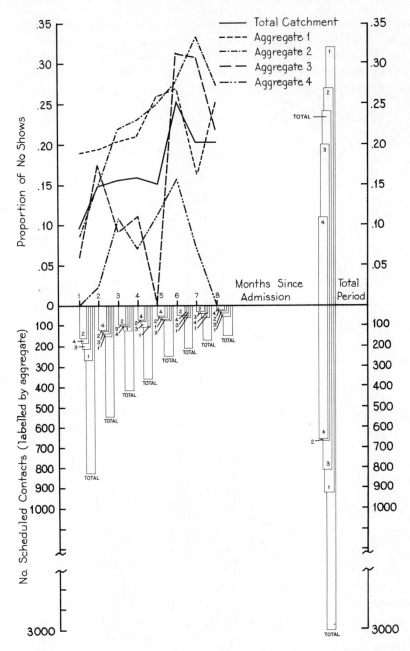

Figure 6   Monthly proportion of no shows and number of scheduled contacts by aggregate.

255

cated but unavailable and (2) unresponsive to referral. A bar graph was drawn (Figure 7) charting the variation of these two indices over aggregations.

The disruption of care measures introduced can be used longitudinally to assess the effects of changes in programming and staffing as well as to compare patterns of care over the social area aggregates.

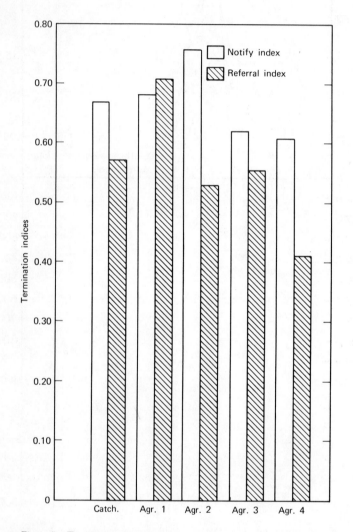

Figure 7   Termination indices.

DESCRIPTION OF THE CATCHMENT AREAS AND THE CENTERS

The four mental health centers participating in this study exhibit extensive differences in terms of the catchment areas they serve, their client populations, the types of services they provide, the length of time they have been in existence, and the size and scope of their therapeutic facilities as well as the way in which MSIS is employed in each center. Because of these intrinsic and fundamental differences, it was felt that comparisons of the centers in terms of the various study measures were not appropriate and accordingly were not made. Differential admission distributions and dissimilar patterns of service utilization are unquestionably due in large part to these differences, as well as to differences among the centers in terms of administrative and clinical philosophies and goals. Therefore each center's data were separately considered. However the methodology and data analysis employed in the evaluative paradigm were found useful as a general approach across all four participating centers.

The qualitative differences among the four centers are summarized below in terms of the catchment areas.

The populations vary tremendously in terms of both size and ethnicity (Figure 8). Area B CMHC services a very large, predominantly nonwhite population (85% nonwhite). Rockland also services a very large population but differs from Area B in that its catchment population is predominantly white

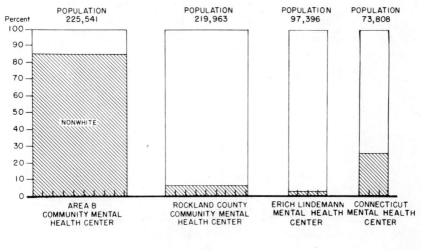

Figure 8   Comparison of catchment areas by population size, excluding group quarters, and ethnicity of four participating community mental health centers.

(6% nonwhite). Lindemann services a population which is less than half the size of Rockland's or Area B's and Connecticut about one-third the size. Lindemann is almost totally white (2% nonwhite) and Connecticut is about 16% nonwhite.

The four catchment areas vary in social rank as measured by median house value/median rent figures (Figure 9). Rockland has the highest median house value/median rent indices, composed as it is for the most part of substantial homes with a few small areas of poverty in an otherwise generally well-to-do community. The Connecticut Mental Health Center has the second largest median house value/median rent indices. These values are much lower than those of Rockland County due to the presence of poverty-stricken urban areas,

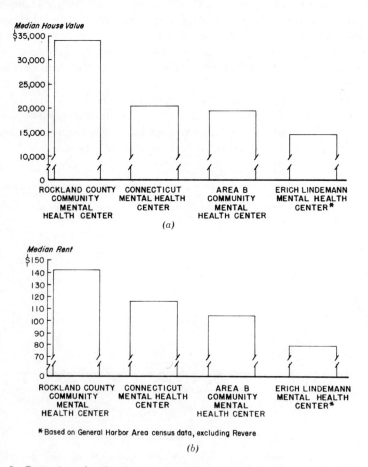

Figure 9   Comparison of median (a) house and (b) rent values of catchment areas of four partici-pating community mental health centers.

particularly in the Hill district, balanced somewhat by more affluent suburban areas in West Haven. Area B Community Mental Health Center, while evidencing house values comparable to Connecticut, shows a lower ranking due to a lower median rent value. Since a majority of dwellings within the city are rented, this lower median rent figure more appropriately characterizes the social level of the inhabitants. Erich Lindemann Mental Health Center has the lowest values of the four participating centers. However it must be noted that median house value/median rent statistics were unavailable for the collection of tracts, including the Revere area, actually used in this study. Catchment area statistics were only available for the general Harbor area, including North End, Chelsea, and Beacon Hill but excluding Revere. If Revere statistics had been available, the Lindemann indices would have been higher, since Revere is a predominantly middle class, outlying area, in some respects comparable to West Haven.

The four catchment areas also differ in terms of degree of urbanization. An urbanicity index was constructed by equally weighting the three urbanicity indicators, percent occupied housing rented, percent multiple-unit housing structures, and percent persons in overcrowded housing (Figure 10). Lindemann is the most highly urbanized catchment area (urbanicity score 52), closely followed by Area B (urbanicity score 46). Connecticut MHC with a

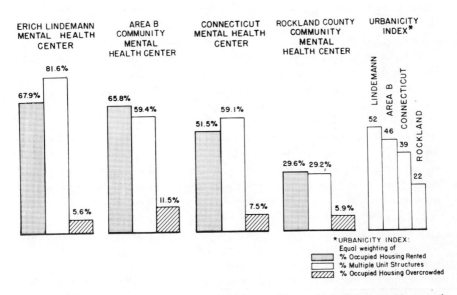

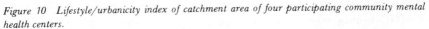

Figure 10   Lifestyle/urbanicity index of catchment area of four participating community mental health centers.

catchment area composed of a combination of central city and suburban area is less urbanized (urbanicity score 39). Finally, Rockland County CMHC has the lowest urbanicity index, as a result of its predominance of owner-occupied, single-unit, uncrowded housing (urbanicity score 22).

Fourteen percent of Connecticut MHC admissions were emergency admissions, while at least twice as many admissions to the other centers were emergency admissions (29 to 38%). It should be noted that Lindemann MHC with the highest proportion of emergency admissions uses its emergency service as a walk-in clinic as well as an emergency service.

Further differences were found in terms of center admissions. These differences strongly reflect the entirely different populations comprising the catchments these centers serve. An overview of the clients served by each of the community mental health centers has been obtained from an analysis of data on the admission record of each client grouped into Admission Summaries for the catchments. The MSIS Admission Form is used by the centers to report various socioeconomic and demographic characteristics as well as relevant data regarding source of referral to the center, prior psychiatric experience, type of admission (whether emergency or not), and some summary material on psychiatric impressions. Admission Summaries of the demographic characteristic of the admitted patients for each catchment area revealed interesting differences in the types of patients seen and the manner in which they came to the centers.

Although the ethnic composition of the catchment area is reflected in the ethnic composition of the admissions, in the three predominantly white areas, the percent nonwhite admission was somewhat higher than the percent nonwhite in the population. For Area B CMHC, which alone of the four centers is predominantly nonwhite, the nonwhite proportion of admissions was slightly less than the nonwhite proportion of the population (Figure 11).

The three predominantly white catchment areas of the Lindemann, Rockland, and Connecticut centers reflect national sex distributions. Admission sex ratios for these three centers tend to be lower than are found nationally (ratios of 79 to 87 for catchment admissions against a ratio of 91, nationally). The predominantly nonwhite catchment area (Area B) had a 2 to 3% lower proportion of males than the other three areas, which may be due to the fact that black males tend to be underreported in censile counts. Thus the highly significant overrepresentation of males in the Center's admissions (sex ratio of 183, which is twice as high as the national figure) was all the more noteworthy.

The four catchment areas varied significantly with respect to the age distributions of their populations, with Rockland County having a greater proportion of children under the age of 15 and Lindemann having higher proportions of persons beyond the child-rearing stage and over 65. The centers themselves differ significantly with respect to the age of patients served, with Rockland CMHC serving twice as many children 14 and under as the other centers.

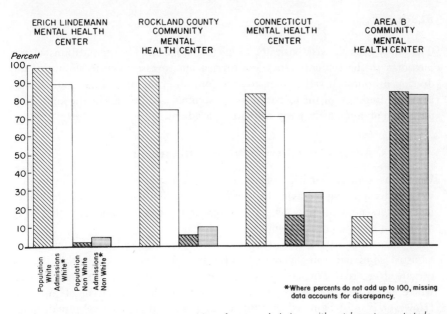

Figure 11   Comparison of ethnic composition of center admissions with catchment area populations (group quarters excluded) of four participating community mental health centers.

Service facilities in Rockland reflect this interest. Area B, on the other hand, serves significantly greater proportions of adults than the other centers, with a strong emphasis on the care of alcoholics. None of the centers spends a significant proportion of its efforts serving the elderly 65 and over.

There were highly significant differences in the educational level of admissions to the four centers, with Area B CMHC and Connecticut CMHC having significantly greater proportions of admissions with less than 12 years of schooling than Rockland County CMHC and Erich Lindemann CMHC. Factors other than age distribution of the catchment population, such as ethnicity and socioeconomic determinants appear to be responsible for the disproportionate representation of admissions not having completed high school in the Area B and Connecticut CMHC admission loads.

The centers differ significantly with respect to the distribution of referral sources of admissions. Connecticut MHC which has been in operation for the longest time had the highest percent of self/family/friend referrals. Area B and Lindemann MHCs, both relatively new to the catchment areas they serve, had proportionately less self-referrals. Area B CMHC received twice as many referrals from police and court agencies as did the other centers. Lindemann MHC received a significantly greater proportion of its referrals from mental hospitals and other hospitals.

RESULTS

The study was viewed basically as methodological. The applications of the measures to the centers' data were carried out to assess the feasibility of the developed approach rather than to carry out an evaluation of the centers. The principal findings for the four centers are summarized to indicate the kind of information obtainable from the evaluative paradigm.

Admission Patterns (Process Objective 1)

While the centers participating in this evaluation suspected that nonwhites were underapplying for available services, admission data indicated that in all four centers nonwhites in general showed adjusted admission rates that were more than twice the rate of whites.

In the three catchment areas that are predominantly white, nonwhite adjusted admission rates increased as the percent of nonwhites within the aggregate decreased. The nonwhite adjusted admission rates were not as high where nonwhites comprised more than 12% of the population of an area. (However it must be noted that this finding is based on relatively small numbers.) This finding is similar to that reported in a previous study indicating rates were "highest for the group which constituted a small minority (10% or less) of the population in a census tract, whether the group was white or nonwhite" (5). It is felt that this finding, which is replicated across the three predominantly white catchment areas, merits further investigation to examine determinants of the greater needs for service of the very small minority nonwhite groupings within the larger white areas. Lack of cohesive social support or structure leading to feelings of "anomie" and increased social stress may serve to create greater needs for mental health services.

In the two catchment areas with relatively long-established service networks, the poorest aggregation in each catchment area showed the highest adjusted admission rates. In the most recently established center, highest admission rates were from the most affluent aggregation. The community mental health center, itself, was on the periphery of this aggregation and seemed to be servicing those in geographical contiguity to the center. However, although this highly serviced aggregation showed the highest socioeconomic level within the catchment area, it exhibited the highest indices of those demographic characteristics commonly associated with high risk of encountering mental illness, such as the highest proportions within the catchment of persons not living in families, the lowest proportions of children in normal families, and a markedly lower youth dependency ratio than the rest of the catchment. These indicators suggest that in spite of the higher socioeconomic level of the aggregate, there was an increased need for service.

The extremes of the age range were underrepresented in the admission populations of all four of the centers. However, in those centers where special programs were targeted toward either children, age 14 and under, or the elderly, age 65 and over, the extent of unequal representation appeared to be smaller. Where no programs existed, the catchment population proportions were from three to five times as great as the corresponding admission proportions. Where special age-targeted programs existed, the population proportion for the age group was only twice as great as the corresponding client proportion. However these age groups may be served by other facilities within the catchment area (such as schools or social service organizations) that are not directly affiliated with the centers.

The three predominantly white centers exhibited peak admission rates for the 15- to 24-year age group, with females utilizing the centers at greater rates than males for all age groups except 0 to 14, where males showed higher utilization rates. The predominantly nonwhite catchment area exhibited a different utilization pattern, in which peak admission rates were found in the 25- to 44-year age group. A most striking finding for the center serving a nonwhite catchment area was the fact that male admission rates were more than double female rates, although males constituted only 46% of the catchment population.

Variations in Type and Quantity of Treatment Received (Process Objective 2)

Modality on Admission. There were significant differences in the way clients presented to the centers related to population characteristics of the various social areas within the catchment. Although each of the centers manifested different usage of various differing admission modalities, the usage pattern could be interpreted in terms of the population characteristics of the different aggregations involved.

Direct Patient Service. Once having been admitted to the center, patients exhibited differential care patterns linked to their social area and ethnicity. Those aggregates across the four catchments that were identified as utilizing significantly different modes of entry to the center were further highlighted as receiving differential treatment patterns once treatment was begun within the center. For each catchment area, the aggregate with a modality on admission pattern which differed from the remaining aggregates within the center received significantly different amounts and types of treatments than did the other aggregates.

In all but Lindemann, the population service rate was highest for the poorest, most highly nonwhite aggregate of the catchment area. However client service rates for the 90-day period in both Connecticut MHC and Rockland

097

County CMHC showed a different pattern. For these two centers the lower middle class, predominantly white aggregates had the highest overall client service rates. In Connecticut whites received service at higher rates than non-whites for the 90-day period, while in Rockland this ethnic differential varied for males and females—male nonwhites receiving service at higher rates than male whites, and the reverse for females.

For the 30-day period in Rockland, Aggregates I and III had the highest client service rates. The high rate of service for Aggregate I was accounted for by service to whites and nonwhite females. Nonwhite males in Aggregate I had the lowest service rate. However nonwhites received service at higher rates than whites in the catchment area as a whole.

In Connecticut for the 30-day period Aggregate II had the highest overall client service rate, with nonwhites receiving service at higher rates than whites.

In Area B, the predominantly nonwhite center, the most highly urbanized aggregates had the highest client service rates for both the short-term and long-term periods. For these periods, nonwhite females received service at higher rates than white females.

In Lindemann, the predominantly white center, the highest socially ranked aggregate had highest client service rates for both periods. This finding appeared to be linked to the particular composition of the population of this aggregate (singles, students, one-family households).

For all centers, it was seen from the Lorenz curve data that 10% of clients received more than 50% of the total service. This 10% of patients will be scrutinized carefully in the near future to determine what population characteristics are represented by this high-utilization group.

Disruption of Care (Process Objective 3)

An analysis of ongoing service patterns to determine the extent and amount of disrupted care of clients while in treatment suggests that sociodemographic characteristics of the patients significantly influenced the extent of disrupted care encountered. For two of the four centers the poorer, more crowded aggregates showed in each month higher proportions of clients who neither kept nor canceled (no show) an appointment at least once. The proportion in each of the aggregates generally increased with time since admission. Proportionately greater amounts of service were offered by the centers to the no-show clients than to those who always kept appointments, suggesting that clinicians expended effort to insure that services were made available to the more difficult-to-treat clients who tended toward a disruptive care pattern.

The termination data indicators created to measure disruption of care in terms of loss of contact with clients and the assurance of care for terminated clients requiring further service were highest in the predominantly white catchments for the more urbanized, ethnically diverse aggregates. As length of time between last contact and termination increased, the values of the indices of disruption of care increased. Only a small proportion of patients in any of the catchment areas had their disposition marked "care indicated but unavailable." The single predominantly nonwhite catchment exhibited different termination patterns of disrupted care. Disruption indicators on termination were similar for the five aggregations of this catchment area. There was a high proportion of terminated clients having the disposition status of "withdrawing and not notifying the facility" across the five aggregates.

CONCLUSION

In the light of competitive requirements for federal funds and legislative requirements of evaluation and accountability, the need to assess the degree to which an agency is fulfilling its goals and objectives has assumed major significance. To measure the extent to which the process objectives of a CMHC are being met is a difficult and ambiguous task. Simply stated but loosely constructed general aims must be translated into more precisely formulated objectives which are amendable to the application of statistical methods. A comprehensive, readily accessible repository of psychiatric data is an important prerequisite.

This study has defined a methodology for evaluating objectives applicable to CMHC data and applied the methodology to the data of four CMHCs. Since all were users of the MSIS, relatively detailed data were already available on computer files, permitting a timely and detailed analysis for this assessment. This study represents a paradigm and thus, theoretically, any CMHC may utilize both the methodology and specifics of this approach.

REFERENCES

1. R. W. Redick, H. F. Goldsmith, and E. L. Unger, *1970 Census Data Used to Indicate Areas with Different Potentials for Mental Health and Related Problems,* Mental Health Statistics, Series C., No. 3, National Institute of Mental Health, 1971.

2. H. F. Goldsmith and E. L. Unger, *Social Areas: Identification Procedures Using 1970 Census Data,* Laboratory Paper No. 37, Mental Health Study Center, National Institute of Mental Health, May 1972.

3. S. Greer, *The Emerging City: Myth and Reality,* Free Press at Glencoe, New York, 1962.

4. C. Siegel, M. Meisner, and E. Laska, "A Look at Equity," in *Proceedings of the Social Statistics Section,* American Statistical Association, 1973.

5. G. D. Klee, E. Spiro, A. K. Bahn, and K. Gorwitz, "An Ecological Analysis of Diagnosed Mental Illness in Baltimore," in R. R. Monroe, G. D. Klee, and E. B. Brody, Eds., *Psychiatric Epidemiology and Mental Planning,* Psychiatric Research Report No. 22, American Psychiatric Association, April 1967.

CLINICAL MANAGEMENT

The Use of MSIS for Utilization Review

OSCAR D. WEINER

When utilization review was merely a glint in the eye of the Connecticut Mental Health Center, there was more than a flicker of recognition that a necessary resource for its ability to be effective would be the use of the Multi-State Information System.

The volume of patients—about 4000 admissions and readmissions annually—dictated that selection of individual cases for review, detection of types and trends of services, analysis of characteristics of patients served, and documentation of rationales for norms of duration of care could only be reasonably accomplished through selective use of the MSIS; certainly such activity was well beyond the manual capability of supportive staff. The potential aid of the computer as an extremely useful means toward helping utilization review become operational was enhanced by prior staff familiarity with the MSIS.

A prerequisite to understanding and interpreting printouts was the broad participation of clinical and supportive staff in the input process, including discussion, interpretation, and negotiation on which MSIS forms were to be filled out. A broad understanding of the pertinence of the data was achieved at the CMHC. Completeness and reliability of the data to be retrieved would derive directly from the quality of the clinical input.

Clinicians representing various service units on the Utilization Review Committee were familiar with MSIS forms and thus were aware of what data were or could be available through the MSIS. Clinicians were also able to be critical in the sense of not simply accepting all computerized data as if it thundered out of the high crags of biblical Mt. Sinai! There was the recognition that except for demographic and other identifying data, printouts were reflections of somebody's judgment.

Key to the CMHC utilization review process are three stages: first is staff awareness of data availability derived from daily exposure to and participation in the input part of the system; second is staff discussions and decisions on what, how, and why specific computer programs should be designed; and the third has been the analysis of the printouts and its relevance to utilization review.

ORGANIZING FOR UTILIZATION REVIEW

The early recognition of MSIS as a potential tool for utilization review (UR) preceded the establishment of a Utilization Review Committee at the Connecticut Mental Health Center. Upon recommendation of the Clinical Chiefs' Committee,* the Utilization Review Committee (URC) was authorized by the Director and Executive Committee* in April 1972. It was fortunate that the Psychiatric Utilization Review and Evaluation (PURE) Project (1), a collaborative research endeavor of the Departments of Psychiatry, Epidemiology and Public Health, Sociology, and Administrative Sciences of Yale University, had already begun to study the problems in performing patient-care evaluation. As part of their effort, this group developed a set of criteria for a number of aspects of patient care from evaluation through treatment. They also developed the Autogroup process, a "man–machine interactive computer system consisting of a user, a database and a computer language which is designed to facilitate rapid analysis of complex medical information" (2). Patients can be grouped into similar categories based upon the selection of dependent variables. As an illustration, an entire patient population can be grouped according to combinations of identifiable characteristics such as age, sex, diagnosis, and treatment modality using, for example, length of stay as the dependent variable. Norms for length of stay are developed for particular segments of the CMHC population. From these norms, cases which were in treatment for longer or shorter than average periods for their defined group are selected for further scrutiny. It is hypothesized that these cases are more likely

* The Clinical Chiefs' Committee recommends policies to the Executive Committee affecting clinical services and formulates procedures that make the policies operational. The Executive Committee adopts policies, rules, and regulations necessary for the direction of the staff in regard to its service, educational, and research programs which relate to patient care and/or CMHC operation.

to represent inappropriate or inefficient instances of care than cases closer to the mean of the distribution for any particular variable chosen.

The CMHC became one of four mental health centers which entered into agreement with the PURE project to permit the latter to study the establishment and operation of its utilization review mechanisms.

In 1971 the Program Information and Analysis Section (PIAS) of CMHC was established. PIAS collaborated with the PURE project in the development of an individual Chart Review Checklist which, "based on predetermined explicit criteria of adequate care, applicable in large measure by paraprofessionals" (3) has given the Utilization Review Committee a useful aid.

Figure 1 is a reproduction of one of the 22 pages of the PIAS Checklist focusing on one of the specific treatment services, "outpatient brief treatment." Other sections of the form are headed "Intake and Evaluation" and "Treatment."

The sections that apply to intake and evaluation include:

Referral Information and Contacts
History of Previous Treatment
Description of Present Illness
Drug and Alcohol Abuse
Mental Status Examination
Diagnosis of Schizophrenia
Medical Evaluation
Assessment for Suicide
Assessment of Support
Formulation, Treatment Plan, Disposition

The sections that apply to treatment include:

Medication
Suicidal Patients
Adolescents
Specific Treatment Services (including criteria for hospitalization and admission to outpatient psychotherapies)

The three levels of PIAS review are subsequently described in detail; however it may be briefly noted that the steps are (1) a review for completeness of charts in the Medical Records Room, (2) a review of the selected chart by a PIAS Research Assistant who circles YES or NO, indicating adequacy or inadequacy for each applicable section, and (3) an additional review by a senior clinician of the CMHC if the previous chart review indicates inadequacy.

PIAS Checklist (sample page)

	PIAS Review	Clinical Review

IV. Review of Specific Treatment Services (Cont.)

C. *Outpatient Brief Treatment*

1. Was patient treated in an outpatient brief treatment unit? ^{55}Yes$_1$ No$_0$ XXXXXXXXXXX

   IF NO, MARK NA IN CLINICAL REVIEW SECTION ITEM 2, AND SKIP TO SECTION D.

2. IF YES,

   a. Was the goal(s) of the present contract defined? ^{56}Yes$_1$ No$_0$ XXXXXXXXXXX

   b. Were the external precipitating factors defined? ^{57}Yes$_1$ No$_0$ XXXXXXXXXXX

   c. During the last year was the patient at least six continuous months without psychiatric treatment? ^{58}Yes$_1$ No$_0$;   XXXXXXXXXXX

   d. If medication was given, were the target symptoms defined? ^{59}Yes$_1$ No$_0$ NA$_9$ XXXXXXXXXXX

IF NO TO ANY ITEM 2.a–d, chart should be subject to clinical review: ^{60}Appl$_1$ NA$_9$ XXXXXXXXXXX

Was the treatment (or choice of treatment) adequate? XXXXXXX ^{61}Yes$_1$ No$_0$

EXPLAIN:

3. Does the chart indicate that the length of the contract (no more than 12 weeks) was discussed with the patient? ^{62}Yes$_1$ No$_0$

XXXXXXXXXX
XXXXXXXXXX
XXXXXXXXXX
XXXXXXXXXX

D. *Continuing Care–Medication Maintenance Program*

1. Was patient admitted to Continuing Care–Medication Maintenance Program? ^{63}Yes$_1$ No$_0$

XXXXXXXXXX
XXXXXXXXXX
XXXXXXXXXX

IF NO, MARK NA IN CLINICAL REVIEW SECTION ITEMS 2 AND 3, AND SKIP TO SECTION E.

XXXXXXXXXX
XXXXXXXXXX
XXXXXXXXXX
XXXXXXXXXX

2. IF YES, does the chart indicate that the goals of treatment were:

XXXXXXXXXX
XXXXXXXXXX

a. to prevent psychiatric hospitalization and/or to prevent acute exacerbation of psychosis ^{64}Yes$_1$ No$_0$

XXXXXXXXXX
XXXXXXXXXX
XXXXXXXXXX
XXXXXXXXXX

b. to help patient keep his job or other social activities with which he is involved ^{65}Yes$_1$ No$_0$

XXXXXXXXXX
XXXXXXXXXX
XXXXXXXXXX

c. to provide social contacts to counteract the isolation due to bad living conditions or other factors ^{66}Yes$_1$ No$_0$

XXXXXXXXXX
XXXXXXXXXX
XXXXXXXXXX
XXXXXXXXXX

Continued . . .

Figure 1   PIAS Checklist sample page.

271

The senior clinician's review focuses on those sections identified by the PIAS Research Assistant as inadequate. If the clinician's review substantiates the finding of inadequacy, the chart is referred to the Utilization Review Committee for its review.

It is believed that focusing upon an aspect of treatment is more efficient than reviewing an entire chart. In short, more work gets done.

The work of PIAS and the URC are closely related. Although the URC has been free to select its own areas of interest, it has primarily focused its work during the initial year and one-half upon cases selected each month by PIAS, either through the Autogroup method using the MSIS data base or haphazardly. A partial listing of criteria used in types of cases selected is shown in Figure 2.

Many of these selection criteria are "loaded" in the sense of providing a probable high yield of cases that may indicate deviance from the PIAS standards of adequacy.

The items "Condition on Discharge" and "Reason for Discharge" derive from the MSIS Change in Status Form, although additional criteria as well could be selected from the data available at MSIS. For example, if one wanted

---

Partial Listing of Criteria Used in PIAS-Selected Cases

Patients with a discharge diagnosis of schizophrenia.

Adolescent patients treated at CMHC for at least 3 months.

Patients whose suicidal potential was assessed as moderate to high at the time of admission to CMHC.

*Patients who signed out against medical adivce (AMA).

*Patients who withdrew from treatment.

*Patients who were considered "worse" upon discharge.

Patients unresponsive to referrals.

Patients treated on more than one unit including Evaluation Unit.

Most recent patients admitted and discharged within a specific time frame.

Sampling of patients from several Service Units.

Patients having transient situational reactions, had agreed to discharge, and condition on discharge was worse.

Patients whose charts lacked a notation on condition on discharge and no more treatment indicated.

Patients who had a diagnosis deferred.

Figure 2   For entries marked with an asterisk, in programming with MSIS, selection criteria would include: codis, condition on discharge (e.g., worse, no mental disorder); reasondis, reason for discharge (e.g., patient went AMA, patient withdrew from treatment).

data on patients who withdrew from the program against medical advice, 'AMAs', one would use the GALS (General Alphabetical Listor) to select those patients who were discharged 'AMA.' This information would be derived from the MSIS Change of Status Form under the category "Reason for Discharge."

One could also be more specific about the criteria used for a patient sample by designating the variables to be used in selecting that sample, for example, female AMAs with a diagnosis of schizophrenia who had had prior hospitalization. This information would derive from the Admission Form, the Change of Status Form, and the Psychiatric Diagnosis Recording Form (PDRF).

PIAS conducts its work through three levels of review (Figure 3). The first level of review, Record Room Review, involves examination of charts on all patients admitted to treatment at the CMHC and is accomplished by personnel in the Record Room. The goal of this level of review is to establish the completeness of the information contained in the chart. Charts found not to meet the minimal standards of completeness as required are returned to the attending clinician for completion.

The second level of review is used on samples of charts selected for intensive review, and it is designed for completion by nonclinical personnel trained in the use of the checklist under the supervision of a psychiatrist. This review establishes the adequacy of the information recorded in the chart for clinical review and whether or not the treatment reflected in the record meets the criteria of adequate patient care set forth in the checklist.

The third level, Clinical Review, is accomplished by senior clinicians on all charts judged to be inadequate at the second level review. The clinical reviewer determines whether adequate patient care has been provided in those instances where the standards prescribed in the checklist were not followed. This level of review also provides a continuing test of the effectiveness of the checklist criteria in discriminating between adequate and inadequate patient care at the second level of review. When the clinical reviewer judges the patient care to be inadequate, he refers the chart to the URC.

The URC has also been reviewing cases judged adequate in accordance with PIAS criteria as a way of testing the continuing appropriateness of the criteria. One result of this review was a finding that while there was an adequate assessment of support in terms of the existing critera, some cases would have been regarded as inadequate if additional criteria specified by URC were included. Subsequently, the additional criteria, more reflective of the needs of the patient population, were added to the PIAS checklist.

Individual review of charts judged inadequate by PIAS clinicians provides the URC with opportunities for educative interventions. URC judgments that differ from those of PIAS provide issues for discussion and clarification. Interactions between URC members and clinicians around cited issues provide a most useful exchange of understanding about the clinical management of the

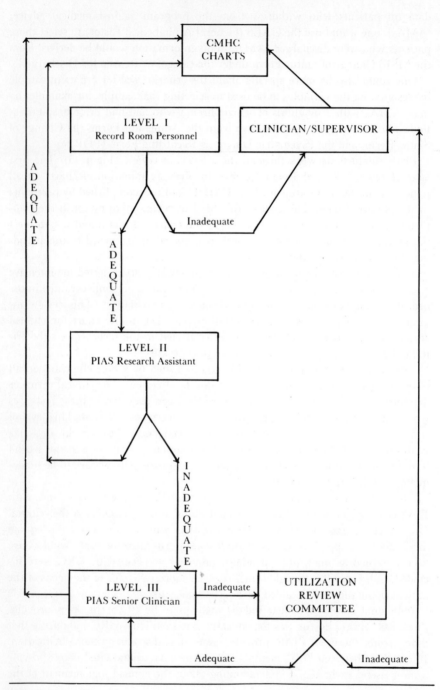

Figure 3

patient. Recognizing the threat that review represents to clinicians, URC members approach their task with appreciation of the educative value of the process and a total rejection of any punitive aspect to their work.

Thus when URC was organized (Figure 4), it inherited the fruits of the PIAS' labors, a yield of identified cases that presented the potential for reviewing inadequate patient care—a basis for a continuing educative, interactive process among URC members, the pool of clinicians, supervisors, consultants, administrators, and consumers of the service.

The Chairman of the URC was appointed by the Director and the Executive Committee for a term of 1 year, and his time was protected so that he could concentrate his primary efforts on URC activities. Committee members were appointed with a view toward reflecting the importance with which the CMHC viewed this work. The Committee included representatives of every kind of service offered patients and included senior clinicians with administrative responsibilities as well as first-line service personnel. A review of the composition of the 23-member committee reveals about an equal number of men and women and a wide range in terms of length of service at the facility. The disciplines of psychiatry, nursing, social work, psychology, administration, pharmacy, and statistics are represented. Members have rotating terms to insure fresh ideas and wide involvement of staff.

MSIS DATA AND UTILIZATION REVIEW

The major work of URC is accomplished through subcommittees and Task Forces, each of which has utilized the MSIS to facilitate its work. For example, the Patient Care Review Subcommittee in emphasizing individual patient care

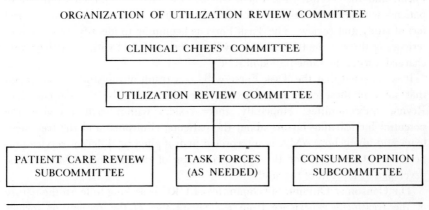

ORGANIZATION OF UTILIZATION REVIEW COMMITTEE

Figure 4

review has intensively studied cases whose stored data satisfy selected criteria for review, as described previously. This subcommittee has selected for review topics of special interest to them, to Unit Chiefs, or to administrators or topics that have been frequently cited by PIAS as recurring areas of inadequacy insofar as chart content is concerned. "Assessment for suicide" and "assessment of support" were the first topics reviewed, resulting in recommendations that have led to an institutional procedure for the reporting and review of deaths, suicides, and suicidal gestures; clinicians are required to provide narrative in the chart when they indicate in the Problem Appraisal section of the MSIS Admission Form or in the Periodic Evaluation Report—Community Version or Mental Status Examination Record that "potential for suicide" is moderate, high, or very high or that suicidal thoughts, acts, or gestures are present. In this linkage, the computerized forms both trigger the clinicians to amplify their assessment of suicide and provide a monitoring instrument that may be used by clinicians, supervisors, administrators, and researchers.

Other recommendations of the URC that are finding their way into practice include material used in orientation, preservice, and in-service training programs for staff and trainees; for example, the Pharmacy Committee will work on guidelines indicating what constitutes a lethal supply of medication dispensed at any one time.

Sometimes charts are reviewed as part of a study of an issue. As mentioned previously, a CMHC administrator suggested a study that would define the characteristics of those patients who leave against medical advice. The Task Force of URC identified those patients who are so categorized by devising a report that would provide the pertinent data using the MSIS General Alphabetic Listor.

Figure 5 displays the logic used to request a report of AMA patients. The report using data derived from the Admission Form, the Change in Status Form, and the Termination Form can be restricted to inpatients only or to patients with selected diagnoses or other combinations depending on the desired foci of study and review. The Task Force is beginning to identify some characteristics of these patients. Such data will also be compared with all patients discharged during the same period of time.

It is expected that the Task Force will, as a result of the study, recommend that some of these cases be subject to intensive review by the Patient Care Review Subcommittee. Hopefully, there resides within such a review the potential for learning factors about the patients, clinicians, and the treatment team and about how AMA is interpreted and applied by different service unit personnel. Guidelines for the appropriate use of the category AMA will be developed as a result of the study.

The Consumer Opinion Subcommittee of URC is seeking to learn the nature of the treatment experience from the perspective of the patient or former patient. In initiating a pilot study of 30 patients to be invited to participate in

LISTING REPORT REQUEST

Title: Patients discharged AMA
Logic: Patients discharged AMA from CMHC July 1, 1973 to September 30, 1973
Sort: By case number ascending order
List: By case number with the following variables:

    Sex
    Ethnic group
    Age on admission
    Education on admission
    Weekly family income on admission
    Number of Persons on income on admission
    Source of referral
    Date of admission
    Date terminated
    Prior inpatient psychiatric service
    Prior service all other types
    Usual address
    Discharged most recent unit
    Diagnosis, primary (most recent)
    Days Stay (gross)
    Condition on discharge
    Discharge without referral

Figure 5

one in-person interview with a member of the Subcommittee, the Subcommittee requested of MSIS a listing of patients who had been discharged since October 1, 1973, and who had had four or more clinical interviews. The Subcommittee requested a listing of case numbers, addresses, last unit of treatment, those discharged with referral, and those discharged without referral. From this list, they will proceed until 30 former patients are interviewed.

In addition to the federal requirements which mandate the review of extended-duration patients in inpatient services, and the interest of other third-party payors in looking more critically at the utilization of beds and services, the CMHC has undertaken a task that will lead to the establishment of norms that will identify too-long or too-brief uses of inpatient and outpatient treatment experiences. All inpatient cases that exceed the norm will be reviewed. Inpatient cases that are in briefer treatment than the norm and outpatient cases that are either too brief or too long in accordance with the norms will be subject to review on a sampled basis.

In approaching this task, opinions of unit chiefs were solicited. Inpatient duration of care was estimated by days; outpatient duration was estimated by number of clinical interviews or by a combination of a number of interviews and days. A grid was constructed that could accommodate any number of clusters of days and interviews, with the horizontal rows depicting length of stay (in days), broken into columns coinciding with the limits of the norms suggested by unit chiefs. The vertical columns depicted the number of interviews held according to the unit chief's suggestion for each modality.

To facilitate comparison of the actual duration of care with the opinion of the unit chiefs, MSIS was requested to provide data regarding patients admitted or readmitted to each unit between July 1, 1973 and September 30, 1973 where a transfer or discharge had occurred. The output has begun to provide an overview of duration of care and documentation for further negotiation with unit chiefs who might wish to revise their suggested norms. It has also given an indication of the potential load for the Utilization Review Committee.

This program will soon be repeated to cover a 6-month period, and then a year's experience. Establishing norms for a service unit and the rationales that have led to those decisions represent only the beginning of this task. Within each modality may emerge subsets of norms affected by diagnosis, severity of illness, race, and economics, which may be used with the same grid.

Figure 6, a printout displaying duration of treatment in the Evaluation Service, is similar to printouts of all other services. Longer norms for particular services contain specified additional rows and columns. In the figure it is noted that 13 cases with more than 4 contacts had a length of stay greater than 44 days.

The Evaluation Unit is the institution's primary portal of entry and has the task of assessing the presenting needs of all applicants to CMHC's clinical services. It was selected for initial study by the Task Force for two reasons: first, it had been operating since July 1, 1973 under an institutional goal of arriving at a disposition within 44 days or 4 interviews; second, this unit screens about 70% of all persons seeking service at the CMHC and involves the services of about 20 clinicians at the CMHC. Thus it was possible to measure duration of care against existing norms and to provide feedback to a large number of clinicians. Since this Unit is a feeder affecting all other units, a study of the Evaluation Unit could have a major impact on the other services.

Length of stay data are displayed in Figure 7, as summarized from the grid. Eighty per cent of the patients ($N = 385$) fell within the expected norms, and the 13 cases exceeding the norms for days' stay and contacts, representing 3% of the patients transferred or discharged from Evaluation Service, provided the cases of special interest to the URC.

The MSIS program also provided a clear statistical picture of patients transferred to different services as well as those discharged (Figure 8). From these data, it is known that somewhat more than half of the patients were discharged from the Evaluation Service. Transfers to the Brief Treatment Unit and Psychotherapies Section comprised 65% of the transfers; 20% of the patients were referred to CMHC inpatient units, 10% to the CMHC Com-

LENGTH OF STAY—EVALUATION UNIT
TRANSFERS/DISCHARGES JULY 1, 1973 TO SEPTEMBER 30, 1973
ROWS = NUMBER OF CONTACTS   COLUMNS = LENGTH OF STAY

	0	Φ	2	3-6	7-12	13-20	21-24	25-35	36-44	45-60	61-74	75-120	Row Sums	Key
0	152	1	1	8	4	3	4	3	1	3	2		182	RAW
	83.516	0.549	0.549	4.396	2.198	1.648	2.198	1.648	0.549	1.648	1.099		100.000	RPR
	100.000	9.091	16.667	21.053	6.897	5.882	14.815	9.677	5.556	10.345	15.385		41.743	RPC
1		9	4	20	30	24	4	4	3	5			103	RAW
		8.738	3.883	19.417	29.126	23.301	3.883	3.883	2.913	4.854			100.000	RPR
		81.818	66.667	52.632	51.724	47.059	14.815	12.903	16.667	17.241			23.624	RPC
2		1	1	10	17	15	7	9	3	6	3	1	73	RAW
		1.370	1.370	13.699	23.288	20.548	9.589	12.329	4.110	8.219	4.110	1.370	100.000	RPR
		9.091	16.667	26.316	29.310	29.412	25.926	29.032	16.667	20.690	23.077	50.000	16.743	RPC
3					5	5	4	7	5	5	2		33	RAW
					15.152	15.152	12.121	21.212	15.152	15.152	6.061		100.000	RPR
					8.621	9.804	14.815	22.581	27.778	17.241	15.385		7.569	RPC

Figure 6

279

LENGTH OF STAY—EVALUATION UNIT
TRANSFERS/DISCHARGES JULY 1, 1973 TO SEPTEMBER 30, 1973

ROWS = NUMBER OF CONTACTS   COLUMNS = LENGTH OF STAY

	0	1	2	3–6	7–12	13–20	21–24	25–35	36–44	45–60	61–74	75–120	Row Sums	Key
4					2	3	7	4	5	2	2		25	RAW
					8.000	12.000	28.000	16.000	20.000	8.000	8.000		100.000	RPR
					3.448	5.882	25.926	12.903	27.778	6.897	15.385		5.734	RPC
5						1	1	3	1	3			9	RAW
						11.111	11.111	33.333	11.111	33.333			100.000	RPR
						1.961	3.704	9.677	5.556	10.345			2.064	RPC
6–10								1		5	4	1	11	RAW
								9.091		45.455	36.364	9.091	100.000	RPR
								3.226		17.241	30.769	50.000	2.523	RPC
Column Sums	152	11	6	38	58	51	27	31	18	29	13	2	436	RAW
	34.862	2.523	1.376	8.716	13.303	11.697	6.193	7.110	4.128	6.651	2.982	0.459	100.000	RPR
	100.000	100.000	100.000	100.000	100.000	100.000	100.000	100.000	100.000	100.000	100.000	100.000	100.000	RPC

Figure 6 (continued)

EVALUATION UNIT

	Contacts 0–4		Contacts 5+	
45+ days stay	31		13	44
	B		D	
0–44 days stay	385		7	392
	A		C	
	416		20	436

Figure 7. Summary of length of stay by number of contacts based on transfers/discharges July 1, 1973 to September 30, 1973. A: 385 patients fell within the expected norms; B + C + D: 51 patients exceeded a norm; B: 31 patients exceeded the norm for days' stay only; C: 7 patients exceeded the norm for contacts only; D: 13 patients exceeded the norms for days' stay and contacts.

munity Support System (Medication/Maintenance), and 5% to other units such as Depression Unit, Alcohol Clinic, and Drug Dependency Unit.

The variations of average days' stay in the Evaluation Unit also lead to further study aimed at identifying factors that cause such variations. For example, what are the factors that cause a 3-day-longer stay for discharged patients (17.44) compared to those transferred (14.37)? Why do patients who are transferred to Brief Treatment have a stay of 4½ days longer (18.11) than those transferred to the Psychotherapies Section (13.45)? To what extent does the transfer to a different clinician contribute to the length of stay in evaluation?

The 13 cases identified as "extended duration" in evaluation were identified through MSIS programs for the purpose of more intensive review and served as documentation for discussion with the unit chief. The Task Force looked for trends such as first admissions compared with readmissions and age, and race factors. Initial impressions substantiated through subsequent discussions with staff identified two broad kinds of reasons for extended duration: one related to incorrect data supplied by clinicians indicating the need for administrative supervision, and the second involved clinical judgments which in most cases justified the extended duration.

Once the extreme cases are identified, characteristics of patients, clinicians' work habits, placement committees' assignment schedules, work loads of the typing pool, and filing time within the Medical Records Room will emerge and provide the basis for education and change.

CONCLUSION

Through participation in the MSIS, the entire review process has been accelerated because the CMHC does not have to rely on manual collation of the

282

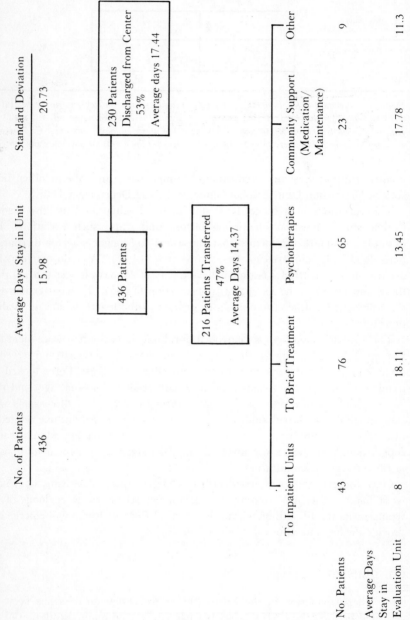

Figure 8

data. The data base has allowed for a rapid analysis of topics such as assessment of suicide, assessment of support, and discharged AMA. As the review process continues, awareness of the need for additional information has led to increased use of MSIS capabilities. MSIS offers a richness of data in patient demography and the movement and activity aspects of patient management.

As the demand for accountability to ourselves, patients, third-party payors, Professional Standards Review Organizations, government, and consumers increases, as it surely will, Utilization Review Committees will be expected to monitor, to inform, and to educate in an effort to improve the quality of care that each facility provides. The volume of patients and the number of clinicians involved in care-giving roles will require from all, increased reliance on the data that are put into the MSIS and more creativity in what is drawn from it.

REFERENCES

1. D. C. Riedel, L. Brauer, M. H. Brenner, P. Goldblatt, C. Schwartz, J. K. Myers, and G. Klerman, "Developing a System for Utilization Review and Evaluation in Community Mental Health Centers," *Hosp. Community Psychiatry*, **22**, 8 (1971), 229–232.

2. R. E. Mills, R. E. Fetter, D. C. Riedel, L. D. Brauer, R. F. Averill, J. H. Carlisle, D. A. Adler, and L. M. Mills, *Autogroup: An Interactive System*, Health Services Research Program, Yale University Institution for Social and Policy Studies, 1973.

3. P. B. Goldblatt, L. D. Brauer, V. Garrison, J. E. Henisz, M. Malcolm-Lawes, "A Chart-Review Checklist for Utilization Review in a Community Mental Health Center," *Hosp. Community Psychiatry*, **24**, 11 (1973), 753–756.

BIBLIOGRAPHY

American Hospital Association, *Quality Assurance Program for Medical Care in the Hospital*, American Hospital Association, Chicago, 1972.

American Psychiatric Association, "Position Statement on Peer Review in Psychiatry," *Am. J. Psychiatr.* **130**, 3 (1973), 381–385.

American Psychiatric Association, *Psychiatric Utilization Review: Principles and Objectives*, American Psychiatric Association, Washington, D. C., 1968.

M. Fitzmaurice, R. Lawrence, and G. Weygant, *Implementation of a Basic Utilization Review Program*, Hospital Administration Program, Department of Epidemiology and Public Health, Yale University School of Medicine, New Haven, Conn., 1968.

H. B. Kedward, M. R. Eastwood, and F. W. Furlong, "Computers and Psychiatric Data Recording: Rationale and Problems of Confidentiality," *Compr. Psychiatr.*, **14**, 2 (1973), 133–137.

B. C. Payne, "Measurement of Effectiveness of Utilization," *J. Am. Med. Assoc.*, **196**, 12 (1966), 1066–1068.

A. Richman, and H. Pinsker, "Utilization Review of Psychiatric Inpatient Care," *Am. J. Psychiatr.* **130**, 8 (1973), 900–903.

D. C. Riedel, M. H. Brenner, L. Brauer, P. Goldblatt, G. Klerman, J. Myers, C. Schwartz, and

G. Tischler, "Psychiatric Utilization Review as Patient Care Evaluation," *Am. J. Public Health,* **62,** 9 (1972), 1222–12228.

T. D. Scurlatis, "Criteria for UR," *N. Carolina Med. J.,* **30,** 9 (1969), 350–353.

R. M. Sigmond, "What Utilization Committees Taught Us," *Mod. Hosp.,* **100,** 2 (1963), 67–71.

R. M. Sigmond, "An Outline of the UR System," *Inquiry,* **3,** 2 (1966), 4–12.

V. N. Slee, "Information Systems and Measurement Tools," *J. Am. Med. Assoc.,* **196,** 12 (1966), 1063–1065.

M. B. Sussman, E. K. Caplan, M. R. Haug, and M. R. Stern, *The Walking Patient: A Study in Outpatient Care,* Case Western Reserve U. P., Cleveland, 1967.

G. L. Tischler, and D. C. Riedel, "A Criterion Approach to Patient Care Evaluation," *Am. J. Psychiatry,* **130,** 8 (1973), 913–916.

A. S. Weinstein, D. Di Pasquale, and F. Winsor, "Relationships between Length of Stay in and out of the New York State Mental Hospitals," *Am. J. Psychiatry,* **130,** 8 (1973), 904–909.

CLINICAL MANAGEMENT

Patient Assessment and Monitoring

JEAN ENDICOTT and **ROBERT L. SPITZER**

Much of the data collected on the Washington Heights Community Service (WHCS) at the New York State Psychiatric Institute has been used for research by the Evaluation Section of Biometrics Research. Both the Mental Status Examination Record (MSER) (see Part 2) and the Psychiatric Anamnestic Record (PAR) (see p. 132) have been used on the WHCS. The Evaluation Unit has a special interest in these instruments, having developed them, and therefore cannot be considered ordinary users of the system. In addition, the research staff is particularly interested in treatment evaluation and problems of patient description and classification, and special studies are often conducted in conjunction with the clinical staff of the WHCS. This paper discusses examples of some of the uses that have been made of the data provided by the therapists responsible for the patients' care rather than that collected by special research personnel.

Each therapist on the WHCS is expected to complete a MSER within a few days of admission for each of his patients. Close monitoring and checking is necessary, to assure that this is, in fact, done. Depending upon particular studies being conducted on the service, the therapist may be asked to complete a PAR as soon as he has sufficient information or to make periodic reevaluations using the MSER on specific study patients.

When these MSERs and PARs are processed, several types of output are available in addition to the computerized narrative. These include MSER T scores, percentile rankings, and "ratings of clinical severity" for 20 summary scales (Figure 1). These summary scales are based upon the results of a factor analysis of 2001 MSERs completed for newly admitted inpatients. Thus the scores for each patient, or group of patients, are compared with this standardization sample whose average score is always a T score of .50. In addition, a computerized diagnosis with the rationale for the main diagnoses is available (Figure 2). The work done to derive the MSER scoring system or the development and validation of the computerized diagnosis programs is described in detail elsewhere (1–4).

In training new therapists in the use of the automated forms, an attempt is made to impress upon them that these scores and diagnoses will be useless for

```
MSER GRAPH** PATIENT NO.   13870,10/15/73,FACILITY NO. 14,RATER NO. 20

     SUMMARY SCALES                 CLINICAL EQUIVALENTS        PER-
                                                               CEN-
                             NONE MIN  MILD MOD   SEV  EXTRM TILE  T

DEPRESSIVE IDEATION AND MOOD. .  XXXXXXXXXXXXXXXXXXXXXXXXXXX    97   76
SUICIDE . . . . . . . . . . . .  XXXXXXXXXXX                   80   54
SLEEP-APPETITE DISTURBANCE. . .  X                             45   42
SOMATIC CONCERN . . . . . . . .  X                             71   45
ANXIETY . . . . . . . . . . . .  XXXXXX                        42   44
INAPPROPRIATE APPEARANCE. . . .  X                             62   44
DISORIENTATION-MEMORY . . . . .  X                             68   45
COGNITIVE DISORGANIZATION . . .  XXXXXXXXXXX                   60   47
HALLUCINATIONS. . . . . . . . .  X                             75   45
UNUSUAL THOUGHTS-DELUSIONS. . .  X                             51   43
SUSPICIOUSNESS. . . . . . . . .  XXXXXXXXXXX                   58   47
ANGER-NEGATIVISM. . . . . . . .  X                             20   42
VIOLENCE IDEATION . . . . . . .  X                             71   45
DENIAL OF ILLNESS . . . . . . .  XXXXXXXXXXX                   57   50
EXCITEMENT. . . . . . . . . . .  X                             63   45
RETARDATION-EMOTIONAL WITHDRAWL  XXXXXXXXXXXXXXXXXXXXXXXXXXX    99   86
ALCOHOL ABUSE . . . . . . . . .  X                             80   45
DRUG ABUSE. . . . . . . . . . .  X                             86   46

                             VERY       ONLY       VERY  EXTRM
                             GOOD  GOOD FAIR POOR POOR POOR
JUDGEMENT . . . . . . . . . . .  XXXXXXXXXXXXXXX               62   53

                             UNRE AVER QUI-        UNUS EXTRE
                             MARK AGE  TE    VERY UALY MELY
LIKEABLE. . . . . . . . . . . .  XXXXXXXXXXXXXXX               84   56
```

   **THE SUMMARY SCALES ARE MADE UP OF ITEMS GROUPED ON THE BASIS OF A FACTOR ANALYSIS OF A REFERENCE GROUP OF 2001 NEWLY ADMITTED INPATIENTS. THE CLINICAL EQUIVALENTS ARE ESTIMATES OF THE LEVELS OF SEVERITY OF EACH DIMENSION. THE PERCENTILE IS THE PERCENT OF PATIENTS IN THE REFERENCE GROUP THAT HAVE A SCORE EQUAL TO OR BELOW THIS SUBJECT. T SCORES ARE STANDARDIZED SCORES WITH A MEAN OF 50 AND A STANDARD DEVIATION OF 10 FOR THE REFERENCE GROUP.

Figure 1   Example of Mental Status Examination Record Scale Score Report.

THE INFORMATION CONTAINED ON THE MENTAL STATUS EXAMINATION RECORD WAS
ANALYZED BY MEANS OF A COMPUTER PROGRAM, DIAGNOIII-MSER, VERSION 2,
NOVEMBER 1972. THE RESULTS OF THIS ANALYSIS ARE GIVEN BELOW AND ARE
INTENDED TO SERVE AS AN AID IN THE DIFFERENTIAL DIAGNOSTIC PROCESS.
BECAUSE THIS PROGRAM DOES NOT HAVE HISTORICAL INFORMATION, SOME
DIAGNOSES CANNOT BE MADE (E.G. PERSONALITY DISORDERS). ALSO, ALL BRAIN
SYNDROMES ARE CALLED ACUTE. IN ADDITION, SOME SCHIZOPHRENIC SUBTYPES
ARE CLASSIFIED AS 'SCHIZOPHRENIA, UNSPECIFIED TYPE' AND SOME SPECIFIC
AFFECTIVE ILLNESSES ARE CLASSIFIED AS 'PSYCHOTIC DEPRESSIVE MOOD
DISORDER'. A MORE DETAILED AND ACCURATE DIAGNOSTIC EVALUATION IS
POSSIBLE BY SUBMITTING A PSYCHIATRIC ANAMNESTIC RECORD ON THIS PATIENT
WITHIN TWO WEEKS, PROVIDING THIS MSER IS STORED ON THE DATA BASE.

PATIENT IDENTIFICATION NUMBER-   13870
FACILITY CODE-   14
RATER CODE-   20
DATE OF MSER EVALUATION- OCT. 15, 1973

THE MOST LIKELY DIAGNOSIS IS-

   295.74 SCHIZOPHRENIA, SCHIZO-AFFECTIVE TYPE, DEPRESSED

HOWEVER, THE FOLLOWING CONDITION(S) SHOULD ALSO BE CONSIDERED-

   296.8   PSYCHOTIC DEPRESSIVE MOOD DISORDER

   300.4   DEPRESSIVE NEUROSIS

   300.0   ANXIETY NEUROSIS

SUMMARY OF BASIS FOR COMPUTERIZED MAIN DIAGNOSIS BASED ON MSER RATINGS

A MAIN DIAGNOSIS OF SCHIZOPHRENIA IS MADE BECAUSE

THERE IS NO EVIDENCE STRONGLY SUGGESTIVE OF AN ORGANIC BRAIN SYNDROME

FUNCTIONAL PSYCHOSIS IS STRONGLY SUGGESTED BY RATINGS OF
       -AT LEAST MODERATE FLATNESS OF AFFECT

ALTHOUGH THERE IS EVIDENCE OF AN AFFECTIVE DISTURBANCE, RATINGS ON
THE FOLLOWING ITEMS SUGGEST SCHIZOPHRENIA, RATHER THAN A MOOD DISORDER
       -AT LEAST MODERATE FLATNESS OF AFFECT (IN THE ABSENCE OF A
        DEFINITE ORGANIC BRAIN SYNDROME)

SCHIZO-AFFECTIVE TYPE, WITHDRAWN, BECAUSE OF RATINGS OF
       -DEPRESSED MOOD AND A SCORE ON AN INDEX OF THE DEPRESSIVE
        SYNDROME (WHICH COMBINES INSOMNIA, LOW ENERGY LEVEL, GUILT, SELF
        DEROGATORY THOUGHTS, REDUCED PRODUCTIVITY OF SPEECH, DECREASED
        RATE OF SPEECH, HYPOCHONDRIASIS, PSYCHOMOTOR RETARDATION OR
        EXCITEMENT, POOR APPETITE, DIMINISHED INTEREST, DIMINISHED
        INTEREST IN SEX, SUICIDAL IDEATION AND THOUGHTS OF DEATH)
           CRITICAL VALUE =   3   PATIENT'S SCORE =   5

Figure 2   MSER computerized diagnosis.

describing their patients if they are not careful in completing the forms. They are told that an item left blank is of necessity counted as a rating of "none" or "absent" in the scoring system. They are reminded that the computerized diagnoses often depend upon single critical items and are advised to look at the rationale for the diagnosis so that they may better evaluate the strength of the evidence upon which it is based.

A controlled study of three treatment modalities for patients admitted to the WHCS who met a number of specific inclusion criteria for the study has been conducted. (5) Patients were randomized into one of three groups: brief hospitalization followed by outpatient care (day care not being available) (brief–out), brief hospitalization followed by day care and then outpatient care (brief–day), and standard inpatient care (i.e., therapist's discretion) followed by outpatient care (day care not being available) (standard-out).

In this study, a MSER and a PAR were completed by the therapist on admission, and a MSER was completed at 3, 12, and 24 weeks and at 12, 18, and 24 months, if the patient was still in therapy. In addition, evaluations of the patients were made and interviews of the families were conducted by the research staff for the same time periods.

Several uses have been made of the therapists' MSERs and PARs in this study. First it was necessary to determine if the randomization had "worked," that is, were the patients in the three groups equivalent in aspects of psychopathology, and so on, which would have obvious prognostic significance. Figure 3 compares the MSER scale scores for the three groups on admission to the hospital and to the study. Only 3 of the 60 possible differences were significant at the .05 level (two-tailed), differences which could occur by chance alone. This finding that the three groups were essentially equivalent on admission psychopathology was in agreement with the results from the research evaluations of the same patients using another instrument, the Psychiatric Status Schedule (6). Table 1 compares the three groups on a number of PAR variables of prognostic significance, again indicating that the randomization had been successful.

At each of the follow-up evaluations the relative improvement of the three groups of patients was compared. Figure 4 shows the improvement made by the three groups 3 weeks after admission to the hospital. An analysis of covariance of the data on which this figure is based indicated that none of the differences in the amount of improvement were significant. Again these findings agreed with those of the research interviewers. Similar analyses will be made for the other follow-up evaluations as long as there are sufficient numbers of patients being actively followed by therapists.

In addition to an evaluation of the relative effectiveness of the three treatments for a heterogeneous sample of patients, the MSER scores will be related to measures of family "burden" and to other outcome indices as part of an ef-

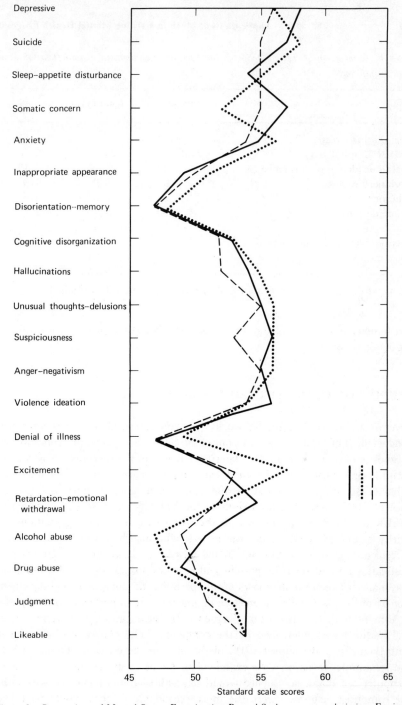

Figure 3 Comparison of Mental Status Examination Record Scale scores on admission. For inappropriate appearance, excitement, and alcohol abuse, one of the three comparisons was significant at the .05 level, two-tailed. Brief out (———) (N = 51); brief day (- - - -) (N = 61); standard (———) (N = 63).

Table 1   Comparison of Three Groups on the Psychiatric Anamnestic Record Items of Prognostic Significance[a]

Items	Brief Out	Brief Day	Standard
Precipitating stress	3.51	3.67	3.45
Age first hospitalized	30	25	26
Overall academic performance	3.24	3.46	3.40
Work performance	3.6	3.9	4.0
Delusions	2.7	2.6	2.5
Hallucinations	2.0	2.3	2.3
Suicide attempts	1.5	1.4	1.5
Overall severity of illness age 12 to last month	3.9	3.8	4.0

[a] None of the differences were significant at the $p < .05$ level, two-tailed.

fort to determine which of the three modalities is most appropriate for different types of patients.

STUDIES OF COMPUTERIZED DIAGNOSIS

Several studies related to the work with computerized diagnosis have been conducted. The first study was completed prior to making the computerized diagnostic output a part of the material returned to the therapist. It was an attempt to assess the degree to which the computer could simulate the diagnostic behavior of an "expert" and thereby act as a diagnostic consultant (3). For each of 100 consecutive admissions to the WHCS, the therapist completed a MSER and a PAR in addition to the usual case history. Each patient was briefly examined by R. L. S., the expert, who also had access to the written case records (but not to the automated forms). R. L. S. made a clinical diagnosis after he had seen the patient and read the initial history. A comparison was made between the diagnoses of the therapist, the computer, and the expert. For 65 of the cases the computerized diagnoses were in perfect or nearly perfect agreement with the therapists' diagnoses. In these cases the therapist merely had his diagnoses confirmed by the computer. (The expert also agreed with both therapist and computer 91% of the time in these cases.) The records for the remaining 35 cases were examined in detail to determine how often the computerized diagnostic advice would have aided the clinician because either the computer diagnoses were the more reasonable or they would have been helpful in reminding the clinician to rule out an important diagnosis.

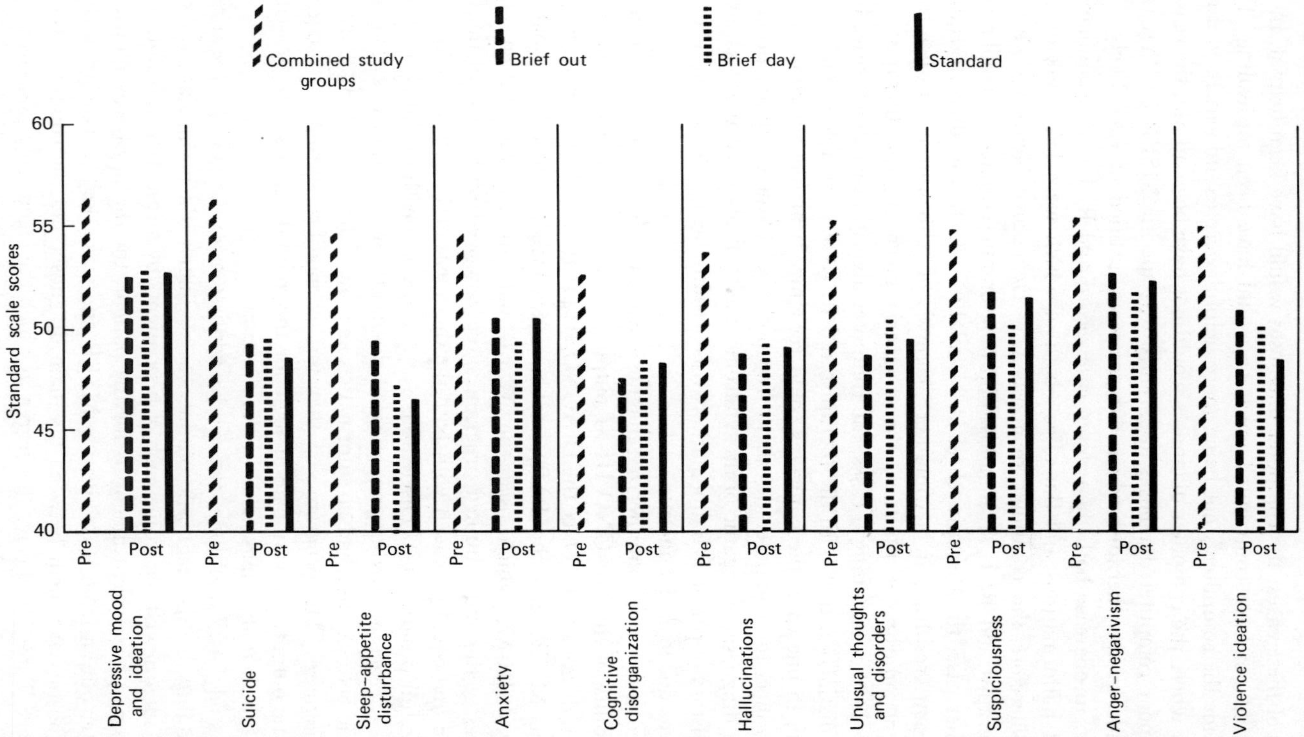

Figure 4 Mean Mental Status Examination Record scores on admission and at three weeks. None of the differences in amount of improvement were significant.

291

In 20 of these cases, the computer diagnoses would have been helpful; in 15 they would not have contributed much or would have been misleading. The reasons for the computer's not being more helpful were examined. In 9 of the 15 cases where the computer diagnoses would not have been an aid, the reason for the poor computer diagnoses apparently was specific MSER or PAR ratings made by the therapist which did not seem justified or even likely. For example, in one case both the written case record and R. L. S.'s examination revealed hallucinations and flat affect, both of which were left blank on the form. Therefore the computer diagnosis was Depressive Neurosis, whereas both therapist and R. L. S. diagnosed chronic undifferentiated schizophrenia. In another case, the therapist checked "echolalia" which was almost certainly not present, resulting in a computer diagnosis of schizophrenia rather than adolescent adjustment reaction, the diagnosis given by the therapist and R. L. S. In the remaining 6 cases, the computer algorithm was insensitive to a clinical distinction that both the therapist and R. L. S. were able to make. For example, in one case, the clinicians could recognize a manic syndrome which failed to meet the computer threshold. In another case, the computer program issued a diagnosis of organic brain syndrome due to alcohol because it assumed that a history of previous hallucinations was accountable by alcoholism when in fact it was due to schizophrenia.

A second study of computerized diagnosis was intended to assess the clinical acceptability of the DIAGNO III-M output accompanied by the rationale for the main diagnosis (4). Once the DIAGNO III program (which used data from both the MSER and the PAR) had been developed, a modified program, DIAGNO III-M, which used the MSER data alone, was written. The diagnoses of this more limited program agree very well with those of the full program and equally as well with both the therapists and "outside experts" as does the full program (7). Discussions with clinicians on the WHCS indicated that their reaction to the computerized diagnostic output was less than enthusiastic because they had no information as to how the computer had arrived at its diagnoses. The program was then further modified so that following the diagnostic output, the rationale or logic for the main diagnosis is presented in terms of the actual ratings made by the clinician.

In a study of 77 additional consecutive admissions to the WHCS, the clinical acceptability of this diagnostic output was evaluated. Each clinician was personally interviewed regarding each of his patients by a research assistant. After determining his current diagnosis for the patient, the therapist was shown the computer output from his admission MSER and was asked to indicate the level of diagnostic agreement between his main diagnosis and the computer's main diagnosis. Table 2 indicates the degree to which the computer's diagnoses were viewed as reasonable. Where applicable, the therapist was asked to indicate why he thought the computer disagreed with him. In the examination of

Table 2   Clinician's Judgment of Degree of Agreement between His Main Diagnosis and that of the Computer (N = 77)

Agreement (%)		Category
	45	Exactly the same
71	13	Same major diagnosis
	13	Just as reasonable as mine
	22	Wrong but not completely unreasonable
28		
	6	Wrong and practically nothing to support it

sources of disagreement for the "wrong" cases, there was often more than one possible reason. However in no case was it because the MSER did not contain an essential item descriptive of the mental status. In 32% of the wrong cases, the therapist had not recorded mental status information on the MSER either through oversight, or deliberate choice at the time he completed the MSER or because the information was obtained later. In 21% of the cases the clinician questioned the logic of the computer; for example, once the computer diagnosed an organic brain syndrome when the clinician considered the patient's disorientation to be secondary to a dissociative state.

For 71% of the cases the therapist stated that the output was helpful on differential diagnosis with comments such as "helped demonstrate a logical and structured approach to diagnosis." Several therapists commented favorably on the listing of diagnoses "to be considered." There was great variability among the clinicians—some found it helpful for all their cases, whereas some found it of little value. It was obvious that much of their response to the computerized output was determined by factors other than the accuracy of the computer. In one instance a therapist expressed a generally negative attitude towards the use of computers in diagnosis, and in psychiatry in general, and stated that the output was not helpful at all even though in all of his cases there was very good agreement between his diagnoses and those of the computer.

Another research use made of the computerized diagnoses was the demonstration that the uniform criteria applied by the computer program probably give a more meaningful description of the relative diagnostic frequencies in two different facilities than do the clinical diagnoses. A comparison was made of the computer distribution of diagnoses (including multiple diagnoses) with the clinical distribution for a group of unselected consecutive admissions to two New York facilities in the Multi-State Information System

Table 3   Computer and Clinical Distribution of Diagnoses (including multiple diagnoses) in Two Facilities

	Facility A N = 162		Facility B N = 122	
Diagnosis	Computer (%)	Clinical (%)	Computer (%)	Clinical (%)
Brain syndrome	33	37	8	5
Schizophrenia	39	31	48	60
Affective psychoses	1	4	4	7
Alcoholism	11	7	5	1
Drug abuse	9	6	17	0

(Table 3). Facility A (WHCS) is a community mental health center, whereas facility B is a voluntary hospital that specializes in the treatment of young adult patients. A comparison of the distributions in facility A shows that there is remarkable similarity between the clinical and the computer diagnoses. On the other hand, the same comparison in facility B shows greater discrepancy, particularly for Drug Dependence because the clinicians never reported that diagnosis. If an administrator had to rely on the reported clinical diagnoses in facility B, he almost certainly would seriously underestimate the prevalence of drug problems. If he were interested in a comparison of prevalence of schizophrenia in the two facilities, he might well exaggerate the true difference if he relied on the clinical difference of 29% (60 − 31) as compared with the computer difference of only 9% (48 − 39).*

DISCUSSION

If research use of the data which is routinely collected on the WHCS is made, some judgment regarding its reliability and validity must have been made. Just how reliable and valid is it considered to be?

This is not an easy question to answer because reliability and validity of data are always specific to the situation in which the data are collected and the use to which they are being put. On the WHCS, the therapists who have provided most of the data discussed in this paper were first- or second-year psychiatric residents, some psychology interns, and occasionally a social worker or a

* Computer diagnoses were used to describe the characteristics of the standardization sample because clinical diagnoses were not available for a large percentage of the subjects.

medical student. They received very little training in the specific use of the MSER, and their motivation and knowledge of psychopathology varied considerably. The MSER ratings and the computer output were not used by the attending psychiatrists in their supervision or in rounds, although the output became part of the clinical record in that it was read and signed by the therapist. During the period of the study, an effort was made to assure that the admission MSER was completed within a reasonable length of time, but there were exceptions. Obviously data collected under these circumstances are not as reliable and valid (regardless of use) as data collected by specially trained research evaluators whose main purpose is the collection of good research data.

An attempt was made to determine how well the routinely collected data on the WHCS agrees with data collected by the research interviewers. In one study research evaluations were made on a series of newly admitted inpatients, and the research interviewers' MSER scale scores were compared with the scale scores for the therapists. The study was not a true test of clinical use because it was not possible to have the research interviewer duplicate the therapist's clinical contact with the patient and his family. The interviewer's contact was limited to an interview conducted when the patient was interviewable. Therefore there are many possible sources of disagreement, such as different access to information and changes in the patient's behavior, that makes it difficult to judge whether the moderate degree of agreement found was due to errors on the part of the therapists or to differences in information available to the two raters (intraclass R range of .82 to .27, with 7 being .60 or higher on the 18 scales on which there was variability). A comparison of two diagnostic groups in that study indicated that the findings of the research evaluators were in relatively good agreement with those of the therapists' in that none of the conclusions would have differed greatly had the research evaluations been used rather than those collected routinely (Table 4). Data from the same study was used to contrast the profiles of a sample of newly admitted inpatients as described by the therapists and by the research evaluators. Again, there was fairly good agreement regarding the characteristics of the patient sample (Figure 5), although the therapist generally reported more pathology, particularly in those areas that are likely to show a great deal of day to day variability or rapid response to drugs.

In one of the studies of computer diagnosis, the MSER ratings were compared with what was known from the case history and personal examination of the patient (3). In only 14 out of the 100 cases, the expert judged computer diagnosis to be incorrect because of an error in the ratings.

The conclusion reached was that while the reliability and validity of the data obviously vary with the individual therapists, data collected on the WHCS are sufficiently "good" to make group comparisons when a finding of relatively large differences would be of importance. A conservative interpretation of

Table 4 *Clinical Severity Ratings from Mental Status Examination Record Evaluations Made by Therapists and Research Interviewers*

Symptom	Paranoid Schizophrenics		Depressives	
	Research Interviewer (N = 22)	Therapist (N = 21)	Research Interviewer (N = 27)	Therapist (N = 25)
Depressive ideation and mood	4.23 moderate	3.71 mild	4.59 moderate	4.80 moderate
Suicide	2.45 minimal	2.62 minimal	2.81 minimal	3.92 mild
Sleep–appetite disturbance	3.23 mild	3.48 mild	4.52 moderate	4.36 moderate
Somatic concern	2.36 minimal	2.67 minimal	2.52 minimal	2.52 minimal
Anxiety	3.86 mild	3.81 mild	3.81 mild	3.76 mild
Inappropriate appearance	2.09 minimal	2.62 minimal	1.26 none	1.68 none
Disorientation–memory	1.55 none	1.52 none	1.33 none	1.80 none
Cognitive disorganization	3.14 mild	3.48 mild	1.48 none	2.16 minimal
Hallucinations	2.50 minimal	2.52 minimal	1.52 none	1.12 none
Unusual thoughts–delusions	2.68 minimal	3.90 mild	1.26 none	1.76 none
Suspiciousness	3.73 mild	4.24 moderate	2.30 minimal	2.84 minimal
Anger–negativism	4.32 moderate	3.57 mild	3.48 mild	4.12 moderate
Violence ideation	2.09 minimal	3.29 mild	1.78 none	2.60 minimal
Denial of illness	2.50 minimal	2.33 minimal	1.81 none	2.32 minimal
Excitement	2.00 minimal	2.43 minimal	2.07 minimal	2.16 minimal
Retardation–emotional withdrawal	3.64 mild	3.19 mild	3.11 mild	3.68 mild
Alcohol abuse	1.55 none	1.90 none	2.26 suspected	2.16 suspected
Drug abuse	1.27 none	1.14 none	1.74 none	1.48 none
Judgment	3.27 only fair	3.57 only fair	2.48 good	3.08 only fair
Likeable	2.27 average	3.57 quite	3.56 quite	3.48 quite

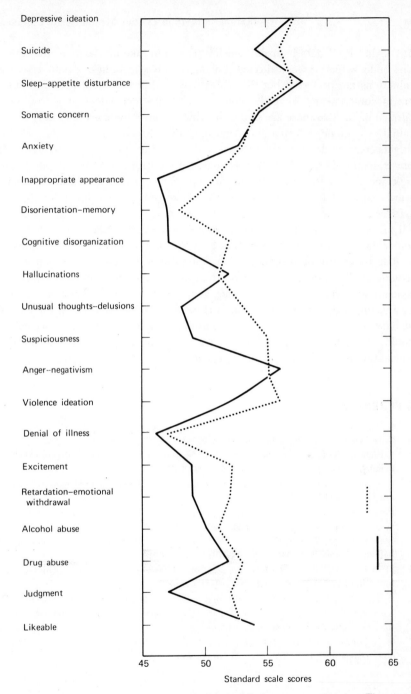

Figure 5 Mental Status Examination Record Standard Scale scores on admission. The research interviewer was limited to information obtained in an interview within a few days of admission. Research interviewer (———); therapist (- - - -); N = 170.

MSER and PAR data is made, which attempts to take into account the conditions under which it was collected. For most research studies, specific research evaluations are preferred but the realities of funding, the need for large numbers of subjects, and so forth make many studies dependent upon routinely collected data. Also there are studies in which, even if there are special research evaluations, some information regarding the therapist's evaluation of his patients may be desired. In such a situation one is apt to get better research data from the therapists if their ratings can substitute for some of the paper work and if they thus provide information that goes into the patient's official record, rather than their being asked to make research ratings in addition to their regular work.

If an individual administrator or research investigator plans to make use of similar data, it is strongly urged that he make efforts to increase the validity of the data by instituting training, encouraging use of the computer output in discussions of the patients, monitoring the quality of the ratings being made by having a supervisor review the ratings, giving feedback to the therapists regarding any use of the data beyond that of clinical records, and so on. If the user of the data has no control over the circumstances under which it is collected, he should, at the least, be quite familiar with what actually goes on and use this information in his interpretation of the data.

REFERENCES

1. R. L. Spitzer and J. Endicott, *Arch. Gen. Psychiat.*, **24** (1971), 540–547.
2. J. Endicott, R. L. Spitzer, and J. L. Fleiss, "Mental Status Examination Record (MSER): Reliability and Validity," unpublished manuscript, 1974.
3. R. L. Spitzer and J. Endicott, "Can the Computer Assist Clinicians in Diagnosis?" *Am. J. Psychiat.*, **131** (1974), 523–530.
4. R. L. Spitzer and J. Endicott, "Computer Diagnosis in an Automated Record Keeping System: A Study of Clinical Acceptability," in J. L. Crawford, D. W. Morgan, and D. T. Gianturco, Eds., *Progress in Mental Health Information Systems: Computer Applications,* Ballinger, Cambridge, Mass., 1974, pp. 77–100.
5. M. I. Herz, J. Endicott, and R. L. Spitzer, "Brief Hospitalization of Patients with Families: Initial Results," *Am. J. Psychiat.*, **132** (1975), 413–418.
6. R. L. Spitzer, J. Endicott, J. L. Fleiss, and J. Cohen, "The Psychiatric Status Schedule: A Technique for Evaluating Psychopathology and Impairment in Role Functioning," *Arch. Gen. Psychiat.*, **23** (1970), 41–55.
7. R. L. Spitzer, J. Endicott, J. Cohen, and J. L. Fleiss, "Constraints on the Validity of Computer Diagnosis," *Arch. Gen. Psychiat.*, in press.

CLINICAL MANAGEMENT

Problem Orientation in Psychiatry*

MYRON PULIER, M.D., GILBERT HONIGFELD, Ph.D. and
EUGENE M. LASKA, Ph.D.

Demands from nonclinical agencies for psychiatric data are rapidly increasing. Government funding sources, community groups, and even law courts (1) are trying to ensure provision of rational and effective treatment to each mental patient. At the same time, the current trend toward a "team" approach to psychiatric treatment calls for closer coordination among staff personnel. As a result inadequate communication processes are becoming a major bottleneck in improving quality of care, in large-scale clinical research, in management of psychiatric treatment organizations, and in monitoring the delivery of psychiatric services. Improvement in the communication process in psychiatry may therefore be crucial to general progress in the field.

Psychiatric communcations are either "horizontal" or "vertical." Horizontal communications pass among the members of a treatment team and concern one particular patient. These communications involve study of past treatment and symptoms, formulation of treatment plans and goals, implementation of therapy, and accumulation of an archival record for possible use by future

* Preparation of this report was supported in part by NIMH Grant No. 14934 (A Multi-State Information System for Psychiatric Patients), National Institute of Mental Health, United States Department of Health, Education, and Welfare.

therapists on behalf of this one patient. Vertical communications are used for evaluation and for general control of psychiatric services. This includes systematic monitoring of the progress of selected patients and comparisons of groups of patients with various psychiatric illnesses. Vertically relevant information flows both upwards towards administrative levels and downward from administrators to clinicians.

The relationships between the horizontal and vertical communications systems are complex. Decision making in the horizontal mode relies on far more accuracy and detail about a single case than does vertical "monitoring." Yet, to the clinician the relatively modest administrative requirement for upward vertical reporting seems an annoying additional burden even though most of the facts demanded by the administration should be known to the clinician anyway. In part, what the clinician resents is being obliged to transcribe this information into vertically transmittable form without gaining any direct and immediate benefit for his patient. The clinician's primary role is in the intensely detailed, rushed, "real-time" clinical milieu where he relies mostly on his memory and on spoken communication. In that context it is inefficient for him to delay urgent clinical (horizontal) work to write down superficial abstractions about the case and feed them into an impersonal slow-moving vertical administrative information system, a system where omissions and inaccuracies concerning this one case would make little practical difference. Recent efforts to improve the quality and quantity of upward flowing clinical data have been at the expense of clinical time. Of course, without such vertical transmission of clinical data, supervision and systematic review of institutional practice are vitiated, efforts at improving treatment methodology are impeded, and public accountability is frustrated. The conflicting aims and requirements of the vertical and horizontal information systems make each compete with the other. Growing vertical demands are driving administrations to impose an increasingly heavy "data tax" on the clinicians.

Lawrence Weed's concept of the problem-oriented medical information system (2) is a way of resolving the horizontal–vertical conflict. Problem orientation can be a pivot whereby horizontally flowing clinical information can be directed up the vertical system without intervention by the clinician. However the special needs of psychiatry call for adaptation of Weed's basic approach.

PROBLEM ORIENTATION

The problem-oriented practice of medicine rests on the formulation of a unique list of "problems" for each patient. This Problem List is displayed in the clinical chart as an index to the treatment record. Progress notes from all sources (doctors, nurses, physiotherapists, etc.) are appended in date order and are not, as in more traditional source-oriented charts, isolated into a separate chart area for each discipline. This integration of the progress notes echoes the integration of the multidisciplinary treatment team.

A progress note is formatted as a set of comments about one or more of the problem areas mentioned on the patient's problem list. The note is divided into sections, each headed by the title of a different problem. Information from any source is entered consecutively as a progress note labeled according to the problem or problems discussed. This differs from traditional medical record-keeping practice which sorts information, primarily according to its source, into separate areas for nurses' notes, doctors' notes, social workers' notes, and so forth.

It is far easier to make sense of a problem-oriented medical record than to grasp what has been going on from a traditional source-oriented chart. A record organized in terms of problems can more clearly show the rationale for each treatment, the relevance of each observation, and the thrust of the overall management strategy. Even if someone who reads the chart disagrees with the particular viewpoint adopted by the treatment team, the requirement that this frame of reference (the problem list for that patient) be explicit facilitates critical analysis of the working formulation without preventing alternative explanations. Thus the record is more readily "audited" by others. Paramedical staff working with the patient get a better idea of what is going on and why particular orders have been issued. A doctor taking over the case or filling in during an emergency is quickly directed toward the essentials and can therefore better manage any particular aspect of the case within the context of the other problem areas. Such explicit clinical charting immediately helps in supervision, medical audit, and peer review.

Problems with the Problem Oriented Psychiatric Record

While problem orientation has aroused the enthusiasm of many physicians and has been adopted by many major medical centers, it has been slow to catch on in psychiatry. This seems mystifying since psychiatry is one of the most institutionalized specialties and is heavily concerned with communications. The resistance to problem orientation results from certain difficulties in the problem-oriented approach that are particularly disadvantageous in psychiatry.

Today's psychiatric practice considers each patient from several angles simultaneously (3), while modern medicine rests upon a single accepted theory of organ systems, recognized syndromes, and disease etiologies. Although the problem-oriented method calls for separate listing of seemingly independent presenting symptoms, as understanding grows the problem list is revised so that related problems are merged into one on the basis of organ system, syndrome, or disease. Thus "facial rash," "lack of spontaneity," "tremor," "greasy skin," "shuffling gait," "rigidity," and "drooling" may be upgraded to "seborrheic dermatitis," "extrapyramidal motor symptoms," "lack of spontaneity," and "drooling." On a medical service these problems might be resolved into a single syndrome such as "parkinsonism" or, on an even higher level into a diagnostic entity such as "rigid form of Huntington's chorea" or "neuroleptic-induced parkinsonism." This progressive abstraction and combination of problem areas reflects the physician's improving grasp of the case. However general psychiatry lacks any single accepted conceptual scheme above the level of descriptive psychopathology. A psychiatrist would be quick to point out that the "lack of spontaneity" in the above example may well be multidetermined, a situation which would be obscured (to the detriment of treatment) by merging that problem into the "parkinsonism" syndrome. The psychiatrist could carry this objection to an extreme and call for a problem list where each psychiatric symptom, indeed each personal idiosyncracy, is separately listed and treated as if it had a life of its own. The resulting progress notes would be fragmented, and clinical communications channeled by this problem list would be confounded. Paradoxically, current psychiatric practice also takes a holistic viewpoint by regarding the patient as having a single complex "problem." Carried too far this approach also can smother interdisciplinary team communications and impede task assignment within the team. Clearly a balance must be struck between differentiation and integration in developing a practical psychiatric case formulation.

Even a problem list optimally balanced between the specific and the general may not fit the diverse settings in which psychiatric services are provided. The problem list (1) unresolved negative Oedipal complex (2) anal eroticism (3) counterphobic defensive structure may be useful to a psychotherapist but will hardly guide the writing of nurses' notes or a report to a probation officer.

A third deficiency of the medical-style problem-oriented record is that it is inadequate for vertical communication needs in psychiatry. Psychiatric practice is largely institutionalized because of the high patient/psychiatrist ratio, the chronicity of many psychiatric problems, the necessity for a multidisciplinary approach, the social stigma, and the enormous cost of treatment. Consequently, administrative and research requirements for information are unusually great in psychiatry. Periodic cross-sectional evaluations of large numbers of patients are now being sought in all types of psychiatric care facilities. These require large amounts of clinical information. The quality of information sent up by the psychiatric clinician depends heavily upon the immediate and direct benefit to him and to his patient of whatever specific data he provides. Information-gathering forms that seem merely an imposition on the line clinician are negligently filled out. Yet more and more "data tax" will inevitably be levied against the clinical services. If there are elaborate problem-oriented record-keeping requirements where the clinician is at the same time feeding the nonreactive generalized vertical system, then clinical, administrative, and research functions must all suffer.

Integration of Psychiatric Communications

Any major improvements in psychiatric information flow will depend on integration of horizontal clinical reporting with vertical administrative reporting. The following four main issues require resolution:

1. The place of oral communication in psychiatry.
2. The wide range in levels of detail and abstraction of the same basic data called for at different places within a facility.
3. The contrast between vertical requirements for regular surveys and summaries of material on many patients versus sudden unanticipated horizontal demands for immediate access to up-to-date details about an individual.
4. The necessity of keeping communications moving during the transition from the dual to the unitary integrated information structure.

Face-to-face conversation is essential to the team process. Yet, to an increasing extent, records must be kept. Problem-oriented records can benefit team discussion by giving team members a common frame of reference and by focusing attention around the patient's specific problem areas. Team deliberations organized around the problem list and the progress note format can easily be reported by some team member other than the psychiatrist.

Differing degrees of specificity versus generalization needed in various settings can be generated by means of "coding," "highlighting," and "rating." "Coding" means categorizing each problem on the problem list into a standard hierarchically structured classification system or "dictionary." The category to which a listed problem belongs tells to a large extent what the problem is. By means of the code for this category it is possible to isolate subgroups of patients with similar problem configurations or to examine which patterns of treatment are associated with the most favorable outcome of each problem. The hierarchical structure of the problem-classification dictionary permits capture of the specificity inherent in tailoring a problem list for the individual patient yet provides the standardization necessary for comparing, contrasting, and aggregating problems on various levels by computers (Figure 1).

Batch-mode computer processing is usually adequate for vertical reporting. Most information need not be fully up to date, and little detail about individuals is required. In contrast, a computer system handling all horizontal communication needs would have to use expensive on-line conversational mode technology since clinical work involves large amounts of highly accurate,

```
ADS/PCPR PRCBLEM CICTICNAFY VERSICN-C7 10FEB73                          PAGE  5

ICODEI FFCBLEM TITLES                        I DEFINITIONS (EXAMPLES)


   IAI-ALAPTIVE ANC COPING

AA.CC  ALCCHCL ABUSE
AA.10     STEADY ALCCHCL BVERLSE
AA.20     BINGE CRINKING              *INTERMITTENT BOUTS OF HEAVY CRINKING
                                        FCR SEVERAL CAYS
AA.30     REACTIVE INTOXICATICN       *DRINKS BPIEFLY AS CHARACTERISTIC RESFCNCE
                                        TO SPECTFIC STRESS TO AVOID FACING
                                        FEELINGS CR RESPCNSIBILITES


AC.00  NEGLECTS SELF CARE             *HYGEINE, CRESS, FEEDING, HEALTH CARE
AC.1C     NEGLECTS HYGEINE
AC.110    NEGLECTS PERSCNAL           *BCCY CDCR, GRCCMING, HAIR, NAILS
            CLEANLINESS
AC.120    NEATNESS CF CRESS
AC.20     DAILY SCHEDULING            *ARISING, SLEEPING, EATING CNTIME ETC
AC.30     FEEDING
AC.40     HEALTH CARE
AC.410    ENCANCERS HEALTH            *EATS CIRTY FCCD, CCESN'T DRESS WARMLY
                                        NEGLECTS TAKING MEDS, OBVIOUS ILLNESS ETC.
                                        (FCR CRUG ABUSE SEE AA,AN,AD FCR SELF HARM
                                        SEE AG)

AC.5C     ACCRNMENT, STYLING
AC.510    STYLE CF CRESS              *HAIRSTYLE CR CLOTHES ARE CDD, INAPPRCPRATE
AC.520    SELF CECCRATION             *TATTCCS, SCARIFICATION, JEWELERY, ETC.

AD.CC  DRUG ABLSE, CTHER             *CCWNS, SECATIVES, TRANQUILLIZERS USED
AD.10     SECATIVES, BARBITURATES     WITHCUT MECICAL DIRECTICN
AD.110    BARBITURATE ABUSE
AD.120    GLUTETHIMICE (DCRIDEN)
AD.130    PARALCEHYDE
AD.140    METHACUALCNE (QUAALUDE)
AD.150    ABUSE CF TRANQUILIZERS
AD.20     PSYCHO-STIMULANT CRUGS
AD.21C    CCCAINE-CERIVED CRUGS
AD.220    AMPHETAMINE CLASS DRUGS     *SPEED, UFS
AD.23C    CAFFEINE ABUSE              *EXCESSIVE USE OF CAFFEINE, NO-DCZ, CCLA
AD.3C     MARIJUANA, CANNABIS
AD.310    MARIJUANA GRASS ABLSE       *REEFERS, GRASS, "TEA", HEMP
AD.320    HASHISH                     *HASH,BHANG
AD.330    THC ABLSE                   *"LIQUID MARIJUANA"
AD.40     HALLUCINCGENS
AD.410    LSC ABLSE
AD.420    MESCALINE ABLSE
AD.430    PEYCTE ABUSE
AD.440    PSYLCCIBIN ABUSE
AD.450    ATROPINE-CLASS ABUSE
AD.5C     FUNE SNIFFING
AD.510    SNIFFS GLUE
AD.520    SNIFFS CASOLINE, KEROSENE
AD.530    ANESTHETIC INHALATICN       *LAUGHING GAS, ETHER, CYCLOPROPANE
AD.540    SNIFFS CLEANING FLUID       *CARBCN TETRACHLORICE
AD.6C     ANALGESIC CRUG ABUSE        *ASPIRIN, APC'S
AD.7C     BRCMIDE ABUSE
```

Figure 1   Problem Dictionary.

"idiosyncratic," and up-to-date information that must be quickly organized and available on demand. Computerization of all psychiatric clinical information is wholly impractical. Automation must be restricted to handling only certain "highlights" of the clinical data, with a complementary manual information system dealing with the bulk of the material. The highlight of each progress note may be skimmed from a special progress note form (Figure 2). This form accepts certain coded data and limited narrative text but allows lengthy narrative material to enter the "manual" portion of the case record. The short narrative should be like a newspaper headline that summarizes the message in the remainder of the note. Only the codes and this highlight are entered into the computer. A carbon copy of the entire note comes through onto the clinical chart where it is immediately available for manual horizontal use. The computer rearranges and processes the material it receives to provide so-

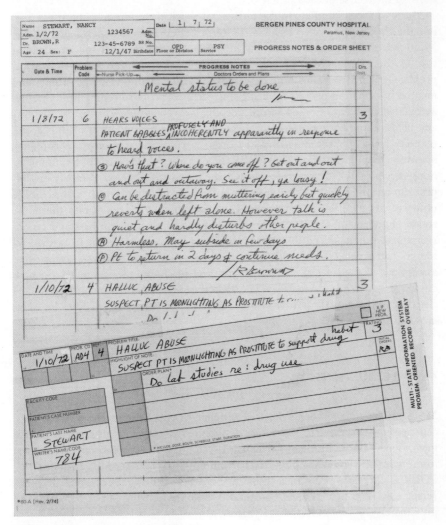

Figure 2   Progress Notes and Order Sheet.

phisticated vertical communications as well as a family of horizontally useful reports. These reports can summarize the course of each problem from various angles and can include several indices to the manual progress notes, such as a display of all highlights in order of date, another display in order of problem, and another arranged in order of type of treatment planned. The inclusion of "ratings" of the severity of each problem on the section of the progress note entered into the computer permits automated graphic display of progress in each area and of the impact of various stressful events and therapeutic interventions on the course of each problem.

Many of these solutions to the horizontal–vertical conflict have been worked into the Problem Oriented Psychiatric Record (POPR) system developed by the Multi-State Information System (MSIS). The POPR permits the amalgamation of the existing MSIS high-volume vertical information network with a problem-oriented organization of clinical practice. Options range from fully manual information processing using unstructured problem coding up to highly automated problem-oriented record keeping with longitudinal progress display and goal-attainment monitoring. These options permit smooth transition from manual source-oriented clinical records to computer-supported problem-oriented communications. The POPR link to the MSIS vertical communications capability provides cross-patient and cross-institutional comparisons of problem-oriented data. Eventually it will be possible to enhance horizontal utility of the POPR by feeding vertical information back down into the horizontal channels for automatic generation of suggested problem lists and target symptoms, automatic enrichment of clinical notes with material from diverse sources, automated search for special dangers and opportunities, automated assessment of the adequacy of treatment and discharge plans, and automated discharge summary production. The POPR is a medium for returning to the clinician, in digested and clinically useful form, the information he sent upwards into the vertical system.

AN IMPLEMENTATION

MSIS has modified Weed's original problem-oriented design to serve the special needs of psychiatric institutional practice. A series of alternative implementations of the Problem Oriented Psychiatric Record concept progresses from manual record keeping to partial automation. An intermediate-level POPR is currently being field tested at Bergen Pines County Hospital in New Jersey, a 1200-bed general hospital whose psychiatric unit services approximately 3000 admissions per year.

Chart Section

The usual clinical chart has two major portions. The first part, the initial work-up, includes the anamnesis, material from old records, and initial examinations and tests. The second portion describes the clinical course, what treatment the patient has received, and the result. This section of the record comes to its fruition in the Discharge Summary.

An important innovation of the problem-oriented concept is the insertion of another portion of chart between the two traditional ones. This new part records the clinical judgment used in the case, that is, the chain of reasoning that led to the diagnosis and the thinking behind the doctors' orders and nurses' interventions. It is the absence of this key information that makes it so hard to piece together from traditional charts just why things were done for the patient. Until now, the lack of access to the clinical reasoning has made it impossible to design a "reasonable" computer-generated Discharge Summary.

Information Base

Before a discussion of the new "reasoning" portion of the chart, a review of the first section of the POPR is in order. This section is called the "Information Base." (Most literature on problem orientation uses the term "Data Base," which is undesirable in this context since "data base" has a special technical meaning in computer sciences.) The Information Base corresponds to the initial workup. It is essentially an outline of the minimum data which should be amassed for every case. This outline is spelled out on various printed forms so that each category of information has a special location where it may be found. The outline is organized in terms of the information itself rather than in terms of its source, be it nurse, psychologist, or doctor. Many of the forms have already been computerized in the MSIS so that the data on these are available for computer-produced reports (see Figure 3).

The Information Base can be thought of as a "shadow board" in a tool shop on which the outline of each tool is drawn. It doesn't matter who hangs the tools up on the shadow board as long as each tool is hung in the right place. The "shadows" also make it quite clear which tools are missing. The effort of putting data in the right location of the chart is repaid by ease of recovering data and ease in keeping track of how well the data are getting into the chart, in individual cases as well as in the treatment center as a whole.

While room is available for more than just the basic data on each case, the formats cry out for at least the minimum. The Information Base is organized to be a springboard for the clinical reasoning section of the chart.

Automated Information Base	
Data Type	MSIS Form
Identifying data	Admission Form
Family history Developmental and social history Psychiatric history Events leading to current episode	Psychiatric Anamnestic Record (PAR)
Drug history	PAR and Drug Order Form
Mental status examination	Mental Status Examination Record (MSER)
Routine tests (lab, x—ray, etc.)	General Application System Forms

Figure 3   Automated Information Base.

Clinical Reasoning Section

The chief of the clinical team abstracts and summarizes the data in the Information Base into a Problem List. This is a tabulation of the major issues the
patient presents to the clinical team. It includes not only diagnoses but such
matters as insufficient funds, difficulty with the family, no place to live, not taking proper care of himself, and other matters which may be considered "problems." This Problem List serves as a capsule summary of the Information
Base, a birds-eye view of the case. In addition, the Problem List is a topic
index for all progress notes subsequently written.

For each listed problem, an initial assessment and initial plans are required.
The writer gives a detailed description of the problem and its underlying causes
as he understands them. He then states what he is going to do about the
problem during the proposed term of treatment and what his tentative aftercare plans are. Thus, instead of one overall formulation and a treatment plan
which is vaguely hinted at in the initial orders, an assessment and a plan for
each separate problem are stated. In addition, a goal is specified for every
problem. The goal is a statement of what each problem is expected to look like
when the patient is discharged or transferred from the service.

In other words, the team writes down *what* is going to be done for the
patient, *why* it is going to be done, and *how* they expect it to turn out in the
end. All of this is spelled out in bite-size chunks, each chunk being a problem
on the Problem List. This makes it clear to everyone on the treatment team and
to anyone called on in an emergency just what treatment is all about for this
patient.

The Problem List is not always complete early in treatment. At any time, even after the initial staffing conference, other problems may be added to the list when recognized. Each new problem gets its own initial assessment and initial plans.

Progress Record

The Problem List directly controls the last major portion of the clinical chart, the Progress Record. In contrast to the traditional source-oriented chart, with segregated sections for nurses' notes, doctors' progress notes, occupational therapy, notes, and so on, all members of the treatment team write notes consecutively in the Problem Oriented Progress Record. Each note is partitioned according to which problem is being discussed. This limitation of the universe of discourse to one single problem area at a time makes it easier to grasp what the writer of the note is driving at. Suppose the topic is "hallucinations," the nature of which has already been described in the record. When a writer merely says "severe," this is sufficient information for the reader to know what he is talking about. This permits the use of a general Rating Scale to describe how a problem is affecting a patient's life at the moment. A single scale value may often be an adequate progress note, so nurses are encouraged to write only a rating number if they really have nothing else to say. Provision for slightly more detail is made via the concept of the "highlight," a very brief abstraction stripped of detail but sufficient to give the gist of what is happening with that problem. Even more information may be entered, but usually a rating and highlight are enough.

Another feature of the POPR is the inclusion of Doctors' Orders as part of the Progress Note. Under a problem title, a doctor writes relevant orders following his highlight, thus making it clear why the orders are being written. A writer can also list plans. The fact that a particular plan is actually a doctor's order is indicated by the doctor's initials in a special location on the note (see Figure 2).

The Progress Note for a particular problem may hold as much detail as the writer desires. After completing the more abstract portion of his note, he can spell out the patient's complaints, requests, or remarks, can detail his own observations or what has been reported to him, can explain his new assessment and viewpoints, and can expand in detail on the plans that were listed in the earlier section of the note on that problem. The earlier abstract or "SCAN" section holds the essence of the entire note so that a reader has the option of scanning the Highlights until he finds something that he wants to read in detail. The existence of this SCAN section makes it possible to computerize the psychiatric record in a convenient and useful way.

The Computerized POPR

A carbon-backed overlay form is used in writing the SCAN portion of the Progress Note. The date, problem code, writer identification, highlight, severity rating, plans, and Doctors' Orders are written through this overlay onto the Progress Note Sheet in the clinical chart so that they immediately become a permanent part of the patient's written record. The overlay itself is then sent for computer processing.

Demographic admission data, the Problem List, initial assessments and plans, and the "meat" of each Progress Note contained in the SCAN portion of the note are sent for computer processing. Several automated reports are returned. One is an "echo" of the information sent in, a chronological listing of problem-oriented highlights, severity ratings, and associated orders and treatment plans. This chronological report shows how things have been unfolding since admission.

A second report provides the same information but is arranged in order of problem and displays the patient's progress within each problem area. The report may be compared with the *New York Times Index* one uses in a library. Under each topic (in the case of the POPR the topic headings would be the entries on the patient's Problem List) are the headlines that touch on this topic, that is, the highlights. One can choose to follow the unfolding story simply by scanning the headlines, but if something looks particularly interesting one can turn to the corresponding issue of the *New York Times* for that date. In the case of the POPR, one turns to the chart under the date given where the problem code points to the complete note which includes the highlight and all the details that were not entered in the computer.

From this problem-oriented computer report, a supervisor can readily find the latest note written about any problem and thus make sure that no problem has been neglected too long.

Discharge Summary

The POPR was designed to facilitate preparation of the Discharge Summary. The Problem List and the description of each problem on presentation are copied directly into the Discharge Summary. The final computer entry for each problem is a description of the status of that problem at the time of discharge. This final status entry, together with the ratings of initial severity, goal, and severity upon discharge show whether the expectations for this problem were attained or whether treatment fell short of the goal (Figure 4).

A narrative of the immediate events that led to hospitalization and some sentences to tie the problems together are added to the Discharge Summary. This narrative material has traditionally been reguired anyway for the initial

Name	STEWART, NANCY		Date	1 2 72

Adm. 1/2/72 1234567 Adm. No.

Dr. BROWN, R 123-45-6789 SS No.

Age 24 Sex: F 12/1/47 Birthdate

OPD Floor or Division PSY Service

PROBLEM LIST & DISCHARGE NOTE
SHEET # 1 OF 1 SHEETS

A-1 R (active, inactive, redefined or referred to . . .)

Problem Status and Date of Status	Code	PROBLEM TITLE (Onset)	Description or Manifestations	SEVERITY RATING Presenting	Goal	Discharge
-- A 12/10/71 -- I 12/28/71	1 (AD.31)	MARIJUANA ABUSE		1	0	0 Goal Met
STATUS ON DISCHARGE		** RESOLVED 12/28/71 **				(YES) NO
--A 12/10/71 --R (#4) 1/5/72	2 (PS)	SLEEP PROBLEMS		3	1	1 Goal Met
STATUS ON DISCHARGE		** SUBSUMED BY PROBLEM 4 **				(YES) NO
--A 1/4/72 --R (#4) 1/5/72	3	AGITATION	Possibly secondary to drug abuse	4	1	1 Goal Met
STATUS ON DISCHARGE		** SUBSUMED BY PROBLEM 4 **				(YES) NO
--A 1/5/72	4 (AD.4)	HALLUCINOGEN ABUSE		2	0	4 Goal Met
STATUS ON DISCHARGE		POLICE PICK-UP; NO ARREST. RETURNED TO FAMILY.				YES (NO)
--A 1/5/72	5 (MC.1)	SUSPICIOUS	of others, esp. co-workers and family members	3	2	4 Goal Met
STATUS ON DISCHARGE		FAMILY REPORTS GETTING BELLIGERENT PHONE CALLS FROM PATIENT				YES (NO)
--A 1/5/72	6 (MP.41)	HEARS VOICES	Content is threatening and accusatory	2	0	5 Goal Met
STATUS ON DISCHARGE		PATIENT STATES VOICES SUGGEST SUICIDE, CONVINCED VOICES ARE REAL.				YES (NO)
						Goal Met
STATUS ON DISCHARGE						YES NO
						Goal Met
STATUS ON DISCHARGE						YES NO

DISCHARGE SUMMARY (describe treatments given and response, complications, unusual incidents, consults)

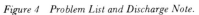

(number) OPD admission (describe)
"This was the 2nd BPCH psychiatric hospitalization of this ... 24 year old single clerk-typist

●Form
[Rev. 2/74]

(OVER)

Figure 4   Problem List and Discharge Note.

311

Name	STEWART, NANCY			Date	1 2 72		BERGEN PINES COUNTY HOSPITAL
Adm.	1/2/72	1234567	Adm. No.				Paramus, New Jersey
Dr.	BROWN,R	123-45-6789	SS No.	OPD	PSY		
Age 24	Sex F	12/1/47	Birthdate	Floor or Division	Service		Psychiatric Discharge Summary
							Side 2

DISCHARGE SUMMARY (CONTINUED) *List treatments, complications, incidents, consults*

who was referred from the Psych. Inpatient Service on 1/2/72 for aftercare.

Pt had been hospitalized for acute psychosis resulting from LSD and marijuana abuse. She improved rapidly on chlorpromazine and was discharged back to her parents' home for followup in clinic by a social worker plus medication maintenance.

COURSE: Pt returned to work but immediately was noted to be hearing voices and talking to herself. Her performance was unsatisfactory and worsening. Attendance at clinic was irregular. Although CHLORPROMAZINE 75mg QID and COGENTIN 1mg BID were prescribed, lab tests showed that the medication was not being taken and that pt had instead resumed abusing various drugs.

When pt was picked up by police obviously incoherent and hallucinated the family notified this clinic. It was clear that at this time outpatient treatment lack sufficient clout to manage the patient.

(Discharge Orders (Please Print)

(cross out one)   (cross out)   (cross out)

~~Discharge~~/Transfer Patient   ~~AMA~~   To custody of ~~self~~   INPATIENT SERVICE

DISCHARGE PLANS *(clinic appointments; name of responsible therapists; long-term recommendations)*

Patient should be kept on at least 400mg of CHLORPROMAZINE and kept in hospital longer than last time. More adequate plans for socialization and more gradual release to the outside will be needed.

MED GIVEN OR Rx'D ON DISCHARGE *(dose, # of tabs given, renewable?)*   CHLORPROMAZINE 100mg QID:

COGENTIN 1mg TID

DISCHARGE DIAGNOSES *(improvements & prognosis of each)*   295.3 SCHIZOPHRENIA, PARANOID TYPE; deteriorated. Prognosis guarded.   294.31 PSYCHOSIS WITH HALLUCINOGEN INTOXICATION, ACUTE; deteriorated. Short-term prognosis good.

Date	Signature (Resident)	Signature (Attending)
1/26/72	R Brown MD	Jan Smith

•60 B (Rev. 2/74)

Figure 5 Psychiatric Discharge Summary.

312

staffing conference so that no extra work is required here at the time of discharge. What does need to be added to the Discharge Summary on termination is a list of the treatments the patient received. Since all treatments and plans have already been entered into the computer, the POPR system generates as its third report a list of treatments showing at which problems each treatment was aimed (see Chapter 00). Working from this report, the clinician can easily summarize treatments and can then comment on their effects.

The Discharge Summary closes with a list of the dispositions made for the patients such as to what further care he is being referred, to whom he is being discharged, what medications he is receiving at the time of discharge, plus the final official diagnoses. Since this information is often required anyway as part of the discharge orders, the discharge orders themselves may be written directly onto the Psychiatric Discharge Summary Form (Figure 5).

CONCLUSIONS

Efforts to improve existing psychiatric communications have exposed fundamental contradictions between the needs of two modes of communication, the horizontal (clinical) and the vertical (research–administrative). While neither communication system can function without the other, supplying data to two independent systems is an unacceptable burden on the clinician who sees little benefit from the "double bookeeping" involved; yet the two systems can support each other. With the vertical system feeding from the horizontal, a utilization review committee could quickly extract desired details of individual treatment, and a horizontal system feeding from the vertical could give the clinician an overview of his patient's treatment and could compare that patient with many similar ones. A problem-oriented structuring seems the best approach toward integration of horizontal and vertical written communications in a stepwise manner which allows each psychiatric facility to upgrade its record keeping at its own rate, moving from simple manual operations to sophisticated computer-mediated methods.

REFERENCES

1. Wyatt v. Stickney, 334 F. Sup. 1341.
2. L. Weed, *Medical Records, Medical Education, and Patient Care.* Case Western Reserve, Cleveland, 1969.
3. R. Michels, *Psychotherapy Social Sci. Rev.,* **6,** 26–27 (1972).

CLINICAL MANAGEMENT

Program Evaluation and the Treatment Support "Package"

MYRON PULIER, M.D.

The evaluation of the effects of treatment or of treatment programs in psychiatry has been fraught with difficulty. Only a very few carefully controlled outcome studies have been acceptable. The current methodology of evaluation is even more unwieldy in the area of program evaluation. We can speak about availability of services, number of patients served, cost per case, and so forth, but do not know what good this all does for the patient or for the community.

A radical change in this state of affairs is now possible because of the existence of the Multi-State Information System (MSIS). This computer-based network allows scores of community mental health centers and state hospitals to feed clinical data on individual patients into one central facility. The communications channels this system provides between clinician and data processing center permit the consideration of an entirely new concept, the treatment support "package." This abstraction fits somewhere between the individual therapeutic intervention and the treatment program. MSIS makes possible the realization of this new concept and allows useful evaluation of therapeutic effectiveness.

The following discussion is divided into a description of the package concept and remarks on how the package can be evaluated.

DESCRIPTION OF THE PACKAGE CONCEPT

A "package" is defined as some coherent concrete body of methodology, instructions, forms, instruments, and so on that can be offered as a whole to several treatment facilities independently and that does not require any further contact with its originators for its operation. An example of this would be a set of training films for state hospital attendants. Duplicates of this set could be provided to various wards or to various hospitals. One way of evaluating this package would be to test the null hypothesis that "Introduction of Package A makes no significant difference to Patient-Improvement-Criterion B." Another example of a package could be an MMPI-interpretive program together with proper forms and instructions. This package could be shipped to various hospitals or hospital wards, and the effect of this shipment on treatment outcome may then be noted.

The reader must be somewhat confused at this point. How does calling something a "package" help us? Let us look at what happens when a package is shipped to a ward. First of all, the personnel may never get around to using the package, or they might use it "incorrectly." Somebody might become very enthusiastic over some part of the package and utilize it in a manner which was never dreamed of by its creators. These creators, the "shippers," exercise no control over how the package is used. They don't force anyone to use it, prevent its abuse, or issue directives or reminders. If the package is not being used or is being used in strange new ways, then what can we measure and what good are our measurements?

We are measuring the effect of shipping the package. We are not considering the package as such. In essence, we are applying a stimulus (package) to a black box (treatment unit) and are observing the effects of what we have done.

The practical consequences of this at once become obvious even though we are thinking in ways not generally applied to medical treatment. If we can show that great positive benefit comes from mailing a package to a state hospital, the precise manner in which this package exerts its effect is immaterial. If the package itself is never used the way it was intended but instead triggers off some bright ideas or innovations, it doesn't really matter; it is still beneficial to send the package around. Of course we are not restricted to such simple-minded conclusions, but could always take a closer look at just how the package "worked" so that we could design a better, more effective package or at least a cheaper one which would do the same thing. Maybe the set of hospital attendant training films was helpful only because the second reel illustrates one useful technique, while all the rest of the films are ineffective. If we somehow discover this fact (such as by experimental manipulation) we could eliminate the useless reels of film. We would then have a new and cheaper package to export. However, even if we didn't know that only one reel is actually required, at least we are in a position to send out a definitely useful product (the whole set of films) despite the fact that most of it is unnecessary. To exaggerate this point, suppose that just getting the attendants together to watch any sort of movie is beneficial. Of course there is certainly no harm in having them watch training films if patient care is thereby positively affected. But if we find that old Mickey Mouse cartoons are even better or cheaper it follows that we should ship those out instead.

The most important attributes of the package concept are its simplicity, its rationality, its generality, and its practical applicability. It allows the originators of each package temporarily to rise above the confusion caused by some therapeutic interventions being useful in certain disorders but not in others, or by the package being effective in certain hands, but not in others. While such might certainly be true about any package or its components, dealing with that problem is for the individual therapist or for the director of the therapeutic unit. Of course, if the originators of a package find that it is useful in retarded depression but harmful in schizophrenia they could develop a new package resembling the old one except that the new package would contain an explanation or warning about the importance of diagnosis. They could then evaluate whether the new package (including the warning) is superior to the old one.

THE EFFECTIVENESS METER

The package concept obviously falls on its face without reliable evaluative techniques. It is essential that the impact of a package be measurable and this is where MSIS comes in.

The more easily understood and acceptable a criterion of efficacy is, the less sensitive this criterion is likely to be. Average length of stay in hospital, for example, seems to be something that we could project onto a "desirable–undesirable" continuum. Yet length of hospitalization depends upon so many variables that whether introduction of a package influences readings along this measure or not would be hard to determine unless the change were dramatic. The marketing of phenothiazines since the mid-1950s may have constituted a package that resulted in a sharply decreased mean duration of psychiatric hospitalization, but many writers dispute this, pointing to the fact that the total state hospital population began to decline before tranquilizers were introduced. Indeed, whether these drugs are really helpful in the long run remains controversial. The apparent short-term symptomatic improvement shown by many psychotic patients who receive these drugs does not necessarily imply that tranquilizers have been beneficial in any global sense. There is clearly a need for some way of measuring "global benefit" so that public health policy decisions (such as regards regulation of tranquilizer usage) can be made more rationally.

The Multi-State Information System gathers data bearing on the clinical status of tens of thousands of patients. Evaluations are made on uniform, standardized checklists that are easily studied statistically. From the information coming in, changes in patients' clinical status may be detected and compared, and the progress of one group of patients may be contrasted with that of other groups. What is particularly relevant to the present discussion is that patient progress on a group of wards may be compared with progress in another group of wards. If we compute the difference appearing on some progress variable averaged over a randomly selected "experimental" group of wards versus the value for a "control" group we have what amounts to an "effectiveness meter" that responds to whatever "experimental condition" we have imposed on the "experimental group." Since measurements are arriving daily we can observe the time course of the effect of the experimental condition on the progress of state hospital inpatients as dramatically as if we were observing a muscle twitch with a galvanometer.

What kind of effectiveness meter should be constructed to begin with? While any criterion is open to severe criticism, a sum of scores on Spitzer's MSER factors (1) may offer the best currently available measure of improvement. This is so mainly because the necessary data are already pouring in from hundreds of state hospital wards. The sheer volume of these data might provide sufficient sensitivity to allow evaluation of the impact of introducing various packages. The availability of all sorts of supplementary data besides the MSER (see Part 2) and the possibility of introducing packages experimentally in balanced or randomized fashion to various treatment units could allow rather sophisticated studies to be done. The effects of patient age, diagnosis, occupational status, intelligence, mood, severity of problem, length of stay, presence of thought disorder, and so on could all be mathematically eliminated so that the effect of introduction of the package could become the major source of variance in our cleaned-up criterion variable, the effectiveness meter.

In the course of time the wealth of data that is flowing into the MSIS central data bank will permit development of increasingly more refined, reliable, and sensitive effectiveness meters. However a new data-collection method would not be required for each new package to be fieldtested. Furthermore, a latin-square overlaid pattern of package distribution will permit evaluation of the effectiveness of many packages at once.

Of what will packages consist? In the near future they will probably be organized around new computer services being developed at MSIS. The communications made possible by the computer network will allow highly sophisticated, flexible and adaptable packages to be fashioned that would have a better chance of being useful in a variety of settings than would such more traditional packages as an issue of the *American Journal of Psychotherapy,* or a drug warning from the FDA, or a pay raise.

The concept of the package illustrates the potential of the computer network as a management information and administrative tool. The basic idea may be modified and expanded, as the examples immediately above are intended to show, to include various administrative maneuvers we don't usually consider therapeutic ploys. Ideally, however, a FDA warning is really intended to improve patient care. Whether or not it is worth the mailing costs is presently unclear. Do physicians actually read the warning, remember it, take it seriously? We may now be in a position to clarify such questions. The MSIS network may be a key to giving us feedback between *what* we are trying to do in mental health and *how well* we are doing.

CLINICAL MANAGEMENT

The Drug-Monitoring System: Managerial and Research Implications

GEORGE M. SIMPSON, M. B., Ch.B., M.R.C.PSYCH.

The Drug-Monitoring System comprises a comprehensive computerized record of the drug history of each patient in the facility. It includes all drugs given since the patient's admission, the reason each drug was administered, the reason dosage changes were instituted, and the reason for the discontinuation of drugs. Its basic function is to provide a readible and accessible record of the patient's treatment history for the patient's chart and for the treating psychiatrists. While this is the most basic and practical application of the system, it has other functions as well. A description is given here of the managerial applications of the Drug-Monitoring System followed by a discussion of its research potential.

MANAGERIAL FUNCTIONS

Each Psychotropic Drug Order written by a physician is immediately recorded in the patient's drug history stored in the computer. At regular intervals, the

321

physicians are provided with a list of the current prescriptions of all their patients so that they have an immediate overview of their patients' current prescriptions. This allows the physician to check that all his orders were instituted or canceled and to insure that no errors in instituting the drugs occurred. It alerts him to the administration of very high or very low dosages of a drug being prescribed which may indicate that something is amiss.

From a managerial point of view, these monthly records permit a monitoring of which drugs are being used (for example, it allows a review of why newer and more expensive drugs are being used on an acute admission ward where patients are less likely to be treatment resistant and can be expected to respond to the older less expensive drugs) and also provides an opportunity to review the multiplicity of drugs sometimes prescribed by psychiatrists. In a Boston study (1), this information was used to monitor changes in prescribing habits following an intensive training program for hospital employees on psychopharmacology. The cost of drugs was reduced by using single daily doses (large-dose tablets, e.g., are cheaper per unit than small dose tablets) even though patient days of treatment increased during the same period. The use of antiparkinson agents also dropped dramatically when they were no longer used prophylactically and were administered only for limited periods of time.

The recording of reasons for changing drugs and of side effects is particularly valuable. In the past a severe or very dangerous side effect would be described in the patient's chart but it might not be immediately accessible to a new physician with the regular chart, particularly if polypharmacy was being used when the reaction occurred and the offending drug was not identified. With the computer system, it would be highlighted on the patient's computer chart and the possible use of a drug which might produce allergies or white cell depressions could be easily avoided.

The drug system, at the moment, is used primarily in hospitalized populations, but with the current change in emphasis towards treatment in the community, the hospital populations are diminishing rapidly without any known change in the number of schizophrenics and with no evidence that the severity of this illness is in any way altered. In an outpatient setting, a chronic patient who has been receiving neuroleptics for some 20 years presents a difficult problem in teasing out all the pertinent data concerning his previous drug treatments. Thus, with hospitalized patients, drugs which were not useful and specific drug allergies, for example, are more likely to be known but these present a much greater problem with outpatients. Here the computerized drug history is a valuable source of material for the outpatient clinicians.

The Drug-Monitoring System also generates a drug inventory including both projected requirements and an ongoing record of what is being used. It thus aids in the ordering of drugs and provides, for each clinical unit, regular estimates of the total cost of drugs prescribed.

RESEARCH IMPLICATIONS

The data in the drug system can be used, at its most basic level and without transformation, to examine actual drug usage in any particular setting. Thus ongoing drug treatments can be evaluated in terms of appropriateness of treatment or generally accepted orthodox practice. Such studies (2) have been carried out at Rockland Psychiatric Center although they are not currently part of the ongoing monitoring system. Thus it was possible to evaluate the total drug usage in the hospital by age, sex, diagnosis, and so on. The studies revealed a very high usage of neuroleptics irrespective of diagnosis, and also a considerable amount of polypharmacy and widespread, long-term usage of antiparkinson agents. It also showed that females received higher dosages of neuroleptics than males in every age group except adolescents where male dosages were higher. This type of study could become an ongoing process associated with an education program.

Beyond this the Drug Monitoring System provides a data base that can be used in a variety of ways. Together with demographic data, the drug system enables a researcher to select subjects on a drug and/or demographic basis for research. Thus the computerized system makes it possible to make the request, "please supply me with a list of all patients receiving 400 mg of chlorpromazine daily with and without antiparkinson medication." The hypothesis that antiparkinson agents lower the levels of blood chlorpromazine could then be tested. One could also ask for a population currently receiving thioridazine at 800 mg per day for a period of 1 year and a separate population who had received the same dosage of thioridazine for a period of 5 years and who had been changed to another drug within the previous year. In this way the chronic effects of thioridazine ingestion on retinal pigmentation, for example, could then be evaluated as well as its possible reversibility. There are obviously an unlimited number of questions one could ask which have to do with selecting patients who have received previous treatments. Thus the suggestion that reserpine did not produce tardive dyskinesia could very easily be evaluated in this manner.

At the moment, the drug monitoring system only includes records from the time the system was developed (approximately 9 years ago) and, hence, the drug history of patients with hospitalization beginning prior to that time is not computerized. In the future, when a large number of patients will have been totally in the computerized system from their first psychiatric contact, a very detailed monitoring system or research system will be available. In the initial medication search in tardive dyskinesia, it was not possible to use the computer system since many patient's records went back to the 1930s and the system was not set up until the late 1960s. However research is possible where the computer files contain long-term historical data to evaluate the usage of individual drugs in relation to side effects such as tardive dyskinesia. One could identify the patients with the side effect and determine how many of them had been receiving one drug, two drugs, three drugs, and so on. By converting all drugs to milligram equivalents of a standard drug, it would be possible to see if more medication was involved in the history of the patients who developed the side effect than in a control group without the side effect and to examine the even simpler question of whether the experimental group received one drug that was never given to the control group. This ongoing drug system allows an immediate screening of the plethora of hypotheses involving psychopharmacology, most of which will probably be disproved; by having such a data bank and, hence, immediate access to a subject pool, an "inexpensive" evaluation can be made prior to the instigation of rigorous, expensive investigations. For example, the problem of drug interaction is becoming more and more prominent and here the availability of a data bank such as this and the printed drug histories already mentioned are invaluable for research. Thus, in the now well known interaction between barbiturates and tricyclic antidepressants where the former produces lower blood levels of the latter, a data bank would allow one to select patients who had received such mixtures of medication and to evaluate whether there was any difference in clinical outcome or in blood levels in comparison with patients receiving the drugs singly and in similar dosage. More frequently there are suggestions or hypotheses involving drug interactions and these could be immediately tested in a pilot study both clinically and with blood levels before developing a sophisticated expensive research design.

Other situations in which the computer drug system has been helpful have involved individuals receiving a drug in which there was interest in evaluating blood levels. Some early pilot work in this area revealed that some patients who were receiving very high dosages of a drug had very low blood levels. Furthermore, it was demonstrated that a patient could show initially high levels of a drug which would become progressively lower and finally disappear over time. The possibility that this is related to clinical responsiveness is obvious, and so a further question was whether patients receiving drugs at very high dosage levels still showed psychotic symptomatology. The probability that these patients might show enzyme induction existed at an even simpler level; the mere fact that the patients had been taking high dosages for a long time with only a slight response makes them good candidates for a trial of a parenteral form. If this involved a new long-acting drug, the possibility that fluphenazine enanthate or decanoate would be the reference drug is very high. However it is possible that in that group of patients there would be one injection of fluphenazine enanthate, and yet this might not be highlighted in his otherwise lengthy chart. Before starting such a study, a drug printout of all patients who had received fluphenazine in any form would be obtained and the reason for their discontinuance checked.

In addition to providing a data base and immediate access to patients (selected on a demographic or drug basis), the computer system also facilitates the selection of control patients to match an experimental group. For example, after a group of tardive dyskinesia patients were identified, it was possible to "ask" the computer to supply a "match" for each experimental subject (same sex, diagnosis, age, length of hospitalization, and race). This selection would have been virtually impossible without the computer data bank.

USE OF COMPUTERS AND DRUG RESEARCH

The availability of a computer means that the large amounts of data accumulated in drug studies can be readily analyzed with appropriate statistics. The Biometric Laboratory in Maryland is an example of a well-developed data analysis system for drug studies. The system is flexible; it can handle a large basic core of rating scales routinely and can be adapted to handle other "unique" rating scales. It also has a library of programs for different study designs, and the final printout of the data analyses compiled in a bound format.

The computerized demographic data means ready access to information pertaining to age, sex, race, diagnosis, and measures of psychopathology, which aids in the selection of patients for drug research projects, permitting the choice of patients who had specific symptoms at least when they entered the hospital. The combination of this with a computerized drug information system permits the correlation of drug usage with any of these variables.

The results of laboratory tests that are usually carried out weekly for any research project can also be entered directly into the computer. The results are printed out with weekly updates so that the study physician can pick out trends before gross abnormalities develop. At the same time, clerical errors are avoided and results are never lost. At the end of a study, a complete printout of all lab test results is available for the study file. The normal ranges for each test are printed at the top of each page and abnormal results are asterisked to facilitate locating abnormalities.

Finally, even the mundane task of writing reports for a drug trial can be computerized. The use of computers for writing reports is well known in the case of the MMPI where a number of programs are available. With the MMPI (an objectively scored personality test), the patient's responses to the 550 questions are entered into the computer, the scores on the various scales obtained, and a personality report is produced. Similarly, when a generic narrative program is developed, the investigator simply supplies certain basic information on a form which is key punched, and a report is produced. With a sufficiently flexible program, a number of different designs can be incorporated, producing the introduction and the method section; if the statistical runs are included, the results section can also be automated. All that is left for the investigator is to write the discussion.

SUMMARY

The practical and managerial functions of a computerized drug-monitoring system have been described. In addition, various research uses of such a system have been proposed. While the practical and managerial functions are indeed valuable, the research possibilities may well have even more ultimate potential. The system provides a ready data base that can be used for specific patient selection to evaluate in a preliminary manner a variety of research questions. In addition, drug histories of different groups can be compared, a task well nigh impossible with written records. Finally, a summary of the more mundane uses of computers in research (statistical analysis, report writing) were described.

REFERENCES

1. A. DiMascio, "Changing Patterns of Psychotropic Drug Usage in Massachusetts Hospitals, *Psychopharmacology,*" **10** (1974), 24–28.
2. E. Laska, E. Varga, J. Wanderling, G. M. Simpson, G. Logemann, and B. K. Shah, "Patterns of Psychotropic Drug Use for Schizophrenia," *Dis. Nerv. Syst.,* **34** (1973), 294–305.

Approaches to the Development of a Management Information System for Mental Health Service Systems

CHARLES W. COBB, Ph.D.

In the spring of 1972 the Connecticut Department of Mental Health (DMH) began an effort to develop a more useful information system. Although the Department participates in the Multi-State Information System (MSIS) (1) and has profited significantly from this participation,* limitations in its scope and evidence of its underutilization prompted an examination of the role of information systems within the Department. The objective for a 1-year planning phase was to build upon MSIS *a design* for a more comprehensive computer-

---

* Over 70 facilities in Connecticut admitting annually approximately 36,000 clients participate in the system.

aided management information system (MIS) to assist state and local management in the provision of cost-effective services.

Although management information systems have been variously defined, the definition employed to guide initial planning was as follows:

> A management information system is a set of procedures and devices for storing and manipulating data which will produce predefined sets of output reports keyed to the information needs of designated managers.

The capability of producing predefined reports is the important characteristic that distinguishes an MIS from the most prevalent type of information system, an information management system (IMS). An IMS also consists of a set of procedures and devices for storing and manipulating data. However it is a passive system that depends upon the initiative and ingenuity of individual managers to manipulate the system to produce information that will contribute to decision making as the need arises. The DMH currently utilizes the MSIS largely as an IMS, although the MSIS has the capability of being utilized as an MIS. The primary objective of this chapter is to share some of the conceptual and logical issues encountered in the design of a comprehensive management information system (MIS) in Connecticut utilizing MSIS.

CONCEPTUAL APPROACHES

The development of an MIS is not an engineering application of an exact science, nor are there existing models that readily lend themselves to a particular environment. One of the first problems was to decide on an approach to delineating the information needed by the DMH for both internal and external reporting, that is, MIS design. (Any public agency has external reporting requirements. These requirements are best met by making the mechanisms for their satisfaction an integral part of the information system. External report requirements, however, will not be separately discussed within this chapter.)

Functional Area Approach

The initial approach selected involved the use of a working list of functional areas to serve as a guide in selecting people to interview with the expectation that their stated information needs would dictate the design of the management information system. For this purpose a functional area was defined as a subset of organizational activities grouped together on the basis of the skills necessary to attain an identifiable organizational objective. This list, conceptualized as types of services, is contained in Table 1 (2). However, the functional area approach to the design of an MIS turned out to have major problems, both practical and logical.

The practical problems were due to the scope of the proposed approach. Required was a set of functions that would be mutually exclusive, would be internally coherent, and would encompass all the activities of the DMH. The magnitude of the task is best seen by recognizing that different organizational units utilize their resources in ways sufficiently different so as to preclude the development of a list of functional areas with attendent activities readily transferable either among major units or even among the smaller service units of the same type (e.g., inpatient). The manpower needed to develop a functional area schema for each organizational unit and then to reconcile the information requirements of each of the units as the basis for MIS design was much greater than that available during the planning year (3). More importantly, however, in the course of efforts to utilize the functional area ap-

Table 1   Functional Areas

Individual-Oriented Services
    Contact services
    Evaluation services
    Treatment services
    Rehabilitation–restoration–habilitation services
    Care services

Community-Oriented Services
    Case-oriented consultation
    Program-oriented consultation
    Public information–education
    Training and continuing education (to other organizations)
    Community planning and development

Intraorganizational Services
    Program planning and evaluation
    Organizing
    Staffing–Recruiting
    Staff training and education
    Supervising–directing
    Procedural administration and housekeeping
    Information collection, analysis, and own program research
    Budgeting
    Fund raising
    Staff enhancement

---

proach, it became clear that a functional area approach provides no assistance in determining the sometimes critical information which management in one functional area needs from another functional area, nor is there a logical way to extend its framework to make this possible. For example, an administrator concerned with resource allocation needs to know from his information collection section how much money he has and from his personnel section, the size and nature of his staff.

In cases of this nature, a functional area approach provides no inherent guides for discovering the information needed; such discovery depends on the ability of the manager to articulate his needs and/or the questioning skill of the system designer. Thus, as the interrelationships of the various parts of a service system are of central importance to its functioning, some of the critical information needed by management would logically be outside the scope of a system generated by employing only the functional area approach.

This limitation led to the search for a different approach and to a consideration of the use of the concept of a hierarchy of organizational objectives (4) as a method of delineating the information needs of the DMH.

Objective Hierarchy Approach

An objective hierarchy (5) consists of a set of statements of objectives explicitly defining what an organization is attempting to accomplish. These statements are developed and organized in such a way that a given objective has a set of subobjectives beneath it that define all the conditions necessary to the attainment of that objective (see Table 2, for example) (6). Thus an upper-level objective will be fulfilled if and only if all of its subobjectives are attained. The subobjectives of a given objective therefore serve as means to the attainment of the end defined by that objective. In a department of mental health, the upper level objectives would define what the department is attempting to accomplish, and the lower level objectives would define what the constituent major units of the department would be attempting to accomplish through individual, community, and intraorganizational services. It should also be noted that an appropriately constructed and utilized hierarchy is closely related to an organization's table of organization. Additional levels of objectives would further define departmental activities.

In employing the objective hierarchy model for MIS construction, the logical relationships among organizational objectives provide the necessary structure for ascertaining the information required to obtain an integrated and meaningful picture of organizational functioning. Thus, although the objective hierarchy example given is confined to high-level objectives, it defines what a department might be attempting to accomplish and begins to define how it will go about doing so. It constitutes a useful starting point for determining the

Table 2   Objective Hierarchy for a Hypothetical State Department of Mental Health

Reduce the prevalence and incidence of emotional disability by a measurable amount through the provision of the most efficient and effective services possible

- **Reduce the prevalence and incidence of emotional disability through the provision of individual-oriented services**
  - Reduce the prevalence of emotional disability by providing appropriate services to those with emotional disability
  - Reduce the incidence of emotional disability by providing appropriate services to those at risk of becoming emotionally disabled

- **Reduce the prevalence and incidence of emotional disability through the provision of community-oriented services**
  - Strengthen community capability to provide individual-oriented services by providing consultation services
  - Increase community understanding of mental health issues by providing information–education services

- **Increase the Cost-Effectiveness of service delivery through the provision of intraorganizational services**
  - Support individual and community-oriented services by providing administrative services
  - Increase cost effectiveness of other services by providing monitoring and evaluation services

kinds of information that should be contained within an MIS to adequately monitor objective attainment, and thereby to manage service delivery. Of course considerable creativity is required in developing useful indices of objective attainment, and the employment of an objective hierarchy approach to MIS design will not solve the measurement problems that continue to challenge the field of mental health. However the clarity in defining what an organization is attempting to accomplish, which this approach facilitates, can do much to assist managers willing to employ it. Managers throughout the service delivery system will more clearly understand organizational objectives, resource allocation decisions can be more carefully organized to be consistent with the attainment of overall organizational objectives and, to the degree that objective statements include specific reference to performance criteria, then performance indices can be developed to assist management in monitoring objective attainment and modifying activities as necessary.

Unfortunately, for purposes of MIS design, this approach also has practical and logical problems whose solutions were beyond the resources of the planning project. The practical problems arise because the DMH has yet to establish a formal hierarchy of objectives. Financial, psychological and political problems have yet to be overcome.

Logical problems arose in examining the relationship between objective hierarchies and MIS design that led to the examination of the role of theoretical models of service delivery for MIS design. A theoretical model of service delivery indicates what kinds of services to provide to which patients at what locations in order to provide the most effective services possible with the resources available. However, it became clear that, first, in order to achieve a set of service objectives in the most cost-effective manner possible, resources should be allocated in accordance with a tacit or an explicit *valid* model of service delivery that would indicate the effects and costs of providing particular services to particular patients at particular locations. Given such a model, the construction of an MIS becomes straightforward, and the data base need only include data on who is receiving what services, where, and at what cost. The task of management then becomes merely employing the MIS to *monitor* service delivery and to insure that services are being delivered to the patients at locations and at costs consistent with service objectives. However the fact that at its current stage of development mental health service delivery is characterized by considerable theoretical heterogeneity attests to the absence of a valid model.

Secondly, in order to insure cost-effective achievement of a set of service objectives in the absence of a valid theoretical model, a hypothetical theoretical model of service delivery is required to assist in determining an information system data base. The task of management in this instance becomes that of employing the MIS *to assess* the effects of services directed toward the attainment of the specified objectives, thereby enabling the hypothetical model to be tested and ultimately validated. The validated model can then serve as the basis for future resource allocation decision making. However, from the point of view of information system design, the information needed to monitor a system of service delivery designed in accordance with a valid model is not necessarily the same information needed to establish the validity of a hypothetical theoretical model underlying a service system. Furthermore, in designing an MIS to monitor service delivery, unless the model is valid, the information purported to be adequate for monitoring service delivery will be misleading or meaningless (to say nothing about the usefulness of the services). Thus, since the construction of an MIS capable of adequately monitoring a system of service delivery is logically equivalent to the construction of a model of service delivery and since the task of the planning staff was not that of building and validating such a model, consideration was then given to a third approach.

Independent Subsystem Approach

An effort was made to identify management or functional areas within the DMH that operate relatively independently of any particular model of service delivery with a view towards designing a limited MIS consisting of a set of subsystems, one for each such functional area.

An independent subsystem is one that can provide useful management information independent (or irrespective) of a particular theoretical model. Examples of independent subsystems would be payroll and purchasing subsystems which fall within the broad functional area "intraorganization support services." A dependent subsystem is one that is dependent for its utility upon an explicit and valid theoretical model. (The utility of both types of subsystems for assessing performance is greatly enhanced if objectives for the relevant organizational unit are explicit, thereby providing a frame of reference for evaluation and/or monitoring.) An example of a dependent subsystem is a system designed for the management of a "treatment service" such as inpatient services, which falls within the broad functional area "individual-oriented services," providing information to managers of those services that directly assist them in monitoring the degree to which program activities are consistent with a valid model of service delivery.

However this approach is limited as is the functional area approach discussed previously, in that it would not lead to an MIS capable of producing a total, integrated picture of DMH functioning reflecting the interrelations of the various components.

Approach Adopted

Because of the limited resources that could be made available, an approach to system design and development was selected that emphasizes the functional area approach, with relatively independent functional areas accorded a high priority and developed as subsystems. In addition, however, an effort will be made to build these subsystems around management objectives, although as yet there are no plans for building in assessment of program effectiveness (or model validation). Thus experientially based judgment will continue to play the central role in management decision making, although buttressed by more information than has previously been available. Two major assumptions underly this approach; (1) the availability of additional information will improve decision making and (2) the tacit or explicit theoretical model(s) underlying management decision making are valid.

The reasons behind limited resource availability are extraordinarily germane to the development of information systems. However a full discussion of the reasons is outside the scope of this Chapter. From the subjective perspective of the author, they include: (1) practitioners are trained as helpers not managers/evaluators (and many administrators are trained as practitioners); (2) funding sources press for more services and survival is still (so far) more dependent on volume of service provided than on improvement in service cost effectiveness; (3) mechanisms for rewarding good performance for individual practitioners or particular service units are inadequate or nonexistent; and (4) the fact that thorough documentation of the cost effectiveness of an MIS requires a long-term investment limits the political appeal of supporting MIS development.

Implications of Approach Adopted

The previously discussed limitations of an approach organized around functional areas will, or course, still apply, a fact that has implications for the way in which the information necessary for system design is gathered. These limitations and their implications are discussed below.

1. *Lack of Generality of Data and Report Requirements across Facilities.* Because of the need to demonstrate the utility of information systems within a short period of time in order to gain support for further developments, the development of a demonstrable cost-effective system within a functional area within a single facility or a limited number of facilities is of greater importance for the long-range development of an information system than the more time-consuming development of a system within a functional area that is immediately generalizable across all DMH facilities. Thus, while a number of facilities will be consulted in the initial stages of system design for each functional area to increase the probability that the developed system will be generalizable, emphasis will be placed on the development and testing of a system in a limited number of facilities in order to permit, with the resources

available, an assessment of its cost effectiveness while minimizing the staff, equipment, and training expenses associated with insuring generalizability. Cost-effective systems will then be expanded to other facilities.

2. *Absence of Guidelines for Determining the Interrelated Information Requirements of Various Functional Areas.* In the determination of the information needs of staff within a functional area, specific questions will be directed at determining the sources of required data and the recipients of data so that functional area requirement interrelationships can be mapped and ultimately included in the design of the total information system, even though the current focus of design may be on satisfying the information needs of one functional area.

Thus, in sum, while a "total plan" dictating the information that should be incorporated within the design of an MIS at first seems most logically desirable, with limited resources, a more modest approach appears not only more feasible, but also more appropriate. The approach adopted will entail less expensive trial and error, provide opportunities to assess the cost effectiveness of each subsystem as it is developed, and thereby enable the placement of the information system development on the firmest possible basis.

The priority to be assigned to the development of each new subsystem has or will be determined on the basis of a combined weighting of a number of criteria. This aspect of system development is not discussed here; the criteria used, however, are listed in Table 3.

Conceptual "Model"

It should be carefully noted that this approach focuses on parts or subsystems of a total information system (modules). The integration of these subsystems into an overall information system remains a major task that cannot be fully structured until additional knowledge is gained through the development and use of the various subsystems, particularly (as mentioned above) with regard to the needs of management for information from more than one functional area. The data base required and some of the ways of aggregating data can, however, be broadly conceptualized. The schematic given in Figure 1 represents the required data base as a three-dimensional matrix that defines the types of data needed by managers (intraorganization support personnel) to manage the services provided by an organization (individual-oriented services, community-oriented services, manpower-training-oriented services, and generalizable research services) to a given target population (e.g., children, adults, drug dependents, alcohol dependents). Note that the list of types of services is somewhat different from the list contained in Table 1. The difference reflects the fact that an improved version of the original list has recently become

Table 3   Criteria for Determining Subsystem Development Priorities

---

Management Need
   Need for more data or information
   Need for more rapid and flexible access to data
   Need to manipulate data to produce information
   Volume of data now processed manually

Payoff
   Direct or indirect contribution to improvement in patient care
   Cost savings in number of personnel or personnel time
   Short- and long-range cost benefit
   Relevance to federal or other reimbursement programs

Feasibility
   Availability of needed data
   Calender time required to develop subsystem
   Clarity with which area can be identified
   Involvability/availability of staff from within functional area
   Degree of routinization of current data handling
   Availability of prepackaged systems
   Cost of development
   Availability of funds (federal or other)

Other
   Relative independence of subsystem

---

available (9, 10). The types of data required by the various managers to manage the various services consists of the data required to answer the basic question "Who needs what services and who receives what services, at what cost and with what effect?" (7, 8). The total information needs of an organization consist of the sum of the data required to manage services to each of the target populations. This could be schematicized as a "super matrix" containing one "block" for each target population served by an organization. However the reader will be spared this schematic. Each small block within the matrix represents an aggregation of data relevant for management. For example, the block in the upper left front of the matrix would contain data required by the Program Planning and Evaluation staff concerning the need for screening services on the part of a given target population.

The data broadly defined and organized by this matrix constitute the data base for the informational system. Thus, from the broadest perspective, the task of information system development can be seen as (1) determining the specific data items that will be collected in each of the blocks in the matrix, and (2) si-

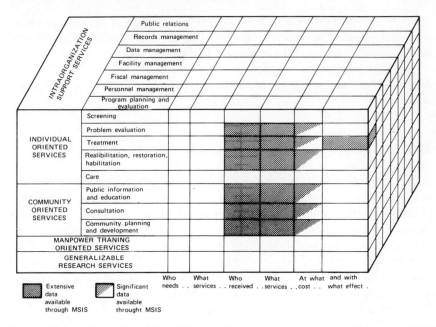

Figure 1   Department of Mental Health Information system—data base schematic.

multaneously determining aggregation of data (frequently from more than one block) necessary for the output reports required by specific management personnel. A distinction will be made within each block between data required by management within the area of responsibility it defines and data required about the area by management in other areas. The distinction reflects the fact that data requirements differ in scope and nature depending upon the level of management. A manager responsible only for food services might only need information from a few blocks, while a manager responsible for program planning for a single facility will require information from all the blocks relevant to the functioning of his (or her) facility but in less detail, and a system manager (a manager responsible for more than one facility), while also requiring information for most or all blocks for each facility, will require even less detailed information.

Future System Development then reflects the following objectives:

1.   Determination of the cost effectiveness of existing applications (which are primarily those available through MSIS) and maximization of the use of cost-effective ones.

2.   Determination of priority functional area subsystems, development of them, evaluation of their cost effectiveness, and institution of those found to be cost effective across the mental health system.

3.   Assistance in the clarification and/or development of department objectives and, insofar as possible, organization of future information system development in support of the attainment of these objectives.

Additional staff are now being added to the task force to in order to attain these objectives.

RELEVANCE OF MSIS TO MIS REQUIREMENTS

It is anticipated that as systems design continues, MSIS capabilities will not only continue to be utilized, but their utilization will increase due to a number of factors inherent within the system. First, the data already contained within the fairly extensive number of forms available is already useful for management purposes, and as the model continues to be developed, the utility of the various existing data items will become increasingly clarified. Second, an important feature of the system is its considerable flexibility in producing reports tailored to particular management needs. Third, MSIS is actively engaged in the development of new applications that increase its utility. For example, the Connecticut Department of Mental Health is collaborating with MSIS in the development of Admission and Termination Forms for children's mental health services, and MSIS has completed a cost-finding/rate-setting subsystem. Fourth, MSIS is continuing to increase its ability to respond flexibly to user needs. In this last connection, a Generalized Application System (GAS) has recently been completed that allows data required by a particular user, which is not available through existing forms, to be entered into the data base and to be manipulated through the system. And fifth, MSIS computing capability is sufficient so that it may be utilized to support an expanding system.

The relevance of MSIS for Connecticut's information needs can be examined in more detail by employing the data base schematic previously presented (Figure 1) as an organizing framework for determining management information requirements that can be satisfied through MSIS. As this schematic implies, the basic question "Who needs what services, and who receives what services, at what cost and with what effect?" can serve as a guide in determining the specific information required for management decisions. The specific data required will differ depending upon a manager's area of responsibility, and the level of detail will vary depending upon the organizational level of the manager, but the basic set of questions are relevant to all managers. For illustrative purposes, this examination focuses upon the information needs of managers responsible for the intraorganization support services of Program Planning and evaluation in support of the delivery of individual-oriented treatment services to a particular target population. MSIS is also oriented toward this set of organizational activities, particularly individual-oriented treatment services for adults, although some of the forms do capture data relevant to the management of other types of services and other target populations, and the previously mentioned Generalized Application System (GAS) allows other data to be gathered as needed. This focus on the part of MSIS is portrayed by the dark boxes in Figure 1. The particular nature of the target population will not be specified in this discussion, although data required for highly focused management decisions will vary as a function of the target population, as the approach to be followed in examining information needs is intended to be generalizable to any target population.

Each part of the above question prompts a subset of more specific questions which can then be employed in examining specific management information needs.

Who Needs . . .
   What is the volume of services requested?
   How does the actual volume compare to the anticipated volume?

What Services . . .
   Are the applicant characteristics appropriate to the services provided?
   Are the applicant characteristics as anticipated?

And Who Receives What Services . . .
   What are the characteristics of the recipients of each service delivered?
   How do the characteristics of the recipients of each service compare to the
      anticipated characteristics of the recipients of each service?
   What are the volume and nature of services delivered?
   Is the volume and nature of the services delivered as anticipated?

At What Costs . . .
   What are the costs of the services delivered?
   How do the actual costs compare to anticipated (budgeted) costs?

And With What Effect
   What is the effect of services delivered?
   Is the effect as anticipated?

The individual-oriented services provided to a client are organized as a sequence of services. Figure 2 illustrates how a client initially becomes involved in screening and then follows any of a number of alternative paths depending upon his needs and/or the availability of services. The MSIS forms available to document information needed by management at various points are also identified on this chart. In the following section, the information needs of intraorganization support service managers regarding individual-oriented treat-

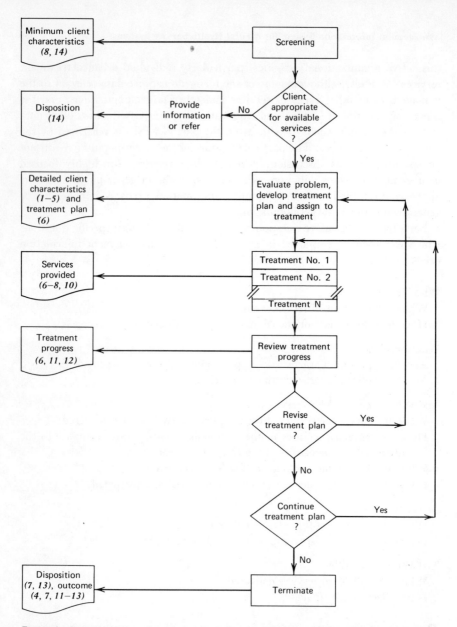

Figure 2 Individual-oriented services—client flow and MSIS documentation available. MSIS input forms: (1) Admission Form. (2) Mental Status Evaluation Record. (3) Psychiatric Anamnestic Record. (4) Problem Appraisal Scale. (5) Psychiatric Diagnosis Record. (6) Problem Oriented Psychiatric Record. (7) Change of Status Form. (8) Direct Patient Services Form. (9) Indirect Patient Services Form. (10) Psychotropic Drug Order Form. (11) Periodic Evaluation Record. (12) Periodic Evaluation Record—Community Version. (13) Termination Form. (14) Generalized Application System (GAS).

ment services that can be satisfied through MSIS are discussed in terms of the above specific questions. This discussion is intended to be illustrative, but not exhaustive, of the relevance of MSIS to management information needs.

"Who needs what services?"

What is the volume of services requested? How does the actual volume compare to the anticipated volume?

Ascertaining the actual volume of treatment services requested (by clients who have come through the evaluation process) is the first step in making planning and evaluation decisions regarding these services. Volume of treatment services requested seen against the anticipated volume which formed the basis for decisions about the resources allocated to the various treatment services is essential data for assessing whether or not these service elements are adequately staffed and/or sufficiently time consuming to warrant further evaluation of whether clinic resources are being utilized in the most appropriate ways in providing these services. (For purposes of this discussion treatment services are not further defined. They may include such major service types as inpatient and outpatient services and/or more specific types such as individual and group therapy.)

MSIS. Documentation of the volume of treatment services requested is not part of the standard MSIS package. However a GAS application can be developed to provide this capability or the standard Admission Form can be coded so as to reflect request for admission to service rather than actual admission. If, for example, the volume of treatment applicants is higher than anticipated, then the decision may be made to perform evaluations answering the following:

Are the applicant characteristics appropriate to the services provided? Are the applicant characteristics as anticipated?

The answers to these questions determine whether management should examine the screening and evaluation process or the treatment services if changes are required. Data required includes the characteristics of clients applying for treatment services, services provided by the organization, criteria governing the types of treatment services appropriate for clients with particular sets of characteristics, and estimates (anticipations) of applicant characteristics.

If the unanticipated high volume of applications are mostly appropriate to the treatment services provided by the organization, then action directed towards the screening and evaluation services to change the types of cases applying for treatment services will not be necessary. This finding may lead to (and provide supporting data for) renewed efforts to obtain additional funding and/or to further evaluation of other service elements within the organization in order to determine whether greater operating efficiencies can be effected (without undue loss in effectiveness) that would enable the organization to provide treatment services to more applicants. If the high volume of treatment applicants contains a significant number of inappropriate applicants and this was anticipated, and an effort was made to change the number of inappropriate applicants, then the effort should be intensified or modified.

If the high volume of treatment applicants contains a significant number of inappropriate applicants, and this was not anticipated, then action is required such as modifying the criteria used within the screening and evaluation services to determine client appropriateness for the various treatment services.

MSIS. Documentation of applicant characteristics, as indicated in the flow chart (Figure 2), is available through an extensive number of MSIS forms. The Admission Form provides data on client demographic characteristics, for example, and the Problem Appraisal Scales and Mental Status Examination Record provide data on client psychological characteristics. MSIS also can provide data on the services provided within an organization through the forms recording services provided, such as the Direct Patient Services Form.

. . . and who receives what services?

What are the characteristics of the recipients of each service delivered? How do the actual characteristics of each of the recipients compare to the anticipated characteristics of the recipients of each service?

Data required to answer the above questions include the characteristics of each recipient of each treatment service and the criteria to be employed in determining the type of service appropriate for clients with various characteristics. If the characteristics of the recipients of each type of treatment service are appropriate, then no further action may be required. If, however, an unanticipated number of clients receive inappropriate services, then further evaluation as to the reasons is required. Discussions with staff leading to clarification and/or revision of criteria are examples of appropriate administrative actions which do not necessarily require new data from an information system once the problems have been adequately documented through the system, unless a more extensive research project is planned to refine the criteria.

MSIS. As discussed above MSIS provides extensive documentation of client characteristics and of the types of treatment services provided to each client.

What are the volume and nature of the services delivered?
Are the volume and nature of the services delivered as anticipated?

Data on the volume and nature of services delivered compared to the anticipated volume and nature of services delivered are critical management information. This data can assist management in evaluating total organization, organizational unit, and individual service provider performance. Data required include the volume of services delivered by type, organization, organizational unit, and individual service provider, and estimates of the volume and type of services to be provided by each.

If the volume and nature of the services delivered by the total organization, each unit, and each individual provider are as anticipated, then no further action may be required.

If however, any of the above are providing more treatment services than anticipated, further evaluation may be required leading to either an upward adjustment in the anticipated level of services to be delivered or an examination of the possibility that other areas of service (e.g., community-oriented services) are being shortchanged.

If less-than-anticipated services are being provided by, for example, the total organization, then further analysis is necessary to determine which organizational units and individuals are performing below their anticipated levels.

MSIS. Documentation of the above areas is extensive. The volume and nature of services provided is available retrospectively through the Termination Form. This form, however, does not identify the individual service provider(s) nor does it enable data to be assembled on active cases. A form that provides data to fill both these gaps is the Direct Patient Services Form.

... "at what costs?"

What are the costs of the services delivered?
How do the actual costs compare to anticipated (budgeted) costs?

The answers to these questions determine whether or not the organization is functioning within its budget and serve as the basis for evaluating resource-allocation decisions. Data required include breakdowns of the various costs associated with service delivery.

If the costs are as anticipated, then no further action may be required. If the costs are lower then anticipated, then further evaluation may be required to determine the reason for the lower costs and to insure that the quality of service has not deteriorated below acceptable limits because of such factors as the *inappropriate* use of less expensive forms of treatment (e.g., group instead of individual therapy) or the *inappropriate* use of less-well-trained and therefore less-expensive staff.

If the costs are higher than anticipated, then either the volume of service will have to be reduced or further cost analyses will have to be performed to determine if cost savings can be effected. These analyses may include examination of personnel costs, types of treatment delivered (individual therapy is more expensive than group therapy per unit of service), and duration of treatment.

MSIS.   Cost data is not part of the standard MSIS package. A cost finding/rate-setting system is, however, nearing completion by MSIS. A currently available system, the Direct Patient Service Form, is nonetheless highly relevant in that it captures staff-time expended for each client by type of treatment activity. Because staff time accounts for approximately 80% of most service organization's budgets, this system can provide legitimate estimates of the cost data required.

. . . "and with what effect?"

What is the effect of services delivered?
Is the effect as anticipated?

The answers to these questions determine whether or not the organization is functioning as effectively as anticipated given the resources available.

If the organization's overall level of effectiveness is as anticipated then no further action may be required. If, however, the overall level of effectiveness is lower than anticipated then further evaluation may be required to discover the program areas performing below anticipated levels. Once these are discovered, then additional questions regarding variables such as treatment approaches used and staffing patterns will need to be raised.

If the organization's overall level of effectiveness is better than anticipated, then some especially interesting questions emerge. For if one or more of an organization's programs are more effective than anticipated, then the possibility needs to be considered that the best balance of service to the organization's community might well be achieved through redeploying some of the resources from the highly effective program to a less effective program. Discussion of this issue, however, is outside of the scope of this paper.

MSIS.   Data on treatment effect is available through a number of forms. Global summary judgments are recorded on the Termination Form, and more detailed data is available through such forms as the Problem Appraisal Scales and the Periodic Evaluation Records. GAS applications can also be developed by organizations wishing to utilize other approaches to measuring effectiveness.

Continued and increased use of the above existing MSIS capabilities is planned, while at the same time new applications tailored to specific Connecticut management information needs will be developed consistent with the overall plan previously discussed. With regard to MIS development in general, the following cautionary section is offered in closing.

ASSUMPTIONS UNDERLYING CONTINUING MIS DEVELOPMENT

It should be stressed that a number of assumptions, underlie the effective use by management of an information system developed in accordance with the above principles. These are listed below.

1.   Management commitment to and understanding of the use of objective data in service management.
2.   A valid (even if untested) theoretical model.
3.   Defined objectives consistent with the model, which can serve as "benchmarks" for monitoring programs.
4.   Predefined uses for information to be generated by the system.
5.   The capability of acquiring and compiling data in a manner appropriate to needs.
6.   Time available to evaluate the implications of data or information for programs.
7.   Administrative ability (authority, resources, skill) to make indicated changes in programs.
8.   Administrative flexibility to reward for achievement.

The degree to which the information system under development will contribute to improvements in service delivery depends upon the validity of these assumptions. Should these assumptions be invalid, then the impact of an information system will be seriously limited and resources invested in hardware, systems studies, and so on might be better spent elsewhere. The potential contribution of this system to the improvement of service delivery is, however, great, in spite of its limitations, if caution in its development and use is exercised. The emphasis on assumptions in this paper reflects the concern that too often information systems efforts have been undertaken without an examination of underlying assumptions. A final assumption: the unexamined assumption is not worth acting upon.

REFERENCES

1.   E. Laska, G. Logemann, G. Honigfeld, A. Weinstein, and R. Bank, "The Multi-State Information System," *Evaluation,* 1 (1972), 1.
2.   This list was adopted from a report of a study undertaken by the Definitions and Classifications Committee of the Southern Regional Conference on Mental Health Statistics (SRCMHS, 1970); the terms used are defined within this report, but are assumed to be sufficiently self-explanatory for the purpose of this paper.

3. Planning project staff consisted of a part-time project director, a part-time assistant, a part-time secretary and a full-time systems analyst.

4. E. A. Suchman, *Evaluative Research*, Russell Sage Foundation, New York, 1967.

5. Stephen Landy, Research Associate in the Connecticut DMH, contributed significantly to this section.

6. Note that the example is included for illustrative purposes and does not represent the objectives of the Connecticut Department of Mental Health.

7. P. H. Person, *A Statistical Information System for Community Mental Health Centers*, National Institute of Mental Health, Mental Health Statistics, Series C, No. 1, March 1969.

8. E. M. Cooper, *Guidelines for a Minimum Statistical and Accounting System for Community Mental Health Centers*, National Institute of Mental Health, Mental Health Statistics, Series C, No. 7, 1973.

9. SRCMHS, Southern Regional Conference on Mental Health Statistics, Definitions and Classifications Committee Report, Definitions of Terms in Mental Health, Mental Retardation, and Alcoholism Programs, (2nd ed.) March 1970.

10. SRCMHS, *Definition of Terms in Mental Health, Alcohol Abuse, Drug Abuse and Mental Retardation*, prepared by the Definitions and Classifications Committee, Southern Regional Conference on Mental Statistics, Southern Regional Educational Board, published by the Alcohol, Drug Abuse, and Mental Health Administration, National Institute of Mental Health, Mental Health Statistics Series No. 8, 1973.

STATE AND NATIONAL PROGRAMS

The Use of Computers by the Ministry of Health in Indonesia

ZEBULON TAINTOR, M.D. and NATHAN S. KLINE, M.D.

The General Purpose Psychiatric Questionnaire (GPPQ), an offshoot of MSIS, has become the standard instrument for all psychiatric hospital admissions in Indonesia. Its use was proposed in 1970 by Dr. Nathan S. Kline, in his role as President of the International Committee Against Mental Illness (ICAMI), and by Dr. R. Kusamanto Setyonegoro, Professor of Psychiatry at the University of Indonesia. Dr. Kusamanto has also been President of the Indonesian Psychiatric Association and Head of the Mental Health Directorate in the Ministry of Health. In the latter capacity, he was in charge of mental health programs for the entire country. Over the last 4 years, the GPPQ has been adapted for Indonesian use and prints patient case histories in both English and Indonesian. In 1972 alone, detailed information was gathered on more than 3600 hospital admissions. Indonesian psychiatrists found that the project enhanced their diagnostic rigor, acumen, and interest as well as provided them with a more detailed overview of local hospital and national activity.

SETTING

Indonesia is a lush, tropical land of 13,367 islands and 120 million people (1). Many of the smaller islands could easily serve as Southseas retreats from civilization. Indonesia includes the spice islands, sought by the Dutch and Portugese navigators in the 16th and 17th centuries, Bali, with its highly developed poetic and artistic culture, Java, one of the most densely populated areas in the world with over 1500 people per square mile, Sumatra, the Celebes, Borneo, and West Irian. The islands have many societies, including a stone age culture on Pnias, off Sumatra; more than 200 languages are spoken. Most of the peasants are nominally Islamic, but are actually animistic; many are mystics. Beliefs in demonic possession and in good and bad spirits are very common. Mineral resources, largely untapped, are extensive, including high-grade oil, nickel, tin, and zinc, but the per capita gross national product is only about $80 per year. The government since 1965 has tried to encourage economic development but has had to cope with the problems of enormous concentration of wealth in Jakarta and high birth rate (2.2%) that, with better health services, is no longer balanced by a sizable death rate.

Western-trained technocrats, most of them in Jakarta, have spent time and effort in selecting and adapting to Indonesian technological advances. The pooling of expertise in Jakarta, however, creates inevitable bureaucratic problems in the running of a country with so many ethnic groups spread out over so many islands. The unreliability of current communications systems and the low wages paid to civil servants exacerbate these problems. For example, a typical Indonesian physician in government service is paid a salary that has a purchasing power equivalent to $60 a month, so he must also maintain a private practice to survive. Because of economic realities, corruption is not uncommon.

The psychiatric care system in Indonesia was developed by the Dutch when Indonesia was a colony and consisted of approximately 7000 hospital beds and virtually no outpatient facilities. Inpatient treatment was largely custodial and is still restricted to severely impaired patients. Virtually no patients seen by psychiatrists have not previously been seen by a native healer (although this situation is changing in the larger cities).

Psychiatric hospitals were initially staffed with general practitioners. Recently psychiatric residency programs at the University of Indonesia, the Airlangga University in Surabaya, and the University of Northern Sumatra in Medan have begun to contribute psychiatric manpower to reverse this situation. Outpatient clinics have been opened in some of the larger cities, and the introduction of a wide range of psychotropic medications has led to more active treatment and a considerable reduction in hospital stays. Modern private psychiatric hospitals have developed in Jakarta.

In summary, Indonesia did not be itself seem to favor the introduction of a computerized psychiatric data system. Indeed, many observers felt that it probably would not be successful.

HISTORY

ICAMI first established a working relationship with the Indonesian Ministry of Health and with the Department of Psychiatry of the University of Indonesia through Dr. Kline in 1963. Initial cooperation in 1964–1965 demonstrated that psychoactive drugs could be used effectively by general practitioners in treating psychiatric outpatients. After Dr. Kline, Dr. Kusamanto, Dr. Laska, and others (2, 3) had collaborated in the development of the GPPQ, it was printed in a computer-readable format for optical scanning. This enabled English-speaking psychiatrists in Indonesia and elsewhere to carry out pilot projects involving the GPPQ. Dr. Kline, Dr. Laska, and Dr. Tenney presented a plan for a recording system using the GPPQ to an all-Indonesian psychiatric workshop in Jakarta in October 1970. Fortunately an IBM 360 computer was available at the Jakarta office of Pertamina, the national oil company that oversees exploration and development of oil and natural gas in Indonesia and that has donated considerable technical assistance as well as computer time for the project. Dr. Laska, who had thought himself bravely optimistic to have brought a tape of the GPPQ processing program with him to that October meeting, was delighted to discover that the program had been installed on the computer the previous night and that GPPQ data could be processed forthwith.

From November 1970 through March 1971, Dr. Ashton Tenney, the first ICAMI–GPPQ program consultant, worked with three Indonesian psychiatrists, Dr. Kusamanto, Dr. Budi Sadono, and Dr. Rudy Salan, and a psychologist, Mrs. H. Noerhardi (4). This committee held seminars with the psychiatric staff of the Grogol State Hospital and the Clinic of the Department of Psychiatry at the University of Indonesia, both in Jakarta. From the seminars emerged standard definitions of terms on the form, a detailed plan of action for the country, and a translation of the optically scannable GPPQ into a key punchable Indonesian language version. Although Indonesian psychiatrists are fluent in English, use English language psychiatric texts, and read American and British journals, translation was made to gain greater local acceptance by both psychiatrists and other hospital staff members and because optical scanning processing facilities were not available in Indonesia. Key punching was done by the National Police.

In December 1970, the GPPQ was introduced for routine use in all cases of first admissions at the Grogol and University Hospitals as well as at psychiatric hospitals in Central and East Java including Bogor, Bandung, Semarang, Surabaya, Lawang, Solo, and Mageland. The GPPQ forms in the Indonesian version were bulky and the number of admissions were large, so packages of the forms were sent using a private parcel post service, the Indonesian postal services being at that time unreliable. The promptness and reliability of this service enabled the hospitals to communicate effectively with Jakarta, resulting in increased use of the GPPQ. Computer-produced narrative histories were returned in English. By February 1971 return visits had been made to the hospitals and the program was regarded as sufficiently secure for further extension.

Further developments in the GPPQ program, until the arrival of one of the authors (ZT), who was the second ICAMI consultant in February of 1972, consisted of the introduction of the system to all the other psychiatric hospitals on Java and to the Bangli Hospital in Bali. Private psychiatric hospitals also came into the system. As a result of initial experiences, suggestions for modifying the GPPQ program to make it more useful included adding diagnostic categories (the original program allowed only 35 choices), island of origin, ethnic group, and religious and housing alternatives. With the arrival of the author, complete debugging of the program was accomplished, and with the assistance of Pansystems, an Indonesian computer software concern, modifications in the computer program were made. Program output was translated into Indonesian so case histories and charts could be produced in Indonesian and in English. The Indonesian printout proved to be remarkably popular with nonphysician hospital workers who were becoming involved with the project.

At the same time the psychiatrists wanted more psychiatric data to be included. Accordingly a problem appraisal list similar to that in the Admission Form of the MSIS was added. It became evident that the diagnostic data produced by the program was only as good as the varying diagnostic skills of the practitioners involved. As a result an *Indonesian Psychiatric Diagnostic and Statistical Manual* was developed. This project required 3 months and many meetings, mostly of the faculty of the University of Indonesia. Copies of the *Diagnostic and Statistical Manual of the American Psychiatric Association,* the *8th International Classification of Diseases* (ICD-8), and other psychiatric glossaries were used as references. Participants drafted definitions and added some specifically Indonesian diagnoses such as koro, latah, and amok.* It was agreed that an annual diagnostic workshop in conjuction with the Indonesian Psychiatric Association meeting should be held and that the diagnostic glossary should be revised yearly. The GPPQ was then reprogrammed to include all diagnoses in the new manual.

* Koro: a man's morbid fear that his penis is shrinking inexorably into his body. Death is thought to ensue when retraction is complete; latah: apparently involuntary repitition of obscenities; imitation of others' words and actions; amok: sudden rampaging; homicidal behavior.

At this time a Termination Form was developed, adapted from the Termination Form of the MSIS. This form included the usual demographic data, statistics about types and duration of treatment, termination alternatives with and without referral, and patient status on termination. It also included estimates of the patient's working capacity, probable duration of disability, family attitude, number of family visits, and the patient's presumed family relationships and living arrangements on discharge. There was a particularly Indonesian problem of monitoring supplies of psychotropic medication, so an extensive section on pharmacotherapy received was included. A persistent problem concerned detection of errors, a clerical operation until recently. The processing program has been and will be further strenghtened to detect and report certain obvious errors and internal inconsistencies in data on particular patients.

During Z. T.'s consultantship visits were made and the MSIS Admission Form instituted at psychiatric hospitals on other islands including Palembang, Padang, Medan, and Banda Acheh in Sumatra, Ujang Pandang, Manado, and Tomohon in the Celebes, Pontianak, Banjarmasin, and Samarinda in Borneo, and Ivapura in West Irian. By the end of 1972 all hospitals except Samarinda and Ivapura were reporting data (5). Acceptance of the Admission Form was very high. Plans were made for introducing the Termination Form and the MSIS Mental Status Examination Record (MSER). Plans for the MSER presently assume pilot trials in the university centers in 1975.

STATISTICS

In the first 8 months of 1971, 18 facilities reported on 1314 patients. In the first 6 months of 1972, 19 hospitals reported on 1380 patients. The most complete statistics and cross-tabulations currently available are for the year 1972 (6). For the second 6 months of 1972, 26 facilities reported on a total of 2274 admissions, ranging from as few as 2 to as many as 337. Of these, 1461 were male, while 806 were female. It was a young population with the largest percentage (23) between 16 and 20 years, and 52% between the ages of 16 and 30. Most were referred by their family (73%) or family doctor (13%); only 5% were referred by psychiatrists, and negligible numbers were referred by patients, courts, police, or clergy. Nominal religion records showed that 69% were Islamic with higher incidences of Protestants and Roman Catholics entering hospitals located in non-Islamic areas. Almost all patients were raised at home and spoke one of the areas' dominant languages. Their upbringing was predominantly rural, but the percentage of rural patients was less than would have been expected from the population distribution. A few more were single than were married, and most were engaged in low-prestige occupations with low income. Historical reconstructions of the rapidity of onset of the present episode found that 11% had occurred within 24 hours, 25% within 1 to 6 days, 17% within 1 to 4 weeks, and only 16% had had symptoms for over a month. (Duration of illness was unknown in 24%.) By diagnosis the largest large nonpsychotic group was that of drug addicts (158) followed by neurotic depressives (23). However almost all other patients were diagnosed psychotic, with about 70% being schizophrenic. There were very few diagnoses of affective disorder. Prognostic predictions followed a bell-shaped curve.

The picture of Indonesian psychiatry that emerges from the data is that it is currently treating predominantly young schizophrenics who have a rather typical acute onset. The data contained relatively few surprises for Indonesian psychiatrists except for the amount of drug addiction. As more data arrives from outpatient facilities, the diagnostic picture is expected to change. Most reassuring thus far is that major diagnostic differences between hospitals have not emerged; however the present programs allow only gross estimation. Introduction of the MSER will allow more detailed evaluation of diagnostic statements as based on presenting problems.

The strength of Indonesian society in caring for its aged is striking. Despite the low average life expectancy at birth (35 years), there are many old people in Indonesia. They are at home with their families, certainly not in hospitals.

The experience in Indonesia is remarkable in that it shows what can be done by determined individuals working in unlikely circumstances. The system generated for Indonesia a wealth of data not usually available in a developing country. Psychiatric planning at all levels can be based on hard facts. The central government in Jakarta can quantitate and understand hospital workloads and plan new services accordingly. The use of the computer program has engendered the development of the Indonesian diagnostic system. The professionalism and objectivity of the psychiatric hospital workers has been enhanced.

This story of hard work and considerable success must be considered, however, against the argument that the development of a computerized psychiatric data system was not then the best use of Indonesian and American resources. A frequently heard objection to the introduction of labor-saving technology in labor-rich countries, such as Indonesia, is that such devices actually worsen developmental problems by depriving clerks of jobs and reducing potential job opportunities for laborers. It is also argued that such complex technology is too problematical for the average professional. The argument is not without merit and carries considerable weight in a variety of developmental fields. For example, the introduction of high-yield rice strains has actually set back agriculture in some villages because of lack of fertilizer. However the arguments as applied to the development of psychiatric data services does not hold on several counts. There are too few workers, there is no surplus of clerks, and certainly there is no surplus of professional personnel to train them. Even if the manpower were available, government resources to employ a large group of statisticians are not. Indonesia, like many other developing countries, has suffered from a drain of talented personnel attracted by more desirable working circumstances in developed countries. A decision not to make the most up-to-date practices of western technology available to Indonesia can only serve to enhance the brain drain. Indonesia's present position of leadership in psychiatric data systems in developing countries provides motivation and interest for its young mental health professionals and computer technicians. To argue that the Indonesians would have to go through technological apprenticeship is to deny them the benefits of development and to insure that they will always lag. What has been done in Indonesia has freed mental health professionals for other activities including epidemiological studies and the development of new services for the psychiatrically ill and has made available computer resources for other research projects.

Another objection to the use of computerized data systems in a country like Indonesia derives from the notion that persons in developing countries are gadget happy and tend to absorb the form rather than the content of western culture. Geertz has described this phenomenon in Indonesia, terming it cultural vagueness (7). For example, houses are built with electrical outlets carefully placed in walls, but without any wires being led to them. The argument runs that the computers are really used as gadgets rather than as providers of significant service. Our experience in introducing the GPPQ and other forms has been quite the contrary. Like many Westerners, Indonesians occasionally exhibited a tendency to regard the computer as magical. However as they worked with the program they demonstrated growing awareness of the exact potentialities and limitations of computers. Rather than serving to distract 100 working psychiatrists (out of a total 6000 physicians) from patient care, use of the GPPQ has enhanced their interest in obtaining more thorough and detailed psychiatric case histories and in making more accurate diagnoses.

Finally, the argument of cost does not hold. Even if computer time had not been donated, the savings in processing and generating accurate reports have been considered in informal comparisons with other Indonesian governmental ministries. The GPPQ produces great quantities of reliable data relatively painlessly. Indonesian officials in other fields are often obliged to spend enormous amounts of time producing less accurate reports. The Directorate of Mental Health has reduced the number of other reports required of its personnel to a bare minimum.

Assuming that the system has been of benefit to Indonesia, what benefits are there for the world? Most prominent is the opportunity to separate the cultural from the biological dimensions of psychiatry. By encouraging the elaboration of an Indonesian diagnostic system consistent with the ICD-8 and obtaining detailed symptom appraisals of inpatients as they present, there is hope of answering questions having to do with the frequencies of paranoid versus nonparanoid schizophrenia in developing cultures, the existence of retarded depression, the incidence of excitement, and the incidence of special entities such as koro, latah, and amok, worldwide epidemiological comparisons are possible. As the system develops further in Indonesia, studies similar to the Stirling County study (8) can be attempted and the strengths and weaknesses of various Indonesian cultural practices assayed, at least as evidenced in their effects on rates of psychiatric symptomatology. As other aspects of the system are installed, international comparisons of the cost of care can also be carried out, and various models for delivering mental health services can be assayed and compared.

REFERENCES

1. Statistics drawn from Far *Eastern Economic Review 1972 Yearbook,* Far Eastern Economic Review, Hong Kong, 1973.

2. N. S. Kline, E. Hacket, and E. Laska, "Evaluation of International Psychiatric Data," *Proc. 7th IBM Med. Symp.,* October 1965.

3. E. Laska, D. Morrill, N. S. Kline, G. M. Simpson, and E. Hackett, "SCRIBE—A Method for Producing Automated Psychiatric Case Histories," *J. Am. Psych. Assoc.* **124** (July 1967), 1.

4. For a full report of Dr. Tenney's activities see A. Tenney, "Activities of the International Committee Against Mental Illness," *Transcult. Psychiatr. Res. Rev.,* **8** (1971), 201.

5. Z. Taintor, R. Salan, and B. Sandona, "Some Developments on the Computerized Recording System Project of Mental Patients in Indonesia," *Proc. 2nd Ann. Meet. Indonesian Soc. Neurol., Psychiatr. Neurosurg.,* Surabaya, Indonesia, **1972.**

6. *Buku Laporan Statistik Pasien Mental Di Indonesia,* 1972 Kirektorat Kesehaten Jiwa, Departemen Kesehatan, R. I., Jakarta, 1974.

7. C. Geertz, *Agricultural Involution: The Process of Ecological Change in Indonesia,* University of California Press, Berkeley, 1966, p. 123.

8. D. C. Leighton, J. S. Harding, D. B. Macklin, A. M. Macmillan, and A. H. Leighton, *The Character of Danger,* Basic Books, New York, 1963.

The MSIS Experience within Israel

MORRIS MEISNER, Ph.D. and CAROLE SIEGEL, Ph.D.

The State of Israel, when founded by United Nations resolution in 1948, experienced an immediate increase in immigration, and the Israeli government responded to the demands of forming workable social welfare policies by inaugurating a system of population registery. An official governmental order was the legal basis for giving each resident a unique identification number as part of this registry. This identification was used not only for voting lists and planning purposes but also served as an identification mechanism for admissions into the country's health system.

Commencing in 1967 with the development of the Multi-State Information System in the United States, a host of foreign visitors curious as to the plans of this information system came to the Rockland Research Center and indicated their interest in the project. In 1968 Dr. Nathan S. Kline, Director, and Dr. Eugene M. Laska, Director, Information Sciences Division (ISD), were invited by the Israeli Ministry of Health to discuss the system with Ministry officials and to begin assessing whether this system might be applicable to the mental health needs of Israel. During the next 2 years international correspondence between the Israeli Ministry and ISD discussed the possibility of collaborative efforts with the International Committee Against Mental Illness (ICAMI), a private agency devoted to improving the care of the mentally ill by providing clinical consultants to government, funding start-up costs of government-sponsored projects, and conducting transcultural research. By 1971 decision was reached to establish a computerized Israeli Psychiatric System patterned and based on the Multi-State Information System.

From an administrative and organizational point of view, psychiatric services in the country are divided into four geographic regions. These are Jerusalem and the southern region, the central region, Tel-Aviv and the surrounding region, and Haifa and the northern region. Within each region a chief regional psychiatrist assumes legal and administrative responsibility for all admissions.

Psychiatric hospitals in Israel are operated under any of four auspices: governmental, those sponsored by the *Kupat Cholim* (Sick Fund), public non-governmental (as represented by the Psychiatric Unit of Hadassah Hospital), and private. The 46 governmental hospitals deliver most of the psychiatric services in the country. Each governmental hospital has a catchment area population of some 150,000 to 200,000 people. Approximately 200 psychiatrists are employed within these governmental hospitals. They provide far more than half of the country's total of 8000 psychiatric beds and each hospital may vary in size from 20 to 500 beds. Over 3000 psychiatric beds exist in private hospitals, although they currently have an excess of patients over official bed capacity. Movement statistics indicate approximately 1100 admissions per month and 1000 terminations per month.

Reporting through admission and termination forms, mandated by law, is uniform throughout all facilities. From the inception of the State in 1948, a card file of each patient entering the Israeli psychiatric system, organized both alphabetically and serially (using the patient's population register number) has been scrupulously maintained. Responsibility for the maintenance and updating of this manual file rests with the Statistical Unit within the Department of Mental Health Services. For 1966–1967 the crucial information on the card files was put onto magnetic tape and statistical reports were issued by the Department of Mental Health Services for these years. This effort marked the first introduction of the use of computer technology for statistical reporting in mental health in Israel. Another department, Statistics and Economic Planning, whose responsibility is statistical reporting necessary for program evaluation and economic planning for the Ministry of Health has, for obvious reasons, a good deal of interplay with the Mental Health Statistical Unit. Nearly all reports are produced manually and contain information taken from the Admission and Termination Forms.

Periodically other forms are initiated in order to compile current statistical data. For example, in 1970, a new form recording contacts for day patients was tested. Ultimately a revised version will be used for all outpatient clinics.

The Electronic Data Processing Department within the Ministry of Health has the responsibility of making computer technology available to all facilities within the Ministry. This technology ranges from automated laboratory tests to census-keeping systems. The department has the responsibility of designing specifications of computer programs for the Ministry of Health and contracting with software houses to carry out these programs.

Accordingly, in introducing MSIS into Israel, three departments played a crucial role. The Department of Mental Health Services responsibile for psychiatric care, the Department of Statistics and Economic Planning responsible for planning, and the Electronic Data Processing Department of the Ministry of Health responsible for all computer-allied technology shared in the developmental efforts of the planned system.

The original agreement between ISD and the Ministry called for implementation of MSIS in three stages: (1) inpatient recording, (2) extension of the data base to outpatients, and (3) incorporation of clinical reporting forms within the system. ISD was to provide some technical support, ICAMI was to assist in funding developmental stages, and the Ministry, of course, was to have overall responsibility for the project.

Since the initial stage of the project dealt with inpatients, a committee representing the three departments of the Ministry was formed to formulate a new Israeli admission form within the scope of MSIS. Israel's interest in epidemiologic research necessitated the inclusion of many items including some dealing with concentration camp experience of immigrants. Accordingly, these items were appended to the form. With the design of the form completed it was submitted to the Israeli parliament, which mandated its completion for all psychiatric admissions.

The flow of information among the facilities, the Ministry central office, and the computer was specified. The new procedures introduced some minor, yet time-consuming, technical difficulties for MSIS. For example, since error checking was to be done by a clerk in the facility, the error report would have to be in both Hebrew and English. Whereas output just in English or just in Hebrew could be easily handled, a mixture of the two languages on one report necessitated modifications within MSIS report software to allow changes in direction of the printing mechanism (Hebrew is written from left to right; English from right to left).

Another technical change involved the mechanisms to protect the data from inappropriate use. The program design of MSIS allows for a series of "locks" ensuring the confidentiality of data base according to American requirements. Israeli custom, however, calls for different portions of a record to be "locked." To date all the technical hurdles encountered have been overcome, and by 1973 all the software was installed on an Israeli computer.

The experience in adapting MSIS to the needs of Israel's psychiatric system illustrates the value of international cooperation. Nations have realized that there is a common basis for human ills, and shared problems can be resolved over international boundary lines. The adaptation of the MSIS technology from one country to the system of another nation took into account differences in culture, language, service delivery, statistics, and research interests.

4. Legal and Social Issues

LEGAL AND SOCIAL ISSUES

Introduction

MYRON PULIER M.D.

It is now generally taken for granted that comprehensive computerized collections of personal information about individuals can pose a serious threat to liberty and privacy. Judging by newspaper articles on data banks, the average citizen is becoming concerned over indiscriminate use of information about such matters as his financial status and his medical condition.

Although great benefit is promised by systematic collection and management of medical data, there has generally been insufficient allocation of funds for preventing loss of control over those data. This is not surprising in view of the lack of any concrete and direct economic return for making a heavy investment in security of medical data. The motive force necessary to construct adequate safeguards for personal medical information must therefore be generated by legislative mandate. Just as governmental intervention is necessary to ensure minimal standards in building codes and in public health, statutory data-safety laws are required to keep the powerful tools of computer technology from being misused.

The issue of computerizing psychiatric information is perhaps the most delicate of all. Psychiatry, of all medical specialities, has been particularly sensitive about guarding the privacy of the consulting room and especially cautious about data banking. The Multi-State Information System stands out as a pioneer not only in implementing procedures to keep the data entrusted to it physically secure, but by helping to create a landmark statute that protects it from having its data directly subpoenaed. This statute, however, is just one brick of the many needed to build a solid legislative enclosure within which massive medical data banks may operate without endangering society.

Laska and co-workers in their chapter, "Data Systems and Mental Health: Recommendations to the World Health Organization" present recommendations that presage extension of large-scale automated psychiatric data banking worldwide even in underdeveloped countries. Westin reviews international developments in the protection of citizens from misuse of data banks and points out that the time for legislation is now, before many large data systems are completed, since modifying existing systems to conform with new legislative standards could become impractically costly. Goldwater reviews the importance of privacy to the American way of life and urges that appropriate legislation be passed. Congressman Goldwater is cosponsoring a privacy bill with Senator Samuel J. Ervin and Congressman Edward I. Koch. Finally, the chapter by Curran and Bank describes the issues faced by MSIS in this area, the model statute developed to protect MSIS data, and the other steps taken by MSIS to ensure adequate protection and control of its data.

These chapters provide a cross section of current thinking on privacy and medical data banks and seem to indicate nearly universal agreement on the broad principles regarding privacy. However, when it comes to implementing these ideas in detail to accommodate the realities of clinical practice and social needs, this unanimity is likely to break down.

As anticipated by Westin, privacy legislation is being fought by "data bank " interests whose current computerized implementations would have to undergo costly modification to comply with proposed standards. In California, for example, "Virtually every state agency affected by the bill (AB2656 which codified the 'Fair Information Practices' recommended by the U.S. Department of Health, Education, and Welfare) said it would cost too much for them to comply with it." Accordingly the bill was killed in Assembly committee after the Senate version was passed 71 to 0.

Although several of the authors favor giving an individual the right to inspect and correct his own file, the details for implementing such procedures are complex and costly. Even if it is acceptable for psychiatric patients to have free access to their entire clinical record (and many would debate this), who should bear the cost of producing a readable copy of the dossier and of confirming or refuting an individual's claim that certain information is wrong? How may a person, a poor and uneducated person, for example, even know that a file is being kept about him? Perhaps printouts from each subject's file should be sent to the subject either at regular intervals or at the time of each update. This would eliminate the problem of repeated nuisance requests for printouts, but raises the problems of finding each individual and confirming that he received his printout and certainly increases the cost of computerization.

The right to sue for damage caused by the inclusion of incorrect information in a file is not an effective tool for ensuring citizens' rights to accurate dossiers since the monetary cost of such damage would be difficult to assess, successful suits would be very rare, and it might be difficult to determine who would be liable.

There are other complications. The second of Koch's "10 Commandments of Privacy" gives each person the right to "supplement" the information contained in his file. Implementing this practically and effectively is difficult. There is no reliable way of ensuring that the questions that define data categories will be fair and that the choice of answers will reflect reality. Furthermore, the right to append a narrative explanation to supplement incomplete and misleading information stored in code form would not be a practical remedy because most computer programs would ignore the textual appendix and would proceed as if the code that was originally entered were to be taken at face value. This problem arises from the process of cramming people into categories, a necessity inherent in medical data processing technology and, therefore, unavoidable.

Finally, there is the issue of specificity in authorizing access to files. As it now stands, patients are usually forced to permit access to any and all information any medical file may contain about them in order to receive certain medical insurance payments. Maximum protection of the privacy of computerized medical data requires classifying each data item into a need-to-know category so that only specifically necessary and specifically authorized information would be released. The technology for this has already been implemented in the business world where money is at stake. In the case of medical information where only privacy is at stake, it would take very involved and technical regulatory legislation plus lots of money to develop, implement, and enforce standards of this sort.

While study of these issues is taking place, only few projects like MSIS take it upon themselves to protect privacy, and medical data banks are proliferating. Unless sufficiently detailed, specific, and comprehensive legislation is prepared now, the confidentiality of medical treatment may well be trampled by a runaway information technology. Westin's pronouncement that the time for federal legislation is now, is an imperative.

LEGAL AND SOCIAL ISSUES

Legal Measures on National Levels to Protect Privacy and Confidentiality

ALAN F. WESTIN

When they were first introduced in the early fifties, computer-based information systems were generally regarded as an unalloyed boon to society. Since the mid-sixties, however, growing international concern about their potentially harmful social effects has been reflected in public debates; legal, political, and sociological writings; parliamentary inquiries; judicial decisions; and the reports of national commissions in most of the nations of the Organization for Economic Co-operation and Development (OECD), which conveniently includes most of the community of Western industrialized democratic nations and Japan, though not the USSR (1).

The issues raised center on concerns about intrusions on the privacy of individuals and associations; the capacity of the press, public interest groups, and the political opposition to gain access to data in government files; and the relatioships between the well-organized and the less-organized elements in modern society. Underlying these issues are more general concerns about the potential effects of broad-scale automation on national culture and social values.

INTERNATIONAL CONCERNS

The most active debates over the issues of computerization and citizen liberties have come in those nations with large per-capita gross national products, highly developed industrial economies, and extensive computer applications in such key areas as commercial credit, government social services, and law enforcement.

These debates and early regulatory responses have not been confined to nations with any particular type of governmental system or legal tradition. Some of the responsive nations have presidential systems while others have parliamentary systems; some have judicial review and others do not; some are common-law countries and others are in the civil-code tradition; some operate under written constitutions and/or bills of rights and others do not. In short, no single type of political system can be considered the leader in early social recognition and response to the computers-and-privacy problem.

There has been a fairly regular developmental pattern within most of these nations, beginning with early-warning literature in the middle 1960s which presented this problem as a new and major challenge to the preservation of citizen rights in an age of high technology. In the United States books by Vance Packard (2), Jerry Rosenberg (3), and Alan Westin (4) were followed by Congressional hearings chaired by Congressman Cornelius Gallagher and Senator Edward Long; television, the press, and magazines also gave extensive coverage to the "Big Brother" data bank issue (5). In Britain the first warnings were sounded by the National Council for Civil Liberties under Tony Smythe, by Lord Ritchie-Calder and Lord Windelsham, by a book decrying *The Data Bank Society,* and in important publications on the topic issued by three major British lawyers' associations (6, 7). Discussion of privacy and technology at UNESCO meetings, meetings of the United Nations Commission on Human Rights, a 1967 conference in Stockholm, and similar events helped spread the initial warnings and stirred analysis and debate throughout a broad international community.

As a result of these deliberations, private study groups and government commissions were established. In the United States there was the National Academy of Sciences' Project on Computer Databanks (8), the 1969 hearings of Senator Sam Ervin's Constitutional Rights Subcommittee (9), and the HEW Advisory Committee on Automated Personal Data Systems (17). In Britain there was a major conference on "The Databank Society" cosponsored by the National Council for Civil Liberties and the British Computer Society, the work of the Committee on Privacy under Sir Kenneth Younger, and a study of government data banks by the Home Office (7). In Norway there was a study under a faculty group at the University of Oslo, led by Professor Samuelson of the Law Faculty (6). In Canada the Federal Department of Communications and Justice conducted a thorough study that produced a series of monographs and an overall task force report in 1971 (10). In Sweden a Committee on Public Access and Secrecy conducted an elaborate census of government and private data banks and their uses, and drafted legislation that became effective in 1973 (11, 12). The French Conseil d'Etat prepared a study and report in 1969–1970. In the Netherlands, West Germany, and the Computer Utilization Group of OECD, studies of varying scope and intensity were conducted by working parties (13, 14).

By 1972–1973 there were two further developments: (1)publication and discussion of the findings of these national and multinational study groups and government commissions and (2) the beginning of efforts to define and install citizen protections through legal and administrative measures.

The major reports issued in 1972–1973 by national study groups, government commissions, and OCED have led to remarkably similar conclusions (15). They indicate that computer technology increases the efficiency of traditional record keeping, provides faster data transmission and more extensive use of information, creates large-scale information-sharing networks, and fosters the growth of large new data bases. They record significant fears among their citizens about such increased power of data processing in the hands of government agencies and private organizations. These fears are intensified by concern in the mass media and among public-interest groups, legal societies, and groups within the professional computer community. However the studies are uniform in reporting that they could not document specific episodes in which the use of computerized files had created new invasions of privacy or denials of due process where these had not previously existed in manual files. Rather, the problem is one of intensification and exacerbation, bringing to the surface many long-standing issues of record keeping and liberty that had been developing for decades. None of the reports sees the problem as a technological one, capable of being resolved merely through the application of better computer security controls. The essential issues are seen as matters of social policy, involving questions of what information should be collected for a given function; how the information collected should be shared within the organization that obtained it and with outsiders; and when individuals should be able to know what is in their records and be able to inspect and challenge this information for accuracy and completeness. The studies uniformly recommend that protective measures be adopted to monitor and control the uses of automated files in the interest of protecting basic citizen liberties.

Based on the momentum and recommendations arising from these studies, legal initiatives to protect citizen liberties in large-scale data systems have been instituted or are pending in about a dozen nations. The middle seventies are expected to be a period of activity during which government bodies, voluntary associations, standards-setting groups, and organizational managers adopt new rules and remedies to deal with the computers-and-privacy issue.

Some nations have gone in the direction of appointing commissions or inspectors with power to pass upon the creation and registration of data banks containing personal information, with authority to supervise their operations so as to assure confidentiality and security, and to provide a complaint mechanism for citizens who believe that their personal information has been misused. With the Hesse Law of 1970 as the earliest model (10), and the Swedish law of 1973 as the most comprehensive and enforceable national legislation to date (7), this approach is under consideration in many other nations, including France, the Netherlands, the Federal Republic of Germany, Canada, and Norway. A recent bill introduced into the United States Congress by Rep. Edward Koch (Dem., N.Y.) would carry the main features of the 1973 Swedish act into American law. Some of these schemes are quite comprehensive, covering all government and private information systems with personal data (Sweden), while others apply only to one level of government (the proposed Canadian commission for federal departments and the municipal data access boards at the local level in the United States) or to one information system (the proposed Netherlands Crown Commission for the central population register). These schemes also vary in how much they predetermine the standards of privacy, confidentiality, and citizen access that are to be met. Some leave these to be empirically developed by the data commissioners, while others are spelled out in legislation.

Other countries follow the model of voluntary guiding principles enunciated by government bodies (the local authorities' and Younger Committee's principles in Britain) or by private groups (the code of practices drawn up by the British Computer Society for computer use in general and for the confidentiality of the national census). Here general legislation is not envisaged, nor are rights enforceable in court being created, and no special commission is being advocated. Rather, protection of citizen liberties is expected to develop through compliance by managers with a set of standards adopted by acclamation and enforced by professional norms and society's traditional pressures for conformity.

Between the extremes of reliance on strict legislated regulatory powers and voluntary codes of proper conduct are a broad middle range of approaches. Some countries advocate laws defining citizen rights and remedies in particular record systems (law enforcement, credit, health, banking, etc.) or the creation of general rights of citizen access to files at a particular level of government (local, regional, national). Others are working toward the development of legally enforceable codes of "fair information practice" that are to be observed by government agencies and by organizations funded by government grants. In some countries the courts are moving to decisions in cases involving the collection and use of personal information, especially by government agencies. These judicial decisions will produce major statements of legal principles about record keeping and citizen liberties and spur further legislative and administrative remedies.

Society as a whole is assuming increasing responsibility for activities that once were the sole concern of the individual, his family, or his immediate community. This trend reflects both a genuine consensus of public opinion that such a shift is desirable and the increase in the physical capability of government to shoulder the administrative burdens this responsibility entails. To a very large extent, that capability rests on the computer.

At the same time the concept of privacy as an inalienable right of the citizen is becoming more and more current in the theory and practice of law as well as in the way the average citizen perceives his situation as a subject of authority. It seems inevitable that the expectations of citizens for more effective and personalized governmental services must at times conflict with the expectations of those same citizens that they will retain, or even increase, the control they exercise over information about their private lives.

Although there are real and obvious technical, managerial, and political dangers inherent in heavily computerized government administration, the sense of anxiety among the public does not always resonate to real situations or to the changes brought about by technology per se. Public reaction and debate is often marked by worries that are basically symbolic. However this public unease about computers is a real element and has the potential for becoming a major *political* force in any of the above-mentioned industrialized democratic countries.

Even though computerized administrative systems are usually planned with the best of democratic intentions, they do furnish the framework for mechanisms of totalitarian control in the hands of antidemocratic forces. It is no coincidence that suspicion of centralized computerization runs deep in countries that were under Nazi occupation a generation ago.

The problem that each nation must face is that of constructing safeguards for the liberty of citizens who are the subjects of data banks, each within the framework of its own legal traditions and structures. These safeguards must secure the present legal rights of citizens in a way that will be clearly understood by the public to represent a recognition by the government of a complex of personal values too subtle to be entrusted to the vagaries of bureaucratic decisions.

UNITED STATES

Efforts are now seriously under way in the United States to bring the uses of computer technology and large-scale record keeping under constitutional rules in order to protect the American citizen's right to privacy, confidentiality, and due process in the use of large-scale information systems by governmental and private ogranizations (16).

Before 1972 many so-called "experts" and the public at large were ill informed about how computers were being used, what problems they posed, and what kinds of regulatory responses were appropriate to the realities of this situation. Later that year the National Academy of Sciences (NAS) completed a project on computer data banks that provided the first empirical, national study of just how computerization of personal records was affecting the rights, benefits, and opportunities of Americans (8). The study concluded that computer processes had not altered existing practices of organizations in their scope of personal data collection, sharing of data with other organizations, and policies concerning giving individuals affected rights of notice and challenge to their files. Computers were responsible for increasing the efficiency of data use in organizations, producing more timely and complete records, faster response time to inquiries, and more extensive processing of data in automated files. This led to the expansion of regional and national data networks and the fostering of larger, more interconnected data systems. Technological advances were foreseen that would bring cheaper, more flexible, and more reliable data processing and communication systems, allowing organizations to store and exchange personal information with greater efficiency.

The NAS report noted that legislation and judicial decisions had failed to keep pace with these technological developments and growing efficiency of data usage, by not promulgating clear standards for data collection, data exchange, and individual access rights. Such standards needed to be defined and installed if the managers of large data systems and the specialists of the computer industry were to have the necessary policy guidelines around which to engineer the new data systems that were being designed and implemented.

The NAS project suggested six major areas of priority for public action: laws to give individuals a right of notice, access, and challenge to virtually every file held by local, state, and national government, and most private record systems as well; promulgation of clearer rules for data sharing and data restriction; rules to limit the collection of unnecessary and overbroad personal data by any organization; increased work by the computer industry and professionals on security measures to make it possible for organizations to keep their promises of confidentiality; limitations on the current, unregulated use of Social Security number; and the development of independent, "information-trust" agencies to hold especially sensitive personal data, rather than allowing these data to be held automatically by existing agencies.

In 1973 a report of the Secretary's Advisory Committee on Personal Data Systems of the Department of Health, Education, and Welfare (HEW) offered a unified conception of how federal and state protective measures might be instituted (17). The HEW report formulated the idea of enacting a "Code of Fair Information Practice" for all automated personal data systems, resting on five basic principles:

> there must be no personal data record-keeping systems whose very existence is secret; there must be a way for an individual to find out what information about

him is in a record and how it is used; there must be a way for an individual to prevent information about him that was obtained for one purpose from being used or made available for other purposes without his consent; there must be a way for an individual to correct or amend a record of identifiable information about him; and any organization creating, maintaining, using, or disseminating records of in-dentifiable personal data must assure the reliability of the data for their intended use and must take precautions to prevent misuse of the data.

Drawing upon these principles, the HEW report called for the development of minimum standards in a federal code (and, by implication, in state codes as well) whose violation would constitute an "unfair information practice," sub-ject to criminal penalties and civil remedies similar to the unfair practices regu-lated in such fields as labor relations, trade practices, and consumer protection. This approach offered flexibility in applying basic principles to a set of sanc-tions that are practical for individuals and groups to enforce against govern-ment violations.

The Right Time for Legislation

The state of computer technology and the growth of data information systems suggest that the present is the most opportune moment for the enactment of pri-vacy legislation.

It is fortuitous that Congress had not drawn up its basic computers/data systems/privacy legislation before the Watergate scandal and its exposure, since that episode holds enormous lessons for the final decisions on privacy legislation. These lessons are that no democratic nation, especially one like the United States, should allow secret files to be built in the name of national se-curity that can be used easily to harrass political opponents, dissident groups, and the press; that any federal instrument created to protect privacy has the potential in it to betray privacy rights and must therefore be tightly circums-cribed; and that the single safest way to protect privacy is to see that much per-sonal information about Americans does not get recorded or preserved at all in organizational files, or that it is destroyed when the useful purposes for which it was originally collected have been accomplished.

There have been some very serious misuses of data, and some data systems have been allowed to come into being that pose grave threats to civil liberties. Many examples of these are contained in the study of federal data systems conducted by the Senate Subcommittee on Constitutional Rights, under Senator Sam Ervin (18). However, since human beings remain in charge of these data systems, and all the hardware, software, and other equipment of which they are composed, it is clear that other human beings can exercise control over potential abuses if there is the will to do so and the informed awareness of where to install the key control mechanisms. Information systems can be made to do exactly what the American people want them to do—and nothing more.

However there is some danger that segments of the public will give up the struggle in the belief that the battle with the Machines has been lost, and computers have already taken over.

> If we assume that computer users are already doing things that they must not, we risk surrendering without a fight the border between properly limited and surveillance-oriented computer applications. . . . The question of what border-control measures should be adopted can hardly be understood and properly considered . . . if the public and opinion leaders assume that the borders are already obliterated (8).

Many leaders of the computer industry, societies of computer professionals, and many of the major computer-user industries recognize the need for such legislative action. Repeatedly, they have been saying:

> It is up to the policy makers—the legislatures, regulatory agencies, courts—to set basic policies as to what personal information should be collected, with whom it should be shared, and when the individual should get to see printouts and/or contest his or her record. With such policy guidelines set by the responsible organs of American society, we—as computer professionals and data-systems managers—can figure out what these rules would entail in costs and in the efficacy of data processing, and can communicate that back to the policy makers, so that sensible measures can be finally settled on. Then, we can design and run systems that embody such rules. But if the policies are not formulated, then it will be natural that we will spend most of our time on getting systems up and running, getting more crunch for the dollar, and paying only lip service to the privacy problems.

In short, most of the computer industry people are ready—even enthusiastic—about the legislature adopting realistic and practical policies such as those recommended by the National Academy of Sciences or the HEW Code of Fair Information Practices. They take this view, in one large measure, because they know that with enough lead time and with sufficient awareness of computer capacities reflected in the legislation, computer manufacturers and applications specialists can accomplish the regulatory objectives, and at acceptable costs in dollars and efficiency. This is especially true if the basic legislation comes now, when applications are spreading into the more sensitive areas of personal record keeping, with more narrative records, and into larger data networks, and also when computer and communications technology is moving into what many call the fourth-generation stage.

To delay Congressional action any further would assure that a large number of new major data systems will be built and many existing computerized systems will be expanded in ways that will make it extremely costly to alter the software, change the file structures, or reorganize the data flows to respond to national standards. And beyond the expense, such late changes threaten to jeopardize many operations in vital public services that will be increasingly based on computerized systems—national health insurance, family assistance plans, national criminal-offender records, and many others. In fact, these systems may become so large, so expensive, and so vital to so many Americans that public opinion will be put to a terrible choice—serious interruption of services *or* installation of citizen-rights measures. At this time a host of political factors, particularly the post-Watergate sensitivity of the American public and of Congress to issues of privacy, make the perceived need for safeguards very strong. But there is no absolute guarantee that this mood will continue. And what can be done at little or acceptable costs in dollars and services today could become unbearable costs 5 years from now.

Critique of Proposed Bills

Some of the bills under consideration by Congress as of mid-1974 present very serious problems that should be avoided. First, the concept of a data registry for all private data systems with personal information, even if limited to automated data systems, is inherently unworkable and unwise for the United States. In Sweden, a nation of 8 million people, with far more governmental direction of private industry than in this country, and with a long-standing tradition of nonpolitical administrative officials who exercise enormous regulatory powers over the citizen, the concept established in the 1973 law of a national data protection board to register and license all data files may make considerable sense (11). But the United States has over 200 million people, some 135,000 general purpose computers in use, and several major types of personal data files typically maintained by each large organization that has or uses computers; it also has a considerable reluctance to give boards or commissions appointed either by the President or the Congress a broad "life-or-death" power over the data collection and exchange on which most organizations depend for their vital operations. In this setting the Swedish approach seems inappropriate. This country does not have the deference to administrative authority that marks the Swedish and German administrative traditions. Furthermore, a registry would necessarily deal, in the United States, with the computer systems that are currently used to process the personal data on members and contributors and officials for a host of political, racial, religious, and ideological groups whose data collection policies could not be put under a federal commission, or any other governmental body, without violating the First Amendment and its guarantees.

Secondly, it would be a political and practical mistake for Congress to attempt to enact a federal measure that would regulate all local, state, and regional government personal data systems. One can argue that the citizen rights involved are national and fundamental and that personal data often crosses state lines and thereby provide the traditional constitutional bases for federal jurisdiction. But a healthy respect for the values of federalism, for the lodging of important decision-making alternatives in the local populations, and the importance of keeping alternative power centers to the federal giant all are important reasons to avoid central federal control over all governmental data systems. In addition, the sheer diversity and variety of such local, state, and regional data systems threatens the uniformity of standards and the sheer feasibility of any single national registration scheme. Such a federal preemption would not be wise policy for those local and state data systems that are basically localized in nature.

The political feasibility of a federal regulatory system is also doubtful. To gain passage, federal legislation will have to run many hurdles and overcome opposition from some powerful interests in government and the private sector. To assure the presence of local and state government officials and political leaders in that opposition camp seems highly unwise and a strategy to be adopted only if there is no other practical way to assure that citizen rights will be protected in such local and state government files. Since there *are* alternative ways to accomplish this, comprehensive federal legislation should *not* attempt to control all local and state data systems in its coverage.

Finally, it would be responsive to the desirability of preserving independence and creative responsibility in the private-association sector to find a way to lead private data system managers to voluntarily adopt policies in keeping with the Code of Fair Information Practices principles. This would enhance the possibilities of genuine compliance and help keep government authority out of the many personal data files that are involved here—a positive protection of privacy in itself. Where major industries or types of organizations did not adopt principles consonant with fair information practices or did not put practical procedures into effect to execute such policies, there would be a need for a mechanism to promulgate law to compel them to do so, as was done under the Fair Credit Reporting Act. The task is for Congress to find the fit instrument to put such pressure on the private sector, police its compliance, and assure remedial action in the case of inadequate response for the public interest.

Concepts for United States Legislation

Writing as of mid-1974, I suggested that the ideal omnibus bill for Congress should have four major sections: (16)

1.   For the federal government, the legislation would require compliance with the Code of Fair Information Act principles for all federal agency systems of personal data used to make administrative or regulatory decisions about indi-

viduals; for all federal agency research and statistical files containing personal identifiers for their data; and for all federal agency investigative files not exempted by the head of the department or agency through a special, public "notice of exemption" procedure set up by the legislation.

The provision of a public-notice exemption procedure for investigative and/or national security files would seem to be an absolute necessity for good legislation. Any blanket exemption of investigative files that allows agency heads *secretly* to exempt them entirely from fair information act principles and procedures would open a huge hole in the protective structure the Congress is erecting. On the other hand, a procedure by which the agency head gives public notice and describes the file he will seek to exempt from parts of the code, the types of information collected, and the uses to which it will be put would establish a formal record of agency testimony as to what it is doing that Congress could periodically review. Furthermore, the law might declare that no federal employee who reports the improper use or operation of an exempted investigative file to a Congressional committee shall be deemed to have committed any offense or misconduct in office; this might provide the "whistle-blowing" incentive to expose such importer uses when and if they take place.

A further provision would make it a criminal offense for any person, public official or private citizen, to seek to obtain personal information that he knows to be held under law or rule of confidentiality. It is not going to be enough to punish those who leak or disclose personal data held confidentially by the government; sanctions against those who seek to pervert the safeguards are also needed.

2.   The second section of the law would apply the Code of Fair Information Practices to all national, intergovernmental data systems, defined as those in which identified personal data is shared—through reporting requirements, regulatory surveillance, or other purposes—among local, state, regional, and federal governmental agencies. The principle here is that national systems of personal data exchange require uniform national standards and procedures to protect citizen rights, and that these can only be installed effectively through federal law and procedures. Covered under this provision would be intergovernmental personal data systems in law enforcement, health, welfare, taxation, motor vehicle licensing-exchange systems, and many others.

3.   The third section of the omnibus law would declare it to be Congress' sense that the states of the nation should adopt legislation to cover their remaining personal data systems—those not operating interstate as part of the intergovernmental networks. There is tremendous diversity in such local and state data systems, and there is a sound reason in public policy (preservation of federalism and limitation on central federal power) to encourage the states to act for themselves in this field. Louis D. Brandeis commented that the states of the American federal system were "little laboratories," able to experiment with

new social, economic, and civil-liberties measures and set legislative trends for other states and the nation. Here Congress would be saying that it was setting its own house in order and was regulating interstate data systems, which would put heavy pressure on the states to come up with similar or even better protective measures. Should states fail to act, it would not be long before their citizens would demand to know why they enjoyed rights of access and contest of records in federal agencies or interstate data systems but not in their state or local files.

To make sure that the states were under the greatest incentive to pass protective legislation for themselves, Congress might write into its omnibus act a provision that a Congressional commission look at the situation as to state laws in 3 to 5 years, to see whether federal regulation was necessary to cover state and local files directly.

4.   The fourth segment of an omnibus bill would deal with the private sector. Here the impracticality and dangers involved in trying to regulate and/or register hundreds of thousands of files of every kind indicate that what is needed is an instrumentality to lead private organizations to adopt codes of fair information practice as their voluntary policies. A national commission on private interstate personal data systems should be given 2 years to examine the conduct of those nationwide personal data systems that affect the rights, opportunities, and benefits of Americans, holding hearings as necessary and with a strong, competent staff to make on-site visits and study the real practices of organizations, not just their formal policies. After such a study, the commission might be directed by Congress (in the initial legislation) to report to Congress whether there were particular industries or fields of organizational activity that should be regulated by Congress, as the credit-reporting industry was by the Fair Credit Reporting Act. Or, the commission might be given regulatory power itself, to give notice of rule making, hold hearings, issue final rules, and enforce compliance through the customary, regulatory-agency mechanisms of compliance hearings, cease and desist orders, and penalties. In either case the commission could be authorized to receive individual complaints and investigate them with an eye toward what they revealed about the need for regulation.

The creation of such a commission would provide an extremely valuable force acting on the private sector. It would push privacy, confidentiality, and due process issues to the top of the organizational agenda and into the design, testing, and operational thinking of data system managers and their staffs. It would move the computer industry and computer professionals into high gear, as consultants to the user organizations, developers of new techniques and materials, and innovators in cost-effective responses.

Legislation based on these four approaches would have Congress moving strongly where it has the greatest responsibility and knowledge, sharing the governmental duty of action with the states where localized action is involved, and acting as a force-for-action and legislator-of-last-resort where the private sector is involved.

This concept would obviously have to be fully and carefully elaborated into a bill, with some features from existing bills on fair information practices, limitation of the Social Security number, control over mailing lists, and similar matters included in its contents. Furthermore the drafting would have to recognize that some problems of privacy, due process, and data systems are probably going to be handled by Congress through other specific legislation—such as the pending criminal justice information system measures amendments to the Federal Freedom of Information Act, and amendments to the Fair Credit Reporting Act, and this omnibus privacy bill should take those more specific federal policies into account.

THE FEDERAL PRIVACY ACT OF 1975

Many of the concepts just advocated were the ones selected by Congress later in 1974, when it did pass landmark privacy legislation—the Federal Privacy Act of 1974.[19] To summarize its main provisions, the Act regulates the information practices of *federal* agencies only; puts these under procedures for public disclosure of data-collection activities; and gives data subjects a right of access to their records. At least once yearly, each federal agency covered must publish a notice about each record system it maintains with personal identifiers, whether manual or automated; this notice must indicate the data system's name, location, categories of persons covered, routine uses to be made and the users, agency policies as to storage, retrieval, access controls, and data retention, and procedures for giving individuals notification, access, and contest rights. Whenever an agency asks individuals to supply personal information, it must tell the person what legal authority authorizes the solicitation, whether supplying it is required or voluntary, the purposes for which and procedures with which it will be used. Information collected must be relevant to lawful purposes of an agency, and no information dealing with the exercise of First Amendment rights may be collected unless specifically authorized by law. Agencies must see that personal information in their files is kept accurate, current, and protected from improper disclosure.

The law gives individuals a significant set of rights: to obtain copies of their records if they wish; to know who else has seen their file; to add a personal statement to the file to correct inaccuracies or stale data, or to explain omitted facts; to have inaccurate data officially corrected; and to sue for civil damages if the individual believes the agency has violated his or her rights under the law.

Exemptions from disclosure and access sections of the Act were made for records of the CIA and investigative files of law enforcement agencies; protective files of the Secret Service; statistical records; and personnel eligibility and investigation files obtained under promise of confidentiality and personnel test records. Limits are placed on further compulsory uses of the Social Security number by government or the private sector, unless authorized by law. A seven-member Privacy Protection Study Commission is created to make a two-year study of state, local, and private data systems, to inform Congress whether federal legislation is needed for any such areas of record-keeping activity. To give federal agencies a chance to get their files and procedures into order, the Act sets September 1975 as its date for going into effect.

CONCLUSIONS

Experiences in many countries suggest that the definition and protection of citizen liberties will not be a simple task. At the base are hard questions of how record systems will be used in the process of setting standards of judgment about citizens for all the gate-keeping purposes of complex societies (education, employment, credit, housing and welfare, medical services, law enforcement, etc.); what procedures will be used in administering such standards; and what combination of managerial autonomy and outside review will be used to regulate computerized information systems. Some of the proposals currently being offered are well-meaning but ill-considered formulations. Their money costs would be staggering; their effects on the conduct of critical governmental and private business might be to halt vital operations entirely; and their protection of citizen interests might well be illusory (given the wealth of personal data that lies outside the computerized record systems, in manual files), promising great protection but actually diverting public attention from the real misuse of data.

In each country proposals for safeguards are inching their way through the regulatory and legislative system. In the meantime, the automation of government continues its accelerating pace, threatening the safeguards with obsolescence before they ever go into effect. Technical approaches of broad international applicability lie unnoticed in out-of-the-way journals while scarce resources are wasted in duplicating their programs and communications systems. The rapid growth of multinational corporations, the increasing mobility of workers across national boundaries, and the explosive development of intercontinental digital communications facilities, all add to the challenges of shaping adequate legal and procedural safeguards by traditional legislative and administrative methods.

Computer and communications technology should neither expand unchecked by the rule or law nor lead us into dangerously unwise regulatory policies that could alter vital balances of power and civil liberties guarantees of our constitutional and parliamentary systems. We stand precisely one decade away from 1984, and the measured excellence of our legislative response will be the best guarantee that the arrival of Orwell's date on the real calendar will not be a cause for sadness at the realization of his bleak prophecy but for satisfaction that our system was able to avoid the abyss.

REFERENCES

1. Materials in this section have been adapted from A. F. Westin, D. B. H. Martin, and D. H. Lufkin, *The Impact of Computer-Based Information Systems on Citizen Liberties in the Advanced Industrial Nations,* A report to the German Marshall Fund of the United States, Washington, D. C., 1973.

2. V. Packard, *The Naked Society,* McKay, New York, 1964.

3. J. M. Rosenberg, *The Death of Privacy,* Random House, New York, 1969.

4. A. Westin, *Privacy and Freedom,* Atheneum, New York, 1967.

5. *Computers and Invasion of Privacy,* hearings before a subcommittee of the Committee on Government Operations, House of Representatives, 89th Congress, U.S. Government Printing Office, Washington, D.C., 1966.

6. *Towards Central Government Computer Policies,* Organization for Economic Cooperation and Development, Paris, 1973.

7. Privacy Committee of the British Computer Society, *Comput. Bull.,* **15** (1971), 5.

8. A. F. Westin and M. A. Baker, *Databanks in a Free Society,* Quadrangle Books, New York, 1972.

9. *Privacy, the Census and Federal Questionnaires,* hearings before a subcommittee on Constitutional Rights of the Committee on the Judiciary, U.S. Senate, 91st Congress, U.S. Government Printing Office, Washington, D.C., 1970.

10. *Privacy and Computers,* a Report of a Task Force established jointly by Department of Communications/Department of Justice, Information Canada, Ottawa, 1972.

11. *Computers and Privacy,* Commission on Publicity and Secrecy of Official Documents, Swedish Ministry of Justice, Stockholm, 1972.

12. C. G. Kallner, unpublished materials presented at a seminar on data security at Columbia University on April 29, 1974.

13. U. Thomas, *Computerized Data Banks in Public Administration,* Organization for Economic Cooperation and Development, Paris, 1971.

14. G. B. F. Niblett, *Digital Information and the Privacy Problem,* Organization for Economic Cooperation and Development, Paris, 1971.

15. *Automated Information Management in Public Administration,* Organization for Economic Cooperation and Development, Paris 1973.

16. Adapted from a statement by A. F. Westin, presented before an ad hoc subcommittee of the Senate Committee on Government Operations and Senate Judiciary Subcommittee on Constitutional Rights, Hearings on Privacy and Government Information Systems in Washington, D.C. on June 18, 1974.

17. *Records, Computers, and the Rights of Citizens,* Secretary's Advisory Committee on Personal Data Systems, Department of Health, Education, and Welfare, Washington, D.C., 1973.

18. Senate Subcommittee on Constitutional Rights, *Federal Data Banks and Constitutional Rights: A study of Data Systems on Individuals Maintained by Agencies of the United States Government,* Volumes 1–6, Washington, D.C. 1974.

19. Public Law 93-579.

Data Systems and Mental Health: Recommendations to the World Health Organization*

EUGENE M. LASKA, Ph.D., CAROLE SIEGEL, Ph.D.,
MORRIS MEISNER, Ph.D., RHETA BANK, AND
BAILA ZEITZ

The proper utilization of data information systems in mental health care can noticeably improve the quality and efficacy of such care. The World Health Organization (WHO) is in a key position to encourage and assist governments in achieving the fullest possible application of knowledge in the development and utilization of such systems to the benefit of the greatest numbers of their population.

This chapter seeks to delineate some of the common information needs of the providers of mental health care, to discuss the feasibility of automated data systems, and to propose ways and means by which the WHO can more effi-

* A Statement prepared by The Information Sciences Division of the Rockland Research Institute at the request of The International Committee against Mental Illness.

ciently coordinate efforts in establishing mental health information systems. Recommendations include establishment of an information clearinghouse on data systems, a group coordinating dissemination of this information, a common pool of specialists in the area, and centralization of computing facilities under the auspices of the WHO.

INFORMATION NEEDS IN MENTAL HEALTH

The magnitude of the economic cost to society of mental illness is immense. The long-term financial requirements for providing facilities and trained staff for treatment and maintenance of the psychiatrically ill is counterpointed by the loss of the productive potentiality of the patient. In the United States almost half of the hospital beds are set aside for the treatment of the mentally ill. In New York State alone over 800 million dollars are spent annually by the Department of Mental Hygiene, not including expenditures by other state agencies, local governments, and private facilities.

The need to know about the mentally ill patients being served and the services being given is universal. On a highly specific patient management level, individual patient records are needed to communicate information to the clinician, to evaluate the care being provided, and to plan future care. In order to plan programs, efficiently allocate available resources, and justify requests for additional resources, vast quantities of aggregate data must be available. Among the most pressing questions are:

Who comprises the population in need of mental health services?

What is the prevalence of mental disorders in the population?

How many and what kinds of manpower are trained in mental health services?

What kinds of physical facilities are available for provision of services?

How much does it cost to deliver various kinds of health care?

Clinical Records.   Keeping adequate, legible records of a patient's condition, basic identifying information, notes on orders, treatment, and progress are fundamental requirements in psychiatry (as well as in general medicine). The primary function of the records is communicating patient information to professionals charged with the patient's care. Thus psychiatrists, therapists, social workers, and others are provided with historical and up-to-date information for planning the most appropriate therapeutic activities.

A clinical record also serves as a basis for review, study, and evaluation of the care rendered to a patient. Such review, conducted periodically by professional monitoring groups, insures that the patient has been receiving the appropriate treatment for his case and that medical professionals utilize the best methods available.

Finally, in the aggregate, the clinical record provides data for use in research and education. No matter what the immediate purpose of the medical record, ease of information retrieval is of paramount importance.

Demography. Demographic information of both the population of an area and those in that population who are mentally ill is crucial for the effective planning and evaluation of programs for the care of the mentally ill. This involves quantitative statistics describing the characteristics of these populations (1). Such data on the general population of an area are usually available from population censuses. At the present time, there are no generally accepted methods for measuring the incidence and prevalence of mental disorders in a population. A number of attempts have been made and the results of some of these studies have been summarized in WHO publications (2).

Information vital to the program planning and evaluation process can be obtained, however, by systematic collection of data on the characteristics of persons coming under care in mental health facilities, including such sociodemographic variables as age, sex, ethnic group, income, and family composition. In addition to aiding in the planning and evaluation of mental health service programs, such data would also provide valuable clues to the distribution of mental disorders in the population.

Resources. While demographic information and descriptions of the population being treated are crucial components of comprehensive planning for mental health care, other information elements are vital as well. Descriptions of manpower (professional, paraprofessional available, nonprofessional available), programs (facilities, services, treatment modalities) in progress, and financial resources are also needed for planning mental health care programs (3). Proper utilization of available resources entails statistics that describe these three factors at the national as well as at the community and the facility levels. Examples of utilization statistics might include the number of beds available per population unit (e.g., per 10,000 persons), the number of days spent in hospital by particular kinds of patients (age, sex, diagnosis), the admission and discharge rates, the services rendered by outpatient clinics, hospitals, and so on, and the number and kind of personnel available per unit of population, classified according to inpatient and outpatient care.

Fiscal Information. Fiscal information is an essential ingredient for controlling, implementing, and evaluating mental health service delivery. One of the most important aspects of a fiscal information system is cost finding: determination of the costs actually incurred in providing various types of mental health care. Needed for cost finding are data on patients, such as age, diagnosis, problem clusters, treatments, and treatment outcome; salaries of health workers, cost of maintaining buildings; cost of general services and other variables (4).

No matter what the method of financing mental health care, cost finding fulfills an important function. In countries where treatment costs are absorbed by the government, such information can be used for the solicitation of funds as well as for justification to legislators and government agencies of the need for those funds, the reasons for decisions such as modifying overall plans (e.g., from inpatient to predominantly outpatient care) or implementing a new treatment modality, and the necessity for more trained personnel, etc. Mental health program administrators are concerned with determining the cost–benefit ratios of various treatment modes so as to enable the most economic allocation of their resources.

Planning and Evaluation. Once a comprehensive data base of information is established, a host of questions may be asked, and the answers provide input for planning on many levels. For example, a new treatment center is being planned. Among the questions to be answered are:

Who are the patients to be served? How many are there? What are their problems?

What are the environmental conditions that support and perhaps cause these problems?

What is the optimal location for the center?

What form should the center take?

Given a particular kind of patient with a particular set of problems, who can deal most effectively with him? a professional? a paraprofessional?

Will he be likely to benefit from psychotherapy? drug therapy? behavior modification techniques?

How long will the patient be likely to need treatment?

Planning and evaluation of programs are inextricably intertwined. Given some of the input with which to answer the above questions, a program would be planned and put into action, and after a suitable period of time, it would be evaluated. On the basis of the outcome of this evaluation, additional planning, including perhaps modification of some programs, reallocation of resources, and introduction of new services would come about.

Two of the essential questions of evaluation are: is the program meeting its objectives? and How well are the recipients of mental health care being served? These are far from simple to answer. In order to assess treatments, a set of goals must be established, and the setting of goals for mental health care is an evolving process. At one time provision of custodial care was paramount, and the "success" of a mental health facility was measured by the extent to which it kept mentally ill patients separated from the community and safe from one another. Today such a program would be considered a failure. Some of today's goals are: providing continuous care as the patient progresses through a treatment program, insuring accessibility of care to all who need it, and providing care equally to all population segments (5).

PROBLEMS INHERENT IN DATA SYSTEMS

Efficient and effective management of the resources devoted to the field of mental health occurs only in the most modern institutions. Few nations maintain data systems that make possible an accurate assessment of the extent and nature of psychiatric disorders or of the impact of different delivery systems in prevention or treatment of mental illness. The notion of maintaining a clinical information system to monitor treatment and to be useful in planning and program evaluation for most nations is probably realizable only at some remote future date.

However the knowledge of the most efficient ways in which to organize a data system as well as of the technology for producing automated computer based systems capable of meeting the financial and clinical management needs in the mental health field is already available. The Multi-State Information System, described in Section 2 is an example of such a system utilizing modern data processing technology and meeting these needs. Portions of this system have already been successfully exported to other countries, bearing out the central contention of this paper, that developments in automation can and should be shared. A selection of other systems currently in operation are also described in Section 1.

Before considering the task of establishing a data system, it is important to enumerate the various problems and pitfalls that frequently accompany such an effort. While none of these problems is insurmoutable, each should be taken into account, so that necessary steps may be taken to insure success.

Manual records are limited in utility for many reasons. They are often impossible to read; those that are readable are usually not systematic. Meticulously kept records are very large and hence create storage problems. Furthermore, even the most legible, systematically kept, and neatly stored records cannot be monitored except by sampling. The collection of aggregate data from manual records is virtually impossible; even sampling methods require armies of clerical workers.

All these problems may in part be solved through automated record keeping, but computerization is accompanied by other problems, including cost, selection and maintenance of hardware, training of technicians, inefficient communication channels, motivation of personnel, and the safeguarding of privacy and confidentiality.

Cost. The cost of a system from its conception through its successful implementation and routine use is undeniably high. If the system is automated, large computers are expensive, and even for projects of moderate size, machine costs are usually matched or exceeded by the manpower costs required to program the system and to keep it functioning smoothly. Thus, for economy and efficiency in the expenditure of research and development funds, simple principles seem to be evolving; information on successful developments should be shared, should be disseminated as widely as possible particularly among participating countries in the World Health Organization, and should be adopted wherever appropriate. Duplication of effort should be avoided; successful solutions to common problems must be made easily available. What is also evident is that nations at every level of development can benefit from collaboration. With the availability of pooled resources (equipment, technology and personnel), each nation can choose that level of participation that is most suitable—whether it is simply more efficient organization of its manual system or full participation in an automated effort.

The question must be asked: Why should a developing country with limited financial resources invest in an automated mental health information system? One often-heard argument against computerization for developing countries is that they have a surplus of relatively inexpensive clerical labor resources. The obvious fallacy in this contention is that, although computers do perform clerical work admirably (and can be partially justified on the grounds that they facilitate accuracy and standardization of information handling), it is in their applications to decision making, resource management, and planning that computerization makes its largest contribution for developing as well as for industrialized countries. Especially in the area of human services such as mental health care, practitioners are likely to attack the allocation of money to computerization of patient records, claiming that the limited money available is best spent in direct service. Thus the emotional value of "helping people" is a primary concern, whereas "gathering information" is seen as a secondary, quasilegal requirement, having little or no direct bearing on patient care. However, without adequate information on the nature of the population being treated, without accurate descriptions of the resources available for treatment purposes, and without adequate data on the outcome of various treatments provided to the patients in question, there is nothing to ensure that the services being provided are indeed services and that the "help" being extended is actually helping (6). In the long run, the development of an information base, its use in the ongoing management of programs, and the subsequent research done on the available data provides direct benefit to patients.

Hardware. While the industrial nations of the world have sufficient computer hardware to run complicated psychiatric record-keeping systems, this is not the case in many of the developing nations (3). Here hardware, especially for health or mental health use, of sufficient capacity may be lacking. Even though the cost of sophisticated computers has gone down (in terms of cost per transaction) and continues to go down, many nations still find such equipment impossible to support except for their most urgent needs. There are possible solutions to this situation. Many underdeveloped nations do have limited computing capacity serving "essential" government agencies. Some pooling of resources could be investigated so that the mental health community could have access, even on a limited basis, to computer technology. For those nations having no computer hardware whatsoever or for whom cost is a major problem, a possible solution is their sharing hardware or using a centrally located computer with terminals that allow communication with many system users including those devoted to serving the mental health community. In either case technologically advanced nations can share their expertise with the emerging nations, enabling them to make the best uses of limited resources.

Technicians. Concomitant with the lack of sophisticated computer hardware in the underdeveloped nations is a lack of trained technical programming and statistical personnel working in the mental health area. Indeed, in many nations not only are computer scientists scarce but mental health professionals are as well. In these cases it is imperative to maximize the number of trained persons within a given nation by using them in many capacities. Data processing personnel in other government agencies and in private industry may be available on a part-time basis to assist mental health agencies in designing and implementing mental information systems.

Communication channels. The utility of an information system depends on the accuracy and completeness of the data contributed to the system as well as on the dissemination of data coming from that system. Often a major problem in underdeveloped nations involves the general communication systems which are not always efficient. Mail and telephone services are often unreliable, and technicians are often not available for long periods of time when equipment is disabled. Solutions to the communications problem are not clear. However it is expected that concomitant with the general rise of the technological level of emerging nations, such communication problems will be alleviated.

Motivation. A universal problem in data systems is motivating personnel to participate. No data system can succeed unless the individuals contributing data see its usefulness in the context of their professional lives. This makes it incumbent upon the manager of the data system to provide motivation to those who are expected to contribute the data. The best motivation possible is feedback from the system in terms of useful reports and rapid response to questions asked by those contributing the data. Further, motivating can take the form of training sessions, seminars, and general information dissemination via printed media.

Privacy and Confidentiality.   Questions of safeguarding the confidentiality of records have arisen in every country, and several, notably England, Sweden, Denmark, Canada and several states in the United States, have prepared position papers or have enacted special legislation defining the limits of the revelation of medical information from the records (7, 11). All professionals share in the desire to safeguard the confidentiality of the patient/therapist relationship and to prevent the revelation of information that would be harmful or embarrassing to the patient or his family (12).

Automated record systems are safer than manual systems from inadvertent or malicious unauthorized use, but the pooling of data from a number of sources into more centralized files does present a threat to privacy and raises a number of questions that must be considered by a profession dealing with sensitive, personal information. The threat to privacy may be safeguarded by technical means (codes, passwords), by physical means (locked repositories), and by legal means (special statutes, penalties for misuse such as professional censure, suspension or revocation of license, or adjudicative procedures). The design of an automated record-keeping system must include the provision of adequate personal safeguards (12).

RECOMMENDATIONS

During the last 10 years, computerized information systems applied to health have multiplied in number and scope. At the same time the problem of dissemination of information on computers has also grown. Although the World Health Organization has sponsored symposia on the use of computers in the health sciences, most of the systems discussed are highly specialized and typically only function at one facility. Such symposia serve to present innovations and sometimes provide proof of the applicability of an idea to a realistic working setting; however we are unaware of a systematic effort to classify, keep track of, and respond to inquiries about the generality or transferability of specific systems. Hence at present there may be unnecessarily redundant efforts in the development of systems having similar objectives, and many facilities with specific requirements for a system may have no idea that one already exists that may meet their needs.

Because the majority of existing systems are facility oriented and because there is no clearinghouse of information on operating systems, an emerging country that wishes to implement a computer system for mental health is at the mercy of the local computer salesman. Under such conditions, lack of knowledge of what exists (13), of what, in fact, is applicable to a country, and lack of technical expertise and equipment (14), the undertaking of the development of a national mental health information system is hazardous. Recognizing this, national officials may opt to postpone the decision and continue to operate without the benefits they could obtain.

A national information system for mental health may be conceptualized on many levels, corresponding to various degrees of system complexity ranging from simple statistical reporting of "head counts" to complex data recording and analyses incorporating every relevant fact concerning a patient. Since different nations are themselves at different degrees of development, they should examine existing systems and consider only those appropriate to their needs. At present little or no help is available to help nations make these choices.

There is a plethora of expensive computing machinery on the market. Choice of equipment can play a major role in the success or failure of a project. Very little information regarding maintenance and service performance, breakdown frequency, operating system efficiency, and so forth, even on well known computers, is available to use in evaluating a particular computer configuration. In addition, whereas successes of computer systems are always reported by manufacturers, failures are virtually never reported. Such information may prove invaluable for an emerging country in increasing the probability of success.

We therefore propose the following recommendations:

1.   A clearinghouse, under the auspices of WHO, should be established to amass material on resources of information systems in mental health. Information on data systems, computer resources, manpower resources, and case studies of evaluations of different information systems would then be housed in a single permanent archive.

2.   A group, under the auspices of WHO, should be charged with the responsibility of disseminating information on data systems; this duty could be fulfilled via an international journal, monographs, newsletters, and/or symposia.

3.   A pool of specialists should be formed to advise and assist nations seeking to establish information systems in mental health. This group would have the additional responsibility of coordinating multinational efforts in establishing mental health information systems.

4.   Regional centralized computing facilities should be made available, under WHO auspices, to the member nations to alleviate the financial and manpower burdens associated with the installation of computer information systems.

No official administrative group beside the World Health Organization currently exists that could provide the necessary leadership and lend support to countries wishing to upgrade their mental health delivery systems by developing a mental health information system. Although there are many examples of cooperative projects among groups within and between individual countries, these can in no way match the impact which the involvement of WHO would have on helping the emerging nations. The need for implementing the above recommendations under WHO auspices, to enable all countries to share developmental efforts, evaluate current systems, and share computing facilities is apparent.

REFERENCES

1. M. Spiegelman, *Introduction to Demography,* Harvard University Press, Cambridge, 1968.

2. M. Kramer, "Collection and Utilization of Statistical Data from Psychiatric Facilities in the United States of America," *Bull World Health Organ.* **29** (1963), 491–510.

3. C. C. Gotlieb and A. Borodin, *Social Issues in Computing,* Academic Press, New York, 1973.

4. J. E. Sorenson and J. E. Phipps, *Administration in Mental Health,* (1972), 68–73.

5. R. D. Bass, "A Method for Measuring Continuity of Care in a Community Mental Health Center," unpublished paper supported by NIH-71-324 1971.

6. R. May, *Treatment of Schizophrenia: A Comparison Study of Five Treatment Methods,* Science House, New York, 1968.

7. *Computers and Privacy,* summary of report (SOV 1972:47) and Draft Data Act submitted by the Commission on Publicity and Secrecy of Official Documents, Swedish Ministry of Justice, July 1972.

8. *Privacy and Computers,* report of a task force established jointly by the Department of Communications Department of Justice, Information Canada, Ottowa, 1972.

9. *Records, Computers and the Rights of Citizens,* report of the Secretary's Advisory Committee on Automated Personal Data Systems, United States Department of Health, Education, and Welfare, DHEW, No. 105, 73–94, July 1973.

10. E. W. Springer, *Automated Records and the Law.* Aspen Systems Corp., Pittsburgh, 1971.

11. C. F. Stroebel and B. C. Glueck, Jr., *Am. J. Psychiatr.,* **126** (1970), 8.

12. W. J. Curran, E. Laska, H. Kaplan, and R. Bank, *Science,* 182, (Nov. 23, 1973), 797–802.

13. D. Twain, E. Harlow, and D. Merwin, "Research and Human Services: A Guide to Collaboration for Program Development," NIMH Grant MH-15860, 1970.

14. *Automation and Data Processing in Psychiatry,* Task Force Report of the American Psychiatric Association, 1971.

LEGAL AND SOCIAL ISSUES

Restoration of Personal Privacy and Individual Rights

REP. BARRY M. GOLDWATER, JR.

Awareness of gradual but growing intrusion on personal freedom is spreading rapidly. Civic and patriotic groups, the academic community, and many members of congress have committed themselves to a crusade for personal privacy and the maintenance of human dignity. Nothing short of a national battle plan must be formulated in Congress, by state governments, and by private enterprise to reverse the insidious denuding of every person's personal privacy and individual rights. Furthermore, the ability of the government and big business to exchange indiscriminately private information about any individual must be stopped.

ZONES OF PRIVACY

A special area of concern is information protection, sometimes called "data surveillance." This is not to suggest that there are no other forms of privacy invasion. All too many violations of personal liberty can be found in the current

391

news:

- "Watergate" was an invasion of privacy.
- The break-in to Dr. Ellsberg's psychiatrist's office was an attack on privacy.
- Unwarranted wiretapping and physical surveillance are intrusions on privacy.
- Behavior modification techniques used on young persons and persons in penal institutions invade the privacy of the individual and deny human liberty.

Similarly, the careless or inaccurate handling of sensitive personal facts and transferring or selling personal files without consent are invasions of privacy.

GROWING CONGRESSIONAL COMMITMENT

For almost a decade a few isolated voices in Congress and throughout America have been proposing remedies to privacy invasion. The commitment has been slow in coming, but there are real signs of its arrival. The recent adoption by the House of Representatives of the privacy amendment to the Federal Energy Administration Bill is a case in point. As far as can be determined, this was the first time an amendment of this nature was included in a measure establishing a new agency of the federal government. The amendment requires the agency to protect and assure the privacy of personal information collected or used by the Administration. It also requires the administrator to establish guidelines and procedures for protecting individual identifiable personal data.

When legislation involving information on individuals comes to the consideration of the House or the Senate, a sufficient number of dedicated Congressmen (most especially me) will act to include in the law specific guarantees of privacy and confidentiality.

CONTROLLING DATA SURVEILLANCE ACTIVITIES

In the modern context privacy means protected rights of personality, that is, the right of the individual to keep certain information about himself or aspects of his personality strictly to himself and not available to others. This concept includes material on his personal history, political views, sexual practices, and so forth. Privacy is invaded when an individual is required or wrongfully coerced to divulge sensitive personal facts about himself.

These invasions of privacy may be found in all areas of life; government questionnaires, applications for public assistance, and credit card requests are a few examples. If the seeking of personal information can be confined to the minimum needed, the threat to privacy is lessened.

Once personal information enters a record system, its confidentiality must be protected. This is the case if the information is used only for the purpose for which it was taken and if data managers take care that it is accurate and valid. Once the need for this information has ended, it is the duty of the users to prevent transfer or release of the data and, in accordance with a specific policy, to purge the data from the system.

Prudent attention to private rights has not been the case. Individual privacy has not been respected. Excesses by both governmental and private sector data collectors and continued unresponsiveness and insensitivity are alarming the public. Technological innovations in the automation of information handling have magnified the privacy dangers. Computer processing and analysis of data as well as wide telecommunications networks give a new dimension to the privacy issue. Confidence in government has failed in part because of distrust in government information practices. Public understanding of this threat to civil liberty has elevated privacy to a priority national problem.

HISTORICAL DEVELOPMENT

A review of the development of Western man and of social order in three cities, Jerusalem, Athens, and Rome, will help to bring a clear understanding of the basis of this attack on personality.

The idea of society and of community in the presence of God came from Jerusalem. The concept of privacy as a human value began when the individual was the basis of society, a social order based on laws, and where men were seeking knowledge, truth, and justice.

The Greeks, especially Socrates, Plato, and Aristotle, believed that social order is founded on the human person and on human relationships and actions. A state, then, would of necessity reflect in outward lifestyle the order or the chaos of its citizens' inner lives. Plato in the *Republic* describes an ideal nation, which sought perfect wisdom and justice. Religion also played an important part in developing the concept of privacy and was vitally important to understanding the ancient family and the society that evolved from it. From it was established marriage, paternal authority, and fixed relationships. The rights of property and inheritance were consecrated during these times. Greek and Roman law evolved from family custom. The family was rooted in the land, the land of their ancestors, which supported the family. So closely related are the origins of law and the love of land that Cicero, a Roman, could write:

> What is there more holy than the house and the land of each individual citizen?
> Here is his altar, here is his hearth, here are his household goods. Here all his
> sacred rights, all his religious ceremonies, are preserved.

Indeed these are the origins of patriotism, a word whose literal meaning is love
of the land and love of our fathers.

Eventually religion enlarged and extended the family until cities were
formed. The city was ruled in the same manner as the family with all the institutions as well as the private law of the ancients. With time the importance of
the family and family love became badly distorted. Instead, a new political
entity was created: the ruler, who was the father image raised to the level of
hero or god. It was then that law was needed to restrain the rulers and to substitute for fear and coercion as the means of ruling.Law was meant to lead men
to cultivate virtue and to insure liberty in an environment where common
interests were considered above special ones. Law was meant to correct injus-
tice. The Greeks and Romans left us the principle of rule by law, respect for
the family, and patriotism. What was not clear within the ancient societies was
moral and ethical direction for the state.

Christianity helped fashion the politics and the forms of Western government. St. Augustine's Philosphy brought together Mosaic Law, Socratic
Philosphy, and natural law. He believed that a state and the politics of a people
should reflect society's understanding of itself. With moral and ethical direction, St. Augustine believed a person's life would be marked by charity, love,
and freedom.

THE DOCTRINE OF FREEDOM

The doctrine of freedom to seek and to gain ends beyond mere things is
essential to privacy. Free will and free choice are essential.

There are enemies of freedom, perhaps the greatest ones lie within ourselves:
fear, desire, and ignorance. People have sold their freedom for money, security,
position, merely short-run benefits. These misled people think freedom is not a
spiritual or intellectual quality, but a material one.

This materialistic blunder can easily lead to the view that men with more
things are bound to be somehow freer and happier than men without them. Life
today seems based on producing and consuming things in ever-expanding quantities. This style of life has impacted our freedom and so our privacy through the
worship of social utility and the disregard of human values for the sake of
expediency.

CHANGE OF DIRECTION

In giving so much importance to material values, our society has sacrificed intellectual freedom. We let big government take over our personal responsibilities and those of our churches and our charities. We let government educate us, house us, and direct our cultural experiences.

Now we wonder why this collapse in our rights to be left alone, after we have permitted, and even asked, the government to relieve us of our duties.

THE MATERIALIST CONCEPT OF MAN

Science and technology are justly credited with giving us bountiful progress, and, in large measure, this has been to our advantage. However, we must look closely to see whether all the new methods and apparatus for development are making us slaves to new masters. Are not many of these political and social techniques to regulate the flow of goods and services really controlling our choices and opportunities?

The modern economic view of man dominates our lives. Every television commercial underscores the consumer society. We are told we will be happy and satisfied through possessions. Moral qualities are seemingly irrelevant; success is measured in terms of monitary assets. This is an immoral view.

TECHNOCRACY OR TECHNOLOGY

This section is not intended as an attack on technology as such. There are really two concepts which should be discussed: technology and technocracy. Technology stands as an intermediary between men and their environment in producing the club and the wheel, for example, and is neutral in the molding of human destiny. Technocracy is the product of that applied science that evolved when the scientists, infected by rationalism, developed solutions, to human problems that they believed would erase suffering, end hunger, provide riches, and generally secure welfare but that were based on the continuous availability of government money.

It is technocracy that limits freedom, for in a technocracy men must choose only the most efficient techniques to achieve desired ends to the possible detriment of every other standard such as beauty or humanity. Determining the most efficient means for a project requires an accumulation of facts and then more facts to explain the ones already collected. So many facts are needed that techniques of fact finding and collecting have become a special field of development; that is, the collection of data has become a vast enterprise.

Another technocratic notion reduces individuality by equating one man with another by suggesting that one man with a technical mind is as able as any other to do a technical job. Everything distinctive, individual, or superior in terms of the qualities of a man's mind is not relevant. Technocracy centers on the quantitative; down with qualitative dimensions or values. If there are no jobs except technical ones, everyone will function according to the same common, and probably, low standard.

THE CYBERNETIC STATE

Another result of the vast accumultation of facts is an extremely complex society, a technocracy. Will it function according to the will of the public? No. Can the mechanisms of society be operated by bureaucrats? No. Only technocrats. Since ours is becoming an essentially mechanical state, it is vital that all its parts operate smoothly. If the flow of mail in one area is interrupted, it is enough to warrant a declaration of national emergency and utilization of the Army as was actually done during the mail strike a few years ago. If some scheduled air flights are disrupted by criminal hijackers, it is enough to subject all to a close search. Now, we probably take the search for granted, as if we had never before traveled freely.

Here we are getting to a major concern: our surrender to the tyranny of technocracy. As our country has been mobilized into a technical society, we have become technocracy's servants. We have been asked again and again to place technical accomplishments at the top of our list of human values.

Technocracy requires order, as absolute as possible. This is one of the root causes of society's demand for the apprehension and punishment of those who disrupt order. A penchant for order has blinded people to the circumstances prompting disorder. A student demonstration, for example, is reported largely for its disorderly characteristics, not for the motivations of the participants. This is not to be construed as condoning disorders or disorderly conduct. But perhaps society is often missing the point by worshipping order.

Our desire for order has led the government to appeal to the technicians to devise the means and the techniques to effect social change, but its agencies are also the chief beneficiaries of the techniques. Technobureaucrats now have tremendous influence and power.

PROGRAMMING THE PROGRAMMERS

The computer–telecommunications era is upon us. There are currently 150,000 computers and some 350,000 remote data terminals in use in the United States.

Predictions indicate there will be 250,000 computers and 800,000 terminals by 1975.

Revolutionary changes in data storage are taking place. It is possible today to build a computerized on-line file containing the compact equivalent of 20 pages of typed information about the personal history and selected activities of every man, woman, or child in the United States. Much of this information can be compiled just by using the Social Security number to trace down the information. In this system any single record can be retrieved in about 30 seconds. Few can deny that we are approaching a data bank society.

Let us not undo or slow down technical advancement, but rather put men *over* machines. Let us insert private rights into the programs of the programmers. Let us restore the principle of human dignity lost in the worship of the gods of efficiency and economy. The dehumanists of technocracy should have the back seat in the reshaping of our destinies.

THE CONGRESSIONAL COMMITMENT

There are now more than 300 members of the United States Congress, both House and Senate, who have sponsored one or more of the 60 different approaches to restoring rights of privacy of Americans.

A recent Department of Health, Education, and Welfare Advisory Commission Report on Automated Personal Data Systems set out good recommendations for a Code of Fair Personal Information Practices. Each of these different remedies strikes at a particular evil or abuse. What is really needed is a broadly framed measure to include all kinds of information-collection practices, whether maintained on computers or with traditional manual filing methods, which incorporates the best of the suggestions. Private organizations and businesses must be required to conform to these standards.

Secretary of Health, Education, and Welfare Casper Weinberger and former Attorney General Eliot Richardson gave me the opportunity to introduce legislation implementing the HEW committee report in the House of Representatives. The basic proposals of this legislation are:

- There must be no personal data system whose very existence is secret.
- There must be a way for an individual to find out what information about him is in a record, and how that information is to be used.
- There must be a way for an individual to correct information about himself if it is erroneous.
- There must be a record of every significant access to any personal data in the system including the identity of all persons and organizations to whom access has been given.

- There must be a way for an individual to prevent information about him collected for one purpose from being used for other purposes without his consent.

EXECUTING THE BATTLEPLAN

The fight for privacy has clearly gotten underway in 1974. For the first time both Houses of Congress recognize the issue of privacy as bipartisan and as having a direct relationship to our basic civil rights and civil liberties. President Nixon called for a review of the plight of the right of privacy in February and established a commission directed by the Vice President (Gerald Ford) to review the situation and to make recommendations for remedying some of the problems by executive action. The commission was at a great disadvantage in that it had to start from scratch, but it has, in my opinion, done very well. The commission has participated with both the Senate and the House in the preparation of legislation that will have application only to the federal government, and it issued an interim report early in July. The activities of the commission have been most beneficial both to the government and to the citizens at large. However, the recommendations of the Vice President's Commission are subject to administrative interpretation and modification or revision and do not have the same force and effect as congressionally mandated law. It is for this reason that the real burden of the privacy flight rests with Congress.

I did meet with the Vice President early in 1974 in Washington and suggested that instead of merely studying the issue further, the committee should incorporate the best ideas from government reports into a bill to be sent to the Congress with the endorsement of the President for July of 1974. After that meeting I prepared, in cooperation with Congressman Koch of New York, a Comprehensive Right to Privacy Act which was introduced in the House of Representatives and referred to the Committee on the Judiciary. The number of that bill was H.R. 14163. The bill was sent out to 50 groups and individuals for their critical comments and evaluation's and we received responses from more than half of those contacted. Many of their suggestions were of great merit and value and were incorporated in a revised draft of the bill which was reintroduced recently. There are several bill numbers for this revision, including H.R. 15524.

Another committee of the House, the Government Operations Committee, had also been holding hearings on personal privacy and invasions of the right of privacy. The committee's area of jurisdiction is restricted to the agencies and activities in the federal government. The Comprehensive Right To Privacy Act was redrafted in an abbreviated form so that it applied only to the federal government and not to state and local governments or private enterprise. That modified draft was then submitted to the Government Operations Committee for their consideration. That committee held 3 days of hearings and has begun subcommittee markup on a privacy act. It was to this committee that the suggestions of the Vice President's Commission were submitted.

In the Senate Senator Ervin has been joined by several of his colleagues in sponsoring a right to privacy bill simlar to our H.R. 14163. Two committees, the Senate Committee on Government Operations and the Constitutional Rights Subcommittee of the Senate Judiciary Committee have held hearings on Senator Ervin's bill. They are in the process of completing staff investigations and are about to begin markup of their piece of legislation. The result of all these activities confirms my belief that the Congress will in fact pass and send to the White House privacy legislation before the closing of this session of Congress.

These activities have important consequences for the individuals in our country. The Congress has accepted the heavy burden of restoring privacy and individual rights, particularly as those rights are affected by the collection, maintenance, use, and dissemination of personal information. The quality of American life will be greatly improved when personal privacy and individual rights are restored to their proper relationship through such activities, and I am confident that this restoration will occur.

LEGAL AND SOCIAL ISSUES

Right to Privacy

EDWARD I. KOCH*

Since 1969 I have appeared before many committees of both the House and Senate out of a concern for the neglected field of citizen privacy. On November 21, 1974, Congressman Barry Goldwater, Jr. and I saw an amended version of our Comprehensive Right to Privacy legislation pass the House of Representatives by a vote of 353 to 1. President Ford signed the Privacy Act into law on December 31, 1974. I feel that, notwithstanding its deficiencies, the Privacy Act represents a monumental breakthrough in the field of personal privacy safeguards.

What the Privacy Act does is to open federal files in many areas. Millions of files that are locked away will become available to the public in September 1975. I am not saying available to the public in terms of seeing somebody else's file, but, as I have indicated, in seeing one's own file, seeing whether the material in it is relevant, seeing whether it is accurate, seeing whether it is current, and, if it is not, providing the mechanism whereby corrections can be made.

In this 94th Congress, Congressman Barry Goldwater, Jr. and I have introduced our Comprehensive Right to Privacy Act—H.R. 1984—which extends privacy safeguards to state and local governments and to organizations in the private sector. It is our intention to have the Congress proceed with hearings on this legislation at the same time the Privacy Protection Study Commission develops its report. This commission was established under the Privacy Act with a 2-year mandate, at the end of which time a report on the impact of privacy

---

* Member of the House of Representatives elected from the 18 congressional district in New York.

legislation on state and local governments and the private sector will be submitted to the President and the Congress. Congressman Goldwater and I have received appointments to this Commission.

It is my hope that by the end of the 94th Congress the Judiciary Committee will have compiled a record of findings in the privacy area and, upon receipt of the report from the Privacy Protection Study Commission, will immediately begin work on marking-up the bills before it and reporting out the necessary corrective legislation.

Some groups in the private sector have voiced the opinion to me that it is not appropriate for the federal government to legislate for the private sector and that dictating what should—and should not—be done with information compiled by private concerns would be an infringement on their rights by the federal government.

I would say to them that we must be concerned that the interests of all the people are served and protected while we attempt to meet the justifiable needs of government and business for information.

It should be your right and it should be my right to know how material on us is used—particularly if decisions affecting our lives are based on that material.

Perhaps my own experience as a private citizen years ago planted the seed from which my legislative efforts have grown. It involved a life insurance company inquiry, but the investigative procedure could have just as well been pursued by a federal agency.

When I was a younger man, I made an application for life insurance, and it was rejected. I couldn't understand why because I felt pretty healthy, and the company did not give me the reason. Because I pressed and pressed, I finally was able to secure an off-the-record statement from the individual who had solicited the account. He said, "Well, we have information in our records that 10 years ago you had cancer." I said, "Well, that is very interesting, but I am not aware of it." I asked what the nature of this cancer was. The records showed it was leukemia. I asked, "Where did you get that information?" The company indicated they had obtained it from a neighbor.

The truth is that I didn't have cancer and of course would have been dead a long time ago had I had it. Had I not pressed on that matter, I wouldn't have known and I wouldn't have been given an insurance policy. I brought this matter to the company's attention and demanded that they analyze their file again and finally they agreed that the information that had been provided them had been given maliciously.

While a City Councilman in New York, I introduced legislation in 1968 to give the citizens of New York City the right to inspect and supplement municipal files. At that time I said my bill was "just a first step taken on a local level in what is really a national problem of protecting the citizenry against unjustified governmental prying into private affairs."

All the national health insurance proposals pending before the Congress will have an enormous impact on the privacy of individuals, whether private carriers or the Social Security Administration run the program.

At the present time there is a data bank used by over 700 insurance companies from which they can receive information on an individual—information that pertains to the physical condition of the person—dealing with psychiatric disorders, sexual behavior, and drinking patterns. The existence of this Medical Information Bureau data bank raises serious questions about this privileged relationship.

We must take care to guard against information on a patient's insurance forms finding its way to the personnel department or to the employee's supervisor. In contracts between employers and insurance carriers—or the federal government—any employer participation in the processing of individual claims should be prohibited.

Furthermore, security safeguards should be established to protect the privacy of an individual during any examination of his medical record under the guise of "program evaluation," "audit," or "cost justification."

Under no circumstances should the Congress permit the unbridled transfer of such family medical or income information, particularly without the written, informed consent of the individual (unless it is a case of medical emergency and then with the most stringent regulations). The individual has a right to know the uses to which information he submits will be put, to whom it will be disseminated, and how its release, or nonrelease, will affect his eligibility for benefits.

The creation of a health credit card, although efficient and easy to use, could, without regulation, lend itself to abuses. The code numbers provide quick, easy access to the individual's medical records. If an individual's health credit card code number can be used by other organizations, the accessing of information from many sources on a given individual is made much easier.

If the Social Security Administration (SSA) is chosen to administer the national health program and if Congress authorizes SSA to use the Social Security number as the health card number, the way will have been paved toward using the Social Security account number as a universal numerical identifier—and the spectre of a national data bank with voluminous material being accessible by the use of one number is made more real.

Let me briefly outline in general terms what I think this legislation should contain with respect to privacy safeguards. These 10 commandments of privacy are:

1. Permit any person to inspect his own file and have copies made at reasonable cost to him.

2. Permit any person to supplement the information contained in his file.

3.   Permit the removel of erroneous or irrelevant information and provide that agencies and persons to whom the erroneous or irrelevant material has been transferred be notified of its removal.

4.   Prohibit the disclosure of information in the file to individuals in the agency or organization other than those who need to examine the file in connection with the performance of their duties.

5.   Require the maintenance of a record of all persons inspecting such files, their identity, and their purpose.

6.   Ensure that information be maintained completely and competently with adequate security safeguards.

7.   Require that when information is collected from him, the individual must be told if the request is mandatory or voluntary and what penalty or loss of benefit will result for noncompliance.

8.   Require that those involved with the collection, maintenance, use, or dissemination of medical information operate with clearly defined data access policies and with adequate data security measures to provide medical confidentiality.

9.   Require that persons involved in handling personal information act under a code of fair information practices, know the security procedures, and be subject to penalties for any breaches.

10.   Prohibit agencies or organizations from requiring individuals to give their Social Security number for any purpose not related to their Social Security account or not mandated by federal statute and prohibit the development of any other universal numerical identifier.

I am hopeful that the bipartisan spirit by which privacy legislation has been initiated, shaped, and refined will continue through the efforts of this Congress in drafting a national health insurance plan because citizen privacy must be everyone's concern—conservative and liberal, policy maker and taxpayer, physician and patient.

The Multistate Information System and Confidentiality and Privacy Protection

WILLIAM J. CURRAN and RHETA BANK

Increasing public exposure to the continuing debate on the proposal for a national data center and on various proposals to consolidate information collection has generated concern over the issues of confidentiality and privacy. These issues were further debated in congressional hearings, in articles in the lay press, and in professional journals. Public fears are enunciated quite clearly, as for example, in an article in *Social Casework*, "It is horrifyingly possible that a punitive government could make arbitrary decisions such as that all people who have had counseling for alcoholism will be ineligible for public assistance or public housing or whatever. The possibilities of misuse of personal information are endless" (1).

Some of the most sensitive data of all collected by any source on the private lives of people is psychiatric information. This point was underscored by precautions taken in a study where sane individuals had for research purposes entered psychiatric institutions as (pseudo-)patients. In the study, pseudonyms were employed, "lest their alleged diagnoses embarrass them later" (2).

Professionals working with this personal data and with the new computer capabilities have the responsibility not only to advance knowledge and techniques for helping people but to evaluate these advancements in the light of professional goals and human values. Such a point of view tempers the use of new knowledge in ways deemed unethical. As Alvin Toffler suggests, rather than fight technology, we must learn to adjust to it and use it, but we must be discriminating in the way we use it (3).

With this national concern as background, technical methods have been devised and legal steps have been taken by the Multi-State Information System to protect the confidentiality and privacy of psychiatric patient records stored in the computers at the Rockland Research Institute but deriving from many states and many legal jurisdictions. Because state mental health departments felt the need for efficient, automated psychiatric reporting systems to justify large budgets and to monitor the use of such funds so that appropriate care for the patients may be insured, the argument for an information system specifically operated for mental health programs and specifically designed for psychiatric data with meticulous safeguards of individual privacy and confidentiality led the National Institute of Mental Health to grant the Information Sciences Division monies with which to develop the Multi-State Information System. Thus, resources expended by the federal government could be useful to many states.

The staff of the Information Sciences Division realized very early that work in safeguarding the information from misuse had to be undertaken even before the system was fully operational and that responsibility for these safeguards belonged to the organization that was exploiting the computers' capacities for storage, retrieval, and analysis of vast quantities of information to service the mental health community. The division wanted to avoid the dilemma that Senator Samuel J. Ervin so carefully defined, "It has been noted that organizations too often seize on a device or technique with the intention of achieving some laudable goal, but in the process may deny the dignity of the individual, a sense of fair play, or the right of the citizen in a free society to the privacy of his thoughts and activities" (4).

One of the first steps in attempting to define the legal needs of the project was to retain the services of a legal consultant. His initial functions were to define in legal terms the concepts of privacy, confidentiality, and privileged communication that govern the information being stored in the data bank, to review the legal framework of the operation of MSIS in all the then participating states, to determine necessary legal steps, and to draft any legislation necessary to protect the confidentiality and privacy of that information being stored at MSIS.

ADMINISTRATIVE AND TECHNICAL STEPS FOR MAINTAINING CONFIDENTIALITY

The threshold problem of protection for MSIS records was the determination that all the data collected by it and stored in the computers of the demonstration project at Rockland Research Institute was confidential. All the data in the computer is compiled from clinical records and by clinical and administrative personnel in psychiatric facilities. Thus the confidential nature of the information itself has already been established. All such information is considered confidential on an ethical basis as part of the physician–patient relationship. The MSIS staff from the beginning of its data collection has respected this confidentiality and permits a facility access only to the data it has stored.

The staff of MSIS set up the system in such a way that each terminal has access only to its own data files (disks and tapes) and not to those of any other terminal. Personnel at each terminal dial the computer when data are ready to be transmitted. A password is required to identify the terminal. Failure to provide the correct password results in the immediate termination of the call. The passwords are known only to a few people at MSIS headquarters, where every possible effort is made to keep the passwords secret. Key personnel at each terminal are aware of the password for that terminal and are responsible for its security. Passwords are changed periodically and as needed. A monitoring program in the computer receives all transmissions and affixes to the incoming data an identifier indicating which terminal sent the information. That same identifier is transferred to the output so that reports are returned only to the terminal that sent them.

Every transaction occurring within the MSIS computers is recorded—entries of data, corrections or updating of records already in the file, requests for reports, and so forth. This file also contains a copy of the messages returned to the terminal. These files are kept on tape for a period of 1 year, after which time the facility may request a permanent paper copy.

Other technical precautions have been taken to avoid accidental access or damage to the data base, including internal programming checks and the use of special codes.

Physical security measures have been taken at MSIS headquarters, the Rockland Research Institute, which is a guarded building where there is constant control of access to the premises. All entrances to the building are attended either by personnel or by electronic security devices. During the business day (8:30 A.M. to 4:30 P.M.), receptionists are stationed at two unlocked doors, so that no persons can enter without being identified. In addition, all visitors are logged in at the time of their arrival and logged out when they leave. During the evening hours and on weekends, access to the building is limited to a single entrance that is manned by security personnel. At these times entrance is permitted only to those showing employee identification cards or special letters of permission from Research Institute department heads.

All unattended entrances, in addition to being locked, are protected by an alarm system. Any movement of these doors sounds a piercing alarm at the location and signals the security guard at his central station. Once triggered, the alarm must be reset by the security guard with a special key. Each door alarm is checked once every 24 hours to make sure it is operating properly.

The computer room within the building is further protected by electronic combination locks, the combinations to which are known only to the computer operations staff. Even MSIS staff are barred from direct access to the equipment.

At each of the participating facilities in which terminals are located, responsibility for security of the terminal room is in the hands of the director of the facility, as is the responsibility for distribution of data received and the propriety of its use. Such locations are generally subject to the same or greater security measures than are medical records rooms, and access is usually strictly limited to authorized personnel.

CONCEPTS OF PRIVACY, CONFIDENTIALITY, AND PRIVILEGED COMMUNICATIONS

Before beginning the detailed analysis, it is necessary to identify three basic concepts in this field: privacy, confidentiality and privileged communication.

"Privacy" is the right of the individual to keep certain information about himself or aspects of his personality strictly to himself and inaccessible to others. Examples include personal history, attitudes, political views, sexual practices, child-rearing practices in a family, and his photograph or signature.

"Confidentiality" presupposes disclosure of private or personal information to another person. In a confidential relationship, the information is given to the other person in trust for special purposes and cannot be disclosed to third parties without the permission of the person who gives it. Examples of such confidential relationships are those of the physician and patient, psychologist and patient, priest and penitent, and attorney and client.

"Privileged communication" is a technical, legal term closely related to confidentiality. Under this privilege, if established by statute in the particular jurisdiction to cover the particular relationship, the client, patient, or penitent can prevent information from being disclosed by the confidant in court or in other legal proceedings by refusing the confidant permission to testify.

HISTORY OF MSIS USES OF LEGAL SAFEGUARDS

A policy statement giving formal support to the practices of confidentiality initially implemented was requested by MSIS from the Commissioner of Mental Hygiene of the State of New York. In a letter dated June 18, 1968, the Commissioner, Dr. Alan D. Miller, responded as follows:

> In answer to your request, I am writing to state formally that the Commissioner of Mental Hygiene will not consent to divulge to anyone, other than the agency submitting the data, any information from that data which would in any way identify individual patients. In particular, information of facilities outside New York State will not be made available to any New York State agency or staff other than the staff working directly on the Multi-State Project in the Information Sciences Division at Rockland State Hospital (now, Rockland Research Institute—eds.).

The action by the Commissioner was taken under the New York State Mental Hygiene Law, Sections 20 and 34 (q) which limit accessibility to Departmental records and state hospital treatment records "except on the consent of the Commissioner or an order of the judge of a court of record."

After reviewing the law and the functioning of the developing system, the legal consultant advised that the policy endorsed by the Department of Mental Hygiene might not be sufficient to cover the volume of data accumulating from other states. The policy, even if fully effective, did not protect the records from subpoena or from other legally authorized discovery procedures. Also, it was thought questionable that the New York State statute referred to records other than those of the Department of Mental Hygiene. Although they were physically stored on the grounds of a state hospital, the equipment and records of MSIS were actually owned by the Research Foundation for Mental Hygiene, Inc., the grantee of the NIMH grant. Therefore the policy could be found inoperative in protecting the MSIS records.

The next step was to consider legal protection for the existing system and its future functioning, particularly if it was to be considered clearly *not* covered by the earlier Departmental policy statement. "The central problem" as Miller has observed, "is to determine how the legal system can best insure that a proper balance is struck between the traditional libertarian ideal embodied in the concept of privacy and the immense social benefit that comupter technology offers" (5).

One approach given lengthy consideration was an interstate compact. Each state would formally join the compact, and provision would be made so that smaller mental health care organizations such as counties or even individual facilities could also participate. The compact would provide an organizational framework for MSIS and guarantee the privacy and confidentiality of the data under the law in each state adopting the compact. At the time this proposal was made (1970), however, MSIS was still in the experimental and demonstration phases, and most states were reluctant to adopt a formal organizational structure so soon. While this proposal has not as yet been implemented, it is a likely conclusion to the development of a permanent, formal MSIS organization.

The approach finally decided upon was to seek a special enabling statute from the New York State Legislature directly declaring the MSIS system and its records stored at Rockland Research Institute but collected from other states to be confidential under New York law. The statute would make it clear that the records were not public records but were private corporate records and not the property of the New York Department of Mental Hygiene.

A bill including these provisions was drafted by the legal consultant. It was submitted to the New York General Assembly early in 1972 by Representative Eugene Levy, member of the State Assembly for the 95th Assembly District, which includes Orangeburg (6). The bill further provided that the records and information stored in the system by facilities located outside of New York then and in the future were not open to inspection by any agency or individual other than the agency or facility submitting them and not subject to subpoena in any court, tribunal, or administrative agency. The prohibition of any subpoena was justified to the Legislature on the grounds that all of these records are secondary sources of the information contained therein. The "best evidence" of that information is in the records maintained at the facility itself in the original jurisdiction. Therefore any subpoena should be addressed, not to MSIS, but to the original-source facility. It was also important to bar access to other governmental inquirers such as state auditors and investigators, and the bill included these groups. With all this protection for the records guaranteed, public accountability of the system had to be assured. Therefore it was suggested that a public official, the Commissioner of Mental Hygiene, be empowered to conduct an annual review of the operation of the system to assure its proper and lawful operation in the interests of the cooperating states and facilities. Upon agreement of the Commissioner to such responsibility, this item was incorporated into the bill. Lastly, the bill spelled out the authority of MSIS to release aggregate data for research and planning purposes so long as all personal identification was removed. This last authority granted to MSIS may be likened to that permitted the Census Bureau which is prohibited from using "the information furnished . . . for any purposes other than the statistical purposes for which it is supplied" (7).

The bill was passed by the General Assembly and was signed by Governor

Nelson Rockefeller on May 15, 1972 (8). It became part of the law of New
York as Section 79 (j) of the Civil Rights Law.

This New York statute is entirely unique in American law in many of its
features, especially in its provision of safeguards concerning privacy and confidentiality of the material stored and in limiting access to authorized parties.
The basic idea for such a protective law for a large, cooperative, computer-
based medical records data bank was first suggested in 1969 (9).

PRIVACY AND CONFIDENTIALITY IN THE VARIOUS STATES

Although a special law now provides direct protection of the records stored at
the Rockland Research Institute under the MSIS program, the basic security of
the information at its source in the institutions is still governed by state law. It
should be clear that the contribution of information into the MSIS computers is
not a "disclosure" of the information to a third party in violation of confidentiality. On the contrary, the MSIS is used by the mental health facilities
and by the state agencies for mental health as a supplementary part of their
own record-keeping responsibility. As indicated earlier, the information stored
by the particular facility is accessible *only* to that facility. MSIS is merely a
guardian of that record on behalf of the facility.

As a part of the service to its participants, MSIS ordered an analysis of the
law in each of these cooperating jurisdictions. Separate reports were prepared
by the legal consultant concerning the law in Connecticut, Hawaii, Massachusetts, New York, Rhode Island, Vermont, and the District of Columbia, the
jurisdictions participating in MSIS in the fall of 1971 and in the winter of 1972
when the analyses were conducted.

THE LAW IN CONNECTICUT

General Medical Confidentiality

There are no statutes in Connecticut establishing a general medical confidential
relationship or privileged testimonial communication. However it should be
noted that physicians are traditionally bound in a trust relationship to their
patients not to disclose indiscriminately outside the treatment situation any information derived from a patient in the course of treatment. This restriction is
contained in the Principles of Medical Ethics of the American Medical Association (10) and in the Hippocratic Oath. A violation of this obligation would be
serious professional misconduct. Connecticut law provides for the revocation,

48527

suspension, or annulment of a physician's license to practice medicine, or for a reprimand or disciplinary action for "immoral, fraudulent, dishonorable, or unprofessional conduct" (11). Connecticut courts have not interpreted this provision concerning disclosures of confidential patient information, but other state courts and statutes have included such improper disclosures in the definition of "unprofessional conduct" (12).

Similar ethical principles apply to other professionals such as psychologists, nurses, and social workers regarding confidential information.

Psychiatric Confidentiality

Connecticut does have specific statutes protecting confidentiality in the relationship between a psychiatrist and his patient. All communications and records of a psychiatrist regarding his patients are made confidential and disclosure is strictly restricted (13).

Since psychiatrists are the only physicians covered by a statutory confidentiality law in Connecticut, it is important to examine the definition in the statute (Section 52-146d):

> "Psychiatrist" means a person licensed to practice medicine who devotes a substantial portion of his time to the practice of psychiatry, or a person reasonably believed by the patient to be so qualified.

The statute thus does not include general medical practitioners or other specialists who occasionally treat disturbed patients or patients with psychosomatic complaints. It also does not include social workers or other professionals who counsel patients or clients concerning emotional problems (however note the next section concerning clinical psychologists). If, however, such other professionals work in "mental health facilities" as defined in the law, or "participate" in the care and treatment of mental patients under the supervision of psychiatrists, the communications to such persons are covered by the law and are confidential under the law. Persons in training are included in the coverage of the law.

The law is very specific and detailed in regard to authorized disclosures of psychiatric patients' confidential information. The exceptions are given below.

1. *Patient's or Patient's Representative's Written Consent.*   The law requires not only that the consent be in writing, but that it specify to what person or agency the information is to be disclosed and to what use it will be put. Each patient must be informed that refusal to consent to disclosure will in no way jeopardize his right to present or future treatment except where disclosure is necessary for the treatment of the patient.

2. *Communications for Further Treatment.* The law allows communication of information and records to "other persons engaged in diagnosis and treatment of the patient" or to "another mental health facility to which the patient is admitted" if the psychiatrist in possession of the record determines that such disclosure or transmission is "needed to accomplish the objectives of diagnosis and treatment." Persons in training are considered as engaged in such diagnosis and treatment.

3. *Communications for Protection of the Patient or Others.* The law allows disclosure when the psychiatrist determines that there is a "substantial risk of imminent physical injury" by the patient to himself or others.

It should be noted that this is highly restrictive language, much more restrictive than the American Medical Association's *Principles of Medical Ethics* (10) or the various court decisions in this area (15). It would not allow disclosure to protect the person from acute public embarrassment or to prevent nonviolent criminal conduct or to protect other persons who are dealing with the patient, except where imminent physical injury is substantially apt to occur unless disclosure is made. This would bar disclosure to persons contemplating marriage or commercial dealings with the patient, for example.

4. *Communications to Hospitalize the Patient in a Mental Health Facility.* The law allows disclosure when necessary to have the patient committed, certified, or otherwise admitted for diagnosis and treatment in a mental health facility.

5. *Communications to Third-Party Payors.* The law allows disclosure of name, address, and fees charged to third-party payors. In any dispute over fees, other information may be disclosed if necessary to substantiate the claim for payment.

6. *Court Disclosures of Mental Condition in Court-Ordered Psychiatric Examinations.* The law allows a psychiatrist to disclose at court or administrative tribunals in which the patient is a party information solely on the mental condition of such party where such was obtained in a court-ordered psychiatric examination. However the court must find that the patient was informed before making the communications that any such commmunications were not confidential.

7. *Civil Court Disclosures.* The law allows disclosure in a civil proceeding (noncriminal) in court only under strict conditions: (*a*) where the patient introduces his mental condition as an element in his claim or defense, or, after the patient's death, where the patient's mental condition is introduced into a proceeding by a party claiming or defending as a beneficiary of the patient; and (*b*) where the court also finds that it is more important to the interests of justice to disclose than to keep the information confidential.

Clinical Psychologists

Connecticut also has a specific statutory provision making communications between a licensed clinical psychologist and patient confidential. The statute contains no exceptions to the required confidentiality for any other situations than court testimony unless the patient "waives such privilege." The court-allowed disclosures are the same as those concerning psychiatric testimony listed as (6) and (7) above.

Patient Records of "Mental Health Facilities"

The records kept by mental health facilities, including patient clinical records, consultant reports, psychological tests, and drug administration records, are maintained by the facility for convenience in treating and caring for the patients. These records are owned by the facility and are the property of the facility (16). They are available to the staff of the facility for purposes of treating and caring for the patients.

All records of mental health facilities in Connecticut are made "confidential," and access is severely restricted by the statutes cited above. The definition of a "mental health facility" is very broad in the statute. It includes all public and private hospitals, clinics, and other facilities for inpatient and outpatient services relating in whole or in part to diagnosis and treatment of "mental condition" and psychiatrists' offices as well. Restricted disclosure applies to all communications of patient records where the patient is *identifiable*, or the substance or any part or parts or any resumé of such records. The statute defines "identifiable" as either: (1) when the name of the patient is disclosed; or (2) when other descriptive data is released "from which a person acquainted with the patient might reasonably recognize such patient"; or (3) when codes or numbers are disclosed that are "in general use outside the mental health facility" that prepared the record.

The Connecticut statutes are highly restrictive concerning the use of mental patient records beyond the necessities of patient care and treatment within the facility itself, at least as restrictive as any other state in the country. The statutes place central records in the facility even in the case of an institution that is a part of the State's Mental Health Department. The statutes seem to give the Commissioner no more access to the records of his own Departmental institutions than to private hospitals or psychiatrist's offices. (This is in part due to the legal draftsman's unfortunate practice here of including all types of facilities and offices in a single definition of "mental health facility.")

The statutes allow transmittal of nonidentifiable records and information from any mental health facility to the Commissioner of Mental Health for purposes of administration, planning, and research. A code developed by and in the possession of the mental health facility must be the exclusive means of identifying patients.

Where the patient record is disclosed to another person or agency it must be labeled "confidential," and where the patient's consent is required, a copy of the consent form must be included specifying to whom and for what specific use the record is transmitted and citing the statutory authorization for the release and the limitations imposed by law on such releases. The statute also covers oral disclosures of information in records. It requires that in such oral disclosures the recipient be informed of the statutory limitations on disclosure in the law, Sections 52-146d to 52-146j inclusive. This is a highly difficult provision, since it would seem to require physicians, nurses, and other personnel in talking to relatives and so on to recite highly technical legal language in eight separate sections of the law! It challenges one's credulity to imagine that this provision is ever complied with in practice. The recitation does not seem to be of any great significance in protecting the patient's rights.

The statutes also provide for injunctive relief in court to prevent a violation of these provisions on confidentiality of mental health records, as well as a civil action for damages.

Research Use of Mental Health Records

The Connecticut law, as noted above, is very restrictive on the use of mental health records. It is significant, therefore, that the statutes contain a specific authorization for access to psychiatric records, including identifiable patient records, where such access is "needed for such research," provided that the records are examined at the facility and are not removed from the facility. The "research plan" must be submitted to and approved by the director of the facility or his designee. The statute requires that no identifiable data be "disseminated" under this section except as allowed by law. Presumably this means that published research should not identify any patients.

Data Banks and Computer Services

Connecticut law, as noted above, is very restrictive on the use of mental health records. It is significant, therefore, that the statutes contain a specific authorization for access to a "data bank." The statute authorizes transmittal of information and records to the Commissioner and in turn allows the Commissioner to make contracts within the state and interstate compacts "for the efficient storage and retrieval of such information and records."

Restrictions are placed on the transmittal to such data banks. The mental health facility itself must remove all "identifiable data" from the patient record before release of the record, and the "code" to identify the patient must remain with the facility, although it is available to the Commissioner for purposes of planning, administration, and research.

Another Connecticut statute refers to data processing (s. 3-116a):

> In accordance with the provisions of the constitution of Connecticut, article fourth, s. 24, the comptroller is assigned the other duties in relation to his office of assuming operating control and direction of all electronic data processing and similar equipment and installations in the budgeted agencies of the state. The comptroller shall determine the manner in which such equipment and installations may most efficiently and economically be utilized and correlated to service the needs of the budgeted agencies of the state. . . .

Participation by Connecticut in MSIS has been discussed with the Comptroller, and such participation has been approved.

Although Connecticut has no legislation creating a right of privacy, its courts have recognized such a right and allow legal remedies for invasion of privacy (17). Moreover, there is indirect legislative recognition of such a right in a 1967 amendment to a statute relating to attachments in actions at law: "No attachment shall be made in any action for slander, libel, or invasion of privacy except upon order of the court to which the writ is made returnable" (18). There is no case law under this statutory provision.

It should be noted, however, that state statutes such as the one cited above and related judicial decisions ordinarily refer to a "private law" right of privacy, as distinguished from a narrower "public law" right, the latter protecting individuals from arbitrary and intrusive action by the state (19). In the public law area, the Supreme Court has indicated that electronic eavesdropping (20) and birth control legislation affecting family life (21) constitute invasions of privacy. The birth control decision, declaring a Connecticut statute unconstitutional, is especially relevant to the concept of privacy in Connecticut.

The existence of a right of privacy does not necessarily depend on specific legislative action as in New York State, but, as in Connecticut, can be derived from judicial determination as well.

Participation in MSIS

By administrative arrangement the State of Connecticut is participating in and using the services of MSIS for the collection and storage of mental patient's records and in the development of research in the computer sciences in the mental health field. Connecticut is the only participating state in MSIS that has explicit statutory authority to contract with intrastate or interstate data banks for record-keeping purposes. Other sections of this comprehensive statute dealing with psychiatric records provide protection for the confidentiality of such records and communications. These provisions specifically permit participation in a system such as MSIS, but prohibit the submission of identifiable patient data. Participation in MSIS currently is in accord with these provisions and the confidentiality of the records is strictly observed.

THE LAW IN THE DISTRICT OF COLUMBIA

General Medical Confidentiality

The District of Columbia recognizes a confidential relationship between physicians and patients in its medical testimonial privilege statute (*District of Columbia Code Encyclopedia*, Section 14-307):

(a)   In the courts of the District of Columbia a physician or surgeon may not be permitted, without the consent of the person afflicted or of his legal representative, to disclose any information, confidential in its nature, that he has acquired in attending a patient in a professional capacity and that was necessary to enable him to act in that capacity, whether the information was obtained from the patient or from his family or from the person or persons in charge of him.

(b)   This section does not apply to:

(1)   evidence in criminal cases where the accused is charged with causing the death of, or inflicting injuries upon, a human being, and the disclosure is required in the interests of public justice; or

(2)   evidence relating to the mental competency or sanity of an accused in criminal trials where the accused raises the defense of insanity, or in the pretrial or posttrial proceedings involving a criminal case where a question arises concerning the mental condition of an accused or convicted person.

The statute exempts a number of criminal cases including those in which the patient's "sanity" is in dispute. Broadly interpreted, this would seem to allow disclosure in a variety of psychiatric cases, which is a most unusual provision. A number of other states have exactly the opposite law; that is, they grant a privilege to prevent testimony in psychiatric cases, but allow testimony in other medical matters. The argument for granting the privilege in psychiatric matters is generally regarded as stronger than in any other medical area since such information is often embarrassing or detrimental to the general reputation or character of the patient.

There is another exemption to the general medical testimonial privilege explicitly articulated in District of Columbia law stating that "a physician or psychiatrist making application or conducting an examination under this chapter (for involuntary commitment to a mental hospital) is a competent and compellable witness at any trial, hearing or other proceeding conducted pursuant to this chapter and the physician–patient privilege is not applicable" (*District of Columbia Code Encyclopedia*, Section 21-583). The purpose of this section is clear: court proceedings under the Mental Health Law would be meaningless without psychiatric testimony.

Taking all exceptions into consideration, the stated policy of the medical testimonial privilege is to encourage full disclosure to a physician without fear of embarrassing consequences (22), but is only applicable in the context of treatment (23). It covers information contained in hospital records pertaining to diagnosis and treatment, but does not necessarily prohibit disclosure in court of a patient's name, address, or age provided that there is no disclosure of treatment or diagnosis (24). Arguably, the existence of a mental hospital record of a particular patient would indicate some general diagnostic information which in turn would be inadmissible.

In addition, it should be noted that physicians are traditionally bound in trust relations to their patients not to disclose indiscriminately outside the treatment situation any information derived from a patient in the course of treatment. This restriction is contained in the Principles of Medical Ethics of the American Medical Association (10) and in the Hippocratic Oath. A violation of this obligation would be serious professional misconduct. Under District of Columbia law, a physician's license may be revoked by a court finding of "misconduct or professional incapacity" (*District of Columbia Code Encyclopedia*, Section 2-123). While this statute does not specifically define "misconduct," other jurisdictions have done so to include disclosure of confidential patient information (12).

Mental Health Records

The records kept by mental health facilities, including patient clinical records, consultant reports, psychological tests, and drug administration records, are maintained by the facility for convenience in treating and caring for the patients. These records are owned by the facility, are the property of the facility (16), and are available to the staff of the facility for purposes of treating and caring for the patients.

In the District of Columbia overall responsibility for mental health and retardation services is placed in the Associate Director of Mental Health and Retardation of the Department of Public Health, established by Org. Order #141, Title I, Appendix III, Department of Public Health, 1964. However there is little specific statutory law relating to record keeping in Org. Order #141, or elsewhere, and still less pertaining to the confidentiality of such records. Section 21-562 of the Code states:

> A person hospitalized in a public hospital for a mental illness shall, during his hospitalization, be entitled to medical and psychiatric care and treatment. The administrator of each public hospital shall keep records detailing all medical and psychiatric care and treatment received by a person hospitalized for a mental illness and the records shall be made available, upon that person's written authorization, to his attorney or personal physician. The records shall be preserved by the administrator until the person has been discharged from the hospital.

Research has disclosed no similar provision requiring private hospitals to maintain such records, although good medical practice would suggest maintenance of complete and adequate records (25). While the confidentiality of a public hospital's records of a mentally ill patient is not explicitly stated in the provision, there is an implied limitation on access of anyone other than the patient's attorney or personal physician, who in turn may only see the record with such patient's written authorization. It should be noted that the hospital may destroy a patient's records upon his discharge from the facility; this is an extremely short time for records to be kept (cf. Massachusetts, which requires that psychiatric records be kept for at least 30 years, Department of Mental Health Regulations, #6.2).

Another provision of the District of Columbia Code requires that ". . . a use of mechanical restraint, together with the reasons therefore, shall be made part of the medical record of the patient" (Section 21-563). This section is applicable to both public and private hospitals.

In contrast to the provisions discussed above, a comprehensive alcoholism law in the District of Columbia enacted in 1968 specifically deals with the confidentiality of records in a detoxification center (*District of Columbia Code Encyclopedia*, Section 24-524):

> (c) The registration and other records of a detoxification center shall remain confidential and may be disclosed only to medical personnel for purposes of diagnosis, treatment and court testimony, to police personnel for purposes of investigation of criminal offenses and complaints against police action, and to authorized personnel for purposes of presentence reports.

The degree of confidentiality of these records is questionable, given the number of authorized disclosures to parties such as the police and the courts.

Privacy Law

Although the District of Columbia has no legislation creating a right of privacy, its courts have recognized such a right and allow legal remedies for invasion of privacy (26).

It should be noted, however, that the judicial decisions such as those cited above ordinarily refer to a "private law" right of privacy, as distinguished from a narrower "public law" right, the latter protecting individuals from arbitrary and intrusive action by the state (19). In the public law area, the Supreme Court has indicated that electronic eavesdropping (20) and birth control legislation affecting family life (21) constitute invasions of privacy. The decisions are, of course, binding on the District of Columbia.

Data Banks and Computer Services

There are currently no statutes or regulations in the District of Columbia concerning privacy or confidentiality in data banks or limiting access to information in data banks or computerized information collection and storage facilities.

Participation in MSIS

By administrative arrangement, the District of Columbia is participating in and using the services of MSIS for the collection and storage of mental patients' records and in the development of research in the computer sciences in the mental health field.

The District of Columbia has little statutory or common law protecting the confidentiality of medical and psychiatric records and communications; thus there appear to be no significant problems in this area with regard to its submitting identifiable patient data to MSIS. Moreover, in the implementation of the Bureau of Mental Health's record-keeping responsibility established by Org. Order #141, MSIS could be utilized as an appropriate and efficient means of carrying out such responsibility. In conjunction with clearly drafted contractual arrangements with MSIS, the existing laws in the District of Columbia do not prevent submission of identifiable patient data to and the Department's participation in MSIS.

LAW IN HAWAII

General Medical Confidentiality

The statutes of Hawaii recognize a confidential relationship between physicians and patients. The licensing law for physicians provides that a license may be revoked or suspended on the ground of a willful betrayal of a professional secret (Hawaii Statutes, Ch. 453-8).

There is also a medical testimonial privilege statute providing as follows

(Hawaii Statutes, Ch. 621-20):

> No physician or surgeon shall, without the consent of his patient, divulge in any civil suit, action, or proceeding, unless sanity of the patient be the matter in dispute, any information which he may have acquired in attending the patient, and which was necessary to enable him to prescribe or act for the patient; provided, that such consent shall be deemed to have been given to any physician or surgeon in every civil suit, action, or proceeding which has been brought by any person for damages or account of personal injuries and in all cases in which a party to a suit, action, or proceeding offers himself or any physician or surgeon or any person as a witness to testify to the physicial oondition of the party.

The statute exempts cases in which the patient's "sanity" is in dispute. Broadly interpreted, this would seem to allow disclosure in most psychiatric cases. As was true in the District of Columbia, this is a most unusual provision. A number of other states have exactly the opposite law; that is, they grant a privilege preventing testimony in psychiatric cases, but allow testimony in other medical matters. The argument for granting the privilege in psychiatric matters is generally regarded as stronger than in any other medical area since such information is often embarassing or detrimental to the general reputation or character of the patient.

The records of mental health facilities, however, are made confidential under the law of Hawaii, as is pointed out in the next section.

Mental Health Records

The records kept by mental health facilities, including patient clinical records, consultant reports, psychological tests, and drug administration records, are maintained by the facility for convenience in treating and caring for the patients. These records are owned by the facility, are the property of the facility (16) and are available to the staff of the facility for purposes of treating and caring for the patients.

The law in Hawaii specifically makes confidential all Department of Health "certificates, applications, records, and reports" which directly or indirectly identify a patient (27). Allowable disclosure of information is spelled out in the statute. Authorized disclosure is permitted in the following cases:

(1) with consent of the patient or his legal guardian;
(2) as deemed necessary by the Director of Health or by the administrator or a private psychiatric facility to carry out the purposes of the chapter (the mental health program of the State of Hawaii); or
(3) as a court may direct upon its determination that disclosure is necessary for the conduct of the proceedings and because it is in the public interest.

This section of the statute further provides:

> Nothing in this section shall preclude disclosure, upon proper inquiry, of any
> information relating to a patient and not apparently adverse to the interests of the
> patient, to the patient's family, legal guardian or relatives, nor, except as provided
> above, affect the application of any other rule or statute of confidentiality. The use
> of the information disclosed shall be limited to the purposes for which the in-
> formation was furnished.

The Department of Health's responsibilities for patient records are established in other provisions of the Mental Health Law. Ch. 333-3(b)(5) states
that "the department shall . . . keep records, statistical data, and other information as may be necessary in carrying out the functions of the Mental
Health Program and the provisions of this Chapter." With specific reference to
patients in state hospitals, Ch. 334-35(4) requires the department to "keep a
medical record of every patient."
All such records of the Department would be subject to the confidentiality
provisions of the statute discussed above.

Privacy Law

Hawaii has no statutory right of privacy, nor any other legislative indication
that such a right exists. However such a right need not depend on specific legislative action as in New York State. In a fairly recent decision, the Supreme
Court of Hawaii recognized a cause of action for invasion of privacy despite the
absence of legislation (28).
In addition, it should be noted that state statutes and judicial decisions such
as those discussed above ordinarily refer to a "private law" right of privacy, as
distinguished from a narrower "public law" right, the latter protecting individuals from arbitrary and intrusive action by the state (19). In the public law
area, the Supreme Court has indicated that electronic eavesdropping (20), and
birth control legislation affecting family life (21) constitute invasions of privacy.
These decisions are of course binding on Hawaii courts.

Data Banks and Computer Services

There is no statute in Hawaii specifically dealing with data banks or electronic
data processing.

Participation in MSIS

By administrative arrangement, the state of Hawaii is participating in and using the services of MSIS for the collection and storage of mental patients'

records and in the development of research in the computer sciences in the mental health field. The state of Hawaii protects the confidentiality of medical and psychiatric records and communications by the specific statutes discussed above. Although Hawaii data is not generally stored at MSIS in New York, they may be sent from time to time for research studies; ergo submission of data to MSIS by the Department of Health would neither violate such confidentiality nor constitute unauthorized disclosure, since the statute permits disclosure of identifiable patient data as "may be deemed necessary . . . to carry out the purposes of this chapter" (*Hawaii Revised Statutes*, ch. 334-5). Among the statutorily mandated responsibilities of the Department are record keeping [ch. 334-3(b)(5)] and research [ch. 334-3(b)(3)]. Participation in and utilization of MSIS and its resources would thus be considered an appropriate and necessary means of implementing the Department's statutory duties. In conjunction with administrative and contractual arrangements with MSIS [in keeping with the statutory limitation that "the use of information disclosed shall be limited to the purposes for which the information was furnished" (ch. 334-5)], the existing laws of Hawaii would not prevent the submission of identifiable patient data to and the Department's participation in MSIS.

THE LAW IN MASSACHUSETTS

General Medical Confidentiality

There are no statutes in Massachusetts establishing a general medical confidential relationship or privileged testimonial communication. However it should be noted that physicians are traditionally bound in a trust relationship to their patients not to disclose indiscriminately outside the treatment situation any information derived in the course of treatment. This restriction is contained in the Principles of Medical Ethics of the American Medical Association (10) and in the Hippocratic Oath. A violation of this obligation would be serious professional misconduct. Under Massachusetts law, one of the grounds for revocation of a physician's license to practice medicine is "gross misconduct in the practice of his profession" (29). In a case of fee splitting between a physician and an attorney (30), the Massachusetts Supreme Judicial Court indicated that the statutory ground of "gross misconduct" indeed included violations of recognized ethical principles of the profession and cited the *Principles of Ethics* of the American Medical Association as a source of such ethical demands. Under the reasoning of this case, indiscriminate and unjustified disclosure of confidential information could constitute a basis for revocation of a physician's license. Moreover, other state courts and statutes have included such improper disclosures in the definition of "unprofessional conduct" (10).

Psychiatric Confidentiality

Massachusetts does have a specific statute protecting the confidentiality of communications between a "psychotherapist" and his patient, at least to the extent of a general testimonial privilege (31). The statute defines a "patient" as "a person who, during the course of diagnosis or treatment, communicates with a psychotherapist." "Psychotherapist" is defined as "a person licensed to practice medicine who devotes a substantial portion of his time to the practice of psychiatry." This statute thus does not cover communications to general medical practitioners or other specialists who occasionally treat disturbed patients or patients with psychosomatic complaints. Neither does it cover communications made to social workers or other professionals who counsel patients or clients concerning emotional problems. The statutory definition of "communications" includes "conversations, correspondence, actions and occurrences relating to diagnosis or treatment before, during or after institutionalization, regardless of the patient's awareness of such conversations, correspondence, actions, and occurrences, and any records, memoranda or notes of the foregoing."

With these definitions established, the statute sets forth the privilege:

> Except as hereinafter provided, in any court proceeding and in any proceeding preliminary thereto and in legislative and administrative proceedings, a patient shall have the privilege of refusing to disclose, and of preventing a witness from disclosing, any communication, wherever made, between said patient and a psychotherapist relative to the diagnosis or treatment of the patient's mental or emotional condition.
>
> If a patient is incompetent to exercise or waive such privilege, a guardian shall be appointed to act in his behalf under this section. A previously appointed guardian shall be authorized to so act.
>
> Upon the exercise of the privilege granted by this section, the judge or presiding officer shall instruct the jury that no adverse inference may be drawn therefrom.

It should be noted that the statute permits the patient to prevent any "witness," including third parties such as a nurse, secretary, medical librarian, third-party payor, and the like who have knowledge of such communications, from disclosing communications between the patient and psychotherapist.

The statute then sets forth the following exceptions to the testimonial privilege: (a) civil commitment proceedings; (b) proceedings involving court-ordered psychiatric examinations; (c) most proceedings, where the patient introduces his mental condition as an element and it is found that disclosure would be in the greater interest of justice; (d) proceedings after the death of a patient where his mental condition is introduced and there is a finding that disclosure would be in the greater interest of justice; (e) child custody proceedings in the discretion of the judge; (f) proceedings brought by the patient against the psychotherapist, and in any malpractice, criminal, or license-revocation proceeding where disclosure is relevant.

Mental Health Records

A new Mental Health law went into effect in Massachusetts on November 1, 1971; among its provisions are several sections dealing with the records of mentally ill and mentally retarded persons. M.G.L. ch. 123, s. 36 states:

> The department shall keep records of the admission, treatment and periodic review of all persons admitted to facilities under its supervision. Such records shall be private and not open to public inspection except (1) upon proper judicial order whether or not in connection with pending judicial proceedings, (2) that the commissioner may allow the attorney of the patient or resident to inspect records of such patient or resident if requested to do so by the attorney, and (3) that the commissioner may permit inspection or disclosure when in the best interests of the patient or resident as provided in the rules and regulations of the department. This section shall govern the patient records of the department notwithstanding any other provision of law.

This provision is more specifically interpreted in the Department's regulation dealing with confidentiality of records. The statute is fairly restrictive of disclosure, allowing some flexibility in disclosure in the best interest of the patient and for research purposes.

Confidentiality of Records (Ref.M.G.L. ch. 123, s. 36)
1. Records of patients or residents shall be private and not open to public inspection except:

   a. Records of patients or residents shall be open to inspection upon proper judicial order. For the purposes of this regulation, "proper judicial order" shall mean an order signed by a justice of a court having jurisdiction or signed by the clerk or assistant clerk of the court on the instruction of such a justice. A judicial proceeding need not be pending for such order to be issued.

   b. Records will not be produced on subpoena unless the request complies with the following:

      i. The Commissioner or his designee may permit inspection or disclosure of the records of patients and residents upon the written request of the attorney of the patient or resident provided that the request is accompanied by the written consent of the patient or resident if the patient is competent.

      ii. The written request of the attorney must be accompanied by the written consent of the guardian of such patient or resident if the patient has been adjudicated incompetent.

iii. The Commissioner or his designee may exercise his discretion to permit inspection or disclosure or records upon written request:

(a) in all cases in which the record will enable the patient or resident, or someone acting in his behalf to pursue a claim, a suit or other legal remedy to enforce a right to to defend himself against such actions;

(b) in all cases in which the treatment of the patient or resident is to be continued by other professional personnel;

(c) to insure that the civil rights of the patient or resident are protected;

(d) to cooperate with state and federal agencies when such disclosure will not adversely affect the rights of the patient or resident;

(e) when such disclosure is in the best interests of the patient or resident in the judgment of the Commissioner;

(f) to persons engaged in research approved by the Department.

Such persons shall submit their research plan to the Commissioner for review and approval prior to obtaining access to patient or departmental records. The Commissioner may establish a review committee or committees in the Department or at a facility to assist him in the evaluation of such research plans. No article or other published results of any research shall identify any patient or patients. Persons engaged in approved research shall send a copy of the final work product of such research to the Department. The Commissioner may issue other guidelines from time to time pertaining to the conduct of research projects utilizing confidential data under the jurisdiction of the Department.

2. All requests and consent required by this regulation shall be kept in the file of the patient or resident.

3. All written requests and consents shall be acted upon within thirty (30) days from receipt.

Since s. 36 of the Mental Health law supersedes "any other provision of law" pertaining to confidentiality of mental patient records, preexisting statutes are negated (32). Section 36 refers to all facilities under the supervision of the Department of Mental Health; presumably, this includes both public and private facilities (since departmental facilities are under both the supervision and control of the department).

Another provision of the Mental Health law relates to patient records: M.G.L. ch. 19, s. 29(b) states that "each facility, department or ward licensed under the provisions of this section shall maintain and make available to the department such statistical and diagnostic data as may be required by the department." This does not preclude the same kind of data from being submitted from public facilities, since the department may require, without statutory authorization, appropriate data from its own facilities.

Additional matters covered by Departmental regulations which pertain to patient records include destruction of records (Regulation 6.2), and content of records for mentally ill patients (Regulation MH 24) and mentally retarded residents (Regulation MR 120).

Privacy Law

Until recently Massachusetts courts had not determined whether a legal right of privacy existed under its law. In a 1940 decision the Supreme Judicial Court stated, that "the present case does not require us to declare whether any right of privacy is recognized by the law in this Commonwealth" (33). However in 1969 the *Titticut Follies* case, involving commercial and unauthorized motion picture photography of patients at Bridgewater State Hospital, impelled the Supreme Judicial Court to recognize a right of privacy in Massachusetts (34). Given the special facts of this case (i.e., criminally committed mental patients), it is difficult to predict how broadly the courts will apply this concept; moreover, because issues of free speech and the public's right to know were involved, this decision—in spite of its recognition of a right to privacy—has been frequently criticized (19).

In 1967 the Massachusetts legislature refused to pass a bill creating a civil cause of action for invasion of privacy and referred it to a committee for further study. This bill has not been passed to date. However, in further response to the *Titticult Follies* case, the legislature, in enacting a comprehensive Mental Health Law, included the following provision: "Each patient shall be granted protection from commercial exploitation of any kind. No patient shall be photographed, interviewed or exposed to public view without either his expressed consent or that of his legal guardian" (35). This provision has limited application to patients in mental hospitals and does not constitute a general statutory right to privacy. It should be noted, however, that state statutes such as the one in New York and related judicial decisions ordinarily refer to a "private law" right of privacy, as distinguished from a narrower public law right, the latter protecting individuals from arbitrary and intrusive action by the state (19). In the public law area, the Supreme Court has indicated that electronic eavesdropping (20) and birth control legislation affecting family life (21) constitute invasions of privacy. These decisions are of course binding on Massachusetts courts.

Data Banks and Computer Services

M.G.L. ch. 29, s. 3 requires the submission of agency budgets to the Office of Administration and Finance. The following provision, related to such submission has been part of each annual general appropriation act since 1965:

> No agency of the commonwealth, except constitutional officers, whether or not the expenditure is made from funds authorized by this act, shall initiate any encumbrance or make any expenditure involving a lease or the purchase of data processing or reproduction equipment or systems without prior request to the budget director under the provisions of ss. 3 and 4 of chapter 29 of the General Laws; the certification by the head of the agency that funds are specifically available for the purpose; the prior approval of the Commissioner of Administration, in accordance with rules and regulations established by him; and notification of such approval to the house of representatives and senate committees on ways and means.

There are no other statutes or regulations in Massachusetts concerning confidentiality or privacy in data banks or limiting access to information in data banks or computerized information collection and storage facilities. However the Department of Mental Health has drafted a proposed regulation pertaining to the confidentiality and privacy of data contained in the Department of Mental Health patient data system.

Proposed Regulation (January 20, 1971)

Regulation regarding privacy and confidentiality of data contained in the Department of Mental Health patient data system on individuals receiving care from the Department of Mental Health and other mental health facilities:

(a)   The data shall have the same degree of confidentiality and protection of the personal privacy of the individual as that which exists for the clinical record of such an individual.

(b)   Total numbers from the system when used without patient identification are freely available for administrative, teaching and research purposes.

(c)   For research purposes approved by the Commissioner or acting commissioner, identification of individuals known to the system may be made to research workers connected with such research if they and the nature of the research are approved by the Commissioner, or acting commissioner and the director of the system or his designee.

(d)   Access to identifying data on individual patients in the system is denied to all except personnel requiring such identification in the maintenance of the system and researchers approved in accordance with parts (c) and (h) of this regulation.

(e)   Inquiries directed to the system about an individual presumed by the director of the system or his designee to be in probable hardship as a result of withholding information from the system or about an individual presumed by the director of the system or his designee to be a serious danger to himself or others, may be further directed so that the inquirer may question facilities that the system suggests the individual may be known to. Written record shall be kept of all such inquiries.

(f) Researchers found to have breached parts (a), (d) or (e) of this regulation shall be reported as having done so to their supporting financial and to their educational affiliations, and shall no longer have access to the system.

(g) Employees working in the system and found by the director of the system not to have adhered to parts (a), (d) or (e) of this regulation shall either be transferred to duties elsewhere or dismissed.

(h) The director of the system or his designee shall assess whether persons seeking employment in the system and whether persons connected with research purposes approved by the Commissioner or acting commissioner understand the above parts of this regulation, and shall provide them with a copy of the regulation, personally apprising them of the importance of confidentiality of records and calling to their attention the pertinent sections of the regulation.

(i) The director of the system is appointed by the Commissioner with the advice of responsible directors of private as well as public mental health facilities.

Participation in MSIS

By administrative arrangement, the Commonwealth of Massachusetts is participating in and using the services of MSIS for the collection and storage of mental patients' records and in the development of research in the computer sciences in the mental health field. Under the new Mental Health Law discussed above, submission of data to MSIS with the permission of the Commissioner of Mental Health would neither violate the confidentiality of psychiatric records established by statute nor constitute unauthorized disclosure; rather such submission of data would be considered an appropriate and efficient means of carrying out the Department's statutory responsibility of maintaining records [M.G.L. ch. 19, s. 29(b)]. Furthermore, disclosure of Departmental records containing identifiable data is explicitly permitted for approved research in a Departmental regulation (see Appendix A). The Department of Mental Health is also developing a regulation to delineate specifically its participation in MSIS. In conjunction with administrative and contractual arrangements with MSIS, these factors indicate that the existing law in Massachusetts allows submission of identifiable patient data to and the Department's participation in MSIS.

THE LAW IN NEW YORK

Confidentiality and Privileged Communication

New York law recognizes and enforces a confidential relationship between patients and physicians, psychologists, nurses, and social workers and grants a testimonial privilege to confidential communications to all four professional groups. Very few other states include all these groups. This situation in the law is of particular importance to record keeping in mental health facilities, since each of these professional groups works with mental patients extensively.

Physicians.   The Education Law of New York, Section 6514(2) states: "the license or registration of a practitioner of medicine . . . may be revoked, suspended, or annulled or such practitioner reprimanded or disciplined if he . . . (g) is guilty of unprofessional conduct."

The Commissioner of Education, under his power to promulgate rules to give effect to this section, has defined "unprofessional conduct" to include [8NYCRR 60.1(d)(3):]

> The revealing of facts, data or information obtained in a professional capacity relating to a patient or his records without first obtaining consent of the patient or his duly authorized representative, except if duly required by a court of competent jurisdiction of statute. Nothing in this part shall prohibit a physician from making such facts, data or information available to a department of State government, providing that such department shall when requesting such facts, data or information notify the physician in writing that such facts, data or information shall be used only for research and study and that their confidential nature shall be maintained; nor shall the revealing of such facts, data or information by a physician or a hospital to attorneys to aid in defense of a suit or claim against them by a former patient constitute unprofessional conduct. . . .

Physicians, Registered Professional Nurses, Dentists.   The Civil Practice Law and Rules of New York, Article 45, Section 4504 provides that, unless the patient waives the privilege, a licensed physician, or dentist, or a registered professional nurse must not "disclose any information which he acquired in attending a patient in a professional capacity, and which was necessary in order for him to act in that capacity." The law allows such professionals to disclose such information concerning "the mental or physical condition of a deceased person" except when to disclose "would tend to disgrace the memory of the decedant," and when the privilege is waived by the personal representative or surviving spouse, or next of kin, or on order of the trial judge in any litigation where the interests of the personal representative are deemed adverse to those of the estate of the deceased, or where the validity of a will of the deceased is in question.

Registered Psychologists. A similar provision (Section 4507 of the *Civil Practice Law and Rules*) extends the confidential relationship and privileged communication to registered psychologists.

Certified Social Workers. A similar provision (Section 4508 of the *Civil Practice Law and Rules*) extends the confidential relationship and privileged communication to certified social workers and their clients.

Mental Health Records

The patient records kept by mental health facilities, including clinical notes, consultant's reports, drug administration records, and psychological test results, are maintained by the facility for convenience in treating and caring for the patients. These records are owned by the facility, are the property of the facility (16), and are available to the staff of the facility for purposes of treating and caring for the patient and are rendered confidential because of the previously mentioned legal restrictions on the professionals handling the records. The New York Mental Hygiene Law and the regulations of the Department of Mental Hygiene have further enforced and spelled out the confidentiality of departmental patient records and the restricted access to those records.

New York Mental Hygiene Law, Section 34 specifies that, subject to the powers of the Commissioner and the rules of the Department, the Director of a Departmental institution shall:

Keep a record in which he shall cause to be entered at the time of a reception of any patient, his name, residence and occupation, and the date of such reception, by whom brought and by what authority and on whose petition certified and received, and an abstract of all orders, warrants, requests, petitions, certificates and other papers accompanying such persons.

The director within three days after the reception of a patient shall make, or cause to be made a descriptive record of such case. He shall also make or cause to be made entries from time to time of the mental state, bodily condition and medical treatment of such patient during the time such patient remains under his care, and in the event of discharge or death of such a person, he shall state in such case record the circumstances thereof and make other entries at such intervals of time and in such form as may be required by the Commissioner. Such record shall be accessible only to the director and such officers and subordinates of the institution as he may designate and to the commissioner and his representatives, except on the consent of the commissioner or an order of a judge of a court of record.

There are also specific provisions in the Mental Hygiene Law regarding departmental (central office) records authorizing the Commissioner to maintain patient records and restricting access to such records (Section 20):

> The Department shall keep in its office, and accessible only to the Com-
> missioner, medical director and such other officers and subordinates of the depart-
> ment as the Commissioner may designate, except by the consent of the Com-
> missioner or an order of a judge of a court of record, such information from the
> case record of each patient, other than informal patients and patients admitted
> pursuant to subdivision 1 of Section 78 of this chapter, admitted to an institution
> within the department or to a hospital as the rules and regulations of the Com-
> missioner may prescribe or as may be required by Art. 5 of this chapter, and also
> the records, papers and reports of examinations of others made by any division or
> bureau of the department. The record of each patient shall show:
>
> (1)   The name, residence, sex, age, nativity, occupation, civil condition and
>   date of admission of every patient in custody in the several institutions for
>   the care and treatment of the mentally ill, epileptic and mental defective
>   persons in the state.
> (2)   The date of discharge of each patient from such institution, whether
>   recovered, much improved, improved or unimproved, and to whose care
>   committed.
> (3)   If transferred, to what institution, and if dead, the date and cause of
>   death.

Section 21 of the same law deals more specifically with the departmental institution's responsibility to furnish information to the Department:

> The authorities of the several institutions . . . [in the Department] shall furnish
> to the Department the facts mentioned in such section, and such other obtainable
> facts relating thereto as the Department may, from time to time, in just and
> reasonable discharge of its duties, require of them, with the opinion of the Direc-
> tor thereon, if required. The director or person in charge of any institution,
> whether public or private, a record of whose patients is kept pursuant to the
> preceding section, must, within ten days after the admission of a person thereto,
> cause a true copy of the petition, medical certificate and order on which such
> person shall have been received, or a copy of the application of a voluntary patient
> to be made and forwarded to the department; and when a patient shall be dis-
> charged, transferred or shall die therein, such director or person in charge shall
> send the information to the department, in accordance with the rules and regula-
> tions, and upon the forms prescribed by the Commissioner.

These sections of the New York law make clear the legislative intention and
state policy to make all patient records in the Department confidential and to
restrict access "by the consent of the Commissioner or an order of a judge of a
court of record." Furthermore, the New York courts have limited accessibility
to the records by court order to the strict categories of the privileged communi-

cation law mentioned earlier concerning medical personnel (36):

> Sections 20 and 34, subdivision 9, of the Mental Hygiene Law do not create an
> exception to the privilege and do not permit disclosure thereof except as may be
> done under s. 354 of the Civil Practice Act. Section 34, subdivision 9, was not
> intended to vitiate s. 352 of the C.P.A.

With particular reference to state facilities, another court similarly held that
(37):

> The Mental Hygiene Law, sections 20 and 34, with respect to records of an
> inmate of a hospital, when read in connection with other statutes such as
> C.P.A. s. 352, which makes communications to physicians privileged, indicated
> the intention of the legislature to protect case records as a privileged communica-
> tion.

The statutory provisions relating to departmental records do not, on their
face, use language imposing stringent prohibitions against disclosure, but
rather limit access to designated persons. The distinction is rather one of emphasis and tone. In this regard, however, the courts have pointed out that
"records of a patient in a mental institution are of a confidential nature and
public policy requires that they do not be revealed except on a clear showing of
legitimate and proper call therefore. Permitting access without such a showing
would constitute an abuse of discretion" (38). Thus the discretionary access to
psychiatric records in the Department which may be given by the "consent of
the Commissioner or an order of a judge of a court of record" under s. 20 of the
Mental Hygiene Law is subject to further judicial scrutiny.

To implement and expand upon these provisions, the Department of Mental
Hygiene has developed guidelines or regulations relating to medical records and
disclosure of information (ss. 2900–2919 of the Department's Policy Manual)
promulgated in 1966 and given the force of law. These regulations are more
explicit with regard to a policy statement; state hospital medical records department; disclosure of information; release of admission papers and case
records in court; release of information on subpoenas; release of information in
annulment actions; release of information to local community mental health
services; release of information to insurance companies and health plan organizations; providing information to the New York City Police Department;
release of information to the press; release of information to Veterans Administration contact officers; release of information to the Veterans Administration
concerning patients of the Veterans Administration; and production of patients'
case records for Workmen's Compensation hearings.

Of special interest is the regulation relating to disclosure of information in general (s. 2902).

DEPARTMENT OF MENTAL HYGIENE POLICY MANUAL

Medical Records and Disclosure of Information 2901–2902

Section 2901—State Hospital Medical Records Department

Medical Records Committee

Each hospital shall have a Medical Records Committee consisting of the Assistant Director (Clinical) and two senior members of the staff and the Medical Records Librarian. This committee is responsible for review of all records at the time the patient is discharged, and for spot review of records at all times. This committee is also responsible for recommending changes in policy and procedures relative to medical records.

Section 2902—Disclosure of Information

a.   Information sent to an outside source regarding a patient as authorized in this section is enclosed in a sealed envelope and both letter and envelope are marked "Confidential and Privileged Communication for Professional Use Only."

b.   Under section 34 paragraph 9 of the Mental Hygiene Law, the case record of a patient cannot be exposed to the public except upon the consent of the Commissioner or by order of a judge of a court of record. The Commissioner has authorized the release of information subject to the following principles:

(1)   All disclosures are made by physicians.

(2)   Patients records are held confidential and may not be made accessible to the public without the consent of the Commissioner or by court order.

(3)   Directors may make accessible an abstract of the case record of a patient or a former patient to the following:

(a)   A reputable physician who is or was engaged to care for a patient or a member of his family.

(b)   A hospital which has, or had, or may have the care of the patient or a member of his family.

      (c)   A representative of a court or other public agency which is properly interested in the patient or his family.

(4)   Physicians who have cared for a patient prior to admission and particularly those who will care for the patient leaving the hospital are considered to have a proper medical interest in information regarding the patient's condition and therapy. Therefore, upon request of any physician properly interested in a patient's condition, or upon request of the patient's family, the Director may provide such physician with information pertaining to the diagnosis, present condition, treatment and prognosis.

      (a)   Information relating to personal and family matters should not be released to physicians without the consent of the patient, if he is capable of giving it; if not capable, this information may be released with the consent of a responsible relative.

      (b)   Physicians who make inquiries which are not considered in the best interest of the patient shall not receive any data as provided in this section.

(5)   Such information may also be released to a recognized social agency which has a proper interest in the patient or his family. However, in the case of a discharged patient, the signed and witnessed consent of the patient should first be obtained by the social agency making the request. If the discharged patient is deceased, the consent of the next-of-kin should be obtained by the agency.

(6)   Ordinarily, an attorney is not entitled to access to a patient's record. The principal exception is as follows:

    An attorney must be given access to a patient and his case record if:

      (a)   the institution director has received written notice from a judge advising that the attorney has been assigned to represent the patient in a proceeding relative to the patient's retention at the institution; or

      (b)   the institution director has received written notice from the patient that he has retained that attorney to represent him in a proceeding relative to his retention at the institution.

    Any other instances meriting exceptions should be referred to the Commissioner, with reasons.

(7)   If a district attorney requests the case record of a patient or former patient in an official investigation or for the Grand Jury, the case record may be made accessible.

(8) Any request made by an insurance company for proper information regarding an insured person who is or was a patient should be granted, provided such information is necessary in establishing the patient's interest in the insurance policy.

(9) The Commissioner has authorized the institution directors to make available to an outside physician the case records of a patient as well as permitting such physician to examine the patient in workmen's compensation matters when the director is satisfied that such examinations will be in the interest of the patient.

(10) Copies of the certification and other admission papers shall be furnished only upon court order.

(11) The patient's welfare should be the controlling consideration in acting on any request for information.

(12) When a patient leaves the hospital and it is known that he may be under the care of a particular physician, it is desirable to send the physician a brief statement regarding the patient's release and advice of the availability of information, if needed, regarding the patient's condition.

(13) If a patient is on drug therapy and the maintenance of this therapy is indicated but cannot be maintained through clinic services, or it is the expressed wish of the patient to return to the care of the family physician, specific information regarding the dosage should be sent to the physician at the time of the patient's release.

This regulation permits disclosure of identifiable patient data for the purposes of treatment (to physicians and recognized social agencies), third-party payment, and, under special circumstances, to attorneys and other legal entities (such as Grand Jury). There is no specific authorization for disclosure for research and planning functions, although the Department of Education's regulation cited earlier defining "unprofessional conduct" does allow such disclosure.

Privacy Law

The first legal exposition of the right of privacy is found in an 1890 article by Louis D. Brandeis and Samuel D. Warren in the *Harvard Law Review* (39). At that time there was no judicial or legislative recognition of a legally protected right of privacy. A few years after this article was published, a New York court refused to acknowledge a common law right of privacy (40), indicating that such a right would require legislative determination and action. The New York Legislature acted promptly the following year, enacting the first statute in the United States protecting the right of privacy.

This statute may be found, in slightly amended form, in the New York Civil Rights Law, Article 5, ss. 50, 51, and 52. Section 50 is penal in nature and states that "a person, firm or corporation that uses for advertising purposes, or for the purposes of trade, the name, portrait or picture of any living person without first having obtained the written consent of such person, or if a minor or his parent or guardian, is guilty of misdemeanor." The legal remedies of injunctive relief, as well as real and exemplary damages, are established in s. 51; the "privacy" of judicial, administrative, and other similar proceedings is protected in s. 52.

There is extensive case law applying and interpreting this statute. Originally these cases emphasized the statute's prohibition against purely commercial use (41); moreover, since the right of privacy was legislatively created, it was given appropriately narrow construction (42). Although this kind of interpretation has continued (43), other courts have expanded the statutory mandate and have adopted a more liberal construction (44). It should be noted, perhaps, that the kind of privacy being protected by this statute and related cases can be categorized as a "private law right" of privacy as distinguished from a narrower "public law" right, the latter protecting individuals from arbitrary and intrusive action by the state (19). In the public law area, the Supreme Court has indicated that electronic eavesdropping (20) and birth control legislation affecting family life (21) constitute invasions of privacy.

A New York penal statute specifically derived from the statutory right of privacy establishes felonious offenses against this right, which offenses include unlawful wiretapping, eavesdropping, possession of wiretapping devices, and so forth (45).

In summary, it can be said that the legal concept of privacy in New York is historically important and clearly articulated in both statutory and case law.

Data Banks and Computer Services

There are currently no statutes or regulations in New York concerning confidentiality or privacy in data banks or limiting access to information in data banks or computerized information collection and storage facilities.

Participation in MSIS

The State of New York protects both the individual's right of privacy and the confidentiality of medical and psychiatric records and communications by the specific statutes, judicial decisions, and Departmental regulations discussed above. Submission of data to MSIS with the consent of the Commissioner of Mental Hygiene would neither violate such confidentiality nor constitute unauthorized disclosure, but would be considered an appropriate and efficient means of carrying out the Commissioner's statutory responsibility of record keeping.

THE LAW IN RHODE ISLAND

Medical Confidentiality and Privileged Communication

There are no statutes in Rhode Island recognizing a confidential relationship or creating a privileged testimonial communication for medical, psychological, or social work professionals. The only privileged communication law in Rhode Island concerns communications between husband and wife (Rhode Island General Laws, s. 9-17-13) and between priest and penitent (R.I.G.L. s. 9-17-23).

Nevertheless it should be noted that physicians are traditionally bound in a trust relationship to their patients not to disclose indiscriminately outside the treatment situation any information derived from a patient in the course of treatment. This restriction is contained in the Principles of Medical Ethics of the American Medical Association (10) and in the Hippocratic Oath. A violation of this obligation would be serious professional misconduct. Under Rhode Island law, a physician's license to practice medicine may be refused, suspended, or revoked for "gross unprofessional conduct." Included in the statutory definition of such unprofessional conduct is "the wilful violation of a privileged communication" (46).

Mental Health Records

The records kept by mental health facilities, including patient clinical records, consultant reports, psychological tests, and drug administration records, are maintained by the facility for convenience in treating and caring for the patients. These records are owned by the facility, are the property of the facility (16), and are available for the staff of the facility for purposes of treating and caring for the patients.

In Rhode Island responsibility for the care and treatment of mentally ill persons in hospitals or other facilities is shared: the Department of Social Welfare exercises responsibility for the admission and custody of the mentally ill (47), while the Department of Health licenses and inspects facilities providing such care and treatment (48). In carrying out these responsibilities, both departments have access to patient records in the facilities. However the Department of Social Welfare appears to be vested with supervisory and record-keeping functions.

Section 40-20-6, subsection 7, of the Rhode Island General Laws pertains to the admission of persons to any mental health facility, and states:

> The director (of the Department of Social Welfare) may make request of the superintendent or official in charge of any such facility to examine at any time a record of admission of said patient. The record of admission shall contain such in-

formation as the director by rule or regulation may require. Similarly, the director may examine records of transfers, discharges, conditional releases, and revocation of conditional releases as well as other dispositions of cases of patients admitted hereunder.

The language of this provision is permissive and seems to concern itself with an occasional inspection of records by the Department of Social Welfare. However another provision of Rhode Island's mental health law relating to involuntary commitments, appears to concretize the former subsection and to establish a record-keeping function in the Department of Social Welfare (49):

> A copy of all orders and decisions of the family court, the district court, and opinions, orders and decisions of the supreme court pursuant to proceedings instituted by virtue of this title shall be transmitted to the director (of the Department of Social Welfare) and become a permanent record in his department, as heretofore provided in subsection 7 of s. 40-20-6, article II hereof.

Despite the statutory references to patient records discussed above, there is no provision in Rhode Island's mental health law relating to the confidentiality of such records.

In contrast, the Health Department, which has access to records of mental health facilities through its licensing responsibility, is specifically restricted in its use of information by another statutory provision (50):

> Information received by the licensing agency through filed reports, inspection, or as otherwise authorized under this chapter, shall not be disclosed publically in such manner as to identify individuals or hospitals, except in a proceeding involving the question of licensure.

In further contrast to the absence of statutory protection of the confidentiality of mental patients' records, there is clear legislative protection for records of obstetrical patients, prohibiting direct or indirect disclosure of (51).

> "the contents of the records prescribed in the regulations, or the particulars entered therein, or the inmates thereof, except upon inquiry before a court of law, investigations of the department of the attorney-general, or for the information of the state department of health; provided, however, that nothing herein shall prohibit the director with the consent of any patient in such (maternity) hospital, disclosing to such proper persons such facts as may be in the interest of such patient or the infant born to her.

Privacy Law

Rhode Island has no statutory right of privacy, nor any other legislative indications that such a right exists. Although some state courts in recent years have recognized such a right without legislative action (52), it has been suggested that Rhode Island is one of three states (along with Texas and Wisconsin) which would not recognize a common law right of privacy (53). It should be noted, however, that state statutes and related judicial decisions ordinarily refer to a "private law" right of privacy, as distinguished from a narrower "public law" right, the latter protecting individuals from arbitrary and intrusive action by the state (19). In the public law area, the United States Supreme Court has indicated that electronic eavesdropping (20) and birth control legislation affecting family life (21) constitute invasions of privacy. These decisions are of course binding on Rhode Island courts.

Data Banks and Computer Services

There are currently no statutes or regulations in Rhode Island concerning confidentiality or privacy in data banks or limiting access to information in data banks or computerized information-collection and information-storage facilities.

Participation in MSIS

By administrative arrangement, the State of Rhode Island is participating in and using the services of MSIS for the collection and storage of mental patients' records and in the development of research in the computer sciences in the mental health field. Rhode Island has little statutory or common law protecting the individual's right of privacy or the confidentiality of medical and psychiatric records and communications; thus there appear to be no significant problems in this area with regard to the state's submitting identifiable patient data to MSIS. Moreover, there is legislative indication that the Department of Social Welfare shall keep records [*Rhode Island General Laws,* s. 40-40-6(7) and s. 40-20-9(12)], and that the Director of the Department "may delegate in writing any duty to a deputy or agent" (s. 40-20-5). Based on these provisions, the Department, by contractual delegation, could utilize MSIS as an appropriate and efficient means of carrying out appropriate parts of its record-keeping responsibility. In conjunction with administrative and contractual arrangements with MSIS, the existing laws of Rhode Island do not prevent submission of identifiable patient data to and the Department's participation in MSIS.

THE LAW IN VERMONT

General Law

Medical Confidentiality and Privileged Communication.   There are no statutes in Vermont recognizing a confidential relationship or creating a privileged testimonial communication for medical, psychological, or social work professionals. The only privileged communication law in Vermont concerns communications made to priests or ministers by persons "under the sanctity of a religious confession" (Vermont Statutes, Title 12, Section 1607).

Nevertheless it should be noted that physicians are traditionally bound in trust relationship to their patients not to disclose indiscriminately outside the treatment situation any information derived from a patient in the course of treatment. This restriction is contained in the Principles of Medical Ethics of the American Medical Association (10) and in the Hippocratic Oath. A violation of this obligation would be serious professional misconduct. Under Vermont law, a physician's license to practice medicine may be suspended or revoked for reasons of having committed "immoral, unprofessional, or dishonorable conduct" (Vermont Statutes, Title 26, Section 1398). The statute does not specifically list disclosure of confidential patient information as unprofessional conduct, but an Attorney General's Opinion has ruled that the meaning is not restricted to the listed grounds (1936 Vt. Atty. Gen. Opinions 425). Other states have defined "unprofessional conduct" to include disclosure of confidential patient information (12).

Similar ethical principles apply to other professionals such as psychologists, nurses, and social workers regarding confidential information.

Department of Mental Health Records

The records kept by mental health facilities, including patient clinical records, consultant reports, psychological tests, and drug administration records are maintained by the facility for convenience in treating and caring for the patients. These records are owned by the facility, are the property of the facility (16), and are available for the staff of the facility for purposes of treating and caring for the patients.

Despite the lack of general law in Vermont concerning professional confidentiality, there are specific statutes making the records of the Vermont Department of Mental Health confidential and restricting access to those records.

Section 7103 of the *Vermont Statutes,* Title 18, Part 8 deals with disclosure of information and reads as follows:

(a)   All certificates, applications, records and reports other than an order of a court made for the purposes of this Part of this title, and directly or indirectly identifying a patient or former patient or an individual whose hospitalization or care has been sought under this Part, together with clinical information relating to such persons shall be kept confidential and shall not be disclosed by any persons except insofar:

   (1)   as the individual identified or his legal guardian, if any (or if a minor, his parent or legal guardian), shall consent in writing; or

    (2)   as disclosure shall be necessary to carry out any of the provisions of this Part; or

    (3)   as a court may direct upon its determination that disclosure is necessary for the conduct of proceedings before it and that failure to make disclosure would be contrary to the public interest.

(b)   Nothing in this section shall preclude disclosure, on proper inquiry, of information concerning medical condition to the members of the family of a patient or to his clergyman, his physician, his attorney, or an interested party.

(c)   Any person violating this section shall be fined not more than $500 or imprisoned for not more than one year, or both.

Section 7402 of Title 18 pertains to records and reports:

> The Commissioner shall keep records of commitment and admissions to a hospital or training school and shall secure compliance with the laws relating thereto. He shall report biannually to the Governor and the general assembly on the condition and discipline of hospitals and training schools and patients therein, their physical and medical treatment and any other matters he deems advisable.

There have been no court interpretations of these provisions and no departmental regulations have further interpreted the meaning of some of the broadly worded authorized disclosures such as the scope of "proper inquiry" about the condition of patients by family, clergymen, attorneys, or "interested parties" under Section 7103(b). It should be noted also that the Department may disclose information on patients under Section 7103(a)(2) when necessary to carrying out the provisions of the law. This is quite a broad provision and allows the Commissioner discretion to disclose in the interest of Departmental objectives and programs. These objectives would include patient care and treatment, administration, planning, and authorized research in the interest of the Department.

Although Vermont has no legislation creating a right of privacy, it recognizes such a right indirectly in a 1961 statute relating to the liability of the State in tort claims: "The State of Vermont shall be liable for injury to persons or property or loss of life caused by the negligence or wrongful act or omission of an employee of the state . . ." except that the "provisions of this chapter are inapplicable to . . . (6) any claim arising out of alleged assault, battery, false imprisonment, false arrest, malicious prosecution, abuse of process, libel, slander, misrepresentation, deceit, fraud, interference with contractual rights or *invasion of right to privacy* . . . (54)." There is no case law under this statutory provision, but its implication is that individuals, including state employees, would be liable to suit for damages for invasion of privacy, but not the State of Vermont.

It should be noted, however, that state statutes such as the one cited above and related judicial decisions ordinarily refer to a "private law" right of privacy, as distinguished from a narrower "public law" right, the latter protecting individuals from arbitrary and intrusive action by the state (19). In the public law area, the Supreme Court has indicated that electronic eavesdropping (20) and birth control legislation affecting family life (21) constitute invasion of privacy. These decisions are of course binding on Vermont Courts.

Data Banks and Computer Services

There are currently no statutes or regulations in Vermont concerning confidentiality or privacy in data banks or limiting access to information in data banks or computerized information collection and storage facilities.

Participation in MSIS

By administrative arrangement, the State of Vermont is participating in and using the services of MSIS for the collection and storage of mental patient's records and in the development of research in the computer sciences in the mental health field. The State of Vermont protects the confidentiality of psychiatric records and communications in the statutes discussed above. There is little or no explicit statutory protection of a right of privacy, nor is there a testimonial privilege for physicians. Submission of identifiable patient data to MSIS would neither violate the statutory requirement of confidentiality nor constitute unauthorized disclosure, since the statute permits disclosure of identifiable patient data as "may be deemed necessary to carry out any provisions of this Part . . ." (*Vermont Statutes Annotated,* Title 18, s. 7103). Record keeping is among the statutorily mandated responsibilities of the Department (Title 18, s. 7402), and participation in MSIS would thus be considered appropriate and necessary to the implementation of the Department's statutory responsibilities. In conjunction with administrative and contractual arrangements with MSIS, the existing laws of Vermont would not prevent the submission of identifiable patient data to and the Department's participation in MSIS.

REFERENCES AND NOTES

1. W. J. Daily, *Soc. Case Work,* **55,**7 (1974), 433.
2. D. L. Rosenhan, *Science,* **179** (1973), 250–258.
3. A. Toffler, *Future Shock,* Random House, New York, 1970.
4. S. J. Ervin, Jr., *Vital Speeches of the Day,* 33, 14 (1967), 421–426.
5. A. Miller, *Michigan Law Review,* **67,** 6 (1969), 1222.

6.   Bill No. 8971a.

7.   *U.S. Code,* Title 13, Section 9 (a) (1).

8.   Laws of New York, Chapter 317 (1972).

9.   W. Curran, B. Stearns and H. Kaplan, *New Engl. J. Med.,* **281** (1969), 241–248.

10. *Principles of Medical Ethics,* American Medical Association, Section 9: "A physician may not reveal the confidences entrusted to him in the course of medical attendance, or the deficiencies he may observe in the character of his patients, unless he is required to do so by law or unless it becomes necessary in order to protect the welfare of the individual or of the community."

11. General Statutes of Connecticut, Title 20-45.

12. See, for example, Maine Revised Statutes Ann'd, Title 32, s. 3203A; Hawaii Revised Statutes, Ch. 453-8(4); Education Law of N.Y., s 6514(2) (g) and the regulations promulgated thereunder (8NYCRR 60.1 (d) (3).

13. General Statutes of Connecticut, Title 52-146d, 52-146e, and 52-146f. See also discussion by court in Felber v. Foote (D.C. Conn., 1970) 321 F. Supp. 85, 88, fn. 8.

14. See discussion by court in *Felber v. Foote* (D.C. Conn., 1970) 321 F. Supp. 85, 88, fn. 1.

15. See, for example, Simonsen v. Swensen, 104 Neb. 224, 177 N. W. 831 (1920); *Clark v. Geraci,* 208 N.Y.S. 2d 564 (S. Ct. 1960); Berry v. Moench, 8 Utah 2d 191, 331 P. 2d 814 (1958).

16. *Pyramid Life Ins. Co. v. Masonic Hosp. Assn. of Payne Cy., Okl.* (D.C. Okl. 1961) 191 F. Supp. 51.

17. *Steding v. Ballistoni* (Conn. Div. A. D.) 208 A.2d 556 (1964); *Korn v. Rennison* (Conn. Super.) 156 A.2d 476 (1959).

18. General Statutes of Connecticut, Title 52-279.

19. "The Titticut Follies' Case: Limiting the Public Interest Privilege," *Columbia Law Review,* 70, 359 (1970), 362, fn. 11.

20. *Katz v. United States,* 389 U.S. 347 (1967).

21. *Griswold v. Connecticut,* 381 U.S. 479 (1965).

22. *Ferguson v. Quaker Life Ins. Co.* (D.C. Mun. App.), 129 A.2d 189 (1957).

23. *Kendall v. Gore Properties Inc.* (4th Cir., 1956), 236 F2d. 673.

24. *Kaplan v. Manhattan Life Ins. Co.* (4th Cir., 1939), 109 F2d. 463.

25. See, for example, the Standards of Accreditation as promulgated by the Joint Commission on Accreditation of Hospitals in April, 1971.

26. *Pearson v. Dodd,* 410 F. 2s 701 (4th Cir., 1969); *Bernstein v. N.B.C.,* 129 F. Supp. 817, especially pp. 829–831 (D.C.D.C. 1953); *Peay v. Curtais Publishing Co.,* 78 F. Supp. 505 (D.C.D.C. 1948).

27. Mental Health Law, ch. 334-5, Hawaii Revised Statutes.

28. *Fergerstrom v. Hawaiian Ocean View Estates,* 441 P. 2d 141 (1968).

29. Massachusetts General Laws ch. 112, s.61.

30. *Forziati v. Board of Registration in Medicine,* 333 Mass. 125, 128 N E. 2d 789 (1955).

31. Massachusetts General Laws. ch. 322, s.203.

32. Massachusetts General Laws. ch. 111, s.70.

33. *Themo v. N.E. Newspaper Pub. Co.,* 306 Mass. 54, 27 N.E. 2d 753 (1940).

34. Commonwealth v. Wiseman, 249 N.E. 2d 610 (1969).

35. Massachusetts General Laws ch. 19, s.29(f).

36. *Joffe v. City of New York,* 196 Misc. 710, 94 N.Y. 2d 60.

37. *McGrath v. State of New York,* 200 Misc. 165, 104 N.Y.S. 2d 882.

38. *Application of Hild,* 124 N.Y.S. 2d 271 (1953).

39. Brandeis and Warren, *Harvard Law Review,* **4,** 193 (1890).

40. *Roberson v. Rochester Folding Box Co.,* 171 N.Y. 538, 64 N.E. 442 (1902).

41. *Jeffries v. New York Evening Journal Pub. Co.,* 124 N.Y.S. 780 (1910).

42. *Wilson v. Brown,* 189 Misc. 79, 73 N.Y.S. 2d 587 (1947).

43. *Cardy v. Maxwell,* 9 Misc. 2d 329, 169 N.Y.S. 2d 547 (1957).

44. *Spahn v. Julian Messner, Inc.* 250 N.Y.S. 2d 529, aff'd 260 N.Y.S. 2d 451, aff'd 274 N.Y.S. 2d 877, vacated on other grounds 384 U.S. 239, aff'd 286 N.Y.S. 2d 832, prob. juris. noted 393 U.S. 818, appeal dism'd 393 U.S. 1046 (1964); also *Selsman v. Univ. Photo Books, Inc.,* 18 A.D. 2d 151, 238 N.Y.S. 2d 686 (1963).

45. *McKinney's Consolidated Laws of New York Annotated,* Penal Law, s.250.00 et seq.

46. Rhode Island General Laws, s. 5-37-4.

47. Rhode Island General Laws, s. 40-20-3.

48. Rhode Island General Laws, s. 40-20-4.

49. Rhode Island General Laws, s. 40-20-9, subsection (12).

50. Rhode Island General Laws, s. 23-26-15.

51. Rhode Island General Laws, s. 23-17-8.

52. See, for example, *Steding v. Ballistoni* (Conn. Civ. A.D.) 208 A. 2d 556 (1964); *Fergertrom v. Hawaiian Ocean View Estates,* 441 P. 2d 141 (1968).

53. Note, *Minnesota Law Review,* 43, 943 (1959), fn. 3.

54. *Vermont Statutes Annotated,* Title 12, s. 5601 and 5602.

Index